www.wadsworth.com

www.wadsworth.com is the World Wide Web site for Wadsworth and is your direct source to dozens of online resources.

At *www.wadsworth.com* you can find out about supplements, demonstration software, and student resources. You can also send email to many of our authors and preview new publications and exciting new technologies.

www.wadsworth.com
Changing the way the world learns®

Critical Thinking and Everyday Argument

✳

JAY VERLINDEN

Humboldt State University

THOMSON

WADSWORTH

Australia · Canada · Mexico · Singapore · Spain
United Kingdom · United States

THOMSON
TM
WADSWORTH

Publisher: *Holly J. Allen*
Acquisitions Editor: *Annie Mitchell*
Senior Developmental Editor: *Greer Lleuad*
Assistant Editor: *Breanna Gilbert-Gambacorta*
Editorial Assistant: *Trina Enriquez*
Senior Technology Project Manager: *Jeanette Wiseman*
Senior Marketing Manager: *Kimberly Russell*
Marketing Assistant; *Andrew Keay*
Advertising Project Manager: *Shemika Britt*

Signing Representative: *Terri Edwards*
Manager, Editorial Production: *Edward Wade*
Print/Media Buyer: *Judy Inouye*
Permissions Editor: *Stephanie Lee*
Production Service and Compositon: *Stratford Publishing Services, Inc.*
Copy Editor: *Michele Lansing*
Cover Designer: *Ross Carron Design*
Printer: *Transcontinental/Louiseville*

For more information about our products, contact us at

Thomson Learning Academic Resource Center
1-800-423-0563

For permission to use material from this text or product, submit a request online at http://www.thomsonrights.com

Any additional questions about permissions can be submitted by email to thomsonrights@thomson.com

Library of Congress Control Number: 2004103348

ISBN 0-534-60174-X

Wadsworth/Thomson Learning
10 Davis Drive
Belmont, CA 94002-3098
USA

Asia
Thomson Learning
5 Shenton Way #01-01
UIC Building
Singapore 068808

Australia/New Zealand
Thomson Learning
102 Dodds Street
Southbank, Victoria 3006
Australia

Canada
Nelson
1120 Birchmount Road
Toronto, Ontario M1K 5G4
Canada

Europe/Middle East/Africa
Thomson Learning
High Holborn House
50/51 Bedford Row
London WC1R 4LR
United Kingdom

Latin America
Thomson Learning
Seneca, 53
Colonia Polanco
11560 Mexico D.F.
Mexico

Spain/Portugal
Paraninfo
Calle/Magallanes, 25
28015 Madrid, Spain

To Phyllis, for her laughter, support, help, and patience with me on this project and everything else, and for being such a good example of critical thinking and positive argumentation in everyday life.

About the Author

Jay Ver Linden is a professor in the Department of Communication at Humboldt State University. He participated in competitive speech and debate throughout high school and college and coached forensics for twenty years before retiring from forensics to become department chair. He was the Director of Forensics at Wayne State College in Nebraska, Simpson College in Iowa, and Humboldt State University in California. He also was president of both the Mid-America Forensics League and the Northern California Forensics Association. He earned his B.A. and M.A. from the University of Northern Colorado and his Ph.D. from the University of Nebraska-Lincoln.

Brief Contents

Contents

Preface

I believe that I was very fortunate to have grown up in a school system that introduced me to interscholastic debate and to have attended a college that allowed me to participate in intercollegiate debate. I believe that my experience as a debater did more than anything else in my educational experience to teach me how to analyze ideas, think critically, find published information, evaluate evidence, consider alternative explanations, generate alternative explanations, organize and present ideas clearly, and construct strong arguments. And it was fun! As I continued through college, and in my academic career and everyday life, the skills that I learned from academic debate often have proven extremely valuable. Because of that experience, I am able to present my ideas and respond to arguments made by others with relative ease, and often I am surprised that others don't feel that they can do the same just as easily.

I would recommend involvement in academic debate for anyone, especially for those who are interested in careers that will involve a good deal of advocacy—and that includes almost every career. I coached debaters and other students in intercollegiate speech competition for twenty years, and during that time I watched them develop both their intellectual abilities and confidence. Because of the repeated experiences engaging in argumentation and receiving constructive criticism, academic speech and debate provide a wealth of experience that cannot be gained in the typical classroom alone. I don't think that there is a better activity for the kind of personal development that will pay off for the rest of one's life.

I also know that, for a variety of reasons, intercollegiate speech and debate are not activities in which everyone can participate. Some students simply don't have the time that participation requires; some don't want to be involved in an activity that tends to be as intensely competitive as debate; and some are intimidated by the idea of having their thinking and speaking evaluated as often as is done in academic debate. Unfortunately, many students aren't lucky enough to attend a college with a speech and debate program, or, if they are, they may not find out about the program until it is too late. Thus many students will not be able to benefit from the program that I took for granted during my schooling.

While my overall opinion of academic debate is quite positive, I also know that it can present some problems. Its competitive nature can lead some participants to overemphasize the need to "win" arguments, at almost any cost. The repeated and intense experiences can inadvertently socialize some people to argue in ways that can be described as more destructive than constructive. Academic debate also can simply reinforce habits that may be appropriate in the competitive arena but not in other contexts. I vividly remember debaters who spent a great deal of time preparing their strategies, those who were quite skilled in exposing weaknesses in their opponents' arguments, who were able to overwhelm those opponents with evidence and reasoning, and who presented their arguments with an intensity that was very convincing in an academic debate forum. I also vividly remember these same debaters using these same techniques in less formal situations, and they came across as overbearing, stubborn, arrogant, threatening, and obnoxious. They simply hadn't learned to adapt their style to different contexts. Learning about argumentation only through academic debate certainly doesn't affect everyone negatively, but there can be detrimental side effects for some people. Unfortunately, those are the people who most easily come to mind when many others think of academic debate.

In addition, I consider myself fortunate because my educational experiences also involved situations that emphasized working with others in cooperative ways and learning techniques to maintain better relations with others. My experience with working in theatre, and learning about interpersonal and small-group communication in classes helped me recognize that there is more to communication than making strong arguments, and that there is more to argumentation than defeating another person or team. Argumentation also can be used positively to get people to work together, to understand one another better, to test ideas, and to maintain relationships. It can, in fact, be done in a constructive way.

Argumentation is also all around us. It happens not only in the context of academic debate but also in conversations, in our private reasoning, in small-group discussions, and the like. As I taught argumentation classes, I felt it necessary to clarify to students that studying argumentation had practical implications extending far beyond academic debate settings.

WHY I WROTE THIS TEXT

This text came about because I couldn't find a good, introductory argumentation text that didn't have large sections on academic debate. The content in the existing texts is good, but students who weren't learning academic debate didn't need all of it. Although I still think that academic debate is very worthwhile, I believe that most students will not pursue debate beyond one class, so they may have difficulty regarding the relevancy of such texts. I felt that there was a need for a text that presents the same valuable content in the context of the argumentation that people engage in during their everyday life, and I tried to address that need.

This text also came about because I felt that there was a need to make a clearer connection between critical thinking and argumentation as it is taught in the communication discipline. Those of us who have been involved in academic debate realize that virtually every concept related to argumentation also is related to critical thinking. We may take it for granted to the point that we assume that others recognize the same connections. Although some texts do include some material on critical thinking, I felt that it could be further developed to make a stronger case that what we teach in argumentation courses is the same as what is expected of critical thinkers.

In addition, my purpose in writing this text is to bring together principles of argumentation and principles of other types of communication. I hope that students who aren't able to engage in academic debate will be able to use this text to improve their argumentative and critical-thinking skills and gain some of the benefits of debate. I also hope that this text will help readers apply the principles of argumentation to their everyday communication, both as the producers and the consumers of arguments.

FEATURES OF THIS TEXT

Along with presenting the basic material about argumentation in a way that makes its application in everyday life more apparent, I believe that there are specific features of this text that set it apart from others.

- **The development of the meaning of critical thinking.** I made a special effort to investigate what scholars who affiliate themselves with critical thinking consider central to doing it. Chapter 2, "Critical Thinking," is meant to develop a more complete understanding of what critical thinking is, and the rest of the text attempts to help students develop the ability to think critically.

- **The development of ethical standards for arguers.** The argumentation texts with which I'm familiar either don't address ethics or only address ethics within the context of academic debate. The latter is understandable, because the texts are academic debate texts, but I believe that a serious gap exists. I feel, as did Wayne Brockriede, that argumentation is done among people, and that ethical standards of argumentation also must relate to how we treat people as we argue with them. Thus, Chapter 3, "Ethics in Argumentation," addresses ethics in educational settings and in interpersonal and public-decision-making settings. Those ethical principles remain in the background throughout the text.

- **The development of fallacies.** For some reason, students seem to love fallacies. When they're given the chance to analyze arguments and are given the choice of any method to use, I find that the majority will turn to argumentative fallacies. I also am aware that many instructors don't care much for fallacies. In this text, I try to present fallacies as useful analytic tools, but not as the only way to think about arguments. I believe that knowing about a wide variety of fallacies will help critical thinkers spot *potential* problems in arguments and will give them reason to think more deeply about the arguments they encounter. I also think that the same knowledge helps arguers avoid making common mistakes in reasoning. I don't think that it matters much that a student can name and define fallacies, although there's nothing wrong with that knowledge, and it is appropriate for someone with a college education. But if one is aware of fallacies, then that awareness can be used to improve one's thinking.

  Chapter 4 introduces students to argumentative fallacies. The rest of the material on fallacies is spread out among many chapters, and the specific fallacies have been placed in the chapters they most relate to. This coverage helps students better understand argumentative concepts, because it will help explain how the concepts are regularly misused. In addition to the material on fallacies covered in the chapters, an extensive glossary of common informal fallacies is included in the book.

- **The application of argumentative principles.** This text, in addition to explaining the principles of argumentation by relating them to everyday experiences, includes chapters that explicitly relate to arguing and thinking critically in specific contexts. Those contexts include making and listening to persuasive public speeches (Chapter 12), critical listening (Chapter 13), dyadic argumentation (Chapter 14), small-group communication (Chapter 15), and using the scientific method (Chapter 16). Those chapters certainly are not meant to substitute for full texts on any of these subjects but rather are meant to help students recognize how they can apply the principles of argumentation beyond the classroom, to both make and have strong arguments. The chapter on the scientific method may seem somewhat strange for an argumentation text, but it helps demonstrate that the material covered also applies to a specific context that many students find mystifying.

- **Writing for students.** I originally created this text for use in a class that I teach, and I really wasn't concerned about making it sound particularly scholarly. I wanted my students to read it and relate to the concepts. The responses that I've received from students over the years have led me to believe that I was successful—several students have commented that they like the writing style, and many have noted that they recognize the principles in their everyday lives. The text is still challenging, and there is a lot of material to cover, but the tone is intentionally conversational and directed toward students.

SUPPLEMENTARY MATERIALS

Critical Thinking and Everyday Argument is accompanied by a Web site and an *Instructor's Resource Manual.*

- **Tutorial Web site.** The book, *Critical Thinking and Everyday Argument,* contains many concepts, and I believe that there is value in a college graduate mastering those concepts and the vocabulary associated with them. However, working on that mastery can take up valuable class time that I think can be better used in activities that allow students to apply the concepts. The Web-based tutorial that accompanies this book provides an opportunity for students to study many of the concepts on their own time and to better prepare themselves for exams, assignments, and class activities. It allows students to check their understanding and repeat their exposure to the ideas often enough so they will better remember them. The Tutorial Link box at the end of select chapters prompts students to go to the Web site to test their knowledge of the text's concepts.

- **Instructor's Resource Manual.** The *Critical Thinking and Everyday Argument Instructor's Manual* includes class activities and an extensive test bank.

PART I

✻

Introductory Concepts

The purpose of this text is to help you develop your abilities to engage in argumentation in your everyday life and think critically about both your and other people's ideas. You engage in everyday argumentation in your relationships with your family and others, in your career, when you use mass communication, when you make daily decisions, and in your involvement in our political system. There are few aspects of your life that do not lend themselves to the principles and skills presented in this text, which is meant to introduce you to some fundamental argumentation theory and help you begin to develop skills you can use the rest of your life.

To accomplish those goals, it will help to begin with an understanding of some basic concepts. This part explains argumentation and critical thinking so you know what the rest of the text will help you develop. This section will also describe ethical guidelines that make for better, more constructive argumentation so you'll know them as you learn how to make strong arguments and think critically. Finally, this section will explain what argumentative fallacies are and why they're worth studying so you will better understand the specific fallacies when they're presented later.

1

※

Argumentation

You live in a world full of arguments. You listen to a weather reporter forecast upcoming weather. You read an editorial in a newspaper. You try to convince your spouse to buy a new car. You listen to a professor explain why a work of art is exemplary. You watch advertisements on television. You tell a friend why she should follow your advice. You read a political advertisement you received in the mail. You listen to a sales representative tell you why you should buy a particular computer. You answer an essay question on an examination. You try to convince your boss to give you a raise.

All of those experiences, and many more, are examples of the kinds of arguments we encounter as we go about our everyday lives. Some arguments are clear, and some are not. Some are explicit, and some are not. Some are well formed, and some are not. Some you will easily recognize as arguments, and some you will not. Some will be about issues that are important to you, and some will not.

Knowing how to recognize and knowing how to make strong arguments are very useful skills. They help you make better decisions, promote your best interests, avoid being deceived by others, and prevent others from taking unfair advantage of you. Developing the ability to make and evaluate arguments is justified as an important part of participating in a democratic system of government. In fact, the need for individual citizens to consider arguments about public policies may be even more important now than in the past, as legislation is increasingly decided by popular referendum. In addition, businesses are increasingly involving employees in the decision-making process, which means that those employees need the skills to work with others, to make their own arguments, and to respond to the arguments made by others. Many people also go into business for themselves, which requires them to regularly make reasoned decisions, because there's nobody to tell them what to do.

Sometimes the importance of argumentation and critical thinking rises above what affects us as individuals. Lives have been ruined because of accusations made and accepted without good evidence to support them. Cultural groups have been persecuted because people have not seen through the faulty reasoning supporting the persecution. Poor public policy has been implemented because influential politicians failed to examine the facts. Businesses have harmed people and the environment because decision makers failed to consider the effects of their decisions. Understanding what makes a good argument, being able to see through manipulative, argumentative tactics, and learning to effectively and ethically engage in argumentation can help avoid such problems.

Everyone learns to make and respond to arguments as a natural part of growing up. Some people grow up in an environment where they learn how to make strong arguments and critically evaluate arguments. Doing so seems to come easily and naturally. Most of us, however, grow up learning to make arguments that are good enough to get by, but often they are not strong enough to stand up to scrutiny. And most of us don't grow up learning to critically evaluate the arguments of others, beyond noting simple agreement or disagreement.

The purpose of this text is to help you develop your skills as an arguer and a critical thinker so you can apply those skills in a variety of situations in your everyday life. This chapter will

- explain what argumentation is.
- discuss the value of studying argumentation.
- present a general overview of argumentation to prepare you for what comes later.

WHAT IS ARGUMENTATION?

Everyone knows what arguments are, right? Well, we may not all have the same idea.

For example, what image comes to your mind when you hear someone say, "I had an argument with my boyfriend last night"? If you're like most people, you don't imagine the couple having an orderly, civil discussion in which they took turns stating and supporting propositions. Most people imagine raised voices, rude comments, and hurt feelings. Many people equate "argument" with **"quarrel"** or "fight." You may have noticed, though, that there were no quarrels involved in the examples of arguments presented at the beginning of this chapter, although there were examples of disagreements.

Many terms that we use every day have legitimate multiple meanings, and argumentation is one of them. As we begin our study of argumentation, we should clarify what we mean when we use the terms *argument* and *argumentation*. While the word "argument" can mean to verbally fight, that is not the primary meaning that argumentation scholars have in mind when they study argumentation. This text is concerned with argumentation as a way of expressing reasoning, trying to convince others to agree with us, and trying to arrive at the best conclusions we can. While people engaged in a verbal fight can do that, the elements required to characterize an interaction as a fight are not necessary characteristics of an argument. This text is meant to try to help you learn how to express yourself in the most convincing *and* the most civil way you can.

In this text, **argumentation** usually refers to a form of communication in which at least one person explicitly or implicitly puts forth a claim and provides support for that claim with evidence and reasoning. Let's take a look at the elements of that definition to explain what it means.

First, the definition indicates that argumentation is a *form of communication*. That means that an argument must be capable of being expressed. Most of the time when we talk about arguments we refer to something someone said or wrote and presented to someone else. Part of the communication process is what goes on in people's minds, though, so it is possible to create an argument that you *could* express to someone else but choose not to. You can also create arguments that you communicate only to yourself or that you fantasize about saying to someone else. While we recognize that there may be occasions when we want to think of arguments that are not expressed, most of the time we will consider arguments that are shared in some way with others.

The definition also indicates that arguments involve *at least one person*. That means that arguments do not happen without some human involvement. Nature doesn't make arguments, even though sometimes we metaphorically say so. Your observation of nature may stimulate you to think of an argument, but *you* make the argument, not nature. This part of the definition also means that only one person is required to make an argument, but many more may engage in an argument by making claims and counterclaims and then supporting them.

The aforementioned definition also recognizes that arguments can be made either *implicitly* or *explicitly*. Explicit arguments are made clearly, with everything presented step by step, while implicit arguments are more open to a variety of interpretations. Sometimes someone might make an argument that is so implicit that you can't tell an argument was made. One skill of argumentation and critical thinking is telling the difference between arguments, explanations, and statements of opinion, which will be discussed later in this chapter.

An argument implicitly or explicitly *presents a claim* and *provides support* for that claim with evidence and reasoning. A claim is the idea the arguer wants to prove, the evidence is the information the arguer uses to prove the claim, and reasoning is the explanation of how that evidence supports the claim. In a fully explicit argument, the claim, evidence, and reasoning are all clearly stated. Most everyday argumentation is not that explicit, however, so you have to figure out one element or another from the cues the arguer provides. Usually the elements are missing because the arguer thinks that they are so obvious that they don't need to be stated outright, but sometimes they are unstated because the arguer hasn't thought through the full argument enough to include everything. Sometimes, however, elements are left unstated, because a crafty arguer knows that he can trick others into accepting his claim if he leaves ideas unclear, and if they were made clear, others would quickly notice the weaknesses in the argument.

The definition of argumentation only generally describes what the term means. It does not indicate ways to tell good from poor arguments. The rest of this text will develop what argumentation is, how to do it well, and how to evaluate arguments in much more detail.

TWO SENSES OF ARGUMENT

Although we're thinking of argumentation as communication in which reasoning is presented, there are other senses of the word that you use every day. Argumentation scholar Daniel O'Keefe (1977) points out that we regularly refer to argument in two different ways. The first sense, which he calls **argument$_1$,** is the sense of *making* an argument. When we think of an argument in this first sense, we think of how well made the argument is—whether it's valid, well supported, logical, and so on. When you tell your boss the reasons you deserve a raise, or when you write an answer on an essay exam, you make an argument.

The second sense of argument, referred to as **argument$_2$,** is the sense of *having* an argument. It's a type of interaction that you might have with someone else, an exchange of ideas. So you might tell your boss you deserve a raise because you're a hard worker. Your boss responds that you have been late to work 25 percent of the time. You say that you had legitimate reasons for being late and worked extra hours that more than made up for lost time. Your boss responds that there isn't enough money in the budget to give you a raise. During that exchange, the two of you are having an argument in the sense of argument$_2$. When you engage in argument$_2$, you may or may not find yourself raising your voice and fighting, but remember, you can also engage in such arguments calmly and civilly.

When you *have* an argument with someone else, you may or may not also *make* arguments. You also may *make* an argument without ever becoming aware of, or responding to, counterarguments. For example, you may make an argument in a paper you write for a class, and no one may ever respond to what you write, so you don't *have* an argument with anyone. But if you don't agree with the grade you receive, you may *have* an argument with your instructor about what the proper grade should be, and during that argument, both of you will *make* arguments in support of your positions. The rest of this text will refer to argument in both senses, and there may be times when you have to determine if the argument described is argument$_1$ or argument$_2$.

Figure 1.1 Often arguments are made implicitly and are misunderstood by the other person.

Arlo and Janis reprinted by permission of Newspaper Enterprise Association, Inc.

ARGUMENT AND NON-ARGUMENT

Sometimes people say things that listeners may take to be arguments but really are not. One of the skills to develop to improve your argumentation is the ability to recognize when people make arguments and when they do not. Remember that an argument includes a claim, evidence, and reasoning, but in everyday arguments, any of those elements may be left unstated. So it is easy to mistake communication that is not intended as an argument for an argument that is not completely stated. Two types of statements that are easy to confuse with arguments are explanations and opinions.

Explanations are communications presented to clarify ideas and improve understanding rather than support a claim. For example, earlier in this chapter a definition of argumentation was presented and then explained to try to help you better understand its meaning. That didn't make an argument in favor of the definition, but developed it further. Sometimes people include explanations as they're making arguments to clarify what they mean, so you have to figure out which parts of their messages are supporting their claims and which parts are explaining their meaning.

Opinions are messages that present an individual's personal beliefs on a subject. Sometimes people include their opinions as support for claims, and sometimes their opinions are their claims, as they present reasons to justify their opinions. Other times they're simply expressing their subjective reaction to something.

The value of opinions varies. The reasoned opinion of someone who has a strong background in the subject under discussion, and who is known to be trustworthy, is worth listening to when reaching a decision. Less-informed opinions are not as worthwhile, nor are those from people known to be deceitful. Even so, the opinions of knowledgeable and trustworthy people may not be correct, and those of less credible sources may turn out to be the best.

Sometimes the way statements are made will give you an indication of whether they're meant as explanations, opinions, or arguments. Phrases such as "for example" or "by that I mean" usually indicate that the statements are explanations. Phrases such as "I think" may indicate that the statements are opinions. Statements that include phrases such as "because" or "therefore" are often meant as parts of arguments. However, we often leave out such phrases, and sometimes we make arguments sound like explanations or opinions in order to appear less confrontational, so it won't always be easy for you to distinguish between explanations and opinions and arguments.

To recognize the difference between explanations, opinions, and arguments, you usually have to consider the context of the communication as well as what is said. For example, after taking a bite of dessert, someone might say, "Mmmmm . . . this is really good. It's sweet and rich and creamy, and the blend of flavors is wonderful." If the speaker is an ordinary person commenting on the dessert at the end of a meal, the first sentence is a statement of opinion, and the second sentence is an explanation of what is meant by "really good." If the speaker is a food critic presenting a professional judgment, then the first sentence is a claim, and the second sentence is the evidence for that claim.

LOGIC, REASONING, AND ARGUMENTATION

Argumentation is strongly connected to logic and reasoning, but the terms do not mean exactly the same thing. Argumentation and reasoning both make use of logic but involve more than traditional logic. The traditional study of logic was the study of **formal logic,** or the study of the logical form that arguments should take, including how premises should lead to conclusions, assuming that the premises are correct. Recently logicians have paid more attention to **informal logic,** which is the study of reasoning from evidence to conclusions, focusing on elements of reasoning other than the form of the arguments. The study of argumentation involves the study of both formal and informal logic in people's communication.

Like the term *argumentation,* there are two senses of the term **reasoning.** In one sense, reasoning is something you *do* as you go through the process of drawing a conclusion. You observe, investigate, think, notice relationships, and arrive at a conclusion. Reasoning in that sense should be done prior to making arguments to try to convince others to accept the conclusions. The other sense of reasoning is something you *use,* in the sense that when you make an argument, you use reasoning to support the claim.

ARGUMENTATION AND RHETORIC

The study of argumentation goes back about 2,500 years, to the time of Plato and Aristotle in Athens. The Athenian system of law and government made the ability to communicate in public forums and persuade very important for all citizens, since they were their own lawyers and legislators. Many of them spent time and money learning how to do it well. They studied **rhetoric,** which was defined by Aristotle (1991) as the "study of the available means of persuasion." Argumentation is a part of the study of rhetoric generally associated with the rhetorical appeal called *logos,* which uses reasoning to influence others, and which we roughly equate with "logic." The other two rhetorical appeals were *ethos* (or the personal character of the individual making the argument, today referred to as "credibility") and *pathos* (or the use of emotions to convince the audience). Most of this text is concerned with *logos* and will help you learn to make strong arguments and recognize strong arguments that other people make. In Chapter 12 you'll learn more about *ethos,* but you should recognize from the start that the ability to make strong arguments also enhances your credibility. In general, *pathos* should be used to enhance the effect of sound arguments, not to replace evidence and reasoning.

The study of argumentation is the study of how to create and present strong reasons for claims that deserve to be accepted. The study of rhetoric is the study of methods that effectively persuade others. That distinction is important, because sometimes people reject an argument that deserves to be accepted for reasons that have nothing to do with the argument, and other times they accept arguments that deserve to be rejected for reasons that have nothing to do with the strength of the argument. As you read the rest of this text, you should keep in mind that the quality of an argument is not based on whether other people agree with it, because there are many ways to create agreement without making sound arguments.

PURPOSE OF ARGUMENTATION

For many people, the purpose of engaging in argumentation is to *win.* That impression is easy to understand, because you do not normally put forth claims unless you believe them. When those claims are disputed, that threatens your ego, and you want to overcome that threat. In addition, in many argumentative situations, such as court trials and political campaigns, winning the arguments is important in achieving the final goal.

When you consider winning the only purpose of argumentation, it tends to distort the practice of argumentation by emphasizing the competitive and sometimes destructive aspects while obscuring the cooperative and constructive aspects. Healthy intellectual competition tests the quality of ideas, so argumentation can be both competitive and constructive. When the ultimate goal is only to "win," however, there is a great deal of temptation to resort to destructive means.

Rather than thinking of winning as the only purpose for argumentation, it is better to think of the purpose as reaching the best decisions we can. When you take that point of view, you can still be motivated to present your strongest arguments, but there is less reason to use questionable methods. You can still "win" if the result is the best decision, even if it isn't the decision for which you initially argued. This perspective is especially productive in argumentation with friends and family, within groups, and when attempting to resolve disputes. The rest of this text is intended to help you learn the skills involved in making and evaluating arguments so you can

- make the strongest arguments.
- recognize when others make strong arguments.
- constructively engage in arguments.
- reach the best decisions.

SPECIALIZED ARGUMENTATION

This text addresses the general principles of argumentation as they are experienced in the day-to-day life of ordinary people. It is not meant to teach you the expectations for argumentation in more specialized fields such as law, physics, or financial management. The fundamental principles of argumentation are the same in both everyday argument and specialized argument, so the material in this text can be applied to specialized fields. However, argumentation in specialized fields is usually expected to conform to rules and conventions that are not expected in other fields.

For example, the specialized field of criminal law has particular methods of introducing evidence in court. Those methods are quite different from the way evidence is introduced in scientific arguments, which are quite different from the expectations in a conversation you have with a friend. The fundamental ways of making strong arguments are the same in all three examples, but the specific expectations differ. Since there are so many different specialized fields, this text cannot begin to address the expectations of all of them, but understanding the basics of everyday argumentation allows you to apply those principles in more specialized situations. As you continue your education and become more of an expert in your field of study, you'll probably learn how you're expected to argue in your field. That will only be part of your life, though, so you need to be able to consider arguments and engage in argumentation in other fields as well.

REASONS TO STUDY ARGUMENTATION

One meaning of rhetoric is the act of using communication to influence others. Various thinkers through the ages have identified several good reasons to study rhetoric, and thus argumentation. Aristotle was one of the earliest to systematically consider why people should study rhetoric. He was partially motivated by Plato's attacks on rhetoric as a skill used to make the bad seem good. Aristotle (1991) argued that there were several values to learning rhetoric, and they all apply well to learning to argue both then and now. He said that knowledge of rhetoric

1. *Helps prevent the triumph of fraud and injustice.* If people are trying to do things that are wrong, then those who know how to argue and persuade can use their abilities to stop them. This may include appeals directly to those who are doing unjust actions, or appeals to others who can prevent the action from being completed. Unless people are willing to speak out, fraud and injustice can continue unchecked. You may be one of those people who speak out to protect others.

2. *Provides a method of instruction to the public.* As people speak and make arguments, they will necessarily have to present information that will support their views. Even though their main purpose is not to inform, they will still have that effect. As you present and receive arguments throughout your life, you will educate both others and yourself.

3. *Makes us see both sides of a case.* People who know how to argue well don't just concentrate on their side of the issue but also think about what the other side might argue. As they look for information to support their side, they also find data that supports the other side, and as they engage in arguments, they listen to what the other side has to say. All of that helps them see both sides of an issue, which will help them to understand the controversy better and will open their minds to new ideas.

4. *Can be a means of self-defense.* When other people say things about you, you may have to defend yourself, and you can do that better if you know how to argue well. Also, as you are subjected to arguments made to convince you to do something, knowledge of argumentation can help you decide which claims have merit so you can better defend yourself against unscrupulous business practices, deceptive politicians, and untrustworthy acquaintances.

Aristotle's ideas certainly have merit for all of us, but his weren't the last words on the subject. St. Augustine, who taught rhetoric before he converted to the Christian faith, also argued that learning rhetoric is valuable, particularly for Christians. At the time, the Church considered rhetoric a pagan art that Christians should shun. St. Augustine (1958), however, said that there were two good reasons Christians should learn rhetoric. His reasons still apply to people today, whatever their faiths or subject.

First, St. Augustine said, learning rhetoric *aids in the search for truth*. People who haven't studied rhetoric are more susceptible to faulty reasoning, so when they learn rhetoric (and argumentation) they are better able to recognize and avoid being fooled by it. Moreover, people who are both schooled in rhetoric and ethics are less likely to resort to trickery in their arguments, because they have the skill and knowledge to make sound cases. Rhetoric can be considered a testing ground for ideas, and those that most closely approximate the truth will be sustained, *if* people on both sides of the issues know how to make their arguments well.

Second, St. Augustine said that knowledge of rhetoric *allows the good to have a voice.* If the people who disagreed with the Church's teachings were the only ones proficient in rhetoric, then they would have an advantage in their attempts to persuade. St. Augustine argued that Christians shouldn't be limited to a reliance on divine inspiration for their words but ought to be responsible for their own persuasion. If one assumes, as he did, that his side of the issue is correct, then that side should have powerful speakers representing it. The same is true in politics, business, education, and other fields.

Both of St. Augustine's arguments are still applicable today, whether we are thinking of religious matters or any other type of issue. People are faced with many significant problems today, ranging from their own personal decisions to social issues such as the environment and the economy. Good argumentation skills help people in their search for the truth and allow their side to have a strong voice.

Still other reasons exist for the value of the study of argumentation. First, it is *something we all do.* We all make and hear arguments daily. It is such a common activity that knowing more about it will simply allow each of us to do it better. Once we know more about argumentation, we should realize that no one is really "illogical." Different people may have different starting places for their reasoning, they may become emotionally involved in what they're talking about, and they may have some flaws in their logic, but they are still being logical. When people call others "illogical," they are generally refusing to deal with others' arguments and are shifting attention away from them. When you deal with other people, it is more useful to try to understand their logic and respond to the errors they may make rather than to call them "illogical."

Second, knowledge of argumentation can help bring about *personal advancement,* both in your education and career. As you go through college, you are going to be asked to do many assignments that are argumentative in nature. Although they aren't stated in such terms, most essay exam questions and term papers call for you to make a claim and support it. If you know how to make good arguments, then you can write those assignments more confidently and won't have to attempt to fool the teacher into thinking that you know what you're writing about.

In your career, you will constantly be faced with the prospect of making claims, supporting claims, defending claims, and responding to others' claims orally and in writing. Whether it's a proposal to a potential client, a defense of your department, or the presentation of a scientific theory, you will regularly make arguments. If you are unsure about how to engage in arguments well, then you are likely to avoid them or present your arguments weakly when you can't avoid them. Or you may try to compensate for your lack of argumentative skill with personal attacks and threatening behavior, all of which will make you appear less competent. If you know how to argue well, then you're better able to make the positive contributions that help advance your career.

A third reason to learn more about argumentation is to allow you to *participate in a representative government*. As you already know, our system of government is predicated on citizen involvement, yet many citizens don't even vote, let alone get more actively involved. There are many reasons for that, but one is that many people don't believe they can be heard. People who have more confidence in their ability to make good arguments are more likely to become involved, whether the politics are local or national. Even if you are not politically active, at some point you're likely to be called for jury duty, and you'll probably feel more comfortable if you have some idea how to evaluate the testimony and arguments presented.

Knowing how to argue is particularly helpful in times of national crisis, because it helps both decision makers and fellow citizens consider different ideas and perspectives. Unfortunately, during such crises, some want to end argumentation because they believe it somehow harms efforts to end the crisis and aids the enemy. Soon after the events of September 11, 2001, some people called those who disagreed with President Bush or opposed military responses "un-American," and they suggested that opposing voices should be silenced. However, it is during such trying times that well-done, ethical argumentation can be most productive. If the dissenters do not have a strong argument, then others should point that out, but if their arguments are strong then their views should be carefully considered. The response to a crisis should not be less thought or less interaction but more well-thought-out arguments.

Personal protection is a fourth reason to learn more about argumentation. We're all subjected to advertising and sales pitches, and it's often difficult to recognize a reasonable decision. If you have a good idea of how to listen for claims and support, and how to evaluate that support, then you can better protect yourself and have more confidence in your decisions. Also, you may need to file a grievance over how you were treated or about a product, and if you understand how to clearly state and support a claim with good evidence, then you're not only more likely to be effective, you're also more likely to register your complaint in the first place.

The fifth reason to learn more about argumentation is for your own *individual problem solving*. Even if you could successfully avoid arguing with others, you will still argue with yourself. Should you stay in school or get a job? Should you stay at this school or transfer? Should you try to improve your relationship with someone else or end it? Should you buy a new car or continue to make do with what you have? The list of problems that each of us face is endless. Thus, a knowledge of argumentation can help you think through those problems to make the best, rather than the quickest or easiest, decisions.

The final reason to learn more about argumentation is because it can *help your relationships with others*. Arguing is a fact of life, but people argue differently. Some people avoid arguing, some stick to the issues, some attack the other person, and some feel attacked whenever they argue. Sticking to the issues during arguments tends to help relationships, because it allows people to bring up differences and try to resolve them without threatening the other. All of the other styles mentioned tend to hurt relationships. Arguing with someone doesn't have to be a negative experience, but many of us experience it as such because we, and the people with whom we argue, don't know how to make it more positive.

The study of argumentation is not just an academic exercise for people who want to engage in intercollegiate debate or who want to become lawyers. It's a practical subject from which everyone can benefit. Part II of this text will help you learn fundamental principles of argumentation that you can use in a variety of situations, and Part III will give you some ideas about how to argue and think critically in public, interpersonal, and small-group contexts.

SUMMARY

You engage in argumentation every day. Sometimes you make the arguments, and sometimes you consider others' arguments, but you regularly engage in communication that expresses reasoning and attempts to gain agreement. Sometimes the arguments are explicit, and sometimes they are not. As you go through your day, you may create an argument about some subject, have an argument with someone else, or make arguments as you have an argument.

You may find it difficult to tell when you're exposed to an argument, because explanations and opinions can appear to be arguments, so it is useful for you to develop the ability to tell the difference between them.

Argumentation is closely related to logic and reasoning, and it is part of the study of rhetoric. You may think that the purpose of argumentation is to win, but it's better to think of argumentation as a way to reach the best decision.

The fundamental principles of argumentation are the same in everyday conversations as in specialized fields, but specialized fields may have additional expectations.

Finally, there are many good and practical reasons to study argumentation and to learn how to do it better.

KEY CONCEPTS

argument₁   arguing in the sense of *making* an argument; putting forth a claim, evidence, and reasoning.

argument₂   arguing in the sense of *having* an argument; an interaction with another person in which each person presents, responds to, and defends ideas.

argumentation   (1) a form of communication in which at least one person explicitly or implicitly puts forth a claim and provides support for that claim with evidence and reasoning; (2) the process of making and engaging in arguments; (3) the study of the process of making and engaging in arguments.

ethos   a rhetorical appeal that uses the personal characteristics of the communicator to influence others.

explanation   a form of communication in which statements are presented to clarify ideas and improve understanding rather than to support a claim.

formal logic   the study of the logical form arguments should take, including how premises should lead to conclusions, assuming the premises are correct.

informal logic   the study of reasoning from evidence to conclusions, focusing on elements of reasoning other than the form of the arguments.

logos   a rhetorical appeal that uses reasoning to influence others.

opinion   a message that presents an individual's personal belief on a subject.

pathos   a rhetorical appeal that uses emotion to influence others.

quarrel   a form of interaction about a conflict, often involving anger, hurt feelings, and the misuse of argumentation to achieve victory.

reasoning   (1) the thought process that leads to a conclusion; (2) the presentation of support for a claim in an argument.

rhetoric   (1) the study of means of persuasion; (2) the act of using communication to influence others.

THINGS TO THINK ABOUT

1. Think of an argument you observed or were a part of in as much detail as you can. Who was involved? What prompted the argument? What was said or written? How would you rate the quality of the argument, using whatever standards of evaluation you think are appropriate?

2. Think of an argument you were exposed to within the past few days. Was it argument$_1$, argument$_2$, or a combination of both? Why?

3. When, if ever, should the purpose of argumentation be to win? When, if ever, should an arguer do everything possible to win? Why?

4. Name three specific situations in which knowledge of argumentation could help you in your future. Why would this knowledge be helpful in each situation?

5. Would our society generally be better if more people had a better knowledge of argumentation? Why or why not?

6. Think of a case when social injustice occurred because of poor argumentation or reasoning. What could have been done to prevent the injustice?

7. Read Colin Powell's speech in the Appendix. Based on what you know at this time, what are the characteristics of argument in his speech?

2

✳

Critical Thinking

Just as you live in a world of arguments, you also live in a world calling for critical thinking. You may think critically about what your friends say; about the ideas of a group as you work on a project; about what you see and hear in mass media; about advertisements; about what peers or authority figures try to get you to do; or about what to do, what to buy, and who to vote for.

Critical thinking is widely recognized as a valuable skill in everyday life. Many colleges and universities require students to complete at least one course in critical thinking, and faculty members in most academic disciplines would say they teach students to think critically. Employers say they want employees who have critical thinking skills.

Critical thinking and argumentation go together well because they have so much in common. Both involve reasoning and analysis, and both are used in problem solving. When you create or evaluate arguments, you use critical thinking. Both call for you to consider the quality of evidence and its relationship to claims to decide what to accept. Argumentation goes beyond critical thinking to express reasoning and overtly respond to others' arguments. Critical thinking goes beyond argumentation to consider whether to accept both arguments and other ideas. You may think critically about a movie, but you don't argue with it. You may make an argument about that movie, though, based on the critical thinking you did about it. You use the same abilities to do both, so learning argumentation helps you become a better critical thinker.

Some people find the idea of critical thinking intimidating because it appears to be difficult. They don't think that they'll be able to find all of the problems in other people's ideas the way some critics do. Most people do it, though, without knowing that's what they're doing. You've probably already picked up some skills without knowing it but may not be entirely confident in your abilities. You may already know how to analyze ideas concerning subjects with which you're quite familiar but don't know how to transfer that ability to other subjects.

Critical thinking doesn't have to be so hard. It is not the easiest thing to do, but it's an ability which you can improve as you learn to apply the principles of critical thinking. One purpose of this text is to provide you with some guidelines to critical thinking that you can use in a variety of situations. This chapter will

- explain what critical thinking is.
- identify the general skills associated with critical thinking.

Chapters 5–11 will provide you with more guidance to develop those skills.

WHAT IS CRITICAL THINKING?

You might think that critical thinking needs no further explanation. Everyone knows what thinking is. After all, we all think almost all of the time. And everyone knows what it means to be critical—it means to find fault with something, right? The meaning of critical thinking should be obvious, shouldn't it?

Among people who have given a great deal of thought to what critical thinking is, however, the meaning is not so simple. A variety of definitions may appear to mean the same thing but have subtle differences. A basic understanding of what critical thinking is can help you learn how to do it, because the meaning we attribute to the phrase will do a lot to determine what we try to teach and learn.

First, we should recognize a common misconception of what critical thinking means. Since an everyday meaning of the word "critical" is to find fault, some people think that critical thinking is thinking that finds fault with other people's ideas. While it is true that sometimes critical thinking does find fault with ideas, that is not all there is to critical thinking. In fact, considering it as finding fault is dangerous, because it can lead to being unnecessarily negative, and it can create the impression that we should not be critical of our own ideas. So let's be clear from the start: *Critical thinking is* not *merely finding errors or weaknesses in other people's ideas.*

Now that we're clear about what critical thinking is not, we should try to determine what it is. Examining the ideas of different scholars will help us understand what they have in common and get a better idea of what is generally considered to be part of critical thinking.

The purpose of this text is not to evaluate all of the scholarly meanings of critical thinking, nor is it to establish the definitive meaning of the term. Only a few definitions of critical thinking are included here, and many others differ from them. In addition, the authors of these definitions typically spend considerable time explaining what they mean, so just reading the definitions will probably not provide you with a full understanding of any of them. However, it is a good way to begin to understand the concept, because it helps provide a sense of how the term is conceived of by different people who have tried to create a precise definition.

Argumentation scholars Frans H. van Eemeren, Rob Grootendorts, and Francisca Snoeck Henkemans (1996) summarized various ideas concerning critical thinking. They note that the idea "traces back to Dewey's (1909/1991) idea of 'reflective thought': 'Active, persistent, and careful consideration of any belief or supposed form of knowledge in the light of the grounds that support it, and the further conclusions to which it tends'" (165). They also refer to Robert Ennis's definition of critical thinking as "reasonable and reflective thinking that is focused on deciding what to believe or do" (184). Turning from what critical thinking is to what critical thinkers do, they present Harvey Siegel's definition of a critical thinker as one who is "appropriately moved by reasons. . . . A critical thinker must be able to assess reasons and their ability to warrant beliefs, claims and actions properly" (185).

Brooke Noel Moore and Richard Parker in their critical thinking text, say that "Critical thinking is simply the careful, deliberate determination of whether we should accept, reject, or suspend judgment about a claim—and of the degree of confidence with which we accept or reject it" (4).

Alan Fisher's and Michael Scriven's definition includes the best ideas of other definitions. They say: "Critical thinking is skilled and active interpretation and evaluation of observations, communications, information and argumentation" (20).

What are some of the characteristics these definitions have in common? First, they all indicate that *critical thinking is not passive or automatic.* They characterize critical thinking as "active," "deliberate," and "careful." In other words, critical thinking takes some conscious effort. As with any skill, some aspects of critical thinking become easier as you master them, but others will always require more work.

Second, they all say that *critical thinking deals with ideas,* including "beliefs," "observations," "communications," "information," and "arguments." We don't think critically about flowers, although we may think critically about our understanding of how flowers grow, the meaning of flowers in our lives, the importance of flowers in an ecosystem, or other *ideas* about flowers.

Third, the definitions show that *critical thinking focuses primarily on reasoning and arguments,* although sometimes we may need to think critically about messages that are not meant as arguments. For example, the news you see on television usually is not meant as an argument, but you still may want to think critically about what is reported and what is left out to decide how much you should believe about what is said and shown.

Fourth, they agree that *critical thinking involves making judgments* about ideas so we can decide "what to believe or do" and whether we should accept, reject, or suspend judgment. Critical thinking is evaluative, but the evaluation doesn't necessarily have to be negative.

Finally, the definitions reveal that *critical thinking involves skills* that allow the thinker to make judgments. Evaluating reasoning goes well beyond "I agree" or "I disagree" and is based on principles of reasoning that have been tested over time. The applications of those principles are the skills involved in critical thinking.

Two other ideas are not apparent in any of these definitions but are very important in understanding what good critical thinking is. First, *critical thinking should be applied both to the ideas of others and to our own ideas.* When Fisher and Scriven explain what they mean by "active" in their definition, they say "the critical thinker must deal in an analytic and evaluative way with material they have authored as well as that coming from others, and . . . this means identifying good and bad sources of information and judgment (on certain topics and under certain conditions)—including oneself" (27). Critical thinking is useful as a way to evaluate other people's ideas, and it can be even more valuable when we use it as a way to check our own thinking.

Second, *critical thinking should be done as a means of approaching truth* on any subject, not simply as a means to support preconceived beliefs. Richard Paul introduced the concepts of "strong sense critical thinking" and "weak sense critical thinking." Eemeren, Grootendorts, and Henkemans summarize the distinction as follows:

> Weak sense critical thinking refers to the ability to criticize arguments in order to attack one's opponent and defend one's own standpoint. Strong sense critical thinking is the capacity to question positions and arguments with a view to exposing their assumptions, as well as one's own unexamined values, in order to get closer to the truth of the matter—even if doing so in the light of a full and open examination of all the relevant arguments requires the abandonment of a cherished position. (184)

Whether or not you agree that truth is "knowable," you should see that taking the time to reflect on your thoughts and reasoning has a better chance of coming closer to the truth than simply accepting the first conclusion you think of. Sometimes the snap judgments we make will turn out to be accurate, and if so, they will stand up to scrutiny. Sometimes, though, the snap judgments will be exposed as flawed once we think about them, and that can lead to much better decisions.

Combining the ideas above leads to the following definition: **critical thinking** is the active application of principles of reasoning to your own ideas and those of others to make judgments about communication and reasoning, to analyze arguments, to expose underlying assumptions, to achieve better understanding, and to approach the truth. The rest of this text is meant to provide you with some tools for critical thinking.

CRITICAL THINKING SKILLS

Now we can take a look at the things people do in order to think critically about a wide range of subjects. Once again, it is instructive to look at what some scholars have listed as "critical thinking skills."

In 1992, the U.S. Department of Education gathered together critical thinking educators to identify what ought to be taught to college students to improve their critical thinking. Diane F. Halpern summarized the results of the deliberations and identified the following five categories of college-level **critical thinking skills:**

1. *Verbal reasoning skills* are skills needed to comprehend and defend against the persuasive techniques that are embedded in everyday language.
2. *Argument analysis skills* are the skills of identifying conclusions, rating the quality of reasons, and determining the overall strength of an argument.
3. *Skills in thinking as hypothesis testing,* which involves the accumulation of observations and the formulation of beliefs or hypotheses, using information collected to decide if it confirms or disconfirms the hypotheses.
4. *Using likelihood and uncertainty* is the correct use of probability.
5. *Decision-making and problem-solving skills* involve the generation and selection of alternatives and judging among them.

Halpern's list of specific skills for each category is found in Table 2.1.

Argumentation scholars Edward S. Inch and Barbara Warnick identify several abilities needed for critical thinking, some of which are essentially the same as those listed by Halpern and some of which are slightly different. They say that critical thinking involves

- clearly stating a question for discussion.
- clarifying the meaning of terms.
- developing and applying criteria for evaluation.
- evaluating the credibility of sources of information.
- refining generalizations and avoiding oversimplification.
- generating and assessing solutions to problems.
- comparing perspectives, interpretations, or theories.
- reading critically, seeking out information that disagrees with one's perspective.
- listening critically, seriously considering views with which one disagrees.

What is the purpose of these lists? Should you memorize every item in them? No. The lists reveal what experts in the field have determined critical thinking involves and provide information to help you determine how you already think critically and how you could improve.

The two lists of abilities are not the final word on what critical thinking involves, but they do help clarify what those of us who teach critical thinking try to accomplish, and what you could learn in a critical thinking course. Teaching all of the skills in the lists is beyond the scope of this text, so the following chapters will focus on three of Halpern's five categories: argument analysis, verbal reasoning, and problem solving.

Critical thinking involves both skills and the **disposition** to use those skills. In other words, you could have the skills, but if you aren't inclined to use them, then

Table 2.1 Categorization of College-Level Critical Thinking Skills

1. Verbal Reasoning Skills

  a. recognizing and defending against the inappropriate use of emotional and misleading language (e.g., labeling, name calling, ambiguity, vagueness, hedging, euphemism, bureaucratese, and arguments by etymology [original word use]);

  b. detecting the misuse of definitions and reification;

  c. understanding the use of framing with leading questions, negation, and marked words to bias the reader;

  d. using analogies appropriately, which includes examining the nature of the similarity relationship and its connection to the conclusion;

  e. employing questioning and paraphrase as a skill for comprehension of text and oral language (i.e., recognizing main ideas);

  f. producing and using a graphic representation of information provided in prose form.

2. Argument Analysis Skills

  a. identifying premises (reasons), counterarguments, and conclusions;

  b. reasoning with "if, then" statements (which includes avoiding the fallacies of affirming the consequence and denying the antecedent);

  c. judging the credibility of an information source;

  d. judging the consistency, relevance to the conclusion, and adequacy of the way premises support a conclusion;

  e. understanding the differences among opinion, reasoned judgment, and fact;

  f. recognizing and avoiding common fallacies such as straw person, appeals to ignorance, slippery slope, false dichotomy, guilt by association, and arguments against the person.

3. Skills in Thinking As Hypothesis Testing

  a. recognizing the need for and using operational definitions;

  b. understanding the need to isolate and control variables in order to make strong causal claims,

  c. checking for adequate sample size and possible bias in sampling when a generalization is made;

  d. being able to describe the relationship between any two variables as positive, negative, or unrelated;

  e. understanding the limits of correlation reasoning;

  f. seeking converging evidence to increase confidence in a conclusion;

  g. considering the relative "badness" of different sorts of errors;

  h. solving problems with proportional and combinational (systematic combinations) reasoning;

  i. determining how self-fulfilling prophecies could be responsible for experimental results and everyday observations.

4. Using Likelihood and Uncertainty

  a. recognizing regression to the mean;

  b. understanding and avoiding conjunction errors;

  c. utilizing base rates to make predictions;

  d. understanding the limits of extrapolation;

  e. adjusting risk assessments to account for the cumulative nature of probabilistic events.

5. Decision-Making and Problem-Solving Skills

  a. listing alternatives and considering the pros and cons of each;

  b. restating the problem to consider different sorts of alternatives;

  c. recognizing the bias in hindsight analyses;

(continued)

Table 2.1 *(continued)*

d. seeking information to reduce uncertainty;

e. recognizing decisions based on entrapment;

f. producing graphs, diagrams, hierarchical trees, matrices, and models as solutions [*sic*] aids;

g. understanding how world views can constrain the problem-solving process;

h. using numerous strategies in solving problems including means-ends analysis, working backward, simplification, analogies, brainstorming, contradiction, and trial and error

Halpern (1994, 33–34).

you won't actually think critically. On the other hand, you may want to think critically, but if you don't have the skills to do so, then you won't be able to. While there is no unanimous agreement that disposition is a necessary element of critical thinking, the dispositions identified in the Department of Education study do help us understand what critical thinking involves. Halpern summarized the list of dispositions to include the following:

- willingness to engage in and persist at a complex task, which involves the willingness to expend the mental energy that is required to begin and complete the task

- willingness to plan, which requires individuals to check their impulsivity and engage in intermediate tasks such as seeking additional information, organizing facts, and generating alternatives

- flexibility or open-mindedness, which is an attitude marked with the willingness to consider new options, try things a new way, and reconsider old problems

- willingness to self-correct, or learn from errors instead of becoming defensive about them

- being mindful, which involves the habit of self-conscious concern for and evaluation of the thinking process

- consensus-seeking, involving high-level communication skills and willingness to find ways to compromise and to achieve agreement

The dispositions aren't characteristics that you either have or don't have. They are inclinations that you can develop to become a better critical thinker and decision maker.

LOCAL AND GENERAL CRITICAL THINKING

All critical thinking is not the same. As you go through school, you should be quite knowledgeable about the subject matter of your major, and that should make critical thinking about that subject easier. Your knowledge should help you recognize common errors in thinking about the subject and how to apply principles of that discipline to particular situations. For example, a history major will find it easier to think of alternative ways to make judgments about historical explanations, because she knows more about different possibilities. She may also be aware of explanations that have already been proven false, so she can evaluate them more quickly and accurately than people with less historical background. Fisher and Scriven refer to learning critical thinking skills by studying a particular subject as **"local" critical thinking.**

There are also many areas of life about which you just don't have time to develop much knowledge. You still have to make decisions, however, so the ability to transfer critical thinking skills from one subject area to another is important. According to Fisher and Scriven, that transfer is better accomplished when you learn general principles of reasoning that apply to all subjects, which they call **"general" critical thinking.**

Both types of critical thinking are valuable. This text takes the general approach to critical thinking and will present many principles that you can apply to a variety of subjects.

OTHER THOUGHTS ABOUT
CRITICAL THINKING

You can think of critical thinking as the act of examining arguments and reasoning to determine if the claims and conclusions are justified. It involves finding both weaknesses and strengths in arguments by examining the assumptions, evidence, and reasoning. The more proficient you become at thinking critically, the easier it will become, sometimes almost second nature. However, even when you are quite skilled and experienced, there will be times when critical thinking will take some conscious effort.

Three general occasions arise when critical thinking seems to be the most difficult. The first is when you are thinking about subject matter with which you are unfamiliar. That includes material that is difficult to understand as well as material that is completely outside of your realm of knowledge. Your lack of knowledge will make it harder to recognize what information is crucial, when necessary information is missing, and when valid principles are being ignored. Being too immersed in the subject matter can lead to problems with critical thinking as well, and that's the second occasion when critical thinking is difficult. Although a wealth of background knowledge usually does lead to better critical thinking, it can sometimes lead to difficulty in considering alternative explanations, unusual hypotheses, and theories that don't fit conventional thinking. The third occasion when critical thinking is more difficult is when you already agree with the claim being made. When that happens, there doesn't seem to be a need to think critically, because the reasoning appears to reach the correct conclusion, but often that's when critical thinking is needed the most. If you recognize the general conditions that make critical thinking more difficult, then you can slow down and carefully consider the reasoning rather than jump to conclusions or give up because it's too hard.

Consider critical thinking as being somewhere midway on a continuum between uncritical gullibility and unbridled skepticism. Gullibility is accepting what people say as the truth without stopping to think about it, and we're all gullible to some extent. At the extreme end of the continuum are people who rarely stop to think if what they're told is really accurate, or if the arguments presented are sound. Those who are uncritically gullible may be told something that they'd realize is outlandish if they only took the time to think about it, but they just accept what they're told. Such people are easy for unscrupulous persuaders to fool. Unbridled skepticism is at the other end of the continuum and involves questioning everything, being unwilling to accept any opinion, belief, or conclusion. People who are that skeptical can avoid making any decision by continually asking for more proof. Critical thinkers do examine evidence and reasoning, but they do so to decide if arguments deserve to be accepted, not to determine if the claim is an unassailable universal Truth.

Critical thinking involves making judgments in the uncertain conditions that characterize everyday life, recognizing that those judgments could turn out to be wrong. When you decide which stocks to invest in, you can't know with absolute certainty the best choices; all you can do is decide which stocks have the highest probability of being the best, given the information you can gather at the time. Critical thinking doesn't guarantee what is right or wrong, good or bad, or valuable or worthless, but it does provide you with a better chance of making decisions that are not based on faulty reasoning.

Critical thinking also involves suspending judgment when that is called for. Sometimes, given all of the available information and after applying sound reasoning, there is no clear answer to a question. At that point, it is appropriate to say, "I don't know the answer." Sometimes you have to make a choice anyway, and if you have given the matter careful thought, then you may have to base your choice on something other than the reasoning behind the alternatives. Some people avoid the decision-making process altogether, because they think that there is always a "right" answer, but don't see an answer that is clearly right, and they're afraid to be wrong. There seems to be some stigma attached to concluding "I don't know," so lots of people don't consider it a possibility. If you really are thinking critically, though, you may realize that "I don't know" is the most appropriate answer.

When you study critical thinking, it can seem as though you're expected to think critically about everything all of the time, but that's unreasonable. You are faced with too much information and reasoning every day to stop to carefully consider every argument and report. Part of critical thinking is deciding when the context calls for critical thinking. Remember, critical thinking takes some effort and usually takes some time, and sometimes it just isn't worth it. For instance, it doesn't make sense to think critically about chewing gum advertisements you see on television if you rarely chew gum. Even if you do regularly buy chewing gum, the distinction between the various brands is so slight and the price so low that critical thinking about the advertisements is not worth the effort. It is more efficient to buy a pack of gum and determine if you like it enough to buy it again than to carefully weigh the competing claims of various brands. Perhaps you should do some critical thinking about the decision to watch television, or the effects of advertising

Figure 2.1 Some people may count on others failing to think critically.

© Dan Piraro. Reprinted with special permission of Universal Press Syndicate.

on yourself and society, or your decision to chew gum, but those are separate issues from the value of analyzing the advertisements themselves. However, if you are tempted to spend large sums of money to call a psychic hotline, buy a particular car, or respond to a variety of other advertisements, then carefully considering their claims and support could be more important because the stakes are higher.

Determining when the context calls for critical thinking also has interpersonal ramifications. Some people love to engage in vigorous discussions in which their ideas are challenged and they have the chance to challenge other people's ideas. Other people like to engage in conversations in which they express their opinions and hear other people's opinions, but they hate being challenged to prove what they say. Many people find both types of interaction undesirable. You should be aware that putting all of your critical thinking skills to use and dissecting what others say during casual conversations could lead to strained relationships.

Although critical thinking does lead to better decisions, it doesn't necessarily make your life easier. Once you develop your critical thinking skills, you may notice problems in reasoning that others miss. You may see that decisions are made because they are expedient rather than clearly thought out. You may find it more difficult to go along with the crowd, and you may find yourself rejecting popular opinions and taking unpopular stands because you are really thinking about the issues. And, you may find it harder to make your own arguments to support your positions, because you recognize the weaknesses in those arguments. Critical thinking can complicate your life, but it's worth the effort.

SUMMARY

Critical thinking is something each of us has the opportunity to do every day of our lives. While there are a variety of definitions of critical thinking, most acknowledge that critical thinking takes effort, applies to ideas, focuses on reasoning and arguments, and involves making judgments and using learned skills. In addition, critical thinking should be applied to both other people's ideas and your own, and it should be done as a way to approach the truth regarding a given subject. Many critical thinking skills have been identified that can give you some guidance as you become a better critical thinker.

Critical thinking can be learned either by studying a particular subject or by studying the general principles of critical thinking, although the thinking skills appear to transfer better when the general principles are the focus of study.

Critical thinking is more difficult when you think about unfamiliar subjects, when you are very familiar with a subject, and when you already agree with what someone says. You can think of it as being midway between uncritical gullibility and unbridled skepticism. It involves carefully considering ideas instead of automatically accepting or rejecting them. Sometimes the best result that a critical thinker may achieve is the recognition that he or she doesn't know what is true.

As a critical thinker, you must decide when to apply your critical thinking skills and when the context does not call for putting forth the effort to think critically. While becoming a better critical thinker can improve your decision making, it doesn't necessarily make your life easier.

KEY CONCEPTS

critical thinking   the active application of principles of reasoning to your own ideas and those of others to make judgments about communication and reasoning, to analyze arguments, to expose underlying assumptions, to achieve better understanding, and to approach the truth.

critical thinking disposition   the inclination to use critical thinking skills when the situation calls for it.

critical thinking skills   abilities that can be learned to improve critical thinking, including verbal reasoning, argument analysis, thinking as hypothesis testing, using likelihood and uncertainty, and decision-making and problem-solving skills.

general critical thinking   critical thinking about subjects with which you are not very familiar, applying the general principles of reasoning

and argumentation to recognize weak or strong reasoning.

local critical thinking   critical thinking about subjects with which you are very familiar so that you can recognize inaccuracies and common faulty thinking about that subject.

THINGS TO THINK ABOUT

1. Think of an example of some critical thinking that you have done. What was the situation, and what did you consider in your critical thinking? How did you use the five categories of critical thinking skills?

2. Which dispositions of critical thinking characterize you? Which of them could you improve? How can you tell which ones you have and which ones you don't?

3. Think of a time when thinking critically was difficult for you. Why was it difficult? How does the difficulty you had relate to the ideas in this chapter?

4. Think of an example of a decision you may have to make in the future for which you cannot reach an absolutely certain conclusion. Why can your conclusion not be certain? How can critical thinking help you reach a decision?

5. Think of a subject about which you do your best critical thinking, and a subject about which your critical thinking could improve. Why do you do so well with one and not the other?

6. What is the relationship of critical thinking to creative thinking? How are they similar, and how are they different? Is critical thinking ever creative?

7. What might be some reasons that people don't think critically? Why do you believe that to be true?

8. Think of a controversial issue about which you have a strong opinion. What could you do as a critical thinker to fairly consider the opposing viewpoint?

9. Find three parts of Colin Powell's speech in the Appendix that call for critical thinking. Why did you choose each part?

3

✳

Ethics in Argumentation

Another issue must be considered before we further examine how to make strong arguments: ethics in argumentation. In fact, you should consider ethics as you learn about every other facet of argumentation, because the skills you acquire can be used or misused to influence others. When you are able to recognize argumentative tricks, you may be tempted to use them yourself.

Acting ethically is, in many cases, hard work. Developing principles of ethics is relatively easy compared to consistently acting upon them. For instance, most people would agree that it is ethically right to tell the truth when making arguments. However, we may have difficulty with this principle in a real argument, when we know that if the whole truth came out, our position would not be as strong. Will we intentionally deceive instead of risk "losing" the argument?

It is important to realize that part of what makes good argumentation is doing it in an ethical, or a morally right, manner. Knowing how to make convincing arguments is a form of power, which can be used to persuade people to act. Argumentation that persuades people to act against their best interests, or those of their communities, is unethical. Even when the intent seems to be in the best interests of the audience, the way the argumentation is done may still be unethical.

Unethical   Ethical

Figure 3.1

When you evaluate ethics in argumentation, it is useful to think of ethical behavior on a continuum, with absolutely unethical behavior at one end, absolutely ethical behavior at the other end, and varying degrees of ethical behavior in between (see Figure 3.1). Our behavior is usually *more* ethical or *less* ethical rather than totally ethical or totally unethical. If we have only two choices—ethical and unethical—then we either have to set the standards too low to be meaningful or too high to achieve. If we think of ethics on a continuum, then we can evaluate an argument as being ethical but capable of being even more ethical.

A good principle to use when thinking about ethics in argumentation is Immanuel **Kant's Moral Imperative,** which can be summarized as "act in a way that would be best if everyone acted that way." Most of us would agree that it would not be best if everyone lied when they argued, and that it would be best if everyone told the truth, for example. So, according to Kant, it would be best to always tell the truth when you argue, even when your argument would be more convincing if you didn't. The ethical standards discussed in the following pages provide some specific directions that meet Kant's Moral Imperative.

This chapter will describe

- a way of thinking about ethical argumentation.
- ethical principles for public argumentation.
- ethical principles for interpersonal argumentation.
- ethical principles for educational argumentation.
- how to use ethical principles to analyze arguments.

Even though the ethical principles have been divided among different contexts, think of them as being applicable to argumentation in other contexts as well.

BROCKRIEDE'S THREE TYPES
OF ARGUER

In 1972, argumentation theorist Wayne Brockriede discussed argumentation ethics using a metaphor that compared three approaches to argumentation with three approaches to sexual relations. In many of his writings, Brockriede stressed that argumentation can value other people or devalue them. His position was that the best argumentation is that which recognizes the inherent worth of other people. His metaphor helps us think of the effects of common argumentative tactics on other people.

Brockriede calls the most ethical type of arguer the **arguer as lover.** People who argue as lovers attempt to present their ideas in the spirit of mutual cooperation. They are willing to reveal all information (even if it may weaken their arguments), grant the legitimacy of the other arguer's claims, and listen with an open mind to the other person's arguments. Most of all, this type of arguer sees the co-arguer as someone to be respected rather than as an adversary to overcome.

That doesn't mean that arguers as lovers don't argue vigorously. They are willing to take a stand and defend it, and won't back down if the counterarguments aren't convincing. However, they argue in a way that does not demean or disparage others. Arguers as lovers take exception to *ideas,* but do not attack the *people* expressing them. They argue in a way that would be best if everyone argued.

Brockriede's second type of arguer is the **arguer as seducer.** The seducer attempts to trick the co-arguer through deception, withholding information, and misusing language, and through other misleading means of gaining assent. The arguer as seducer sees the co-arguer as someone to be manipulated rather than as a person to treat with respect.

Arguers as seducers also clearly fail to act in a way that would be best if everyone acted that way. They don't have enough faith in their ideas to present them honestly and clearly, so others can't evaluate the true merit of their arguments. Seducers don't try to win arguments at any cost, but they will stoop to deceit and flattery to achieve their goal.

Brockriede's third type of arguer is the **arguer as abuser.** He actually used a different word than "abuser," but the term he originally used has such strong, negative associations for so many people that another term seems necessary. I chose "abuser" because it captures the harm in the behavior. You should remember, regardless of the term used, that this style is harmful to others and is considered unethical. To paraphrase what Brockriede wrote:

> Arguers can have the abuser's attitude toward other people, arguers can have an intent to abuse, and the argumentative act itself can constitute abuse. The argumentative abuser views the relationship as a unilateral one. His attitude toward coarguers is to see them either as objects or as inferior human beings. So the abuser's intent in a transaction with such people is to manipulate the objects or to violate the victims. The abuser wants to gain or to maintain a position of superiority—whether on the intellectual front of making his case prevail or on the interpersonal front of putting the other person down. (2)

The arguer as abuser attempts to overpower the co-arguer, trying to win the argument through force, intimidation, fabrication, monopoly of communication channels, or other unfair advantages. This type of arguer sees the co-arguer as an enemy to be conquered rather than as a person. Abusive arguers aren't interested in determining truth but in dominating others.

The detrimental effects of this type of argumentative style should be obvious, yet it is too commonly used. People attempt to win arguments by shouting louder

Figure 3.2 Seductive arguers can get us to do things that aren't exactly in our best interests.

Soup To Nutz reprinted by permission of Newspaper Enterprise Association, Inc.

than others or by calling other people names and casting doubt on their competence. Bosses try to win arguments by threatening their employees' job security. Protesters try to win arguments by denying their opponents any opportunity to be heard. Arguers as abusers obviously violate Kant's Moral Imperative, yet they justify doing so because they "know" they are right.

Brockriede's metaphor emphasizes that there is nothing positive about the arguer as abuser by stressing that such arguers are promoting power, not argument, and that profound damage can result from such behavior. He makes clear that certain ways of arguing can cause serious psychological damage to others.

As past students applied Brockriede's three types of arguers to actual argumentation, they made it clear that a category of arguer was missing. How do you classify an arguer who is not as overpowering as the arguer as abuser but who is not as subtle as the seducer? Where would you put an arguer who mixes in sarcasm and name-calling with sound arguments and honest expressions of a viewpoint? How do you categorize someone who clearly is not an arguer as lover but who does not fit into the other categories either? Thus there is a need for a fourth type: the **arguer as harasser.**

Sexual harassment is a term that wasn't widely used when Brockriede wrote his article, but it is in most people's vocabularies now and fits in well with Brockriede's metaphor. The arguer as harasser belittles or ridicules the co-arguer or the subject of the argument but is less forceful and less obvious than the arguer as abuser. The arguer as harasser may defend such practices as being "all in fun" or as making the argument more interesting. The effect, however, is to create a "hostile argumentative environment" in which the targets of the humor are reluctant to engage because they are personally attacked—often in a "lighthearted" way that can make them seem unreasonable if they object.

An individual is usually not the same type of arguer in every argument or even during a single argument. We may argue as a lover one day and as an abuser the next. Of course, some people are more consistent than others, but most of us change with the context. It's very important to remember that these four types are more useful to describe argumentative *behavior* than they are to label specific people.

Some variations of a conversation illustrating the four types of arguers are presented in Sidebar 3.1.

Brockriede's types of arguers provide a useful point of view for argumentative ethics in general, but we also need to identify standards of ethics that are specific to the context in which the argumentation takes place. We will look next at three contexts: argumentation in public decision making, argumentation in interpersonal communication, and educational argumentation. As you read about them, keep in mind that the principles described in each context also apply to the other contexts, depending on the circumstances.

ETHICAL ARGUMENTATION IN
PUBLIC DECISION MAKING

A good deal of argumentation happens in public discourse. Judicial proceedings involve public argumentation to determine guilt and innocence, legislative debate involves public argumentation to decide public policy, commentary in magazines and newspapers makes public arguments about all kinds of issues, and scholarly journals publish arguments to influence theory in every discipline. Even advertising is often argumentation or pseudo-argumentation intended to influence purchasing decisions.

The purpose of argumentation in public decision making is to search for the "truth" about a particular issue, whether it's factual truth, evaluations, or the best course of action. Such argumentation is done in an open forum to test ideas and positions and to reach conclusions based on reasons and evidence. Such ideals are the basis of our system of government and justice. Of course, the system doesn't always work the way it should, but that's usually because the system is misapplied, not because the goal is wrong. So part of what we'll look for are acts that will promote the search for truth (which would be on the more ethical end of the continuum) and acts that will hinder the search for truth (which would be on the less ethical end of the continuum). That leads us to five standards for ethics in public-decision-making argumentation.

1. *Argumentation in public decision making is more ethical when honest evidence is used.* When evidence used in argumentation is not honest, then the truth can be approached only by accident. Dishonest evidence can only lead to conclusions in which we can have no reasonable faith. Honest evidence must not be *fabricated* (the advocate can't just make it up), must not be *distorted* (the advocate can't edit it in ways that change its meaning), and must be *complete* (the advocate should provide enough background and context so listeners can judge its worth).

Sidebar 3.1 Types of Arguers

The four brief dialogues that follow illustrate types of arguers based on Brockriede's metaphor. The characters are college students and roommates. When they started rooming together they agreed that they would take turns each week keeping the apartment clean. Casey feels that Tina hasn't done her share for a while and wants her to clean the apartment. When she sees Tina leaving one day, she decides to bring it up. As you read the examples, remember that you don't know if Tina has done her share or not, only that Casey feels that she hasn't.

Arguer As Lover

Casey: Where are you going?

Tina: I'm just going over to Jeff's.

Casey: Oh. There's something I wanted to talk to you about sometime.

Tina: OK. I have some time right now if you want.

Casey: All right. Well, do you remember when we first moved in together that we'd agreed to take turns cleaning up each week?

Tina: Yes.

Casey: Lately I've felt like I've been doing more than my share. Like when it's my turn, I try to make sure things are kept clean, but it seems like when it's my turn again it's a lot messier than I left it for you.

Tina: You know, I really haven't noticed that. I thought I'd been keeping it pretty clean.

Casey: I understand that you'd think that because I don't think you're purposely trying to leave it messy. And I understand that it's natural for different people to have different expectations. Maybe you're just not used to keeping things as spotless as I am. This is something that's pretty important to me, and I hope we can work it out.

Tina: Sure we can. I didn't realize it was bothering you. How about if you let me know when things aren't as clean as you want so I know what to fix?

Casey: That sounds good. And you can let me know if my standards seem too extreme for you.

Tina: Yeah. I'm glad you brought this up. I'll see you later!

In this dialogue, Casey is straightforward about what she wants, is careful to avoid attacking Tina in any way, and shows that she's interested in maintaining her relationship with Tina. If this is typical of their way of handling problems, then they're likely to maintain a healthy relationship.

Arguer As Seducer

Casey: Tina, where are you going?

Tina: Oh, I'm just going over to Jeff's.

Casey: Oh . . . well . . . there's something I wanted to talk with you about. I guess it could wait until later, though.

Tina: That's OK. We can talk now.

Casey: I was wondering if you could do a favor for me. . . . Well, maybe I shouldn't ask.

Tina: That's OK. Go ahead.

Casey: You're always so nice. I'm really glad we're roommates.

Tina: Me too. (Pause.) What did you want to talk about?

Casey: Well . . . you know I haven't been feeling well lately, and on top of that I'm behind in all my classes.

Tina: Yeah. How are you doing?

Casey: Oh, things aren't going too well for me right now. That's why I was wondering if you could do a little more to keep the apartment cleaned up. I don't have the time or energy to do it myself, or you know I would.

(continued)

Sidebar 3.1 *(continued)*

Tina: You really think it needs to be cleaned up? I thought it looks pretty good. I vacuumed on Monday, and I just washed the dishes last night.

Casey: Yeah, I guess you did. (Sigh) Maybe I'll work on it while you're gone instead of resting or doing my homework. You go have fun.

Tina: You don't have to do that. I have to go now, but I'll do what I can when I get back.

In this dialogue, Casey tries to get her way by flattering Tina and making Tina feel sorry for her. Casey may be someone who socializes and procrastinates a lot, so it may be her own fault that she hasn't been feeling well and is behind in her classes. She tries to keep that information hidden from Tina, though, and she tries to use it to manipulate Tina into doing more. She may be right that Tina should do more, but she uses the strategy of a seducer. If Tina finds out that she's been manipulated, then it's likely to harm their relationship, especially if this is typical of Casey's way of getting what she wants.

Arguer As Abuser

Casey: Where do you think you're going?

Tina: Oh, I'm just going over to Jeff's.

Casey: (Angrily) I don't think so! Look at this place. It's a mess! It's your turn to clean it up, and you're *gonna* do it! You're always going off somewhere instead of doing what you should and I'm SICK of it.

Tina: Well, I can . . .

Casey: Don't "well" me! You're gonna get off your lazy behind and clean up. I've been taking my turn *and* your turn for weeks, and it's going to stop or else!

Tina: But I thought . . .

Casey: (Shouting) *You* thought? Ha! You *thought* you could get away with doing nothing and I'd take up your slack. You're just plain lazy and irresponsible, and I'm *sick* of it! You think your pathetic little life is so important that nobody else matters, but you're wrong. You can forget about going anywhere until you get this mess cleaned up. Do you understand, or am I going too fast for you?

In this dialogue, Casey's way of making her argument is to insult, threaten, and cut Tina off so that she can't present her side. Casey tries to overwhelm Tina and is only concerned with "winning" the argument. If this is Casey's typical way of arguing, then Tina may decide to terminate the relationship.

Arguer As Harasser

Casey: Where are you going?

Tina: Oh, I'm just going over to Jeff's.

Casey: Well, you know this is your week to keep the apartment cleaned up.

Tina: I don't think it is. Didn't I do it last week?

Casey: *Didn't I do it last week?* Well, I seem to remember doing a lot of cleaning last week. HELLO? (Laughs)

Tina: You might have done some cleaning, but I'm sure I did most of it.

Casey: (Smiling) Oh, you're *sure,* huh? Like you were *sure* you paid the electric bill a couple of months ago? I'm glad we don't have to depend on your memory for everything. (Laughs)

Tina: OK. So you're pretty sure it's my turn?

Casey: DUH!

Tina: OK, I'll get on it when I get back.

Casey: Well, I'll believe *that* when I see it. (Laughs)

Casey ridicules and teases Tina into agreeing with her in this dialogue. She may laugh a lot and roll her eyes to lighten the mood, but she's arguing as a harasser. Tina may accept it as Casey's way of expressing herself, but if it happens often, there is a good chance that she will eventually find the relationship less valuable.

2. *Argumentation in public decision making is more ethical when opposing sides make their best cases, which requires knowledge of how to do argumentation.* For public decision making, it isn't enough to present ideas in a passionate, but an unprepared, way. Advocates have a responsibility to make their *best* arguments, particularly when they're arguing on behalf of someone else, such as a lawyer does in a trial. Making your best arguments depends on such things as knowing how to discover information, both in the library and from other sources; knowing how to discover lines of argumentation to cover the issues that need to be covered (discussed in Chapters 7 and 8); knowing how to use evidence to make the arguments strong (discussed in Chapter 9); knowing how to effectively and ethically present arguments so that they make sense and are compelling (discussed in Chapters 11 and 12); knowing how to refute the opposition (discussed in Chapter 11); and putting forth the effort to make a strong argument. This text is a starting point toward doing all of that, but you'll need to sharpen your intellectual skills through lifelong learning and make conscious commitments to make your best cases.

3. *Argumentation in public decision making is more ethical when both sides have an opportunity to be heard.* A lot of people don't want to admit it, but no one has a monopoly on the truth. Fallible human beings have fallible ideas, and one of the best ways to test those ideas is to expose them to public scrutiny. People who have a dogmatic belief that they are absolutely right and don't allow their opposition to have a turn deprive everyone of the chance to weigh the arguments. Most people become indignant when they hear of a dictator silencing his opposition but have no problem when someone with whom they disagree is shouted down. The side of the cause that you're on doesn't affect the ethics of such behavior.

   When considering this standard, it's important to realize that it refers to the *opportunity* to be heard. It doesn't say that anyone has the ethical responsibility to make the opposition's case for her or him, nor does it say that the opposition can't be refuted once the case is made. So if you present one side of an issue and allow others their chance to present their side, then you've met this ethical obligation. On the other hand, if you try to prevent the other side from being heard by shouting down another speaker, for example, then you've violated this principle of ethics. Sometimes it's difficult to stand by and let ideas with which you strongly disagree be expressed, but if you want your ideas to have a chance, then you have to extend the same courtesy to others.

4. *Argumentation in public decision making is more ethical when parties in the argument do not deceive or intentionally manipulate.* Too often advocates spend their time trying to figure out how they can give the appearance of a convincing argument instead of working to develop one. Deception and manipulation may effectively fool people into believing the advocate's claims, but they don't promote the search for truth. And, as we've seen so often in politics, deceptions ultimately backfire, leaving people suspicious and cynical.

5. *Argumentation in public decision making is more ethical when decision makers pay attention to the arguments.* The first four standards refer to the people making the arguments, but the people who listen to them and make the decisions have ethical responsibilities as well. Decision makers who have their minds made up in advance and won't listen to contrary arguments are hindering the search for truth as much as anyone who presents false evidence. Certainly decision makers come to the argument with some preconceived ideas, but they should come with open minds, ready to listen to evidence and reasoning and to change their minds if warranted.

Sometimes professional ethics may appear to conflict with the ethical standards above, but such appearances are misinterpretations. For example, defense lawyers have an ethical responsibility to try to get their clients acquitted, but that duty does not extend to fabricating evidence or unlawfully preventing the prosecution from making a case. Certainly there are lawyers who try to do such things, just as there are people in every profession who behave unethically. They may use professional ethics to rationalize their actions, but that doesn't make them ethical.

ETHICAL ARGUMENT AND INTERPERSONAL COMMUNICATION

A second general arena of argumentation is interpersonal communication. While public communicators try to influence large numbers of people, or people who are essentially strangers, only a few people are involved in interpersonal communication, and the communicators know each other or are in the process of developing a relationship. Interpersonal communication is usually face-to-face, but it may be over the telephone, through letters, or by e-mail.

The emphasis in interpersonal communication is on "personal," regardless of the subject being discussed. There may be only two people involved, or there may be a small group. The typical example of interpersonal communication is a conversation. The topic, however, doesn't have to be "personal." Two people arguing over their relationship would communicate interpersonally. So would a group of friends arguing about the president's justification for a military action.

Interpersonal communication has many implications for the well-being of the participants that are not shared by public communication. Because of the personal nature of the communication, there is a much greater chance for feelings to be hurt or helped, for the communicators to become angry or pleased, and for relationships to be damaged or improved. The ethical standards for argumentation as interpersonal communication are derived from the nature of interpersonal communication and what would be the best ways for all people to treat each other. As it turns out, the ethical standards also lead to better argumentation.

The initial perspective we take toward argumentation as interpersonal communication is that argument is a form of human communication. While public decision-making communication is primarily concerned with argument$_1$, interpersonal argumentation is equally concerned with both argument$_1$ and argument$_2$. There are two important implications to this perspective. First, we should be concerned with the human beings involved and how we treat them, not just with the arguments or the topics. The goal should be both to find the truth about the subject and to treat others with respect and dignity. Second, certain characteristics distinguish interpersonal communication from other forms of communication, such as making requests, asking questions, and presenting instruction. This perspective toward argumentation leads to five standards of ethics for argument as interpersonal communication.

1. *Interpersonal argumentation is more ethical when each arguer treats the other with respect.* It would be nice if this idea was self-explanatory, but it isn't. It's not enough to think that you respect the other, or say that you respect the other, if your actions don't show respect. So what can you do to treat another person with respect?

   First, you can give the other person a chance to speak without interruption. Some interruptions are a natural part of conversation, but if you find yourself interrupting another person, then you should pause and let her finish. Second, really listen to what the other person says. That means you really try to understand the other—you don't just listen for errors to exploit, you don't just pretend to listen, and you don't ignore what the other person is saying while you're planning your own response. Third, you shouldn't distort the other's ideas. Honest misunderstandings happen, but it's not ethical to knowingly twist the other's ideas to try to gain an advantage in the argument. Finally, don't resort to intimidation. Such tactics include name-calling, yelling, and physical threats. It's one thing to raise your voice because you really care about what you're saying, but it's something entirely different to shout down someone. Intimidation tactics can also include calmer expressions of superiority that still threaten or disparage the other arguer.

2. *Interpersonal argumentation is more ethical when each arguer recognizes the legitimate place that emotions have in an argument.* Contrary to the wishes of people who would like us all to be coldly logical, people are emotional as well as intellectual. The fact that people are emotionally involved in what they're talking about doesn't necessarily mean their reasoning is poor. Refuting an argument by saying "Oh, now you're just getting emotional" discounts a very real part of that other person and evades the issue.

3. *Interpersonal argumentation is more ethical when each arguer strives for equality in the relationship.* Equality in a relationship means that no one acts as though she or he is superior to another. There will always be differences in knowledge of a subject, ability to make arguments, and level of social status, but none of those are differences in human worth. Too many interpersonal arguments degrade into opportunities to harm someone's sense of self-worth. Striving for equality means inviting the other person's ideas, giving the other person a fair hearing, avoiding dismissing the other person's ideas, and avoiding

demeaning comments. This principle also means that it is best to actively try to create a sense of equality, not just try to avoid creating a sense of inequality.

4. *Interpersonal argumentation is more ethical when each arguer recognizes the legitimacy of the other person's perspective.* The very fact that you are engaged in an argument indicates that there is a difference of opinion, and it's natural to believe that your opinion is correct and the other person's is incorrect. But the other person's perspective is how she perceives the world, based on her experiences, and that's legitimate. Recognizing the legitimacy of the other person's perspective means trying to understand that perspective and acknowledging that the other person has a right to it. You don't have to agree with it, but recognizing its legitimacy for the other person helps your interaction, helps your relationship with that person, and helps confirm the value of the other person. Besides, it might be your perspective that needs changing.

5. *Interpersonal argumentation is more ethical when each arguer concedes the other's valid points.* Too often we think of arguments, even with people we care about, as some kind of battle to be won. And in that battle we think we weaken our positions if we give up any ground. As a result, we do our best to avoid admitting that the other person said anything that's right. The problem with that kind of attitude is that it tends to make other people feel worthless, as though their ideas couldn't possibly have any value. People who admit that other arguers say things that are true show the other arguers that they have some worthwhile ideas and create a much better atmosphere for interpersonal communication. As an arguer, you don't always have to be right, and it's usually better to admit that the other person is right than to try to dogmatically hold a position that is wrong.

ETHICAL ARGUMENTATION AS AN EDUCATIONAL EXERCISE

The third forum of argumentation is argumentation as an educational exercise, such as the arguments you make for class assignments. The perspective we take is that educational argumentation is a learning situation. Unlike the other two contexts, educational argumentation isn't necessarily "real" advocacy of a position. Its purpose is to develop the ability to effectively engage in arguments rather than sway people to agree with your position. It's somewhat experimental; you try out positions, even some with which you may personally disagree.

In educational argumentation, you can argue against a position you hold because you can learn much by doing so. You'll probably face severe time constraints so you won't be able to reveal all possible information supporting your position. When you have an opposing arguer, you will try to anticipate her arguments and generate counterarguments to learn how to do this better. As you present your best arguments, you will become more proficient, and your opponent will learn to respond to stronger arguments.

Educational argumentation often takes a competitive form, such as academic debate, so it's easy to think that winning is the only thing that's important. Keep in mind, however, that the competition is only a way to learn to argue better. Many people are motivated to try harder and do more in a competitive atmosphere than they would otherwise. However, winning educational arguments by no means justifies straying into ethically questionable behavior. The perspective of educational argumentation as a learning situation leads to the following standards of ethics, some of which overlap with previous standards.

1. *Educational argumentation is more ethical when evidence is accurate.* As in public argumentation, the evidence should be neither fabricated nor distorted. Allowing inaccurate evidence will not help you learn to discover good evidence or use the best evidence you can find. In all forums, honesty is a valued part of argumentation.

2. *Educational argumentation is more ethical when evidence is available to all.* This means that others should be able to find the same evidence you found; your evidence should not be from a "personal" source. This ethical standard puts all of the arguers on equal ground. Personal letters or conversations can't be verified or even known about in advance, so it's unfair to let anyone use them. This standard also means that an ethical arguer will not try to monopolize sources of evidence by checking out everything on a subject from the library or tearing out articles from magazines in the library so his opponent can't use them.

3. *Educational argumentation is more ethical when no one engages in personally harmful argumentative strategies.* Most people engaged in educational argumentation have enough trouble mastering the basic skills, so they don't think about harmful strategies, but a few would rather win at all costs than have a straightforward argument. Some of the strategies they use include purposely trying to confuse the opponents, personally attacking the opponents, and intentionally using undue emotionalism in their language or delivery. Sometimes those things happen inadvertently in a learning situation, but when they are done on purpose to avoid argumentation and to engage in gamesmanship, then they are considered both poor argumentation and less ethical.

A GENERAL ETHICAL STANDARD

One important ethical standard that was not directly mentioned is that *it is more ethical to give credit where credit is due.* This means that when you get an idea or information from someone else, you should identify the source to clarify that this was not your original idea. This is known as "citing sources." If you use information or ideas without crediting sources, then you are technically guilty of plagiarism, which is widely recognized as a breach of ethics.

You should cite sources regardless of where you received the information. If you heard an idea from someone else, then you should say so. If you received information from a printed source, television, or radio, then you should say so.

And if you found information on the Internet, then you should identify the Web site from which it came. Citing sources is usually easier to do in written arguments than in oral arguments, because you can use footnotes. Even so, be sure to cite sources for any information that is not your own.

ANALYZING THE ETHICS
OF ARGUMENTS

When you evaluate the ethics of any argument, you must not confuse ethics with agreement or argumentative competence. Students often say that an argument is unethical, but they explain this by saying that it advocates a position with which they disagree, or that it does not include issues that they think conclusively refute the argument. Failure to address potential counterarguments may be a valid criticism of the merits of an argument, but it is an ethical issue only if you can prove that the arguer purposefully tried to hide the counterarguments to gain some kind of an advantage.

In most cases the issue of competence as an arguer is also separate from that of ethics. Making a mistake in an argument isn't proof that the person is arguing unethically. Some poor arguments are argued ethically, and some strong arguments are argued unethically.

As you analyze the ethics of an argument, it's also important to consciously try to be fair-minded. Avoid accusing someone of being unethical unless you have compelling proof. The proof may be in the language used, such as the demeaning language of the arguer as abuser. Or, you may find proof of distorted evidence if you go back to the sources that the arguer used. Rather than leveling charges of ethical violations, stop to think if there is another explanation.

There will be times when the possibility of other explanations will leave an argument in an ethical gray area—neither clearly ethical nor clearly unethical. When you're evaluating an argument, it's perfectly acceptable to say "It's not completely unethical, but it could be more ethical" and then provide evidence and reasoning for that judgment. Many times such a position is preferable to an absolute judgment. Students who can see both the ethical strengths and weaknesses of an argument usually have thought more critically than those who try to take a more absolute and extreme position.

Once you've consciously decided you're going to be as fair as you can, then it's time to read or listen to the argument to get a general sense of what the arguer did. At this point you're not evaluating it yet, only trying to understand it. After you've done that, you can decide which evaluative standards to use. Brockriede's types of arguers encompass ethical standards that can be applied to any argument. If you use them, look for evidence of each type in the argument. Keep in mind that an arguer may show signs of all of the different types in various parts of the argument. If so, you should acknowledge the good with the bad and show that the arguer was *primarily* one type but had characteristics of other types.

You also can analyze the ethics of an argument according to its context: public, interpersonal, or educational. Most of the time you will examine public decision-making arguments, so you will look for evidence that the arguer did or did not fulfill the ethical obligations for public argumentation. Sometimes it can be quite difficult to tell if the standards are met. For instance, you'd have to find the arguer's sources of information and read them to conclusively determine if she fabricated or distorted evidence, although you can argue that based on what she did say and what you do know, it is unlikely that she fabricated or distorted the information. You don't want to make claims that you cannot support, but you also don't want to make claims that are so bland that you really aren't saying anything.

In any event, keep in mind that when you are evaluating the ethics of an argument, you are making an argument yourself, so you not only need to provide support for what you claim, you need to meet high ethical standards yourself.

SUMMARY

Ethics are important to consider when learning about argumentation, because virtually every argumentative encounter calls for you to make ethical choices, and because part of what makes your argument good is how well you conform to ethical standards. It is useful to think of argumentative ethics on a continuum instead of as an ethical-unethical dichotomy. One way to think of argumentative ethics is Kant's Moral Imperative, which states that we should act in a way that would be best if everyone acted that way.

Brockriede described three types of arguers by using a metaphor of sexual relations to help identify ethical and unethical behavior. For him, people who argue abusively or seductively are unethical, while those who argue as lovers are ethical. The arguer as harasser was added as another type of less ethical arguer.

The ethics of argumentation can be evaluated in three contexts: public, argumentation, and educational. Although all of the contexts share some ethical standards, other standards are specific to each context.

Striving for higher standards of ethics makes you not only more ethical but also a more effective arguer. Arguments that conform to high standards of ethics usually are more effective, because people recognize that the arguer is taking pains to be ethical, and they attribute greater credibility to such a person. The best arguments are both ethical and well reasoned. The rest of this text will address how to make sound arguments, but always remember that the best arguers also are ethical.

KEY CONCEPTS

arguer as abuser   an unethical approach to argumentation in which the arguer sees the co-arguer as an enemy to be conquered and tries to win the argument through force, intimidation, fabrication, monopoly of communication channels, or other unfair advantages.

arguer as harasser   a less ethical approach to argumentation in which

the arguer sees the co-arguer as an inferior to be ridiculed, belittled, and annoyed into agreement or withdrawal.

arguer as lover   a more ethical approach to argumentation in which the arguer sees the co-arguer as someone deserving of respect and attempts to argue in as honest and open a way as possible.

arguer as seducer a less ethical approach to argumentation in which the arguer sees the co-arguer as someone to be manipulated for the benefit of the seducer and tries to win the argument by deceiving, withholding information, mis-

using language, or gaining assent through means other than clear, sound argumentation.

Kant's Moral Imperative an ethical principle that can be summarized as "act in a way that would be best if everyone acted that way."

THINGS TO THINK ABOUT

1. Think of an argument that you were involved in or observed in which one or more people argued as an abuser, a seducer, or a harasser. Why do you consider the behavior to be in that category? How would the argument differ if the arguer had argued as a lover?

2. Why do people not argue completely ethically?

3. Are there any occasions when someone is justified in arguing unethically? Why or why not? What arguments might others make to contradict your position?

4. Identify a profession or career in which argumentation ethics may be an important issue. How should

someone argue ethically in that profession or career?

5. Can you think of any additional standards for ethical argumentation in public, interpersonal, or educational argumentation? What would those standards be, and why should they be followed?

6. Identify any area of argumentation other than public, interpersonal, or educational argumentation for which there should be some ethical standards. What is that area, what standards would you suggest, and why would you suggest them?

7. Analyze a television commercial, an infomercial, or a print ad according to the ethics of its argumentation.

4

✤

Introduction to Argumentative Fallacies

Studying fallacies is a widely accepted way of improving both your ability to make arguments and think critically. When you're aware of the various common ways that arguments can go wrong, then you can better create your own arguments and better analyze those made by others. Knowledge of fallacies isn't the only skill you need, but it can be useful.

Fallacy traditionally has been defined as an argument that appears to be sound reasoning but, in fact, is flawed. Some people purposely use fallacious reasoning to trick others into agreement and compliance, but often people simply don't realize when they make a mistake in reasoning.

Studying fallacies is valuable because it provides a way to evaluate the arguments you make, hear, and read. If you are able to recognize a variety of common ways people make arguments that appear to be strong but are, upon closer examination, weak, then you have a better chance of recognizing weak arguments when you encounter them. Even if you do not remember the names or definitions of all the fallacies, and even if you cannot identify exactly the type of fallacy in an argument, you can identify weaknesses in arguments because you've gotten into the habit of noticing the characteristics of unsound arguments.

This chapter is a general introduction to fallacies. It will

- describe how the concept originated and how it can affect the study of fallacies.
- describe the difference between formal and informal fallacies.
- explain the meaning of a general kind of fallacy.
- explain how to use knowledge of fallacies to examine arguments.
- warn you of some dangers to avoid as you study fallacies.

Since you should try to avoid fallacies as you create arguments, descriptions of specific fallacies are included in Chapters 5–11. As you read those chapters, you will learn how to make strong arguments, and the fallacies in each chapter will help you understand how the principles can be misused, which will also help you evaluate others' arguments.

BACKGROUND OF FALLACIES

Imagine standing in a public place, watching one person question another, similar to a scene of a prosecutor questioning a witness in a courtroom drama. Imagine that it is a familiar sight. It's a common intellectual game that is both educational and entertaining, and you know the rules well. The person being questioned agreed to publicly support a claim and to truthfully answer questions put to him, and to answer with some variation of yes or no. Saying, "It depends," or explaining answers, is not allowed. By strategically using questions that he puts to the other, the person asking the questions attempts to show that the claim cannot be supported. In this game, called **sophistical refutation,** the person asking the questions is "refuting" the claim that the other person agreed to support.

Variations of such scenes were common in Athens during the time of Socrates, Plato, and Aristotle. If you read some of Plato's dialogues, you can get a sense of what they were like. Some people, known as sophists, were quite skilled in attacking and defending claims, whether they thought they were true or not.

Aristotle (1955) became interested in the way sophists engaged in such disputes. He studied them and then wrote a book about them, *On Sophistical Refutations.* In that work, he categorized and described "what appear to be refutations but are really fallacies instead" (278). He identified thirteen types of fallacies at that time, dividing them into those dependent on language and those outside of language. Since his time, many more fallacies have been identified by various authors, using different categorization schemes. Table 4.1 lists a standard treatment of Aristotle's original fallacies.

Through the ages, the idea of fallacies has changed from those found in sophistical refutations to logical or argumentative fallacies. Since the original fallacies were strategies used in an intellectual game involving questions and yes-or-no answers, some of their original meanings do not make much sense any more. Authors writing about them commonly take one of Aristotle's original fallacies and adapt it to try to make it fit an argument made by one person. For instance, one of the original fallacies is "amphiboly," which happens when a statement

Table 4.1 Thirteen Standard Fallacies

Fallacies Dependent on Language

1. Equivocation: changing the meaning of terms during the argument.
2. Amphiboly: using language in a way that allows statements to have more than one meaning.
3. Composition: saying that what is true of an individual part of something is true of that entire thing.
4. Division: saying that what is true of an entire thing is true of each individual part of that thing.
5. Accent: using vocal emphasis to create statements with more than one meaning.
6. Figure of speech: treating figurative statements as if they were literal.

Fallacies Outside of Language

7. Accident: treating an inessential quality of something as if it were an essential quality.
8. *Secundum quid:* arguing for a generalization without sufficient basis for the generalization.
9. *Ignoratio elenchi:* ignorance of the rules and procedures of refutation.
10. Begging the question: asking the respondent to grant the very proposition in dispute.
11. Affirming the consequent: in the argument form "If A then B," getting the respondent to grant "B" and using that concession as proof of "A."
12. False cause: falsely identifying one event as the cause of another.
13. Many questions: explicitly or implicitly asking multiple questions at once, so a straightforward yes-or-no answer cannot answer all the questions.

Adapted from *Fallacies* by C. L. Hamblin (London: Methuen & Co.,1970, 9–40).

NOTE: Hamblin's (1970) titles and explanations for the fallacies of composition, division, and s*ecundum quid* refer to the way Aristotle's original fallacies are treated today. E. S. Forster's (1955) translation of *On Sophistical Refutations* refers to a "combination of words" (21), a "division of words" (23), and "the use of words absolutely or with some qualification" (27).

has more than one possible meaning, depending on grammar or punctuation. In Aristotle's time, the questioner could use that strategy to confuse issues, leading his opponent to a logical inconsistency that would refute the claim. However, you rarely find an example of such a fallacy in straightforward propositional arguments today. The examples you might find include a sign in a window of a clothing store that reads: "Sale on shirts with 16 necks." Such statements are amusing and may lead to disputes about what they mean, but they don't show up in argument$_1$ very often.

Some of Aristotle's original fallacies are only faulty when you try to follow the rules of sophistical refutation. For instance, a fallacy called "complex question" refers to a question that includes two questions in one in a manner that makes a straightforward yes–no answer impossible. Many contemporary students don't think that this is a problem, because they quickly realize that they can simply point out the complexity of the question, or answer with an explanation that answers both questions independently. Doing so would violate the rules of sophistical refutation but is clearly an option in modern, everyday arguments.

Some of the original fallacies simply do not translate well. For instance, one of Aristotle's original fallacies is the fallacy of accent, which happens when a different emphasis is placed on syllables in words, changing their meanings and, therefore, changing the meaning of the question. Since it is one of the original thirteen fallacies, it usually is included in lists of fallacious reasoning. The use of accent in that way may confuse meaning in spoken Greek, but in English, changing the emphasis doesn't often change the meaning much. Some English words change meaning when the emphasis is changed from the first syllable to the second, including: produce, project, rebel, reject, contest, and invalid. If one switched from one pronunciation to another during an argument he might commit the fallacy of accent but probably wouldn't gain an advantage. English language examples of the fallacy of accent usually rely on emphasizing certain words in sentences, and the change in emphasis usually sounds sarcastic, not very tricky. They're still classified as fallacies, but they're different from what was meant by the original concept, and it's usually hard to imagine anyone being fooled into thinking that they're good arguments.

Sometimes examples of fallacies don't seem realistic. Usually if the fallacious example is clear then it doesn't seem like a very convincing argument, so it's hard to see why anyone would be fooled into accepting it. If the example seems convincing, the fallacy is often not very clear, so it doesn't work well as an example to help understand what the fallacy means. Keep in mind that most examples are chosen to help clarify ideas as the fallacies are introduced, and understand that they're much more subtle in everyday arguments.

In addition, reasoning that meets the definition of a fallacy isn't always faulty. For instance, the contemporary fallacy of argument from authority happens when someone uses an expert's opinion as evidence that a claim is true. If the authority is speaking about something outside her area of expertise, then the reasoning is faulty. But if the authority is talking about her area of expertise, then it is often quite reasonable to rely on her opinion as the support for a conclusion, especially if her expertise is in an area that calls for specialized knowledge. For example, if a physician examines you and says that you ought to have a tetanus shot, in the absence of reasons to disbelieve her diagnosis, it would be reasonable to accept her suggestion. So it's important to realize that an argument that fits a particular fallacy isn't necessarily faulty.

Aristotle started with thirteen fallacies, and through the centuries scholars have added dozens more. Sometimes authors use different names for the same fallacy, because some of the original names are either in a language other than English, or the traditional English name doesn't make as much sense now as it did earlier, due to the natural evolution of language. Some authors divide a common fallacy into different types because it makes discussing fallacies more precise, but others lump all of the fallacies together as one type. As a result, you may read something here that goes by a different name in another text. This text includes multiple names for some fallacies, so you can be more familiar with the variations, but you may see different names in other sources.

Finally, you may realize that a single argument may involve multiple fallacies. Three people may look at the same argument and each may say that it is an example of a different fallacy, and all three may be right! That can be confusing if you think there must be a single correct answer to any question.

The important thing to remember is that learning about the different fallacies does not just involve memorizing a list. Each fallacy will remind you of a different potential problem in reasoning. The more of the potential problems you are able to recognize, the better chance you have to think critically about a wide variety of issues and to make stronger arguments.

FORMAL AND INFORMAL FALLACIES

Two general kinds of fallacies exist. Most of the fallacies that Aristotle and other fallacy theorists are concerned with are called "informal" fallacies. **Informal fallacies** are arguments that are flawed because of mistaken assumptions in the premises, errors in language, misuse of evidence, or violation of principles of argumentation. Another classification is called "formal" fallacies. **Formal fallacies** are fallacies that occur because of mistakes in the logical structure of the argument.

In Chapter 5 you will learn about the formal structure of an argument and the requirements to make it logically valid. If any of those requirements are violated, then the argument contains a formal fallacy. Arguments that have the correct form but that rely on false assumptions are known as informal fallacies.

For example, you could make the following argument:

Costliest products are the best, and the shirt I like is the costliest. Therefore, the shirt I like is the best.

That argument uses the correct form of a valid argument, so it does not contain a formal fallacy. However, the opening statement raises some problems. The idea that the value of a product is based only on how much it costs is a questionable assumption. This is an example of the *ad crumenum* fallacy, which occurs when money is assumed to be the way to measure the worth of something or someone. If the first statement turned out to be correct, then the argument might be an example of the fallacy of accident, which happens when you start with a correct generalization but the particular case you refer to is an exception to that generalization. In this case, the expensive shirt has an unnoticed defect, so it really isn't the best, even if it is the costliest. If you are not aware of the fallacies of accident or *ad crumenum,* then you are less likely to recognize the weakness in the argument.

To avoid confusion between formal and informal fallacies, when this text refers to fallacies it means informal fallacies. If it refers to a formal fallacy, it will include the term *formal.*

THE *NON SEQUITUR* FALLACY

So many fallacies go by so many different names that this text cannot include them all. You shouldn't expect the list of fallacies here to be comprehensive, although many fallacies are explained in Chapters 5–11.

If all of the fallacies were presented at once, then you would probably be overwhelmed. So as you learn about other concepts in argumentation and critical thinking, you will also learn about fallacies that are associated with those concepts. Remember, this doesn't mean that this way of classifying fallacies is the only correct way. It's just a way of dividing them to make it easier for you to learn.

One fallacy doesn't fit well with any particular set of concepts, because it fits all of them. It's known as the **non sequitur fallacy.** *Non sequitur* means "does not follow," and the fallacy happens when the evidence and reasoning for an argument don't really pertain to the claim, or when the response to an argument doesn't really relate to what it's meant to respond to. In other words, the conclusion does not follow from the premises, or the answer doesn't follow the question.

For example, someone once argued that burning the American flag should be illegal because one of his ancestors fought in the Civil War. While he adamantly believed what he said, it does not follow that the acts of an individual over 100 years ago should determine the legality of unrelated acts. While you may be able to develop an argument that makes the connection, that was not the argument made at the time.

The *non sequitur* fallacy fits with all of the concepts of argumentation and critical thinking, because almost all informal fallacies are specific names for *non sequitur* arguments. It's sort of a miscellaneous category, so if you don't know the name for a fallacy, but you can tell that the argument doesn't really make sense, then you can label it *non sequitur*. That is not as useful to a critical thinker as an awareness of more specific fallacies is, but you are likely to hear the phrase occasionally, thus you should know what it means.

EXAMINING ARGUMENTS
FOR FALLACIES

The purpose of learning about fallacies is to help you recognize errors in reasoning. Recognizing such errors is a three-step process and calls for you to stop to think critically about the arguments you examine.

The first step is to figure out what the argument is. In the next section of this text, you will learn more about how to do that. Sometimes it's fairly easy, and sometimes it takes a lot of work, but until you have an accurate idea of what someone's claim, support, and reasoning are, you can't really tell if there is a fallacy.

The second step is to recognize whether or not there is a *potential* fallacy in the reasoning. This is where knowledge of the different kinds of fallacies is valuable. If you are aware, for instance, that using money as the only indicator of the value of something is a particular kind of fallacy, then you are likely to be more sensitive to problems with that sort of reasoning. At this point, you are only looking for the potential for a fallacy to exist. You don't yet know if you have come across an actual problem in the argument. Market forces may be such that for a particular type of product, its cost is a reliable indicator of its value, so there really isn't a fallacy for a particular product. You can't know that until you think about the argument though.

The third step is to think more about the particular argument to determine if it really is faulty reasoning. If the arguer answers the problems that would make something a fallacy, then you may conclude that there really is no fallacy. If, upon closer examination, you come to the conclusion that the reasoning is faulty, then you should also think about how the fallacy affects the entire argument. If the part of the argument that has a fallacy is removed, is there still enough support left to justify accepting the claim? If so, even though part of the argument is a fallacy, the rest is still acceptable.

The important thing is to not get into the habit of noticing that someone reasons in a way that corresponds to a certain fallacy and then *automatically* conclude that it is a fallacy. Instead, stop to critically think about the argument.

DANGERS OF STUDYING FALLACIES

Studying fallacies can help you think critically, make better arguments yourself, and better evaluate arguments made by others. There are some dangers to avoid though. Some people have even suggested that fallacies should not be studied as part of learning argumentation and critical thinking. That would go too far, however, and the value of knowing fallacies would be lost. The problems associated with learning about fallacies can be avoided if you're aware of them from the start.

The first danger is that you might get into the habit of only looking for errors in other people's argumentation. Critical thinking and argument analysis should involve finding *both* the strengths and the weaknesses in arguments. Focusing on fallacies tends to prevent people from recognizing what is good in arguments, which also can lead people to quibble over the exact way arguments are expressed instead of dealing with the core substance of the arguments.

The second danger is that you could become rigid in the way you apply the knowledge. You may notice a fallacy in an argument and dismiss everything else in the argument because of that fallacy. One fallacy, the **fallacy fallacy,** happens when someone decides that the conclusion of an argument must be wrong because there was a fallacy in the reasoning. A fallacy in an argument does weaken the argument, and finding one should reduce your confidence in the conclusion, but an argument with fallacies may still include enough support to accept the claim and may still come to a correct conclusion even without support. Think of recognition of a fallacy like a warning sign: it indicates that you should stop to think about the argument more carefully, but you shouldn't automatically reject the conclusion.

The final danger in learning about fallacies is that you may become frustrated with all argumentation. It is hard to find arguments of any complexity that don't contain any fallacies. Sometimes people making the arguments don't realize that they've committed a fallacy. Sometimes the forum doesn't allow the arguer to say enough in support of a claim to avoid fallacies. And, sometimes the arguer decides to allow some fallacies to avoid losing an audience that won't exert the effort to follow a complicated argument. When thinking about arguments, it is worthwhile to think about the fallacies, but you shouldn't stop there.

The answers to the dangers just described are not to avoid learning about fallacies but to apply what you learn thoughtfully. Don't just look for what people do

Figure 4.1 Changing the subject and flattering the other arguer are both fallacious ways that some arguers throw another arguer off the subject.

Luann reprinted by permission of United Feature Syndicate, Inc.

wrong in their arguments, but also look for what they do well. When you recognize a fallacy, stop to ask yourself how that fallacy affects the entire argument. What happens if you eliminate the part that's fallacious? Do you still have a worthwhile argument, or does the elimination of the fallacious portion leave you with inadequate support for the claim? Understand that perfect arguments don't happen very often, and that part of critical thinking is determining the strength of flawed arguments.

SUMMARY

The study of fallacies has a tradition that goes back to the time of Aristotle, when it was based on a particular type of question-and-answer interaction. Since then, many new fallacies have been added, and the focus has shifted from question-and-answer fallacies to those done while making arguments.

Studying fallacies is useful for improving your own arguments and critically thinking about arguments made by others. Fallacies have been defined as "arguments that appear to be sound but are not." Often you cannot tell that an argument is really fallacious until you've given it more thought, however, so fallacies can be thought of as indicators of potentially flawed arguments.

You will learn about many types of fallacies in the following chapters. One general type of fallacy is the *non sequitur* fallacy, which happens when the conclusion of an argument does not follow from the premises. Since the conclusions of many fallacious arguments do not follow from their premises, the term *non sequitur* applies to almost any fallacy.

You can use knowledge of fallacies to examine arguments. To do so, look for answers to the following questions: What is the argument? Is there a potential fallacy anywhere in the argument? Is the potential fallacy really faulty reasoning? If so, how does the fallacy affect the entire argument?

Learning about fallacies can lead you to be overly critical, rigid, or frustrated as you notice fallacies in arguments. To avoid these problems, look for both strengths and weaknesses in arguments, consider the overall effect that a fallacy has on the quality of arguments, and understand that perfect arguments are rare.

KEY CONCEPTS

fallacy   an argument that appears to be sound reasoning but, in fact, is flawed.

fallacy fallacy   deciding that the conclusion of an argument must be untrue, because there is a fallacy in the reasoning.

formal fallacies   arguments that are flawed because they do not conform to the proper structure or form of a valid argument.

informal fallacies   arguments that are flawed because of mistaken assumptions in the premises, errors in language, misuse of evidence, or violation of the principles of argumentation.

non sequitur **fallacy**   an argument in which the conclusion "does not follow" from the premises. The fallacy happens when the evidence and reasoning for an argument doesn't really pertain to the claim, or when the response to an argument doesn't really relate to what it's supposed to respond to.

sophistical refutation   (1) an intellectual activity engaged in by sophists in ancient Greece that involved attacking and defending a proposition by asking and answering questions; (2) the title of a text by Aristotle in which the concept of fallacies was first analyzed.

THINGS TO THINK ABOUT

1. Find a simple argument such as a newspaper editorial or a letter to the editor. What are some of the ways in which the reasoning in the argument may be flawed?

2. Recall someone who has made a weak argument. Think of a name and definition of that weakness, as though it is a fallacy.

3. Watch a TV talk show in which people get into a heated argument. What is an instance of someone in the show committing a *non sequitur* fallacy?

4. What might be a hypothetical instance of someone committing a fallacy fallacy?

PART II

✻

Creating Arguments

Now that you know more about argumentation and critical thinking, the principles of ethics in argumentation, and the general meaning of fallacies, it is time to learn to make solid arguments. In this section you will learn the basic principles of argumentation so you can make better arguments, recognize strengths and weaknesses in arguments, and argue well with others. You will learn to create a logically valid argument and recognize the parts of arguments made in everyday life. You will learn ways that people reason when arguing, as well as three general types of arguments and the common issues to address for each type. You also will learn what to look for in evidence used to support arguments, how language is used in arguments, and how to respond to arguments that others make. In each chapter you also will learn about several fallacies associated with the concepts in that chapter.

5

Formal Logic

The Classical Structure of Arguments

One way to begin the study of argumentation and critical thinking is to learn how to properly structure an argument. You've probably made arguments most of your life without realizing how they're put together, and you've probably done it reasonably well. Knowing more about how to put an argument together can help you make more solid arguments and evaluate the arguments that you hear and read.

The basic building blocks of an argument consist of a claim, support for that claim, and reasoning linking the claim and support. The claim is whatever you're trying to prove, and the support is whatever information you use to try to prove that claim. Making everyday arguments is a lot more complex than that, though, because we often use the conclusion of one argument as the support for another and usually don't present arguments completely.

For centuries, the study of argumentation, reasoning, and logic has begun with the study of the **classical structure of an argument,** which is the logical form that an argument should take. That structure was used by the ancient Greeks and codified by Aristotle.

When you make arguments, your goal is usually to convince someone to agree with you, and you do that by making the strongest argument you can. Strong arguments have two characteristics. One is using the best evidence and reasoning that you can (which future chapters will explain). The other is making the argument the most logically valid that you can. A **valid argument** is properly structured, and all of the logical components fit together correctly. The rest of this chapter explains what is involved in making valid arguments. The material here describes the fundamental building blocks of arguments. Mastering it is necessary to make full use of the principles that will be discussed later.

This chapter will

- describe the two general types of arguments.
- explain the differences between deductive and inductive reasoning.
- distinguish between material truth and formal validity.
- identify the logical requirements of three specific types of argument.
- explain how to use formal logic to analyze arguments.
- describe several informal fallacies based on formal logic.

SYLLOGISMS AND ENTHYMEMES

The basic structure of an argument, according to Aristotle (1991), is called the **syllogism** (pronounced "sil-uh-jiz-um"). A syllogism is **deductive reasoning,** which means that the conclusion is included in the premises. That is, the argument reasons from premises that are already known to a conclusion that is the inevitable result, because it is already contained in the premises.

A syllogism also must contain three distinct parts. The first part is the **major premise,** and it is an unequivocal general statement about the subject of the argument. "Unequivocal" means that it is presented as an absolutely certain statement; it is not "probable" or "possible" but certain. Don't make the mistake of thinking that it is the first statement in the argument, because the parts come in any order. The second part of a syllogism is the **minor premise,** which is a statement about a specific case, related to the generalization of the major premise. The third part is the **conclusion,** which is the *inevitable* outcome of accepting the major and minor premises. The conclusion is the claim being made, the minor premise is the support, and the major premise is the reasoning linking them.

In the syllogism, the conclusion must be a certainty; that is, if the major premise and the minor premise are true, then the conclusion must certainly be true. It cannot be a probability based on the major and minor premises. For example, the classic syllogism, used in many texts, is as follows:

> **All human beings are mortal.** (Major premise)
> **Socrates is a human being.** (Minor premise)
> **Therefore, Socrates is mortal.** (Conclusion)

The major premise in this case is an unequivocal, generalized statement about a characteristic of all human beings. The minor premise is a statement that the particular case is a member of the group about whom the generalized statement is made. Given those two premises, the certain conclusion is that the particular case (Socrates) definitely has the same characteristic (mortality) as all of the members of the group (human beings) to which he belongs.

So a syllogism is an argument that has all three parts *and* comes to an unconditional conclusion. However, most everyday arguments don't do all of that. Incomplete or conditional arguments fit into Aristotle's (1991) other classification of arguments, called the **enthymeme** (en-tha-meem), which is an argument that is missing at least one part of the syllogism, comes to a probable conclusion, or does both. If one or more of the parts of a syllogism is missing, then we would call the argument an "enthymeme," which is often described as a "truncated" syllogism. If all three parts are present but the conclusion is only probable instead of certain, then the argument is also an enthymeme. An enthymeme may also have a part missing *and* come to a probable conclusion. Any argument that comes to a probable instead of an absolute conclusion, or that reasons from known premises to an unknown conclusion, is called **inductive reasoning.**

Thus the classic structure might be expressed in an argument as any of the following enthymemes:

All human beings are mortal.
Therefore, Hilary is mortal.

Most human beings are mortal.
Hilary is a human being.
Therefore, Hilary is probably mortal.

Hilary is a human being.
Therefore, Hilary is mortal.

All human beings are mortal.
Hilary appears to be a human being.
Therefore, Hilary is probably mortal.

Most arguments you encounter in everyday life are enthymemes. Most people make arguments about matters for which they cannot reach an absolute conclusion, so they have to make arguments about what is probably true. For instance, we often make arguments as part of the process of deciding which actions to take. We can't know for certain what the results of our actions will be, so we have to argue which actions will *probably* have the best results. The form of valid, inductive enthymemes is the same form for valid, deductive syllogisms, with the language of the premises and conclusions adjusted. So an enthymeme might state the following:

Exercise is usually good for a person like me.
Running is exercise.
Therefore, running would probably be good for me.

In addition, when people make arguments, they commonly assume that their audiences are able to fill in the missing parts, so they don't include all three. When you engage in an argument, part of your task is to figure out what the missing premise or conclusion might be, decide if the argument is valid, or make sure that the arguer doesn't shift from probable premises to a certain conclusion.

MATERIAL TRUTH AND FORMAL VALIDITY

When we evaluate syllogisms or enthymemes, we can consider whether they are formally valid or materially true. **Material truth** means that the argument reaches a truthful conclusion, or uses true premises, as much as "truth" can be determined. When analyzing the material truth of an argument, you should examine all premises to see if they are true, as well as the conclusion. **Formal validity** means that the argument has the correct structure or "form."

A materially true syllogism doesn't have to be formally valid, and an argument may be formally valid without being materially true. One common mistake that people make when they're evaluating arguments is to assume that if the conclusion appears true, then the reasoning must be valid, or if the conclusion seems untrue then the reasoning must be invalid. People also commonly think that if an argument appears formally valid, then the conclusion must be true. The concepts of material truth and formal validity don't really affect each other, although they do affect the quality of the entire argument. For example, the following argument is clearly not materially true, but it is formally valid:

All fruits are apples.

A chimpanzee is a fruit.

Therefore, a chimpanzee is an apple.

Both premises and the conclusion are obviously untrue, but the *form* is correct, so it is formally valid. If the premises are accepted, then the conclusion inevitably results, so the argument is formally valid. Consider the following argument:

If you sleep sitting up and facing southwest, then you will pass the next exam you take.

You ate a lot of chocolate last night.

Therefore, you will pass the exam today.

The argument is clearly silly, but if you do, indeed, pass the exam today, then the conclusion turns out to be materially true. However, since the minor premise has nothing at all to do with either the major premise or the conclusion, the argument is formally invalid. Of course, invalid arguments in everyday life are rarely as obviously ridiculous as this example.

DON'T BE FOOLED INTO THINKING THE REASONING IN AN ARGUMENT IS VALID JUST BECAUSE YOU BELIEVE THE CONCLUSION TO BE TRUE.

The distinction between formal validity and material truth is emphasized when you realize that the logical structure of arguments is often presented using letters or other symbols with no meaning attached to them. Thus you might have the following argument:

Every p is an r.

q is a p.

Therefore, q is an r.

There is no way to tell if that argument is materially true or not, because the symbols used have no meaning. However, you can determine if the argument is formally valid.

A **sound** or **cogent argument** is one that is both logically valid and uses materially true premises. An arguer who meets both conditions may have faith that the argument does reach a conclusion as true as can be. If either condition is not met, then there is no reason to believe that the conclusion is true. Sound arguments are stronger, and you should strive to make them.

TYPES OF SYLLOGISMS

To determine the validity of a syllogism or an enthymeme, you must first decide which *type* of syllogism it is. (From now on, assume that what is said about the validity of syllogisms also applies to enthymemes, adjusting for the differences in the two kinds of arguments.) The three types are categorical, disjunctive, and hypothetical, and each has its own requirements for formally validity.

Figure 5.1 Just because we say something is logical doesn't mean it really is.

© Baby Blues Partnership. Reprinted with special permission of King Features Syndicate.

Categorical Syllogism

The first type of syllogism is called the **categorical syllogism.** Its major premise establishes categories in which the subject of the minor premise should fit. In the categorical syllogism, the major premise uses some sort of absolute or universal term, such as "all," "every," or "always." The major premise of the categorical enthymeme might use provisional terms, such as "some," "usually," or "probably." Sometimes no such qualifying term is used, and you have to decide if it would be most fair to consider that premise as absolute or probable. Technically, the lack of a qualifying term that indicates uncertainty would make the premise absolute. That is, the statement "Apples are fruits" means "*All* apples are fruits." In a lot of everyday argumentation, it would be a mistake to be that technical unless you want to be considered a pest.

The following is the basic form that the categorical syllogism takes:

All As are Bs.

X is an A.

Therefore, X is a B.

You could expand that to say:

Everything that belongs in category "A" also belongs in category "B."

Something we call "X" belongs in category "A."

Therefore, what we call "X" must also belong in category "B."

You can substitute any terms or phrases you want for A, B, and X, and as long as it follows the same form as the example above, you have a *valid* categorical syllogism, *even if the premises and the conclusion are obviously false.*

A categorical argument has three terms. The **major term** appears in both the major premise and conclusion and is the category into which both the minor term and the middle term fit. The **minor term** appears in both the minor premise and the conclusion. It fits into the middle term and, therefore, it also fits into the major term. The **middle term** appears in both the major and minor premises and is the category into which the minor term fits. The form of a categorical syllogism follows:

All "middle terms" fit into the category "major term."

"Minor term" fits into the category "middle term."

Therefore, "minor term" fits into the category "major term."

You can think of the three terms or categories as containers; the major term is the largest, which the others fit into, the middle term is the middle-size container, which the minor term fits into and which fits into the major term, and the minor term is the smallest container.

A categorical syllogism has to meet seven requirements to be valid. If it fails to meet any one of them, it is invalid, no matter how true the argument seems.

The first requirement is that the categorical syllogism *must have exactly three "terms."* Those terms are the major term, the minor term, and the middle term. A "term" may be an entire phrase (such as "professors in the Department of Communication"), a single word (such as "dog"), or an abstract symbol (such as "X"). It can even be a compound phrase (such as "Democrats and Republicans"), but the entire syllogism must have exactly three of them. So, in the example presented earlier, A, B, and X are the three terms. If you took out term "A" and had only two terms, then you'd have an argument such as the following:

All Xs are Bs	*or*	**All dogs [Xs] are hairy [B].**
X is a B.	*or*	**The dog [X] has hair [B].**
Therefore, X is a B.	*or*	**Therefore, the dog [X] has hair [B].**

That argument just goes in a circle. If you had four terms then you'd have an argument such as the following:

All As are Bs.	*or*	**All dogs [As] are hairy [B].**
X is a Y.	*or*	**Fido [X] is a banana slug [Y].**
Therefore, ????	*or*	**Therefore, Fido [X is] . . . ?**

Given that major premise and minor premise, you can't reach a conclusion that makes sense, and it is invalid. Think of it like this: The major premise of any argument establishes everything you know about the universe, for the purpose of determining formal validity. If the minor premise doesn't refer to something within that universe, then you can draw no conclusion about what is in that minor premise, and the syllogism cannot be formally valid.

The second requirement of a valid categorical syllogism is related to the first, because *every term must be used exactly twice.* So you can't have a valid argument if you say something such as the following:

All dogs are hairy.

Fido is hairy.

Therefore, Fido is hairy.

The three terms are *dogs, hairy,* and *Fido,* but *dogs* is only used once and *hairy* is used three times.

The third requirement is that *a term may be used only once in any premise.* It will sound pretty trivial if someone in an argument said something like "All dogs are dogs," which doesn't say anything that you could build on, thus you'd be arguing in a circle. (You also probably would not have three terms, and you wouldn't use each term exactly twice.) It gets trickier, though, when people start using *equivalent terms,* as most people do when they actually make arguments. An equivalent term would be a word or phrase that means the same thing as another term used. Let's say that "dog" and "canine mammal" are equivalent terms. In that case, a premise that says "All dogs are canine mammals" sounds like it is saying something, when actually it just repeats itself. One of the judgments that you have to make as you engage in argumentation is whether the language used by any arguer is a new term or an equivalent term.

The fourth requirement is that *the middle term must be used in an unqualified or a universal sense.* Recall that the "middle term" is the middle category that you've established in your premises. If the premises say "All As are Bs" and "C is an A," then C fits into A, which fits into B, and so A is the "middle term." For a syllogism to be valid, that middle term must not allow any exceptions. Thus the following would be invalid:

Some mammals are dogs.

Fido is a mammal.

Therefore, Fido is a dog.

The conclusion could state, "Fido might be a dog," but that wouldn't be a syllogism. That same argument would be a valid *enthymeme,* because an enthymeme can come to an uncertain conclusion.

The fifth requirement is that *a term may be in the conclusion only if it has been in the major or minor premise.* This means that the conclusion cannot refer to anything that hasn't already been in the premises. For example, you can't validly say the following:

All liberals favor welfare.

Jack is a liberal.

Therefore, Jack is a communist.

Some people may use *liberal* and *communist* as equivalent terms, but they aren't the same. So the term *communist* was included in the conclusion when it wasn't in either premise. You probably already noticed that this example has four terms and that two of the terms are used only once.

The sixth requirement is that *at least one of the premises must be stated in a positive way. Both* premises may be stated affirmatively, but to be valid, at least one has to be affirmative. If you say:

No As are Bs.

X is not an A.

you cannot reach a conclusion. Your major premise created a universe in which you know nothing in category A will fit into category B, but you don't know anything about the category of things that are *not* As. They could be anything. They might fit into the category of Bs, or they might not; you just can't know, given the major premise you began with. You might make the following argument:

No Democratic senators will vote for this bill.

Senator Elliot is not a Democratic senator.

Therefore, Senator Elliot will . . .

Since the only behavior you can predict, based on what you know of the universe from your major premise, is the behavior of people who *are* Democratic senators, then you cannot come to a valid conclusion about anyone who is *not* a Democratic senator.

The final requirement is that *if one premise is negative, then the conclusion must be negative.* Let's change the previous example to make the argument valid.

No Democratic senators will vote for this bill.

Senator Elliot is a Democratic senator.

Therefore, Senator Elliot . . .

What must the conclusion be? Given the premises, we can validly conclude that Senator Elliot *will not* vote for the bill. To say that Senator Elliot would do anything else would either contradict the premises or introduce a term that hasn't been in either of the premises.

One way to help you determine the validity of categorical syllogisms is to use **Venn diagrams.** Venn diagrams are pictorial representations of a syllogism that help show which terms fit into which categories. For example: "All As are Bs, C is an A, therefore C is a B." In the Venn diagram in Figure 5.2, a small circle would represent C (the minor term), a larger circle would represent A (the middle term), and an even larger circle would represent B (the major term). So you would have the following:

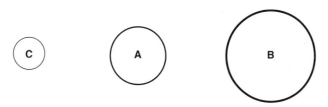

The major premise says that circle A is entirely within circle B.

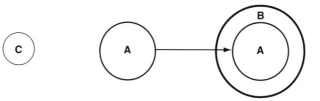

The minor premise says that circle C is entirely within circle A.

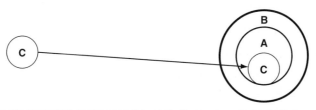

So, since circle A is already within circle B, your conclusion is that circle C is entirely within circle B.

Figure 5.2 Diagram of a Categorical Syllogism

Depending on what the major and minor premises say, you could end up with lots of other diagrams. When you use Venn diagrams to determine the validity of categorical syllogisms, it helps to turn the terms into As, Bs, and Cs, which are easier to sketch than full sentences. Then sketch out how the elements fit together, according to the major and minor premises. Venn diagrams are useful when you analyze a categorical syllogism, because some arguments seem clear until you really think about them, and some seem unclear right from the start. The diagrams simplify what you're working with.

Disjunctive Syllogism

The second type of syllogism is the **disjunctive syllogism.** Its major premise presents two or more mutually exclusive alternatives. "Mutually exclusive" means that you can have one alternative, but that you cannot possibly have more than one at the same time. When the major premise is stated, it usually includes some kind of a phrase such as "either _____ or _____."

In a valid disjunctive syllogism, *the minor premise must either accept one of the alternatives in the major premise or reject all but one of the alternatives.* Once that choice is made, *the conclusion must either reject all of the remaining choices or accept the only alternative not rejected.* A simple disjunctive syllogism could take the following forms:

Either A or B.   **Either A or B.**
I choose A.   **I do not choose A.**
Therefore, I do not choose B. **Therefore, I do choose B.**

Either A or B.   **Either A or B.**
I choose B.   **I do not choose B.**
Therefore, I do not choose A. **Therefore, I choose A.**

You can plug in any terms or phrases for A and B and expand the statements to full sentences and have formally valid disjunctive syllogisms. If there were qualifying terms (such as "probably") in the premises, then you would need to have appropriate qualifying terms in the conclusion to have a valid enthymeme. Keep in mind that none of the requirements for a categorical syllogism apply to a disjunctive syllogism.

So, if the argument were

We must either raise taxes or reduce services.
We are philosophically opposed to raising taxes.
Therefore, we must reduce services.

then it would be valid, because the minor premise rejected one alternative, and the conclusion accepted the other. If the minor premise accepted one alternative, then the conclusion must reject the other alternative. Thus:

We must either raise taxes or reduce services.
We will raise taxes.
Therefore, we won't reduce services.

A more complex disjunctive syllogism could have the following forms, among many others:

Either A or B or C or D.
Not A, not C, and not D.
Therefore, B.

Either A or B or C or D.
Choose B.
Therefore, not A, not C, and not D.

Remember, to determine the *formal validity* of a disjunctive syllogism, you do not consider whether the premises are correct but merely consider whether the conclusion logically follows, *assuming the premises are correct*. To determine the *soundness* of an argument, think about both the formal validity and the material truth of the premises.

There are a couple of simple things to consider to determine if a disjunctive argument is sound in addition to being formally valid. First, *the major premise of a sound disjunctive argument must contain all of the possible alternatives.* Remember, to decide if a syllogism is formally valid, you must accept the premises as true, so you don't ask if the major premise contains all of the alternatives. You do ask that question when considering the soundness of an argument. So if it says that we must accept one of two possibilities, then there cannot be a third possibility that isn't in the premise. The major premise could have twenty different alternatives, as long as the minor premise considered them all. If you were to say "we must either raise taxes or reduce a particular service," then you may be leaving out the possibility of reducing a different service or gaining revenues in ways other than increasing taxes. For example, in the following argument, if you accept the major premise, then the reasoning is valid:

We must have either wine or beer at our party.
We can't get any wine.
Therefore, we must have beer.

Wine or beer at a party doesn't come close to exhausting all of the possible alternatives. You could have soft drinks, hot chocolate, or something else, so the argument is weak, but valid, given the premises. Sometimes conditions dictate that there are only two alternatives when there would otherwise be more. If those conditions are specified or clearly understood, then the argument would be stronger. For instance, in the prevous example, if the arguers were members of an organization that had met earlier and already determined that the only choices for refreshments at the party would be wine or beer, then the major premise would be true, and the argument would be sound. If you don't know that such constraints exist, then don't assume they do if you can reasonably think of alternatives that haven't been considered. This is important in becoming a good critical thinker, because if you stop to think of other possible alternatives, you may discover a better idea that hadn't been thought of yet.

This consideration becomes more important in significant situations. For instance, imagine that you work for a business that isn't doing very well. You attend a meeting to try to decide what to do, and an important company official says that people must either be laid off or prices must be raised. Those may be viable alternatives, but there may be many others, some of which are better. If no one at the meeting recognizes that the alternatives presented are not really comprehensive, then those may be the only choices considered, and a poor decision may result.

The other requirement for a *sound* disjunctive argument is that *the alternatives in the major premise must be mutually exclusive.* If the solution to a problem in our first example could be to raise taxes *and* reduce services, then the major premise cannot cogently say *either* one *or* the other. Considering whether the alternatives are mutually exclusive involves questioning the material truth of the premise. No reason was given for the hosts not having *both* wine and beer at the party, or why the company could not *both* lay off workers and raise prices, so the examples violate this requirement. The more alternatives there are in the major premise, the more thinking you'll have to do to determine if they are actually mutually exclusive.

Hypothetical or Conditional Syllogism

The third type of argument is the **hypothetical syllogism,** which is another name for the **conditional syllogism.** The major premise presents a hypothetical condition and its outcome. Often the major premise will have some phrase such as "if _____, then _____," or "when _____, then _____," or "_____ if _____." The hypothetical condition (the "If _____" phrase) is the **antecedent.** The outcome (the "then _____" phrase) is the **consequent**. The order in which they appear in the sentence doesn't make any difference, so it may say "_____ will happen, if _____ happens." The antecedent specifies the conditions necessary for an outcome, and the consequent is the outcome of those conditions. When determining the validity of the argument, remember that the major premise establishes everything you know about the universe. Even if you personally believe something different, when you evaluate the *formal validity,* you cannot go beyond or alter what was said in the major premise.

The two basic forms of a valid hypothetical syllogism are as follows:

> **If *antecedent,* then *consequent.***
> **Affirm antecedent.**
> **Therefore, affirm consequent.**

> **If *antecedent,* then *consequent.***
> **Deny consequent.**
> **Therefore, deny antecedent.**

The first requirement for a valid hypothetical argument is that *the minor premise must either accept the antecedent or contradict the consequent.* If the minor premise does anything different from those two choices, then the argument *cannot* be valid, because those are the only two things you know anything about. Given the way the major premise is stated, you only know what will happen if the antecedent *does* come about (that the consequent will have to come about), and what will happen if the consequent does not happen (that the antecedent must not have happened). Beyond that, you don't know anything about the universe. Thus you could have the following argument:

If we raise taxes, then we won't have to reduce services.

We've raised taxes.

Therefore, we don't have to reduce services.

That argument accepts the antecedent, and it can lead to a valid conclusion. In the following argument, the consequent is contradicted:

If we raise taxes enough, then we won't have to reduce services.

We have to reduce services.

Therefore, we didn't raise taxes enough.

You probably realize that in the real world governments might raise taxes and still have to reduce services, but if the stated major premise is accepted, then that is not a possibility. You must accept the major premise when determining validity.

Now let's see what happens if you contradict the antecedent or accept the consequent.

If we raise taxes, then we won't have to reduce services.

We didn't raise taxes.

Therefore, we have to reduce services.

It seems to make sense, doesn't it? However, since the *only* thing you know about the universe is what would happen if you *did* raise taxes, then you can draw no valid conclusion about what would happen if you *didn't* raise taxes. It could be that taxes weren't raised and that services were maintained through deficit spending. The point is, given the stated major and minor premises, you just cannot know for sure. The same sort of thing happens if you accept the consequent, as in the example that follows:

If we raise taxes, then we won't have to reduce services.

We didn't reduce services.

Therefore, we raised taxes.

Once again, it sounds plausible. But in terms of the formal validity of the argument, you cannot draw a conclusion based on knowing that the consequent *did* come about. It *may* have come about because the antecedent came about, but it may have come about for some other reason. Remember, the major premise states that if the antecedent happens, then the consequent had to happen, but it doesn't say anything about what must have happened if the consequent happens. You can reason to that kind of conclusion, but that would require adding more syllogisms in a chain of arguments.

The second requirement for a valid hypothetical argument is *if the minor premise accepts the antecedent, the conclusion must accept the consequent.* Conversely, *if the minor premise contradicts the consequent, then the conclusion must reject the antecedent.* Consider the following argument:

If it rains today, then we won't go to the beach.

It's raining today.

Therefore, we won't go to the beach.

The only thing you know about the universe is what will happen if it rains today. And the only thing you know about that is if there is rain, you won't go to the beach. You have absolutely no idea what will happen if it doesn't rain, and you have no idea what you *will* do if it does rain. You only know one thing you will *not* do if it rains. The argument, then, accepts the antecedent, and the conclusion accepts the consequent, so the argument is formally valid.

The mistake many people make in evaluating the validity of hypothetical arguments is thinking that if the antecedent is rejected, then the opposite of the consequent must happen, or the consequent must be rejected. So they *think* the following would be valid:

If it rains today, then we won't go to the beach.

It's not raining today.

Therefore, we will go to the beach.

However, the minor premise did not accept the antecedent, nor did it contradict the consequent. It contradicted the antecedent. Since the only thing you know about the universe is what will happen if it *does* rain, then you cannot come to a conclusion about what will happen if it *doesn't* rain, thus the argument is invalid. If it doesn't rain, then you still might not go to the beach, but for some reason other than the rain. Your major premise gives you no help in deciding what will happen if the antecedent is rejected.

Now consider the following argument:

If it rains today, then we won't go to the beach.

We're not going to the beach.

Therefore, it rained today.

A lot of people would say that that is a valid argument, but it isn't. The major premise only established that you know what will *not* happen if it rains, but it doesn't establish that rain is the *only* reason that you wouldn't go to the beach. Something else might come up, even though it's not raining. So by accepting the consequent, you still don't know anything about what will happen with the antecedent.

However, if you *reject* the consequent, you *do* know something about the antecedent: you know that the antecedent *didn't* happen. So, the following is valid:

If it rains today, then we won't go to the beach.

We're at the beach.

Therefore, it didn't rain today.

The major premise establishes that you know rain would keep you away from the beach, so if you went to the beach, the one thing you would know is that there wasn't any rain. By denying the consequent, you know that you can also deny the antecedent.

Most arguments are much more complex than these examples. Instead of the simple phrases used as major and minor premises in the examples, the premises of everyday arguments may get quite complex, with conditional phrases, compound premises, and unstated premises. In a real argument, there is usually a chain of reasoning, with the conclusion of one syllogism the major premise of another, the conclusion of an enthymeme the minor premise of another, and so on. And, in everyday arguments, the premises and conclusions may be stated quite vaguely, if they're stated at all, and they won't necessarily come in an order that makes them easy to recognize. So don't worry if you have trouble figuring out the logical structure or making decisions about the formal validity of everyday arguments.

USING FORMAL LOGIC
TO ANALYZE ARGUMENTS

If you can follow the forms that were described to create your own arguments, then you're likely to make arguments that are stronger, harder to dispute, and more convincing. You also can use your knowledge of the classical structure of arguments to evaluate the worth of other arguments.

The first step in using classical structure to evaluate an argument is to become familiar with it by listening carefully if it's an oral argument or by reading carefully if it's a written argument. When you evaluate an oral argument, it helps to take notes so you can refer back to them later, or tape-record the argument if you can. After becoming familiar with the argument, you should then decide on the primary claim, which would be a statement that the entire argument is trying to support. Don't assume that the primary claim will be clearly stated in the argument; often it is not. The primary claim would be the same thing as the conclusion.

After you've figured out the primary claim, you must decide how the claim was supported. So you'd return to the argument, or your notes, to identify all of the statements made that could be considered support. Then you'd need to determine which statements would be considered part of the major premise and which would be part of the minor premise. Keep in mind that either premise may be unstated, and that you must state them the best you can. Also remember that the premises may be more complicated than those used in the examples.

You must decide which statements could be considered "part of" the premises, because a statement that would be a major or minor premise may at the same time be the conclusion of a subordinate argument. Other statements may be the major or minor premises for that subordinate argument, and so on. You may find that one part of the primary claim is completely presented, while another part is implied, but you need to figure out how the entire argument fits together.

Once you've figured out all of that, you can decide which type of argument and subordinate argument you have: categorical, disjunctive, or hypothetical. If the major premises are stated in the arguments, then you would use what the arguer said to determine the type of argument. If the major premises are not stated, then you would try to decide what they would be, given the claims and evidence presented. When determining what any unstated parts are, always be as fair to the arguer as you can. Don't create a ridiculous major premise just because that will make it easier to say that the argument is flawed if you disagree with it.

After you've decided what the premises are, how they fit together, and what type of argument you have, then you are ready to evaluate the argument's formal validity by applying the requirements for each type of syllogism to the argument that you're studying. If it meets the requirements, then it's formally valid; if it fails to meet the requirements, then it is formally invalid.

Analyzing the formal validity of arguments is only one step in evaluating them. An argument should be formally valid to be strong, but it should be more than that. An argument that is formally valid but is not materially true has little to recommend it. Later chapters will describe ways to evaluate the probable truth of the information that goes into the premises.

INFORMAL FALLACIES ASSOCIATED WITH CLASSICAL STRUCTURE

Now we can look at some common informal fallacies related to the structures of argument. These fallacies are grouped together because they have something in common, and it's better to introduce just a few fallacies at a time. When a fallacy has more than one name, a common English title is used for the main label, with other names included in parentheses.

ACCIDENT (sweeping generalization, *dicto simpliciter*)—concluding that a legitimate generalization necessarily applies to a particular case.

Most generalizations used in everyday argumentation are not absolute; they are statements that are usually true, and you must be careful that your conclusion is no more universal than the premise. The fallacy of accident happens when you begin with a probable major premise and arrive at an absolute conclusion. For example, you might start with the generalization "Most attempts to rehabilitate criminals have failed" and conclude that attempting to rehabilitate a particular criminal will necessarily fail. Assuming that the generalization is correct, if you conclude that the attempt is *likely* to fail, then there is no fallacy, but if you conclude that it *will* fail, there is a fallacy.

The fallacy of accident is exemplified in the following report from a student:

I have a friend who made it through college even though he had a severe drug dependency. When I was telling my mom about it she said that she didn't think he had a drug problem because he did so well in college. Her reasoning was that one cannot do well with a drug dependency. But he was an exception.

In this example, the legitimate generalization is that people who have a drug dependency usually do not do well in school, but the mother didn't recognize that some drug-dependent individuals are still able to accomplish what they want.

The fallacy of accident is the name of one of Aristotle's (Hamblin) original fallacies, and the meaning has changed over time. For Aristotle, the fallacy meant mistaking a nonessential quality for an essential quality. As Hamblin explains, though, distinguishing between essential and nonessential qualities of anything or anyone is difficult enough to make the original definition almost meaningless (27). The common contemporary meaning is the failure to recognize an exception to a generalization.

LAUDATORY PERSONALITY—reasoning that a person couldn't do something bad, or must have done something good, because he or she has some good qualities or occupies a prestigious position.

This is a particular type of fallacy of accident, which reasons that people who possess positive qualities generally do not do bad deeds, or that people in prestigious positions generally do not do bad deeds, concluding that a particular person or officeholder could not have done a bad deed. It also can happen when someone argues that a person who has positive personal characteristics or who holds a prestigious office must have done a good deed. As with the fallacy of accident, there are exceptions to the general rule that good people and officeholders don't do bad deeds.

An example of this kind of reasoning occurs when someone in a community is accused of a crime and the people who know her say things such as, "She couldn't have done it. I've known her for years, and she's always been so kind." While that may be true, it does not necessarily mean that she couldn't also have some negative characteristics of which others were unaware.

When a religious leader, for instance, is accused of wrongdoing, and someone says that he couldn't have done it because he is a religious leader, it is an example of the second form of this fallacy. Religious leaders, teachers, police officers, government officials, and others are still human and may have failings. Although most of them do no wrong, their positions do not guarantee that they won't.

Notice that in both examples people say that the individuals *couldn't* have done wrong. If they say they are surprised, or think it's unlikely, that the person did wrong, there isn't a fallacy. When dealing in likelihood instead of certainty, one recognizes both the legitimacy of the generalization and the possibility of encountering the case to which the generalization doesn't apply.

REPREHENSIBLE PERSONALITY—reasoning that a person couldn't do something good, or must have done something bad, because he or she has some negative qualities or occupies a particular position.

This specific type of fallacy of accident is similar to that of laudatory personality but changes the qualities of the person to negative instead of positive. With this fallacy one might say that someone couldn't have done something good, because he's such a jerk, or that a politician couldn't tell the truth because she's a politician. People have a mixture of good and bad characteristics. Expressing surprise that a person would act so out of character would not be a fallacy, and predicting that someone would probably behave in a particular way because it is in keeping with the way he has acted in the past usually is not fallacious. However, arguing that the person *could not* have acted any other way would take the generalization too far.

GUILT BY ASSOCIATION—a particular type of fallacy of accident that reasons that someone or something necessarily shares all of the same characteristics of those with which it is affiliated.

It is said that people are known by the company they keep, and that "birds of a feather flock together." Those sayings are at the heart of the guilt by association fallacy. It assumes that people share the characteristics of others in their group. Thus if several members of a group have a certain characteristic, then you might incorrectly reason that any individual member of the group will have that characteristic.

If it is known that Elaine has several friends who don't take school seriously, then someone might infer that Elaine doesn't take school seriously. If the person has no other information about Elaine, then that conclusion should be quite provisional. If it is taken as an absolute, then it would be a fallacious argument. As with other types of fallacies of accident, the problem arises if you take a probable premise and arrive at an absolute conclusion.

The name "guilt by association" implies that the characteristic must be negative. The same kind of reasoning can be done if the characteristic is positive, such as concluding that someone is necessarily a good athlete because he or she is friends with some good athletes. The point is, an affiliation with others does not necessarily confer their traits on anyone. In addition, the same erroneous reasoning can occur when the association is only with one other person.

The associations do not have to be among people but can be among objects as well. You might conclude that because a particular product is sold in a store that sells a lot of poor-quality merchandise that the product you're looking at is definitely shoddy. However, it might be one of the few quality items that the store sells, so your conclusion would be faulty. On the other hand, if a store generally sells high-quality goods, that doesn't necessarily mean that a particular product is high quality. The other items sold at either store do provide you with information to help you arrive at a probable conclusion, but not an absolutely sure conclusion. Examining the specific product is a better way to determine its quality than looking at the other products in the store.

FALSE DILEMMA (false dichotomy, either-or fallacy, bifurcation, black-or-white fallacy)—incorrectly assuming that one choice or another must be made when there are either other alternatives or the choices are not mutually exclusive.

This fallacy is associated with the major premise of the disjunctive argument, in which the choices are identified. The major premise might be incorrect in two ways. First, it may not identify all of the possible choices. Second, the choices in the premise may not be mutually exclusive. This fallacy reminds us to carefully consider a disjunctive premise before accepting a conclusion based on it.

For example, if someone said, "We have to either go to the zoo or go skating. Since you don't like to skate, we'll go to the zoo." There are certainly many other choices of activities in addition to going to the zoo and skating, so the major premise sets up a fallacious argument. In addition, there may be no reason that the people couldn't both go to the zoo and go skating, along with a variety of other activities. If the individuals had already decided that all other possibilities were unacceptable, and they only wanted to do one of the two possibilities listed, then this would not be a fallacy. But if someone starts off by limiting choices then it's quite reasonable to point out that other choices should be considered. The same would be true if someone made an argument about public policy, such as "We must go to war or be unsafe."

The false dilemma fallacy reminds you to stop to think about the premise whenever you hear an either-or argument. You should ask yourself if the situation really is correctly characterized as "either-or."

BEGGING THE QUESTION (circular reasoning, *petitio principii, circulus in probando, circulus in demonstrando*)—arguing in such a way that the support of a conclusion is a restatement of that conclusion.

The fallacy of begging the question happens when the conclusion restates one of the premises, or when the acceptance of a premise depends on accepting the conclusion. When the conclusion restates a premise, it usually uses slightly different wording, so the circular reasoning isn't obvious. This type of argument essentially says "X is true, because X is true." Although "X" may be true, a strong argument will provide some other support.

An example of an argument that restates a premise is if someone said, "Obviously compact discs are the best sounding of all recordings, because nothing else sounds as good." The premise is "nothing else sounds as good [as compact discs]," and the conclusion restates it as "compact discs are the best sounding of all recordings." The premise didn't present any information to lead to the conclusion, it just reworded the conclusion.

Another example is "I know I can trust my girlfriend because she told me she wouldn't lie to me." In this case, trusting the girlfriend is dependent on her saying she wouldn't lie, and accepting the truth of that statement is dependent on trusting her. There is no evidence or reasoning that she deserves to be trusted included in this argument, so it isn't really sound.

SUMMARY

The classical structure of arguments provides a way to determine if an argument is valid, that is, if the parts of the argument fit together the way they should. The two types of arguments covered by the classical structure are the syllogism and the enthymeme. The syllogism includes a major premise, a minor premise, and a conclusion, and it arrives at an absolutely certain conclusion. The enthymeme is missing at least one of the parts of a syllogism, arrives at a provisional conclusion, or does both. Syllogisms are deductive arguments, and enthymemes with provisional conclusions are inductive. An argument that is formally valid may or may not be materially true, and a materially true argument may or may not be formally valid.

The three types of arguments are categorical, disjunctive, and hypothetical. Each has a different form and different requirements to be valid.

KEY CONCEPTS

antecedent   the clause in the major premise of a conditional argument that establishes the conditions that will lead to an outcome; the "if" clause in the major premise of a conditional argument.

categorical argument   a syllogism or an enthymeme with a major premise that establishes categories in which the subject of the minor premise will fit. The major premise takes the form "All As are B."

classical structure of an argument the logical form that an argument should take.

cogent argument   another term for a sound argument.

conclusion   the statement in a syllogism that is the inevitable outcome of accepting the major and minor premises. It must be absolute in a syllogism and may be provisional in an enthymeme.

conditional argument   a syllogism or an enthymeme with a major premise that establishes what will happen if particular conditions exist. The major premise takes the form "If A then B." Also called a "hypothetical argument."

consequent   the clause in the major premise of a conditional argument that establishes the outcome if the conditions of the antecedent are met; the "then" clause in the major premise of a conditional argument.

deductive reasoning   argumentation in which the conclusion is included in the premises; an argument that reasons from what is known with certainty in the premises to a conclusion that is known with certainty.

disjunctive argument   a syllogism or an enthymeme with a major premise that establishes alternatives from which to choose. The major premise takes the form "Either A or B."

enthymeme   an argument that is missing at least one part of the syllogism, comes to a probable conclusion, or both.

formal validity   having the correct structure or "form."

hypothetical argument   another name for the conditional argument.

inductive reasoning   an argument that comes to a probable instead of an absolute conclusion, or that reasons from what is known in the premises to a conclusion that is unknown in the premises.

major premise   the part of a syllogism that is an unequivocal general statement about the subject of the argument.

major term   the term in a categorical argument that appears in both the major premise and the conclusion; the category into which both the minor term and middle term fit.

materially true argument   an argument that reaches a truthful conclusion or uses premises that are true, as much as "truth" can be determined.

middle term   the term in a categorical argument that appears in both the major premise and the minor premise; the category into which the minor term fits.

minor premise   the part of a syllogism that is a statement about a specific case, covered by the generalization of the major premise.

minor term   the term in a categorical argument that appears in both the minor premise and the conclusion; the term that fits into the middle term and, therefore, fits into the major term.

sound argument   an argument that is both materially true and formally valid.

syllogism   a deductive argument that includes a major premise, minor premise, and conclusion and which comes to an absolutely certain conclusion that is the inevitable result of accepting the premises.

valid argument   an argument that is properly structured, in which all of the logical components fit together correctly.

THINGS TO THINK ABOUT

1. Think of an example of a deductive argument that someone else made, and another example of an inductive argument someone else made. What would each be, if turned into a syllogism or a three-part enthymeme? Why is one deductive and the other inductive?

2. Create a deductive argument and an inductive argument.

3. Think of a valid categorical syllogism, a valid disjunctive syllogism, and a valid conditional syllogism about different, significant topics. Then think of invalid syllogisms for each type of argument. Which requirements are violated to make each invalid?

4. Choose part of Secretary Powell's speech in the Appendix. How would it appear as a syllogism or as an enthymeme that includes all three parts?

5. Think of a syllogism or a three-part enthymeme about a significant topic. Which other syllogisms or enthymemes would develop subordinate arguments whose conclusions are either the major premise or the minor premise for part of the main argument?

6. In your opinion, what are the strengths and weaknesses of the classical model of argumentation in your everyday experience with argumentation?

TUTORIAL LINK

Go to *http://communication.wadsworth.com/verlinden* and complete the tests for the following tutorials:

Formal Logical Structure

Formal Validity Requirements

Validity and Invalidity

Informal Fallacies Set #1

VALIDITY PRACTICE

Identify the type of syllogism in each of the following examples, whether it's valid or not, and if it's invalid, why. Answers follow.

1. The Department of Motor Vehicles (DMV) always has long lines. I have to go to the DMV. Therefore, I will have to wait in a long line.

2. The DMV always has long lines. I can make an appointment. Therefore, I won't have to wait in line.

3. If everyone recycled, then the earth's resources would last longer. Everyone has begun to recycle. Therefore, the earth's resources will last longer.

4. If everyone recycled, then the earth's resources would last longer. Everyone hasn't started to recycle. Therefore, the earth's resources won't last longer.

5. Recycling always saves energy. Marilyn recycles. Therefore, Marilyn saves energy.

6. Recycling might save energy. Pete recycles. Therefore, Pete saves energy.

7. If I take a nap right now, then I will not finish my homework. I finished my homework. Therefore, I did not take a nap.

8. If I take a nap right now, then I will not finish my homework. I did not take a nap. Therefore, I finished my homework.

9. Either the color of her eyes is real, or she wears colored contacts. She doesn't wear contacts. Therefore, the color of her eyes is real.

10. Either the color of her eyes is real, or she wears colored contacts. Her eyes are green. Therefore, she doesn't wear contacts.

11. Everyone will either pass or fail this class. Paul did not pass this class. Paul failed this class.

12. Everyone will either pass or fail this class. Paul never studied. Paul failed this class.

ANSWERS TO THE VALIDITY PRACTICE

1. This is an invalid categorical syllogism. While it may seem reasonable, the minor premise doesn't address what we know from the major premise. The minor premise gives no reason to believe the speaker has to go to the DMV to conduct business (and thus wait in a line); she may be going to work there, she may pick someone up, or she may do something else. Given this major premise, the minor premise might be, "That building is the DMV," and the conclusion might be, "There will be long lines in that building."

2. Another invalid categorical syllogism. It too may seem reasonable, but the parts don't fit together. The minor premise introduces two new terms: "I" and "make an appointment." That makes a total of four terms, which violates the rules for categorical syllogisms.

3. This is a valid hypothetical (or conditional) syllogism. The minor premise affirms the antecedent, allowing you to affirm the consequent.

4. This is an invalid hypothetical syllogism. The minor premise denies the antecedent, which means that you can come to no valid conclusion. While it may seem reasonable, the only thing you know about the universe is what will happen if everyone does recycle. When you say that people aren't recycling, you can't come to any conclusion, given only the information in the major premise.

5. This is a valid categorical syllogism. Everything fits together just like it should.

6. This is an invalid categorical syllogism. Since the major premise says "might," you can come to no certain conclusion as this does. If the conclusion were, "Pete might save energy," then it would be a valid enthymeme.

7. The major premise sets up the universe that you know about. While there may be other reasons you would not finish your homework, you know that if you had taken a nap, it would not be done. Since it is finished, you know that you cannot have taken a nap. The minor premise contradicts the consequent, and it's a valid hypothetical syllogism.

8. This one is not valid. According to the major premise, you have no idea what would happen in a world in which you don't take a nap. Since your minor premise states that you didn't take a nap (denying the antecedent), you can't come to a valid conclusion.

9. This is a valid disjunctive syllogism. The minor premise eliminates one alternative, and the conclusion picks the other.

10. This one is invalid. The minor premise doesn't pick or eliminate either alternative, so you can't come to any conclusion.

11. This argument is valid but not sound. It is valid because it meets the requirements for a disjunctive syllogism. It is not sound because the major premise does not include all possible alternatives, including withdrawing from the class or taking an incomplete.

12. Another invalid disjunctive syllogism, because the minor premise doesn't say anything about either of the alternatives in the major premise.

6

The Toulmin Model of Argumentation

In the late 1950s, British philosopher Stephen Toulmin decided that the formal structure of argument was not an accurate depiction of how people really argue. The classical model was quite good for philosophers and mathematicians but not for examining everyday arguments by people using natural language. So in his book *The Uses of Argument,* Toulmin presented a different model that better reflected real-life argument. Unlike the classical model, with a major premise, minor premise, and conclusion, his model has six parts, some similar to those in the classical model, and others added to it to present a more complete model of how people argue.

Toulmin's model of argumentation also has the advantage of working better with inductive reasoning than the classical Aristotelian model. If you try to fit an inductive argument into the syllogism, it often is virtually impossible to do without violating some of the requirements for the syllogism.

Toulmin noted that, as with Aristotle's (1991) enthymeme, most arguments do not explicitly include all of the elements in his model. In everyday argumentation, the person who makes the argument implies some of those elements, or the person receiving the argument infers some. When we make the elements explicit, we can more easily decide whether the argument deserves to be accepted, but we shouldn't expect the person to make all parts of her argument fully explicit.

This chapter will

- describe the elements of the Toulmin model.
- explain Toulmin's idea about fields of argument.
- explain how to use the model to both make and analyze arguments.

ELEMENTS OF THE TOULMIN MODEL

The six parts of Toulmin's model are the claim, grounds, warrant, backing, modal qualifier, and possible rebuttal. The **claim** is the proposition that the arguer is supporting. In a lengthy argument, there may be several claims that are then used as other elements to prove the primary claim. So what could be a claim in one part of the chain of argumentation may then be the grounds for another part. The **grounds** (which are also sometimes called **data**) are the specific evidence used to support the claim, which makes them similar to the minor premise of the classical model. The **warrant** is the explanation of why the grounds legitimately support the claim, and is similar to a major premise. If stated, the warrant explains the connection of the grounds to the claim, but often the warrant is only implied. When warrants are implied, receivers may accept the argument as reasonable when, if the warrants were stated, the reasoning wouldn't seem so strong. **Backing** is the justification for believing the warrant. Depending on the subject, backing may come from the history of scientific experimentation, art theory, generally accepted cultural beliefs, and so on, or from specific statements of why the particular evidence fits the particular claim. Another part of the Toulmin model is the **modal qualifier** (often just referred to as the **qualifier**), which is any term or phrase associated with the claim that indicates the strength of the claim. Words such as "certainly," "probably," and "possibly" would be modal qualifiers. Sometimes in everyday argumentation the qualifier will not be stated, but the arguers understand that no one is arguing a position as absolutely certain. Other times, however, it may be unclear how certain the arguer intends the claim to be, because there's no agreement on how qualified it is. The final element in the Toulmin model is the **possible rebuttal,** which is a statement indicating under what circumstances the claim may not be true. Think of the possible rebuttal as a kind of "unless" statement. The arguer is saying "X is certainly true *unless* Z happens," or "A is probably true *except when* B is involved." Toulmin's model was created with argument$_1$ in mind, so the possible rebuttal is something that the arguer making the claim says, not the objections other arguers or listeners have regarding the claim.

Soon after Toulmin presented his model, critics noted that the backing for the grounds is as important as the backing for the warrant, but Toulmin left them out. Rather than confuse backing for warrants with backing for grounds, we'll refer to backing for grounds as verifiers. **Verifiers** are implicit or explicit justifications for believing the grounds. If, for example, the grounds are statements of eyewitnesses, then verifiers may be the receiver's belief in eyewitness testimony in general or trust in the specific witness presenting testimony. If the grounds are statements made by a member of a research organization, then verifiers would be the reputa-

Figure 6.1 The possible rebuttal indicates why the claim may not be true.

© Baby Blues Partnership. Reprinted with special permission of King Features Syndicate.

tion of the research organization that discovered the information, as well as the details of how the research was conducted. If the grounds are assertions made by a friend during a conversation, then verifiers may be how well the assertions fit with other beliefs and the credibility of the friend regarding that topic. An arguer may explicitly state them by source citations, identifying credentials, and so on or imply them through language or nonverbal suggestions. The receivers may infer them by comparing the grounds to other knowledge, attributing credibility to the source, and so forth.

Think of the elements in the Toulmin model as answers to questions in an argument. After you've made a claim, you might be asked what proof you have to support the claim, which the grounds would answer. Then you might be asked, "What do those grounds have to do with the claim?" The warrant answers that question. Then you might be asked, "Why should we believe either your grounds or your warrant?" The verifiers and backing are the answers. You might be asked how certain your claim is, and the modal qualifier answers that question. Finally, you might be asked if there are any conditions that would make your claim untrue, and the possible rebuttal answers that question. Anticipating such questions in advance helps you answer them as you make the arguments rather than wait for the questions to be posed.

For example, we can use an earlier argument to illustrate the elements of the Toulmin model:

All human beings are mortal.

Hilary is a human being.

Hilary is mortal.

The claim is "Hilary is mortal," and the grounds are "Hilary is a human being." The reasons those grounds can be used to support that claim are the warrants "All human beings are mortal" and "What is true of all human beings in the past will be true of any current human being." The unstated backing might be "Mortality is defined by death, and all human beings throughout history have been mortal" and "The future tends to resemble the past." The verifiers would be the receiver's trust in the person making the argument, or the receiver's personal knowledge of Hilary. There is no modal qualifier, so the claim is certain. The possible rebuttal might be "Unless we are speaking figuratively (i.e., 'She lives on in history') or of some religious or mythical figure." When you examine an argument using the Toulmin model, you often have to fill in parts with reasonable statements if they haven't been explicitly stated, and you can't ask the arguer to fill them in for you.

What might be the various elements that support a meteorologist's claim that "We will probably get rain in Kansas City tonight"? Try filling in the possibilities that follow:

Grounds:

Verifiers:

Warrant:

Backing for Warrant:

Modal Qualifier:

Possible Rebuttal:

The following is one of many possible answers:

Grounds: Whatever the atmospheric conditions are when the prediction is made, such as barometric pressure and whether it's rising or falling, the presence of a high or low pressure system, the existence of moisture from the Gulf, and so on. (*Note:* If someone other than a meteorologist is making the claim, then the grounds might be something quite different, such as "There are dark clouds in the western sky.")

Verifiers: The data are from the National Weather Service; our faith in its ability to collect and report such data.

Warrant: "These particular weather conditions usually result in a rainstorm."

Backing for Warrant: Past experience with weather observations.

Modal Qualifier: Explicitly stated as "probably" (and oftentimes even more precise by stating something like a "70 percent chance").

Possible Rebuttal: Something like, "Unless the high pressure system to the east becomes stationary."

Let's try another example. Assume you are in a class that uses a point system to determine your final grade, and if you get more than 92.5 percent of the possible points, then your final grade will be an A. Now try working out the elements for this claim: "I deserve an A in this class."

Grounds:

Verifiers:

Warrant:

Backing for Warrant:

Modal Qualifier:

Possible Rebuttal:

Once again, there are many possible answers. One follows:

Grounds: The scores you have for all of the assignments and exams, and the scores possible on those assignments and exams, which show that you have more than 92.5 percent of the total possible points.

Verifiers: The physical evidence of the assignments with the scores written on them, and the mathematical calculations used to arrive at your percentage.

Warrant: Something like, "A cumulative score that is more than 92.5 percent of the possible points indicates that an A for the course is deserved."

Backing for the Warrant: A copy of the course syllabus that states that standard.

Modal Qualifier: There is no modal qualifier, because you say you definitely deserve an A.

Possible Rebuttal: Something like, "Unless the course isn't finished and there are still more assignments or exams to be completed, or unless some information about the scores was left out." If the claim is made after the class is over, then a possible rebuttal might be, "Unless I (the student) violated some course policy that justifies a lower grade."

A popular topic in argumentation classes is support for the idea that hemp should be legalized. For that claim, the grounds usually are that hemp can be used to make paper, clothing, energy, and oils. Students also often say that hemp is more environmentally friendly than other resources. The verifiers for those grounds are historical examples and testimony of hemp advocates or scientists, and trust in those sources. The warrant usually is unstated but might be, "Useful resources that are environmentally beneficial should be legal." The backing for the warrant would be past experience with other resources and beliefs about sound public policy. The claim usually is unqualified, although most people would assume that the claim is highly probable rather than absolutely certain. No possible rebuttal is presented, but one might be "Unless hemp is found to have other significant problems."

This example is a little more complex than the first two, and the elements are also a bit more complex. For instance, establishing the grounds and their backing may require full arguments rather than simple statements, as might the backing for the warrant. When you make arguments, you have to decide how much you need to say about each element. For some audiences you don't have to state an element at all, while for others you will need to carefully present all of the evidence and backing.

It might help to think of the parts of the Toulmin model in terms of the analogy illustrated in Figure 6.2. Imagine you have a river. One side of the river is your grounds, and the other side is your claim. You need some way to get from your grounds to your claim, so you build a bridge. That bridge is your warrant. In various places in the river, you install columns to support the bridge/warrant.

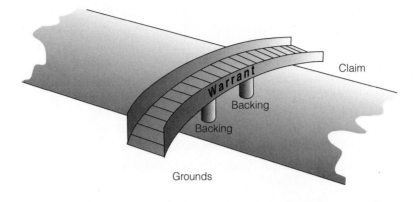

Figure 6.2 The warrant bridges the gap between the grounds and the claim, and the backing supports the warrant.

They are your backing. Verifiers are the tests done to the grounds to make sure that they're solid. Modal qualifiers and possible rebuttals would be signs on the "claim" side of the bridge that help you understand that side of the river.

FIELDS OF ARGUMENT

Along with revising the model of argument, Toulmin made a second major contribution to thinking about argumentation, the concept of **fields of argument.** The classical notion of the structure of arguments assumed that the arguments remain the same regardless of context. Toulmin said that different fields of endeavor have their own sorts of rules for what constitutes good argumentation. Those "rules" include things such as what questions are worth making arguments about, what counts as evidence or grounds, what warrants will be used, what counts as worthwhile backing, and how strong a claim must be to be considered worthwhile.

For example, questions that atomic scientists ask are not those asked by lawyers, art critics, or anthropologists. Evidence that lawyers use is different from that used by atomic scientists, art critics, and anthropologists. Warrants that art critics accept would be rejected by anthropologists, atomic scientists, and lawyers arguing within their fields. And backing that anthropologists use would be unacceptable to atomic scientists, lawyers, and art critics. The task, then, of someone evaluating an argument would be to try to understand how argumentation is done within that particular community and to try to decide if the argument meets that community's standards rather than applying standards from one field to another or a universal set of standards to all fields. An extension of that idea would be to critique the standards for particular fields to determine whether other standards would better serve each field.

This doesn't mean that common argumentation standards do not exist across fields. The basic structure remains the same in all fields, as does the need for all of the elements to fit together well. But the acceptable use for each element varies from field to field.

USING THE TOULMIN MODEL
TO MAKE ARGUMENTS

When you have a chance to carefully prepare an argument, you can use the Toulmin model as a template to ensure that you make a sound one. To do that, start by identifying all of the elements, both for your main argument and for any subordinate arguments. Ask: What is my claim? What are my grounds? What are the verifiers? What is the warrant? What is the backing of the warrant? What is the modal qualifier? What is the possible rebuttal? What arguments are needed to support any of these?

After you have determined the elements of your argument, ask yourself if they all fit together well, and if they are all reasonable. For example, you think of a warrant that fits well with your grounds, but to make it fit the warrant would have to be so ridiculous that you realize you need different grounds to make a sound argument. After you determine how well all of the elements fit together, decide if any need to be changed to strengthen your position. While you do that, you also can think of the possible objections that an arguer who disagrees with your claim may bring up.

Finally, determine which elements of the model must be expressed. You probably want to explicitly state your claim, including the modal qualifier and your grounds, but you have to decide if you need to state the warrant, any of the backing or verifiers, or the possible rebuttal. You should make that decision based on what you think the audience already knows, what you think an opposing arguer might bring up, how clearly the elements in your argument fit together, and if more developed arguments will help make your reasoning clear.

USING THE TOULMIN MODEL
TO ANALYZE ARGUMENTS

Using the Toulmin model to analyze arguments can help you determine whether the argument really makes sense or not. The first step is to determine the major claim of the argument. That can be tricky, because arguers often will say or write things that seem like claims, but they don't support them and go to some other subject. Sometimes they don't state the major claim at all, or they state it so late in an argument that you didn't realize what the person tried to support. So don't decide what the claim was until you've heard or read the entire argument. This step is very important, because warrants and grounds also sound like claims, or they may be claims for subordinate arguments, and if you choose the wrong claim, then the argument won't make sense when you analyze it. This also is a good time to look for the modal qualifier, since it is always associated with the claim.

After determining what the claim is, you can look for all of the grounds or evidence used to support that claim. You may have to decide which statements are used to support the claim, which are used as verifiers, and which are used just to try to make the argument more interesting. Once you decide what the grounds are, you can determine what is used to verify the grounds. Explicit verifiers, such as source citations, come right out and say why you should believe the evidence, while implicit verifiers hint at it. Receivers supply inferred verifiers, so also consider what the receivers might think would verify the grounds. Since verifiers do not have to be explicitly stated by the arguer, there is always some sort of verification for grounds, even if it isn't stated in the argument.

Next you can figure out the warrants for all of the grounds and the backing for each. As you do this, keep in mind that the warrants often are unstated, so you may have to decide what the warrant *should* be, given the claim and the grounds. Be sure to be as fair as possible when you decide this. Resist the temptation to make a warrant seem ridiculous if you disagree with the claim. Once you have the warrants, decide on the backing. As with grounds, there will always be some backing but it won't always be stated explicitly.

Finally, determine if any possible rebuttals are mentioned in the argument. Keep in mind that possible rebuttals are ideas expressed by the person making the claim, not things that others could possibly say against the argument.

So far all you've done is describe the argument. The next step is to evaluate how solid the argument is, which is the whole point. Try to answer the question "Does this argument *deserve* to be accepted?"

This part of the analysis has two steps. You must first evaluate how well the argument holds together. Ask questions such as the following:

Are the grounds acceptable to a reasonable person and a critical thinker?

Do the warrants make sense to a reasonable person and a critical thinker?

Do the grounds and the warrant fit together?

Is the claim fully proven or does it require more qualification?

The answers to some of these questions could involve reasoning using other concepts, such as formal validity, to see if the grounds and warrant do fit together. Others require reasoning using deeper knowledge of the subject matter. Identifying the elements of the model will help you make these decisions, because it allows you to focus your attention on the elements.

The second part of evaluating the argument is to determine how well it fits the field of argument in which it belongs. If it's an argument about science, does it argue using scientific grounds, warrants, and backing? If it's an artistic argument, does it argue using artistic grounds, warrants, and backing? If it doesn't argue using the standards of the field, then how does that affect the quality of the argument? Finally, given all of these considerations, does this argument deserve to be accepted?

Toulmin's model advances the classical model of argumentation by presenting a more accurate representation of what people actually do when they make arguments. It doesn't replace the classical model entirely, though, because the determination of how well the grounds fit with the warrant to support the claim depends on understanding the classical model. Using the two models together helps you both make stronger arguments and think critically about the arguments you hear and read.

SUMMARY

Stephen Toulmin developed a different model of argumentation to better reflect what people actually do when they make arguments in everyday life. The model originally had six elements: claim, grounds, warrant, backing, modal qualifier, and possible rebuttal. Verifiers were added to address the need to provide backing for the grounds.

Toulmin also developed the idea that different fields of argumentation argue in different ways. When making or criticizing an argument in a field, use the standards of that particular field.

You can make stronger arguments by applying your knowledge of the elements of the Toulmin model. This also will help you evaluate arguments made by others by giving you a better idea of what to look for.

KEY CONCEPTS

backing   the element in the Toulmin model of argumentation that justifies believing the warrant.

claim   the element in the Toulmin model of argumentation that is the proposition the arguer supports.

data   another name for grounds in the Toulmin model of argumentation.

fields of argument   subject-related communities of arguers with argumentative "rules" specific to each community.

grounds   the element in the Toulmin model of argumentation that is the evidence used to support the claim.

modal qualifier   another name for the qualifier in the Toulmin model of argumentation.

possible rebuttal   the element in the Toulmin model of argumentation that is a statement indicating under what circumstances the claim may not be true.

qualifier   the element in the Toulmin model of argumentation that is any term or phrase indicating the strength of the claim.

verifiers   the element added to the Toulmin model of argumentation that provides justification for believing the grounds.

warrant   the element in the Toulmin model of argumentation that explains why the grounds legitimately support the claim.

THINGS TO THINK ABOUT

1. Write an outline for an argument about a significant subject that includes all seven parts of the Toulmin model.

2. Find an example of a brief argument. What are the parts of the Toulmin model that are explicitly stated in the original argument? What statements could be added for each part of the Toulmin model that were not explicitly stated?

3. Think of an argument made in a field with which you are familiar. How do the rules for making arguments in that field differ from those of other fields?

4. Find one of Secretary of State Powell's arguments in the Appendix. How does it exhibit the seven parts of the Toulmin model, explicitly and implicitly?

TUTORIAL LINKS

Go to *http://communication.wadsworth.com/verlinden* and complete the tests for the Toulmin Model of Argumentation tutorial.

7

❋

Forms of Reasoning

You use both reasoning and evidence to support claims. **Reasoning** is both the thought process that leads to a conclusion and the presentation of support for a claim in an argument. In the classical model, the reasoning is generally found in the major premise and the evidence in the minor premise. In the Toulmin model, the reasoning is in the warrant and the evidence is the grounds. A critical thinker finds an argument that uses good evidence and poor reasoning and an argument that uses good reasoning and poor evidence unacceptable. When you understand the components of the classical and Toulmin models of argument, you have the foundation to understand more complicated arguments.

The two general types of reasoning are deductive and inductive. You'll remember from Chapter 5 that **deductive reasoning** draws a conclusion that is already known from information in the premises. **Inductive reasoning** draws a conclusion that is not known from information in the premises. Deductive conclusions are certain, and inductive conclusions are provisional. For example, if a teacher knows for certain that all of the students in his class share a particular characteristic, and knows that a particular person is a student in his class, then he can be certain that that person has the characteristic. On the other hand, if he knows that *some* of the students in his class have a certain characteristic, then he may conclude that all of the students in the class *probably* have that characteristic, or that an individual student *might* have that characteristic. Knowing something about some members of the class may lead to a conclusion, but it cannot be certain.

Most everyday argumentation is inductive reasoning, because we rarely know enough about the subjects we argue about to start with absolutely certain premises and proceed to absolutely certain conclusions. Even when people state their claims absolutely, they probably do that for effect, or because they mistakenly believe that their warrants are absolutely true. If you stop to think about their claims and grounds (or their premises and conclusions), that then you'll realize that they cannot know their claims are absolutely true.

This chapter will

■ identify five specific forms of reasoning that you may encounter or use in an everyday argument.

■ explain what to look for to evaluate arguments using each form.

The ideas that follow are adapted from the work of argumentation scholar Austin J. Freeley (163–77), with the exception of reasoning by criteria.

REASONING BY EXAMPLE

The first form is **reasoning by example,** which involves inferring a conclusion from specific cases (which are your examples). The inference may be drawn from one case, but stronger arguments draw from multiple examples. Reasoning by example is inductive reasoning, because you draw a conclusion about either an unknown member of the group or about the group as a whole, based on what you know about particular members of the group. We'll keep referring to members of a group, although you also could be reasoning about parts of a whole, or about future behavior based on past behavior, and so on.

Realizing that the conclusions of reasoning by example are generalizations can help you identify this form, which uses a limited number of examples of the members of a group, or a limited number of examples of a phenomenon, to conclude a generalization about a specific member of the group or a specific phenomenon. Sometimes it may seem as though the conclusion is not a generalization, but that's because there are two steps in that reasoning. For instance, someone might reason that a few members of a group have a particular characteristic, so another member will also. In everyday argumentation, people commonly go straight to the final conclusion without articulating the opening argument. The argument, if expanded, might look like the following:

Warrant: Something that is true of many members of a group is likely
            to be true of the other members of the group.

Grounds: X is true of members 1, 4, 5, 8, 9, and 12.

Claim: Therefore, X is probably true of the other members of the
            group.

Then

Warrant:	X is probably true of all of the members of the group.
Grounds:	7 is a member of the group.
Claim:	Therefore, X is probably true of member 7.

Reasoning by example is something we all do almost every day. For instance, you might decide that all history classes are interesting, because the history class you took was interesting. Or you might predict that a friend will want to go to a party, even though he has a test the next day, because the last time he had a test he was eager to party the night before. Both the history class you took and your friend's prior behavior are examples that you use to reach a conclusion. Since you don't already know about other history classes or your friend's future acts, the reasoning is inductive.

Scientific reasoning is, in general, reasoning by example. Scientists perform experiments on specific subjects, reason that what is true of the specific subjects is also true of other subjects similar to those in the experiment, and draw generalized conclusions. Whether they're physicists, biologists, psychologists, anthropologists, or other scientists, the basis of what they do is reasoning by example. Unlike most of us, however, scientists make much more rigorous efforts to ensure that their examples are chosen in ways that lead to sound arguments. Scientists also generalize from the findings of experiments to theorize. They know the results of those experiments, and from those known results, they predict what would happen in other unknown cases, and why.

Opinion polls and surveys are extended cases of reasoning by example. Since it's impractical to find out what every person's reactions will be to something, researchers pick a sample, find out what their reactions are, and use them as known examples to predict the unknown reactions of the rest of the population.

Reasoning by example is necessary, because we often need to draw conclusions before we know much about something or someone, and it's impractical to get all of the relevant information about the entire group or the specific case. For instance, when discussing welfare reform, we can't wait until we know everything about everyone on welfare to determine what to do. Reasoning by example, therefore, is always provisional; you can infer what will probably happen, but you can't infer what is certain to happen.

When you encounter examples presented by others, you must decide if they're reasoning by example or using examples to clarify a point. For instance, the examples above try to help you understand concepts, but they don't support an argument. If a person, for instance, presents examples to try to help you understand what she means, and you interpret them as examples to support a claim, then you're likely to find fault with her argument when she wasn't making an argument.

Reasoning by example must meet several requirements to be considered strong. If an argument relies on reasoning by example and fails to meet any of the requirements, then you should question the argument and think about it some more. The conclusion *could* still be correct, but you should have less confidence in it than you would if the reasoning met the requirements.

The first requirement is that *the example must be relevant.* That is, the subject of the known example must be directly related to the subject of the unknown conclusion. If the example and the conclusion do not refer to the same thing, then the example doesn't support the conclusion. For instance, you can't say, "Using nuclear power to meet energy demands is too dangerous. Just look at what happened in Hiroshima and Nagasaki." The examples concern the use of nuclear *weapons,* and the conclusion refers to nuclear *power generation.* Nuclear power plants and nuclear weapons are different enough that one isn't relevant as an example for the other. Nuclear power generation and nuclear weapon production do share some common hazards, such as what to do with nuclear waste, but the *use* of nuclear weapons and nuclear power generation are significantly different.

Another way of putting it would be to say that you may not draw legitimate conclusions about apples based on what you know about oranges. They're not the same thing. You might think that apples and oranges have enough in common that you can draw some conclusions about one by using the other as an example, but you can only make that argument after you already know something about both apples and oranges. Remember, reasoning by example uses a known example to draw a conclusion about something that is unknown. If you already know enough about apples to say that they are comparable to oranges, then you're doing reasoning by analogy, which we will discuss later.

The second requirement for reasoning by example is that *there must be a reasonable number of examples.* Remember, the whole idea behind reasoning by example is that you draw a conclusion about an entire group without going through the trouble of examining *every* member of the group. If you examined every member of the group, you would not be drawing a conclusion about something that isn't known. It may be impractical to examine every member of the group, but a sound conclusion requires several examples. If you rely on only one example, then you may have picked one that is abnormal.

Imagine, for instance, that you have a bag of marbles but that you don't know what kind of marbles are in the bag. You can feel the marbles through the bag and can roughly guess that there are about fifty. You reach into the bag and pull out one of the marbles, and it's blue. Would it be reasonable to conclude that the bag contained only blue marbles, or that the next marble you'd pull out would be blue? Most people realize that the color of one marble doesn't tell you anything significant about the rest of the marbles. If you pulled out fifteen blue marbles in a row, then you could start to have more confidence in saying that all of the marbles are blue, or that the next one picked will be blue. However, if six were blue, four were clear, and five were green, then you'd draw a very different conclusion.

Unfortunately, we create problems for ourselves and others by drawing conclusions based on too small a sample. For example, we encounter someone once and decide that he's an awful person based on that one encounter, or we meet someone and decide that everyone who generally looks like her will act like her. Or, we combine both, and we decide, based on one encounter, that everyone who looks a certain way will always act the way that person did the one time we encountered him or her. Misusing reasoning by example is a basis of stereotypes and prejudices. If you find yourself making conclusions based on just a few examples, then it's a good idea to remember to make those conclusions provisional. That is, draw a conclusion, but recognize that the reasoning is weak, and be ready to revise it.

The third requirement for sound reasoning by example is to *use typical examples* that are representative of the group under consideration. Of course, you don't really know if the examples are typical until you have a reasonable number of them, but once you have a reasonable number, don't use the unusual examples to draw conclusions or make your argument. When others make their arguments, you shouldn't accept them if they use examples that aren't typical.

Using atypical examples is one way that people try to misuse evidence to prove what they want. They find a few examples, for instance, of people who are 100 years old and have smoked multiple packs of cigarettes every day for 80 years, and then they argue that those examples are proof that smoking cigarettes isn't harmful. They know that many more people have smoked far less and have developed serious heart and lung disease, but they ignore that evidence in favor of the few examples that prove their point.

Typicality is one reason medical researchers don't rely on testimonials to prove that treatments work. Someone may have lost weight on the latest diet plan, for example, and wants to tell the world about it. However, that person's testimony may come from the only person in the world for whom the diet has ever worked. The people selling the diet plan may know very well that the other thousand people who used the plan didn't lose any weight, so they try to sell it based on an example that isn't typical of all of the users. (Along with using an atypical example, they're also using an unreasonably small number of examples.) In fact, whether the argument is about medical procedures or anything else, be skeptical when only testimonial examples are used for support.

A fourth requirement for reasoning by example is that *the examples must cover an appropriate period of time,* that is, the examples used to prove a point should come from a time period that is most appropriate for the topic being argued. Examples of failed attempts to fly that come from a time period before the Wright brothers flew at Kitty Hawk are hardly appropriate to support a claim that flight is impossible. Or, examples of harmful activity that occurred before legislation was passed making the activities illegal are not legitimate to use to call for further legislation.

The final requirement for reasoning by example is that *contradictory examples must be unimportant.* "Contradictory examples" means examples that deny the claim. For instance, if the claim is "Smoking cigarettes is unhealthy," and it is supported by examples of studies showing that people who smoke have more health problems than people who don't smoke, then a contradictory example would be a study that shows that there are no health differences between those who smoke and those who don't. This requirement says that such examples must be unimportant to the conclusion. To determine if they're unimportant, apply the first four requirements of reasoning by example. In the case just discussed, the negative example is unimportant, because it is only one example and is not typical. If the contradictory example were a much better study than all of the others, then it would be an important one, because it has something to recommend it over the others. Also, if someone, for instance, were refuting the position that smoking cigarettes is deadly by raising the example of his grandfather who smoked heavily and lived to be ninety, then we could say that example is unimportant because it's only one example, and it's not typical.

REASONING BY ANALOGY

A second kind of reasoning is **reasoning by analogy,** which makes a comparison between two similar cases and infers that what is known about one is also true of the other.

Analogical reasoning is similar to reasoning by example in that they're both inductive reasoning. However, reasoning by example doesn't compare two cases to draw a conclusion. Rather, it builds case upon case to either reach a generalization or to predict characteristics of a future case. Reasoning by analogy uses perceived similarity to reach a conclusion that the two things being compared are alike, or that what is true about one known case should be true about a similar case. For instance, reasoning by example might be used to argue that using illegal drugs is dangerous by describing several examples of people who used drugs and suffered. Reasoning by analogy could be used for the same claim by comparing your brain to an egg and drug use to a hot frying pan. Reasoning by analogy is used so often that we can easily fail to notice it. The general argument, if presented completely, might be the following:

Warrant: Case A and Case B are similar, so what is true of case A is true of Case B.

Grounds: X is true of Case A.

Claim: X is true of Case B.

or

Warrant: Keeping your car functioning well is similar to keeping your body functioning well.

Grounds: To keep your car functioning well, you need to have it examined regularly.

Claim: You need to have your body checked regularly.

People who use reasoning by analogy usually do not make the argument that the things being compared are the same. The similarities usually are assumed. So, for instance, when Arnold Schwarzenegger ran for governor of California, he wrote, "The problem is overspending, and the deficit must be closed by getting spending under control. Our first order of business is to get California's operating deficit under control. I will ensure that California's government lives within its means—something working families manage to do every day—and rein in spending to close the operating deficit" (Schwarzenegger). He didn't take the time to argue that management of the California budget is the same as managing a family budget. He simply asserted that they are the same, leading to the conclusion that what is done with one ought to be done with the other.

Reasoning by analogy comes in two forms. First are **literal analogies,** which compare cases that belong in the same classification. Second are **figurative analogies,** which compare cases in different classifications. For instance, to say that a government program will work in San Francisco because it worked in Los Angeles is a literal analogy, comparing two cities. To say that your brain is like an egg is a figurative analogy—for *most* people, at least. Is the comparison of managing a state's budget to managing a family's budget literal or figurative?

Reasoning by analogy is basic to legal reasoning. When court cases establish precedents, they are used as the basis of deciding future cases. When cases are litigated, one attorney says that the current case is analogous to one precedent-setting case, while the other attorney says that the current case is not analogous to that precedent at all but is to another case. The specifics of all of the cases will be somewhat different, so the court has to decide, based on the argumentation, which precedent-setting case is similar enough to the current case.

Some say that all reasoning by analogy is logically weak, because when you compare two things there will ultimately be some critical differences. Even when comparing two cities, there will be differences in the demographics of the populations (ethnic makeup, political affiliation, religion, etc.), climate, history, economic base, size, and so on, and those differences could mean that the comparison isn't valid. That is important when trying to reach an absolutely certain conclusion, but in the realm of everyday argumentation, where we are usually interested in probable conclusions, reasoning by analogy is still very useful. So we don't reject analogical reasoning automatically, but we do examine it carefully to see how well it holds up so we can reach conclusions that have a high probability of being correct. To do so, you determine if the argument meets the four requirements of sound analogical reasoning.

The first requirement is that *there must be significant points of similarity* among the items being compared. The more alike they are, the better able you are to argue that what is true of one is true of the other. The significance of the similarities may be both quantitative and qualitative, that is, there should be many points of similarity, and those similarities should be among important qualities. So a comparison between Los Angeles and San Francisco probably would have more significant points of similarity than a comparison between San Francisco and Omaha. Two cities from the same state, both on the Pacific Coast, with similar histories and cultures probably will have more in common with each other than with a smaller city in the Midwest with a different historical and cultural background. That doesn't mean that a comparison cannot be made between San Francisco and Omaha, only that you'd have to be careful that the similarities truly exist.

The second requirement is that *the points of similarity must be important to the comparison*. For instance, reasoning would be poor if you drew a negative conclusion about Charlie Chaplin's character based on the similarity of his mustache to Adolf Hitler's mustache. The existence of a mustache is simply not relevant to personal character. Maybe you've heard of all the supposed similarities between

Abraham Lincoln and John F. Kennedy and their assassinations presented as though some kind of a meaningful conclusion could be drawn from them. Similarities between people, institutions, governments, and other things can be found; the question is whether or not those similarities matter. As a critical thinker, you would not automatically assume that the similarities are critical.

Since reasoning by analogy compares two different things, there inevitably will be differences between the two. Sometimes those differences are important, and sometimes they are not. So the third requirement of sound reasoning by analogy is that *the differences must be unimportant* to the comparison being made. For instance, if you were to argue for educational reform because public schools are like prisons, the your reasoning would run into problems when the differences between schools and prisons were discussed. While there is regimentation and authoritarianism in both institutions, there also are important differences, such as students get to leave school at the end of the day, and the purpose of schools is different from that of prisons.

The fourth requirement of analogical reasoning is that *only literal analogies should be used as logical proof.* Sometimes arguers use figurative analogies to help others understand. As long as enhancing understanding is the purpose of a figurative analogy, there is nothing wrong. But if you use a figurative analogy as a way to support your conclusion, then there will be too many differences for a sound argument. Often it's hard to recognize when you, or others, use figurative analogies, because they become such an accepted part of our language and way of thinking that we no longer think of them as analogies. An example would be the analogy between the brain and a computer.

CAUSAL REASONING

The third type of reasoning you may use is **causal reasoning,** which argues that one thing or event in the past caused another thing or event to happen, or will cause something to happen in the future, or an action taken in the future will cause a particular outcome. Please note that this is "causal" reasoning, as in "cause and effect." It is not "casual" reasoning.

Causal reasoning should be central to any kind of legislative argumentation. Legislators decide which laws to pass based on what significant problems exist and can be solved. They have to decide what causes the current problems and what new laws will cause. For instance, legislators in favor of health care reform want to decide which problems in health care can be solved with federal health care reform, while those opposed to such reform focus their attention on potential problems that health care reform will create. That assumes that they are making their decisions based on what is best for the country, not on what will make them popular in the polls. Even basing decisions on what will cause them to be popular is a form of causal reasoning, though. Causal reasoning also is done when a mechanic tries to figure out what is causing problems with your car, when a manager tries to figure out why subordinates aren't performing well, or when you try to determine why someone is angry with you. An explicitly stated argument might be the following:

Claim: People imitate violence because they see it on television.

Grounds: People see violence on television.

Warrant: People tend to imitate behavior they see.

The first requirement of causal reasoning is that *the alleged cause must be relevant to the effect described*. Meeting this requirement may be more difficult than you'd think, and a lot of argumentation may center on whether the cause and effect are actually related. A few years ago a major news story covered the mysterious deaths of several Navajos in New Mexico and similar illnesses that occurred elsewhere. The physicians trying to determine the cause had to determine whether the suspected causes had any connection to the illnesses. In doing so, they probably rejected a large number of potential causes without even thinking of them (such as the position of the stars when the victims were born, and the malevolent acts of supernatural beings), and others after seriously considering them, because they are irrelevant to the illness. People often make causal arguments by presenting possible or plausible causes, but they still may be irrelevant. However, you may not be able to tell if they're relevant until they've been examined.

The second requirement of causal reasoning is that *the cause must be capable of producing the effect*. You may not know this until you've seriously examined the alleged cause. There was a time when the existence of microorganisms wasn't accepted, and even when it was, few people believed that they could possibly cause serious illness. After all, how could something so small you can't even see it make something as large as a human being sick? Germ theory wasn't generally accepted until it was explained how germs were capable of producing their effects. So if you make a causal argument and can't show how your cause is capable of producing the effect, then that's likely to be perceived as a weakness in your argument.

The third requirement of causal reasoning is that *the cause(s) cited must be the sole or distinguishing causal factor*. If you are arguing that pesticides are causing illness, then you need to show that pesticides are the only significant difference between people who get sick and people who do not. Naturally there will be many differences between the two populations, so if an opposing arguer shows that another cause is as likely as pesticides to be responsible for the illnesses, then your argument is weakened. This requirement doesn't mean that there can't be multiple causes of something, but it does indicate that all of the causes need to be accounted for in the argument. If some causes are addressed but others aren't, then you may be ignoring the actual cause.

When you engage in causal reasoning, *the cause(s) cited must be necessary and sufficient*, which is the fourth requirement of causal reasoning. "Necessary" means that the effect cannot be produced without the cause you cite. "Sufficient" means that nothing more than the cause you cite is needed for the effect to occur. You do not have to argue that a single cause produces an effect; you might argue that a combination of factors is necessary and that any one of these factors is not sufficient. So the "cause cited" means the totality of the causes that an arguer says produces the effect.

The idea that multiple factors are necessary to cause an effect is important when thinking critically about public policy issues. Often everyone can agree that a problem such as violence in society exists, but the cause of the problem is so complex that a single cause can't reasonably be found. For example, depending on who is making the argument, social violence has been said to be caused by: easy access to handguns, television programming for children, alcohol, drugs, the lenient sentencing of convicted criminals, the lack of a death penalty, the presence of a death penalty, the process of appeals made by convicted criminals, the absence of traditional family values, unemployment, racism, patriarchy, music lyrics, the number of police, genetic traits, lack of religion, and so on. Perhaps all of the advocates are correct to a certain extent, and the question becomes which, if any, of the causes are both necessary and sufficient to produce the amount of violence in our society? If you want to create a policy that can remedy violence, then you won't be successful if you merely try to eliminate one minor cause; there will still be enough other causes left that violence will continue.

Closely related to the idea of necessary and sufficient causes is the requirement that there be *no counteracting cause.* A counteracting cause is a factor that *prevents* the effect from coming about. For instance, a high-calorie diet would be a cause of someone becoming overweight, but a high level of exercise would be a counter-acting cause that would prevent the weight gain. Strictly speaking, a counteracting cause would not deny the effect of a cited cause, but it might make that cause irrelevant when choosing a course of action. The counteracting cause might indi-cate that there is a better way to solve a problem than the policy advocated, or that the cause originally cited will become irrelevant.

Whenever you're thinking about causal reasoning, keep in mind that *correlation* is not the same thing as *causation.* Correlation means that two events happen together, either simultaneously or in some order. When there is a high degree of correlation, the two events happen together most of the time; when there is a low degree of correlation, the two events don't happen together very often. A high degree of correlation, with one event preceding the other, may lead us to erro-neously think that the first event caused the second.

There are three basic ways that you may have correlation without a strong indication of causality. First is coincidence. Just by chance, two events may be closely related in time, so it looks like one caused the other. A tragic example of this is when someone blames himself for a friend's suicide, thinking his actions earlier in the day caused his friend to take her life. The decision to commit suicide, though, isn't based on one encounter; it's likely just a coincidence that both events happened the same day.

Second is that the event cited as the cause may be so common that it could be seen as a cause of almost anything. Viewing television, for instance, may have caused all of the ill effects that people attribute to it, but it may also simply be an easy target. Since so many people watch so much television, it's hard to think of anything we do that isn't correlated with television viewing. We could probably determine that Americans' life spans have increased as the average television viewing hours have increased, but you're not likely to hear anyone argue that television leads to longer life.

Finally, two events that are highly correlated may have a common cause, so one event doesn't cause another, but they are both caused by a third event. For example, thunder and lightning don't *cause* rain, and rain doesn't cause thunder and lighting. They're all caused by atmospheric conditions.

Other examples of conclusions that are the results of everyday causal reasoning that are problematic because correlations are used to prove causality include the following statements:

Chocolate causes acne.

Childhood trauma causes mental illness.

Guns cause murders.

Electromagnetic radiation causes cancer.

Judas Priest's music causes suicide.

Pornography causes rape.

To say that those conclusions are problematic doesn't mean that they are necessarily wrong but that the evidence and reasoning behind them, as well as opposing them, should be considered carefully.

SIGN REASONING

If someone disagreed with you forcefully in a loud voice, with eyes bulging and face flushed, and jabbing his hands in the air, then you probably would conclude that he is angry. In reaching that conclusion, you've taken a group of signs that by themselves could indicate a variety of emotions but added together indicate a particular state of mind. When that happens, you engage in the fourth type of reasoning, **sign reasoning.** Sign reasoning argues that two variables are so strongly related to each other that the presence or absence of one may be taken as an indication of the presence or absence of the other. For example, a swollen stomach, nausea, and diarrhea are all signs of food poisoning. We find sign reasoning when a doctor makes a diagnosis, when economists argue over the condition of the economy, and when individuals make judgments about others. One of the key characteristics of sign reasoning is that it uses signs (clues, indicators) that can somehow be observed to draw a conclusion about something that cannot be observed.

An example of sign reasoning might be the following:

Grounds: Gary has been spending a lot of time with me, smiles at me a
           lot, looks in my eyes, and has bought me several gifts.

Claim: Gary likes me, because . . .

Warrant: When someone spends a lot of time with you, smiles at you, looks into your eyes, and buys you gifts, those are signs that that person likes you.

Notice that the person making the argument can observe all of the grounds but not the claim, so must infer it based on the grounds.

Another key to sign reasoning is that the signs, if true, naturally occur as a result of the existence of a claim. It doesn't matter whether anyone notices them, draws a conclusion based on them, or even knows that a conclusion could be based on them. The way a person acts around someone he or she likes is naturally occurring behavior (even though it is culturally learned), so this is a sign of his or her state of mind.

As with the other types of reasoning, there are several conditions that sign reasoning must meet. First, *the alleged sign must be relevant to the conclusion.* That means that the sign must really be a sign of what the arguer claims it is. For example, some people believe that they can tell when a person is lying by nonverbal behavior they see. Often such behavior is really related to nervousness, and it may or may not be a sign of deception. Since some people don't get nervous when they lie, they are able to do so without showing any signs. And since some people get very nervous when they think that they may be suspected of lying, they'll give all of the signs when they're really telling the truth. (It's somewhat reminiscent of the alleged medieval idea that a witch would float when tied up and dumped into water, while someone who is innocent of witchcraft would sink. That idea was spoofed in *Monty Python and the Holy Grail,* when villagers reasoned that since wood floats, and ducks float, a sign someone is a witch would be if she weighed the same as a duck.)

An example of sign reasoning comes from the old saying "Where there's smoke, there's fire," at least if you take the saying literally. As an absolutely certain statement, it may not be true, because it's possible to create smoke without a fire. But as a statement of probability, it holds up; the presence of smoke is an indication of the probability of fire.

The statement becomes a problem, however, when used figuratively but taken literally. For example, women's moral characters often are questioned—by both men and women—based on the clothing they wear. The reasoning behind the conclusion usually is based on a figurative application of the idea that "where there's smoke, there's fire." This time it could be stated: "If she dresses that way, then she must be promiscuous." That is, certain clothing styles are signs of certain character traits. Of course, there is no necessary relationship between appearance and sexual behavior. (By the way, men's appearances are taken as character signs too, whether the length of their hair, preferences for suits or leather jackets, or other stylistic choices. It seems that with every change of fashion, someone is ready to say that people wearing the new styles have some character flaw that is indicated by their clothing.) Some people tend to take a sign that is, at best, a weak indicator of character and behavior and treat it as though it were an extremely dependable predictor, without looking for other signs to either confirm or disprove their conclusions. So the first step is to determine whether there is a legitimate sign.

This leads to the second requirement of sign reasoning, that *the relationship between the sign and the subject must be inherent.* In other words, it must be necessary and consistent. For instance, we could make the argument that you are a good student because you attend classes regularly. For that argument to hold up, we would have to agree that regular class attendance is not only a sign of a good student but that good students inherently attend class regularly. Assuming that this argument doesn't depend on defining a good student as one who attends classes regularly, we might wonder if class attendance really is an *inherent* characteristic of a good student. If we define a good student as someone who masters the course material and performs well on exams, then is it possible to be a good student without attending classes regularly? Yes. And is it possible to attend classes regularly and not be a good student? Yes. While we know, generally, that students who get higher grades tend to attend classes more regularly than students who get lower grades, class attendance alone is not an inherent indicator of student quality.

Many factors are associated with being a good student besides class attendance, including motivation, self-discipline, lack of distractions, natural ability, and self-confidence. To make a strong argument about a good student, an arguer should point out a variety of such signs, which leads us to the third requirement of sign reasoning: *sign reasoning should be cumulative.* That means the that arguer is taking into account multiple signs to arrive at the conclusion.

When doing sign reasoning, the signs are your evidence. You might reach a conclusion that is true based on only one sign, but your *argument* would be weak, because you don't have enough evidence to support the conclusion. A critical thinker should not accept the argument without more convincing evidence. To make your argument stronger, you must "accumulate" more signs that will all lead to the same conclusion.

If the same set of signs legitimately leads to several different conclusions, then the only conclusion you can have faith in would be very general. For instance, reporting to your doctor that your stomach feels funny may be a sign of many different illnesses, a sign of nervousness, or a sign that you ate too much. A doctor who argued that you should have your appendix removed based only on that sign will not be very compelling to someone who is familiar with the signs of appendicitis. The doctor will examine you and look for other symptoms that when taken together add up to the eventual diagnosis.

The final requirement of sign reasoning is that *there should not be a counter-factor to disrupt the relationship.* A counter-factor would be some information that would indicate the relationship between the sign and the attribute is weak. For instance, in the argument about being a good student, you might point out that the student doesn't pay attention when he comes to class, which is a sign that he is not a good student. Since it is a sign for a different conclusion, the reasoning needs to meet the same requirements as the original sign reasoning. However, as a counter-factor that disrupts the original relationship, it casts doubt on the original claim.

Figure 7.1 Some people don't recognize signs and draw conclusions as well as others.

Dilbert reprinted by permission of United Feature Syndicate, Inc.

REASONING BY CRITERIA

The final type of reasoning that we'll examine is **reasoning by criteria.** This type of deductive reasoning happens when an arguer applies preexisting standards to a subject and makes a judgment based on how well the subject fits the criteria. The preexisting standards are either created or identified as a way to reach a conclusion. For instance, teachers establish criteria for the assignment of final grades, such as, a student who gets more than 90 percent of the total possible points gets a final grade of A. At the end of the semester, the reasoning to determine the final grade simply applies this criteria to the student's score.

A good deal of legal reasoning is reasoning by criteria. If someone is accused of a crime, then legal statutes define conditions that must be met to find her guilty of that crime. The prosecution tries to prove that the defendant met all of those conditions. The defense tries to show that whatever the defendant did, the actions do not meet the legal definition of the crime. Reasoning by criteria is also referred to as reasoning by definition, because definitions often are used as the criteria to determine what something is.

Reasoning by criteria is similar to reasoning by sign. When doing sign reasoning, the arguer usually looks for evidence of naturally occurring signs with an inherent relationship to the attribute. When reasoning by criteria, the arguer applies standards devised by humans. For example, overturned furniture in a room may be a sign of a struggle, and a corpse with a bullet in the heart may be a sign that the person was killed rather than died of natural causes, but neither one is a sign of murder. Humans created the legal concept of murder, and various standards have to be met for a killing to be considered a murder.

Another example is that physical symptoms are signs of a particular disease. The disease and the symptoms would occur whether or not a physician ever gets involved. The existence of the symptoms also may be used as criteria to determine treatment. While the symptoms may be the same, the *reasoning* is different. In the first case, the physician uses sign reasoning to draw a conclusion about what exists in conjunction with the symptoms. In the second case, the physician uses reasoning by criteria to determine the correct course of action to treat the disease indicated by the sign reasoning.

An example of an argument using reasoning by criteria might be the following:

Claim:	Brian's confession is inadmissible in court.
Warrant:	If a criminal suspect was not advised of his Miranda rights prior to questioning, then any information from the questioning is inadmissible in court.
Grounds:	Brian was not advised of his Miranda rights prior to confessing to the crime.

When you reason by criteria, the criteria may come from several different sources. They may be arbitrarily imposed by an authority or agreed upon by some parties. They may come from a preexisting *definition* from a reputable source, or they may come from some *principle* of art, morality, law, fairness, and so on. In many arguments, the decisions of which criteria to use are so important that the arguers spend almost all of their time arguing over them, since once the criteria are established, the conclusion may be inevitable.

The first requirement for reasoning by criteria is that *the criteria must be adequately established*. Adequacy has two characteristics: clarity and authority. Clarity means that whatever the criteria are, they are clear to the parties involved in the argument. Objective, observable criteria are the easiest to apply, but sometimes more subjective criteria are more appropriate. For example, courts strike down unclear laws because reasonable people wouldn't know if they were breaking the laws. But criteria for judging art are not as precise because of the nature of what is being judged. That doesn't mean that there are no standards for evaluating art, or that subjective standards are necessarily flawed; they are appropriately clear for the field of art.

The consideration of authority means that something more than the arguer's opinion and assertion is behind the criteria. As an arguer, you don't just make up criteria for judgment but use criteria that have some reasoning behind them. Even criteria that seem somewhat arbitrary have reasons one standard was set rather than another, and those reasons can give the criteria value. Criteria for judging art have been established through centuries of experience with art, through philosophical reasoning, and through arguments among art experts. Similarly, criteria for legal decisions are based on the wording of laws, the legislative history behind the writing of the laws, and by precedents set in court decisions. If there is no support for criteria, then criteria are vulnerable to rejection upon examination.

The second requirement is that *the criteria are the best available.* Why use a criterion for judgment if better criteria exist? Determining which are the best criteria is easier said than done. Take, for example, an argument about the quality of a film. What criteria might you use? Is popular appeal at the box office the best? Is the majority opinion of film critics a better standard of judgment? Or can you apply other artistic standards, regardless of the reactions of audience and critics? If you argue over the quality of a film, and your opponent says that the way to determine quality is by how much money the movie made at the box office, then your response might be that there are better ways to determine the artistic merit of a film. You also might point out that there is a difference between the artistic and financial merit of a film. The criterion of financial success is very clear and easy to apply, but it probably isn't the best in this case.

Part of determining if the criteria are the best available is to ask if the criteria are actually relevant to the conclusion. For instance, the criteria that are relevant in determining the quality of a scientific article are irrelevant in determining the quality of a poem, and vice versa.

Once the criteria are established, though, the next requirement is that *the subject of the argument must meet the criteria.* Whatever criteria are chosen, the subject of a sound argument must have the characteristics called for. If the legal definition of a crime includes criminal intent, then the prosecution must prove that there was criminal intent. Sometimes criteria are very complex, and sometimes very simple, but your argument must show how the criteria are fulfilled by the subject, or it will be weak and vulnerable to refutation.

The subject may not completely fulfill the terms of the criteria. If so, you must ask if that is significant. The more precise the criteria are, the more significant any failure to meet them will be. When criteria are more vague, however, there may be room for some error without creating a problem for the argument as a whole.

ANALYZING REASONING

Using the forms of reasoning to evaluate an argument is both straightforward and rather complex. You begin by determining what kind of reasoning is being used in the argument. That may seem easy, but most arguments will make several points using the same general kind of reasoning and several others using other kinds. You must go through the entire argument and determine each individual form of reasoning. Once you've determined which arguments are made and the reasoning they use, you can determine if they meet the requirements for each kind of reasoning by asking the questions in Table 7.1.

Once you analyze the particular arguments and decide if the reasoning is sound, you consider the entire argument. Just because an arguer makes subarguments that meet the requirements for their forms of reasoning doesn't mean that the reasoning is sound when strung together. Conversely, problems with a few individual subarguments may not necessarily invalidate the entire argument.

As with any other analysis of arguments, when you analyze forms of reasoning you should separate yourself from your agreement with what the arguer says. Someone can make a very good argument with which you strongly disagree, or can make a very poor argument with which you do agree.

Table 7.1   Testing Forms of Reasoning

Reasoning by Example

Is the example relevant?

Are there a reasonable number of examples?

Are the examples typical?

Do the examples cover an appropriate time period?

Are contradictory examples unimportant?

Reasoning by Analogy

Are there significant points of similarity?

Are the points of similarity critical to the comparison?

Are differences unimportant to the comparison?

Are only literal analogies used as logical proof?

Causal Reasoning

Is the alleged cause relevant to the effect?

Is the cause capable of producing the effect?

Are the causes cited the sole or distinguishing causes?

Are the causes cited necessary and sufficient?

Are there counteracting causes?

Sign Reasoning

Is the alleged sign relevant to the conclusion?

Is the relationship between the sign and subject inherent?

Is the sign reasoning cumulative?

Is there no counter-factor to disrupt the relationship?

Reasoning by Criteria

Are the criteria adequately established?

Are the criteria the best available?

Does the subject meet the criteria?

USING REASONING

You use the types of reasoning to make arguments by determining what you're trying to prove. Sometimes that will provide a strong cue about the kind of reasoning to use. For instance, if you want to prove that a decision will lead to negative consequences, then it is clear that you need to use causal reasoning. Keep in mind, though, that within that argument you also may use other kinds of reasoning. For example, you might argue that the decision will lead to negative consequences because it is similar to another decision that led to negative consequences, using reasoning by analogy to develop your causal argument.

Sometimes the form of reasoning you should use is determined by the field of your argument. If you make legal arguments, then you are more likely to make arguments by analogy and from criteria. If you make arguments about legislative actions, then you're more likely to use causal reasoning. If you're a physician making a diagnosis, then you're more likely to use sign reasoning, and so forth.

After you've decided what you're trying to prove, you should look at the available evidence to figure out what kind of argument it can support. You may have definitions, you may have examples, or you may have signs, etc. Use the evidence to create an argument, supplying the warrant that connects the grounds to the claim. By this time you should be able to discern which form(s) of reasoning your argument uses.

Finally, apply the requirements of the form of reasoning to the argument that you've constructed. Ask yourself if the argument meets the requirements, and avoid being lenient when you answer the question. If the argument does meet the requirements for the various forms of reasoning you use, then you're likely to have a strong argument. If not, then you probably ought to revise it to make it stronger.

FALLACIES ASSOCIATED WITH FORMS OF REASONING

HASTY GENERALIZATION (overgeneralization, converse accident, *secundum quid*)—Arguing that what is true of a few members of a group must be true of all members of the group.

The fallacy of hasty generalization is flawed reasoning by example, in which a conclusion about an entire group is made based on only a few examples. This fallacy can occur in two ways. First, the arguer may have too small of a sample of the entire group, coming to a conclusion without having enough information. An example would be to draw a conclusion about all sorority members based on the characteristics of one member of a sorority. Second, the arguer may use examples that are unrepresentative of the entire group, choosing to support a conclusion with examples that are the exceptional cases. An example would be a school promoting its quality by referring to only one successful alumnus.

Hasty generalization is the opposite of the fallacy of accident, described earlier, thus the alternative name "converse accident." The fallacy of accident takes a legitimate generalization and applies it to a particular case in an absolute manner. The fallacy of hasty generalization takes a particular case and applies it to the entire group when there isn't enough information to apply it to that whole group.

A hasty generalization may simply be poor reasoning. When someone knows that the sample is small or unrepresentative, though, it is not only poor reasoning but also unethical argumentation.

ANECDOTAL EVIDENCE—a particular type of hasty generalization in which individual stories are substituted for a larger sample as support for a generalization.

Anecdotes are stories that people tell about something that happened to them or others. They often are useful for illustrating ideas or for demonstrating something about the person telling the story. They are not very good, however, for drawing conclusions beyond the particular story.

For instance, advertisers regularly use individual testimonials about the quality of their products. Usually they are interesting stories that gain attention and that the audience can relate to. The problem is that there is no way a consumer could know if the experience of that individual is typical of what the consumer can expect from the product. Assuming that the individual story wasn't made up by the advertiser, it may relate to one of a large number of satisfied customers or one of only a few satisfied customers.

HASTY CONCLUSION (jumping to a conclusion)—drawing a firm conclusion without enough evidence to support it.

The fallacy of hasty conclusion is similar to hasty generalization, but the argument doesn't necessarily make a generalization. It may involve any type of reasoning, and a conclusion is drawn based on little evidence. For example, a person may note that the Dow Jones average dropped for two days straight and decide that a recession has begun, without looking at other signs of the health of the economy. Or someone may have a headache and decide that she has a brain tumor without considering other symptoms. The conclusion may be correct, but the reasoning used to arrive at it is flawed.

DIVISION—arguing that what is true of an entire object must also be true of every individual part of that object.

The fallacy of division is the failure to recognize that the components that make up something may have different qualities than the entire object. So someone might conclude that every department in a university is good because the university is good. The quality or reputation of an entire university is not necessarily the same for every individual department.

The fallacy of division is similar to the fallacy of accident, discussed earlier, except accident refers to members of a group while division refers to parts of a whole. Using the example just described, you might have a fallacy of accident if your reasoning was that a particular department is good because most of the departments at the university are good. The individual department is one member of the group of departments. However, the university is a whole made up of many parts, including departments, faculty, students, administrators, and more.

Sometimes it can be tricky to distinguish between division and accident, because we think of members of a group as parts of a whole. When we talk about members of a group, we are saying that each member can be placed in the same classification. When we talk about parts of a whole, we say that the individual parts combine to create something else.

COMPOSITION—arguing that what is true of an individual part of an object must be true of the entire object.

The fallacy of composition is the reverse of division. It argues that an entire object must have the quality that an individual part of it has. Arguing that since an individual department in a university has a good reputation then the entire university has a good reputation would be the fallacy of composition.

The fallacy of composition is similar to hasty generalization in the same way division is similar to accident. Hasty generalization draws a conclusion about all of the members of a group based on the knowledge of some members, while composition draws a conclusion about an entire entity based on the knowledge of its parts. If you pick up one piece of paper, notice that it is light, and conclude that the weight of each piece of paper in a stack is light, then you made a hasty generalization. If you note that the weight of one page of a book is light and conclude that the book is light, then you made a fallacy of composition.

FALSE CAUSE (questionable cause)—arguing that one event caused another without sufficient evidence of a causal relationship.

We regularly need to determine what caused events to happen, or what future outcomes our actions will have, often without having much information to go on. When we do that, and when we don't recognize the very tentative nature of our conclusions, then we have committed the fallacy of false cause. For example, if you conclude that a friend intentionally hurt you without any evidence of intention, then you have committed the fallacy of false cause.

It is possible to incorrectly identify the cause of something without committing the fallacy of false cause. For instance, if evidence is accumulated using the best means available, and if that evidence leads to a reasonable conclusion, then the reasoning would not be fallacious if new methods of gathering evidence later proved the original conclusion false. Scientific conclusions often are revised when new evidence indicates that a conclusion is faulty in some way. That doesn't mean that the original argument was fallacious, only that new evidence was discovered to change the reasoning.

False cause is the common name for this fallacy, but "questionable cause" may be a better name. When you're examining the reasoning, you may not be able to determine if the cause cited is false or not, but you can question it. The term *questionable cause* reminds us to slow down and think about the causal reasoning rather than accept it as true or reject it as false.

POST HOC (*post hoc ergo propter hoc*)—a specific kind of false cause fallacy that argues that because one event preceded another event the first event must have caused the second event.

The *post hoc* fallacy is the most well known false cause. In a world of simple cause and effect, one can easily tell what the causes of events are by observing them. Whatever happened just before the event is obviously the cause of that event. For example, if you have a row of dominoes, then you can watch one domino knock over the next to see the cause and effect. The trouble is, most events that happen in sequence do not necessarily establish causality. Washing a car doesn't cause rain, even though it may seem like rain always follows. Going out in cold weather without bundling up well doesn't cause a cold; a virus causes it. So if someone tells you that an event caused another, then you should examine that person's reasoning to see if there is more to it than one event happening before the other.

CONCOMITANT VARIATION (joint variation, joint effect, *cum hoc ergo propter hoc*)—a particular type of false cause fallacy that argues that since two events happened at the same time, one event caused the other.

Someone who commits the fallacy of concomitant variation mistakes correlation for causation, thinking that because events are correlated that one must have caused the other. Many events are independent of each other, though, and others share a cause but don't influence each other. The rate of skin cancer in the United States has risen during the same time period that we've explored space, for example. Therefore, space exploration causes skin cancer, right? Or maybe skin cancer causes space exploration. In this case, the two events are probably independent of each other.

COMPLEX CAUSE—a specific type of false cause that involves mistakenly attributing an event to a simple cause when the cause is really more complicated.

People are tempted to simplify causal relationships, because that makes it easier to think about them. However, many causal relationships are more complex than they appear. Did a car accident occur because there was ice on the road, because the driver wasn't paying attention, because the driver was driving too fast, because it was hard to see at dusk, or because the driver slammed on the brakes instead of pumping them? The combination of all of those factors may have caused the accident, but many of us would be tempted to argue that there was only one cause.

The complex cause fallacy is easily combined with the *post hoc* fallacy when we reason that an event that immediately preceded a second event caused the second event, without considering that many other factors were involved in addition to the first event.

The fallacy of complex cause reminds us to look for multiple causes of events rather than to settle on a single cause that seems the most obvious.

FALSE ANALOGY (questionable analogy, wrongful comparison, imperfect analogy)—drawing a conclusion based on an analogy, when the items being compared are not similar enough to sustain the analogy.

The nature of an analogy is to compare the similarities between two things that are not alike, so there will inevitably be differences. When the similarities are insignificant, or when the differences are significant, the analogy doesn't hold up to scrutiny, and the fallacy of false analogy is committed.

Analogical reasoning is necessary to get through the day. When we encounter a new situation, we compare it to one or more previous situations to make sense of it. We usually do that quickly, because there is no time to consider the new situation in detail. Analogical reasoning usually works well enough that we don't question it, but other times it doesn't work so well.

For example, when an adult has a fever, it is common practice to treat it with aspirin. One could easily make the analogy that a child's fever is like an adult's fever, and give the child aspirin. Even if the dosage is adjusted for the size differences, though, the aspirin can cause a serious and potentially life-threatening reaction, Reyes syndrome, among children and teenagers.

False analogy is similar to both the fallacies of hasty generalization and accident. The difference is that false analogy reasons that what is true in one case is true in one other case, while hasty generalization reasons that what is true in a few cases is true in all cases. Accident reasons that what is generally true in many cases must therefore be true in a single case.

NATURAL LAW FALLACY—a specific type of false analogy that reasons that what is true about nature must be true about humans.

Sometimes what is true about nature is true about humans, and sometimes it is not. The natural law fallacy reminds us to stop to carefully consider conclusions based on similarities between nature and humans, and vice versa.

For example, sometimes people argue that monogamy is the proper relationship among humans, and they use monogamous birds as proof that it is natural. But if what is true of birds is also true of humans, then maybe we should migrate during spring and fall as well. If one aspect of bird behavior is applicable to humans, then why aren't others? And if birds make a good analogy, then why not other animals? Grizzly bears have been characterized as "wildly promiscuous." Since bears and humans are both mammals, shouldn't we look to them for proper analogies before we turn to birds? The point is, neither analogy is really correct in this case, even though either may seem appropriate depending on what you want to conclude.

This doesn't mean that analogies between nature and humans cannot be sound, only that critical thinkers ought to carefully consider them before accepting them.

FALSE SIGN (questionable sign)—drawing a conclusion based on sign reasoning when there is not really a direct relationship between the alleged sign and the subject of the conclusion.

Sign reasoning is based on the assumption that there is a direct relationship between a sign and whatever is signifies. Sometimes signs can be manipulated, though, or can be signs of different things.

For example, for some people, clothing is a sign of prosperity. Wealthy people wear more expensive clothing than others can afford. So, if you see someone wearing obviously expensive clothes you can safely assume that person is rich, right? Well, credit cards do allow people of more modest means to buy what they want. So the person you see may have average wealth, possess little self control over spending, and be on the verge of personal bankruptcy. On the other hand, someone else might dress very inexpensively, even though she is extremely well off, because she prefers inexpensive clothes.

AD CRUMENUM—a specific type of false sign that reasons that there is necessarily a direct relationship between cost and quality, concluding that something is necessarily of higher quality because it costs more, or of a lower quality because it costs less, or that someone is necessarily a better person because he or she is wealthy or highly paid, or a worse person because he or she is poor.

High-quality products may cost more to manufacture because more costly materials and more difficult manufacturing processes are used. As a result, high-quality products often cost more than lower-quality products. However, sometimes higher-quality goods actually cost less than lower-quality products, due to a variety of factors. Thus it is not always true that cost is directly related to quality or worth. When people reason that something is certainly better just because it is more costly, they commit the *ad crumenum* fallacy.

People also commit this fallacy when they conclude that others are necessarily better because they are wealthier or make more money. Wealthy and highly paid people probably have strengths and weaknesses just like everyone else, and their financial status doesn't really indicate much about their character.

The *ad crumenum* fallacy is also committed when one concludes that something is necessarily worse because it costs less, or that a person is necessarily worse because she is poor. Money is not an infallible sign of either quality or character.

AD LAZARUM—a specific type of false sign that reasons that there is necessarily an inverse relationship between cost and quality, thus concluding that something is necessarily a better value because it costs less, or someone is necessarily a better person because he or she is poor, or a worse person because he or she is wealthy.

This is the opposite of the *ad crumenum* fallacy. Bargain hunters may erroneously conclude that something is a better value because it is less expensive. If everything else about the product is equal, then that is a reasonable conclusion. But if something is poorly made, or made of inferior material, then it may be a very poor value, even if it is considerably cheaper than competitive products.

Just as the character of a person is not necessarily better because she is wealthy, it is not necessarily better because she is poor. Certainly some poor people have good character, while others do not. The ability or inability to amass wealth indicates how well people are able to amass wealth, not necessarily anything more.

AD ANTIQUITATEM—a specific type of false sign that reasons that something is necessarily better because it is old or worse because it is new.

Sometimes people say things like, "They just don't make things as well as they used to." Sometimes they're right and sometimes not. Age is not necessarily a sign of quality. Some old clocks were very well made, and some were junk. Some of grandma's recipes produce wonderful meals, and some are better forgotten. Older people aren't necessarily wise just because they are old.

Someone also commits *ad antiquitatem* when he argues that something new couldn't possibly be any good. Improved techniques and material don't matter, the reasoning goes—if a product is new, then it can't be as good as the older product.

In any case, the age of something rarely indicates its value. Worth is conferred by a variety of other factors. Even antiques aren't valuable just because they're old, but because they are rare, well made, and in good condition.

AD NOVITATEM—a specific type of false sign that reasons that something is necessarily better because it is new or worse because it is old.

This is the reverse of the *ad antiquitatem* fallacy. Newness is taken as a sign of positive value, and age is a sign of negative worth, so advertisers promote products based on their being "new," and people are rejected for jobs because they are "old." However, it is not the age that makes something more or less valuable but the characteristics that the subject has in addition to the age.

There isn't necessarily a fallacy if the age of the subject is combined with other characteristics. Advertising something as "new and improved" indicates that the value is enhanced because of the improvements rather than age, or a young college graduate who is rejected for a job because he is inexperienced is missing an important quality.

The *ad novitatem* and *ad antiquitatem* fallacies remind us to slow down and consider whether the age of something or someone really has a bearing on the conclusions we reach.

FALSE CRITERIA (questionable criteria)—reasoning that applies irrelevant standards to the subject of the argument.

Whenever you argue by criteria, you have to decide which criteria are appropriate to apply. Using irrelevant criteria innocently or by design creates fallacious reasoning. This fallacy reminds you to stop to think about criteria presented in arguments and determine whether they are appropriate or not.

For example, a teacher should base a student's grade in a class on the quality of the student's work and on whether the student fulfilled the requirements of the class. Arguing that the grade should be based on how well the teacher likes the student, on whether a higher grade will help the student achieve some goal, or on feeling pity for the student engages in fallacious reasoning by applying criteria that are irrelevant to the situation. Applying those criteria may reach a conclusion that the arguer wants, but they should not be applied in the first place.

SUMMARY

People use several different forms of reasoning when they make arguments. Each form of reasoning has requirements that should be met for that reasoning to be considered strong. The forms of reasoning include reasoning by example, reasoning by analogy, causal reasoning, sign reasoning, and reasoning by criteria. Table 7.1 on page 105 lists things to think about when deciding if the reasoning is sound.

KEY CONCEPTS

causal reasoning   reasoning that argues that one thing or event in the past caused another thing or event to happen or will cause something to happen in the future, or that an action taken in the future will cause a particular outcome.

deductive reasoning   argumentation in which the conclusion is included in the premises; an argument that reasons from what is known with certainty in the premises to a conclusion that is known with certainty.

figurative analogy   an analogy that compares cases in different classifications.

inductive reasoning   an argument that comes to a probable instead of an absolute conclusion, or that reasons from what is known in the premises to a conclusion that is unknown in the premises.

literal analogy   an analogy that compares cases within the same classification.

reasoning   (1) the thought process that leads to a conclusion; (2) the presentation of support for a claim in an argument.

reasoning by analogy   reasoning that makes a comparison between two similar cases and infers that what is known about one is true of the other.

reasoning by criteria   reasoning that applies preexisting criteria to a subject and makes a judgment based on how well the subject fits the criteria.

reasoning by example   reasoning that involves inferring a conclusion from specific cases.

sign reasoning   reasoning that argues that two variables are so strongly related to each other that the presence or absence of one may be taken as an indication of the presence or absence of the other.

THINGS TO THINK ABOUT

1. Outline a series of brief arguments, each using one form of reasoning. How does each argument meet, or fail to meet, the requirements for that form of reasoning?

2. Think of an argument that you have encountered in your everyday life. Which kind of reasoning did it use? How well did it meet the requirements for that reasoning?

3. Pick a section of Secretary of State Powell's speech from the Appendix. Which form of reasoning did he use for that section? How strong is the argument, based on the tests in Table 7.1?

4. Think of a time when your reasoning, or the reasoning of someone else, committed one of the fallacies discussed in this chapter. What made the reasoning fallacious?

TUTORIAL LINKS

Go to *http://communication.wadsworth.com/verlinden* and complete the tests for the Informal Fallacies, Set #2 tutorial.

8

Propositions and Stock Issues

Some people are not confident in their ability to argue because they don't know what to include or listen for. There are always surprises, but it helps to have an idea of what an argument should encompass. We now turn our attention to making more extended arguments concerning things about which people normally argue.

This chapter will explain the three general types of arguments and some issues that typically arise with each, regardless of the field of argument. These typical issues are **stock issues.** Arguments that address all of the stock issues usually are stronger than those that don't, which does not mean that an everyday argument *will* address all of the issues, or that it *needs* to address all of them in a particular situation. This chapter will introduce you to an alternate way to make a strong argument and will explain what to look for when evaluating other people's arguments. If you are familiar with stock issues, then you'll have a basic outline to make, respond to, or critically think about an argument.

Part of engaging in critical thinking is considering the unstated assumptions of both your own and others' arguments. An awareness of these propositions and stock issues gives you a tool to do so, because the unstated assumptions often are stock issues that have not been made explicit.

This chapter will

- explain what propositions are.
- describe the basic responsibilities of advocates.
- describe the stock issues for the three basic types of propositions.
- explain how to use your knowledge of propositions and stock issues to make and evaluate arguments.
- identify argumentative fallacies associated with propositions and stock issues.

PROPOSITIONS

The starting place for deciding which issues should be addressed in an argument is determining what kind of proposition you have. A **proposition** is the declarative statement that an advocate intends to support in the argument. Some propositions are stated formally, some informally, and some just implied. For example, intercollegiate debate propositions are worded formally and might read, "Resolved: That United Nations implementation of its Universal Declaration of Human Rights is more important than preserving state sovereignty." In everyday conversation, you might state the proposition, "Gays should be allowed to marry." You also might argue about a subject without ever clearly stating a proposition.

The proposition for an argument is the same thing as a "claim" in the Toulmin model or a "conclusion" in the classical model. However, when making an argument, usually several claims are used in support of the proposition, so the terms are not always synonymous. Think of the proposition as the overall claim that an arguer tries to prove, and think of claims as the subordinate claims developed to support the proposition. Many of the stock issues themselves are claims in support of the proposition, while others clarify the proposition.

Sometimes it helps to think of a proposition as a statement that answers a question about the subject of the argument. For instance, the question "What should be done about inflation?" can be answered by the proposition "The Federal Reserve Bank should raise interest rates." The question "How good is the movie *American Wedding*?" can be answered with the proposition "*American Wedding* is an excellent movie." And the question "Who will win the next presidential election?" can be answered with the proposition "The Republican candidate will win the next presidential election."

Stating a proposition, either formally or informally, is generally a good idea, because the proposition specifically states what you are trying to prove. Most of us have had the experience of arguing with someone, only to find that we really agreed with the other person, or discovered that we weren't even arguing about the same thing. This will happen less often if both people know the specific proposition from the start.

The specific nature of propositions often is unclear, because arguers don't always clearly state their claims or sometimes state them late in their arguments. Don't expect propositions to always appear early in arguments. One of the basic skills in argumentation and critical thinking is to figure out what someone is trying to prove.

There is a difference between a "proposition" or a "claim" and an "assertion." Claims and propositions are supported with either reasoning or evidence, or both. An **assertion** is a claim that has no support. So an assertion could turn into a claim if it was supported, but without support, it doesn't help make a very sound argument. For example, someone might support the proposition "The U.S. invasion of Iraq is unjustified" by saying "George Bush just wants to get Iraq's oil for his friends in the oil business." Whether or not others accept that statement, if the arguer offers no proof that it is true, then it is only an assertion, thus the argument for the proposition is weakened.

Some ideas in most arguments have to be asserted, because there isn't enough time or space to fully support them, the arguer doesn't have the information needed for support readily available, or the arguer expects the listeners to accept the assertions. Realize that assertions weaken arguments and thus should be used sparingly. When making your own arguments, your assertions usually should be statements that other arguers are likely to agree with from the start and that you have no reason to believe are untrue.

BASIC RESPONSIBILITIES
OF ADVOCATES

After you figure out what the proposition is, you can then determine what needs to be done to support it well. Anyone who argues in favor of the general proposition has **the burden of proof** for that proposition, which is the responsibility to provide sufficient evidence and reasoning to justify acceptance by a critical thinker. In other words, "She who proposes must prove." The more the proposition deviates from what is commonly accepted, the greater the advocate's burden of proof. Those who argue against the proposition have the benefit of **presumption,** which is the perspective that the proposition should not be accepted until sufficient evidence and reasoning have been provided to justify acceptance. In some fields, presumption is formalized, such as the legal field's explicit recognition of the presumption of innocence. It's important to keep in mind that presumption doesn't mean the proposition is necessarily false; it only means that critical thinkers won't accept it until its advocate fulfills the burden of proof.

Imagine that you are living in an apartment and that a few months remain on your lease. One day a stranger comes to the door and says, "You have to move by Saturday." Would you just say "Okay" and move out? Probably not. You would believe that you have a right to stay until you're given some good reason to move. You would take the position that presumption is in your favor, that things should remain as they are until there is good reason to change. You would recognize that it is the other person's obligation to say why you should move, not just to show up and tell you to do it. That is, the other person has the burden to prove that you should no longer occupy the ground you occupy.

Or, say you were walking home one night and the police arrested you for robbing a store downtown. When it came time for your trial, would you want the court to take the position that you're guilty, and then you have to prove that you're not guilty? Probably not. You would want the benefit of the presumption that you are innocent until the state has provided enough evidence to convince others that you did commit the crime. The concepts of presumption and burden of proof apply to any argument, in any field. Arguers in science, art, history, politics, and other fields all need to overcome presumption for their arguments to prevail.

The first requirement for fulfilling the burden of proof is to present a **prima facie case.** *Prima facie* means "on its face," and it refers to an argument that presents enough evidence and support that a person thinking critically ought to accept the proposition, at least until the argument is refuted. Until a *prima facie* case is presented, opposing arguers have no responsibility to dispute the proposition, because the advocate has the burden to prove the proposition

Once a *prima facie* case has been presented, the opposition has the **burden of refutation,** which is the responsibility of those opposed to the proposition to dispute the claims, evidence, and reasoning that the advocate has presented. When a *prima facie* case is presented, argumentation about it can proceed. Presenting a *prima facie* case does not mean that the argument *will* stand, only that enough has been done to justify accepting the argument if no one disputes it. An advocate will generally have a *prima facie* case if she provides evidence and support for each of the stock issues for that type of proposition. That is why knowing the stock issues helps you construct, respond to, and think critically about arguments.

While the person arguing in favor of a proposition has *the* burden of proof, everyone who puts forth a claim during the dispute has *a* **burden of proof,** which is the responsibility to provide evidence and reasoning for each claim put forth. Each claim that the advocate makes in support of the proposition requires evidence and reasoning to support it, and each claim the opponent makes against the proposition requires evidence and reasoning to support it. Thus everyone in an argument has *a* burden of proof.

A working knowledge of the concepts of presumption, burdens of proof, *prima facie* case, and burden of refutation is quite useful to engage in and think critically about arguments. If you stop to consciously ask, "Who has presumption?" "What is the advocate's burden of proof?" "What does it take to have a *prima facie* case?" and "What is needed to fulfill the burden of refutation?" then you are on your way to being more prepared for an argument. When you evaluate arguments, the concepts provide guidelines for thinking.

For instance, if an advocate doesn't make a *prima facie* case, then you would realize that it wouldn't be reasonable to accept the proposition based solely on what the advocate said. Or, if the advocate did make a *prima facie* case, then you would know that it is reasonable to accept the proposition unless someone successfully fulfilled the burden of refutation.

Often people are frustrated when they hear two evenly matched opponents making equally good or poor arguments, and they can't decide who "won." These concepts help provide a way of breaking such ties. If at the end of the argument you're not sure that the person in favor of the proposition prevailed, then she has not overcome presumption, and the proposition is defeated. The person in favor of a proposition must prevail to win. The person opposed to the proposition should win if there is either a "tie" or if she clearly made better arguments.

There are three general types of propositions that anyone in any field might argue about. Each has a set of stock issues that, if addressed well, will generally establish a *prima facie* case. The three types are propositions of fact, propositions of value, and propositions of policy. As each type is explained, you should realize that the forms of reasoning described in Chapter 7 may be used to argue for them.

PROPOSITION OF FACT

The first type of proposition is the **proposition of fact.** When an advocate argues in favor of accepting a statement that something is factually true, was factually true, or will be factually true, then she supports a proposition of fact. It doesn't make a difference if the factual statement is good or bad, or even if we can do something about it. The advocate simply provides reasons to believe the statement. So someone might say, "HIV is not the cause of AIDS," and that would be a proposition of fact. Remember, this is a *proposition* of fact, so it is a statement that requires support; it is not, in and of itself, necessarily factually true. Sometimes students get confused and ask how it can be argued if the proposition is a fact. When they ask such questions, they're forgetting that whether the proposition is true or not *is what the argument is about;* it's not accepted as a fact to begin with. In a criminal trial, the prosecution tries to convince the jury that the defendant committed the crime, while the defense tries to prove the opposite. The proposition of fact is that the defendant committed the crime, but it's up to the jury to decide whether the burden of proof has been met for that proposition by listening to the arguments.

Arguing a proposition of fact indicates that the truth of the statement is in doubt, regardless of the time frame of the statement. Such a proposition may be a *proposition of past fact,* in which you argue about something that happened in the past, such as "A meteor caused the dinosaurs' extinction." It may be a *proposition of present fact,* in which you argue about what "is" at the present time, such as "Businesses are leaving California at an unprecedented rate." Or, it may be a **proposition of future fact,** in which you argue about what "will be," such as "Weather patterns will dramatically change during the twenty-first century." Some propositions of fact are fairly easy to resolve by looking at the record. Others are not so easily resolved and call for argumentation leading to probable conclusions.

The stock issues for a proposition of fact answer the following three questions:

1. What does the proposition mean?
2. Which standards should be used to determine if the proposition is true?
3. How do those standards apply to the subject?

The first stock issue for a proposition of fact is **definition and distinction.** When addressing this stock issue, the advocate defines what the proposition does and does not mean. In formal settings, this may involve providing authoritative definitions for each important term or phrase of the proposition. In a less formal setting, it may simply involve saying, "What I mean is . . . " For example, if you supported the proposition "The United States will experience a recession next year," then you might have to say you mean that the majority of states in the United States will experience the recession, although some may not. You would define what you mean by "recession," and you probably would want to state that the recession will happen during some part of the following year but will not necessarily last from January 1 to December 31. In addressing this stock issue, the opposition may argue that the definition of the "United States" means the entire country, not just parts of it, so the proposition, as stated, isn't proven if there's reason to believe that any of the states will not have a recession. The opposition also might want to specify what is meant by "experience," because it does not want the proposition to be interpreted as "to be affected by a recession in a foreign country."

Definition and distinction is an important issue, because both the way a proposition is worded and the way that wording is interpreted are the basis for the entire argument, giving an advantage to one side or the other and establishing how to decide which side should prevail. Definition and distinction doesn't prove the proposition; it merely explains it more fully so that there is less chance of misunderstanding.

Basically, you might use two kinds of definitions to address this issue. You could read the definition that you want to use from a dictionary or from some expert source on the subject, which is an **authoritative definition,** or you could use an **operational definition,** which means that the meanings of the terms will become clear by the way you use them in your argument, or that you will explain what you mean as you go along.

Authoritative definitions have the advantage of being relatively precise but have the disadvantage of making you argue on very narrow grounds. Operational definitions have the advantage of giving you more leeway but the disadvantage of creating the potential to shift from one meaning to another during the argument. Either way of defining terms runs the risk of inconsistency of use. If you use evidence that includes the term you defined, then the source might not have used the same meaning as you, and if you use more than one source, then they may not mean the same thing. If that happens, then the evidence doesn't really support the proposition that you are arguing.

The second stock issue for the proposition of fact is the issue of **criteria.** This issue seeks to establish how to determine whether the proposition is true or not. In the example above, how do we tell if the United States is likely to experience a recession? Economic definitions of the term refer to a period of reduced economic activity, but that would tell you how to determine whether a recession *has* happened, not if one probably *will* happen. So during the criteria argument, the advocate might say, "It would be reasonable to conclude that the United States will experience a recession in the next year if the national inflation rate rises by more than 2 percent and if bankruptcies increase in the remainder of this year." However, simply saying that is not enough. The advocate still has the responsibility to argue that the criteria actually are accurate predictors of a recession. Such argumentation doesn't have to be accepted by the opposition, who can argue that the proposed criteria are poor predictors and that other predictors are more worthwhile. However the argumentation proceeds, it should answer the question, "How should we determine the truth of this kind of proposition?"

It's best to argue the criteria without referring to the particular proposition being argued. For instance, the criteria in this example should say how to predict a recession at *any* time, not just next year. The criteria argument should present a set of guidelines that can be applied to any specific proposition on that subject. So, instead of saying "The best criterion to tell if Joe Cool will win the next election is . . . " you might say "The best criterion to tell if someone will win an election is . . . "

The final stock issue for a proposition of fact is called **application.** During the application phase of the argument, you argue that the criteria are being met, were met, or will be met, so the proposition is true. In the recession example, the advocate would want to show that the inflation rate is rising and that bankruptcies are increasing, so we should conclude that there will be a recession. The opposition would argue that there is no good reason to believe inflation and bankruptcies will continue to rise and might go on to argue that even if they do rise, they are normal market fluctuations that may lead to an economic slowdown but not to an actual recession.

Notice that the stock issues for a proposition of fact can be put in the form of a syllogism. The major premise is the criteria ("If certain conditions are met, then the proposition is true"), and the minor premise would be the application ("those conditions are met"). The conclusion, then, would be the proposition, as interpreted by the definitions. Further argumentation would be directed to the material truth of the stock issues and the formal validity of the syllogism.

A generic outline of an argument in favor of a proposition of fact using the Toulmin model would be the following:

Claim:	A statement is probably true.
Modal qualifier:	"Probably."
Warrant:	If certain criteria are met, then the statement is true.
Backing:	Expert testimony, past history, accepted theory, etc.
Grounds:	The criteria are met.
Verifier:	Source citation, subordinate arguments, etc.

PROPOSITION OF VALUE

Imagine that you are a sales representative for a company and are trying to convince a potential customer that your product is better than a competitor's. What kind of arguments would you make? If you were to address the stock issues for a **proposition of value,** the second general type of proposition, then you would more likely be effective.

When arguing a proposition of value, you support an evaluation about something, such as how good a product is. The sentence structure of a proposition of value is the same as that for a proposition of fact, so the two aren't always easy to tell apart. Some would even say that a proposition of value is a type of proposition of fact. The important distinction is that a proposition of fact isn't concerned with determining what is good or bad, worthwhile or worthless, and so on. It is only concerned with what was, is, or will be. A proposition of value will include some term that indicates that an evaluation is made. It might say, "Cutting old growth forests is wrong," which is an evaluation on a right-wrong scale. Or, it might say, "Eating vegetables is better than eating meat," which makes a comparative evaluation between the consumption of vegetables and meat on a better-worse scale.

Propositions of value may address the same subject matter as propositions of fact but focus on evaluating the subject. So a proposition from a previous section could be adjusted to read "Business regulations in California are bad for the state." To support the proposition of value, the claims of fact may have to be argued and would be subpropositions to the major proposition.

As a critical thinker, when you evaluate an argument that someone else made, then you are developing the arguments for a proposition of value. In a way, you're arguing to yourself that the argument was strong or weak, ethical or unethical, or somewhere in between.

The stock issues for a proposition of value answer the four questions that folllow:

1. What does the proposition mean?
2. Which value should be used to evaluate the subject?
3. Which standards should be used to tell when the value is met?
4. How do those standards apply to the subject?

Four stock issues are involved in value propositions, and three are the same as propositions of fact. First is definition and distinction, or defining what the proposition does and does not mean, just like the proposition of fact.

Second is the **value,** which is an argument of which value or set of values is the most important in drawing a conclusion about this subject. For the proposition "Eating vegetables is better than eating meat," a variety of values might be used, so the advocate explicitly argues for some or implies them in the rest of the argument. The values could be taste, health, life, quality of life, freedom of choice, or morality. The advocate would present a value that supports the proposition, while her opponent would defend a value that would help deny the proposition. This is an important issue for both sides, because the value used determines the effectiveness of the rest of the argumentation. If the value were health, then the advocate would try to prove that eating vegetables is healthier than eating meat, and her opponent would need to prove that eating vegetables is not healthier. Remember, the advocate has the burden to prove that eating vegetables *is* healthier; her opponent doesn't have any burden to prove that eating meat is healthier, although that is one choice.

Since the opponent might have trouble proving that eating vegetables is not healthier, then he might be better off arguing that quality of life is a more important value than health. Then the opponent could try to prove that for people who enjoy eating meat, it is part of a higher quality of life. The idea here is that something might be considered "worse" if it violates the important value but wouldn't be considered worse if it were consistent with a more important value. So whenever you make a value argument, you have a better chance of being effective if you address the most important value you can. Keep in mind that if you argue against the proposition, then you do not have to accept the advocate's value; you can argue that a higher value should be used.

In everyday argumentation, the issue of which value is the most important usually is implied by the argumentation. If you argue that something is wrong because it causes needless deaths, then your value is human life, and that might seem so self-evident that you don't even consider arguing for it. Sometimes, though, your value might be something less obvious, so it would be a good idea to establish its importance at some point in your argument. Sidebar 8.1 contains a list of value terms that someone might use to support a value proposition. Naturally, different values will be appropriate for different subjects, and a lot more terms could be used. This list is only intended to give you a better idea of what is meant by "values."

Values usually are fairly general terms, though, so something specific is needed, which is where the third stock issue, criteria, comes in. The criteria issue in value argumentation is similar to the criteria issue for the proposition of fact, except that in value argumentation it establishes how we know when a particular value is being achieved. For instance, the value of health might be met when people are free from illness or live longer than the norm. The value of quality of life may be met when people report that they are happy or content. As with the proposition of fact, the criteria for a value argument should be applicable regardless of the specific subject of the proposition. We should be able to use the same criteria to evaluate health whether we're talking about eating meat or vegetables, getting exercise, watching television, or using different forms of transportation. The opponent can still accept it or argue for different criteria, but specific criteria should be established to decide the issue.

As with the proposition of fact, the criteria usually establish the warrant and are often not explicitly stated in everyday argumentation. You will often have to figure out what the criteria are and whether they are appropriate.

The fourth stock issue in value argumentation is the issue of application, just as in the proposition of fact. At this point, the advocate tries to show that when the criteria are applied to the topic being considered, the value is met and the proposition proven. In the example, the advocate may argue that people who eat

Sidebar 8.1 Sample Value Terms

Life	Health	Wealth	Freedom
Justice	Liberty	Patriotism	Knowledge
Truth	Honesty	Success	Compassion
Courage	Peace	Quality of life	Fun
National sovereignty	Capitalism	Democracy	Religion

Figure 8.1 The value that will be used to evaluate the subject can make all the difference in the outcome of a value argument.

Reprinted with special permission of King Features Syndicate.

meat are subject to more heart disease and die earlier than do vegetarians; thus, eating vegetables results in better health, which proves the proposition.

The structure of the argument for a proposition of value is a bit more complex than that of a proposition of fact. For this proposition, the argument proceeds in three general steps, many of which are probably not stated explicitly.

Step 1 (value) might argue the following:

- *The most important value should be used to evaluate a subject.*
- *Health is the most important value.*
- *Therefore, health should be used to evaluate this subject.*

A subpart would argue something like:

- *Something that is necessary to enjoy other values is the most important value.*
- *Health is necessary to enjoy other values.*
- *Therefore, health is the most important value.*

Step 2 (criteria) might argue the following:

- *The best criterion is one that predicts overall health.*
- *Absence of heart disease is the best predictor of overall health.*
- *Therefore, rates of heart disease are the best criteria to determine health.*

Step 3 (application) might argue the following:

- *People who have lower rates of heart disease are healthier.*
- *Vegetarians have lower rates of heart disease than people who eat meat.*
- *Therefore, vegetarians are healthier than people who eat meat.*

and

- *If vegetarians are healthier than people who eat meat, then eating vegetables is better than eating meat.*
- *Vegetarians are healthier than people who eat meat.*
- *Therefore, eating vegetables is better than eating meat.*

Any of those statements can be disputed, and several need support and reasoning to be accepted, but this is an example of how the argument could be structured.

The argument also can be outlined using the Toulmin model. A generic outline might be the following:

Claim:	A particular judgment is correct.
Warrant:	X is the most important value for this subject.
	If particular criteria are met to uphold value X, then the judgment is correct.
Backing:	Expert opinion, philosophical arguments, etc.
Grounds:	The criteria are met.
Verifier:	Explanations of studies, etc.

PROPOSITION OF POLICY

Imagine that you're a member of a group and think that the group ought to do something different than what it is doing. What would you say to convince the group to change? Whenever you argue that some change of action should take place, you are arguing a **proposition of policy.** In the discussion that follows, most of the examples will be related to public policy topics, such as laws, but remember that the same stock issues are used for more personal situations, such as how to spend your family's money. The specifics are adjusted, though, when the argument is over something that concerns only a few people compared to the public policies that may affect millions.

The proposition of policy is quite different from the other two types of propositions. This type calls for some kind of action and should argue in favor of some action that isn't already being taken. Policy propositions attempt to change the ***status quo,*** a term that refers to the existing state of affairs. The *status quo* includes all of the existing laws, regulations, court decisions, attitudes, beliefs, values, and ways of doing things as they are right now. When arguing in favor of a proposition of policy, you argue that the *status quo* is flawed and that the policy should be implemented to correct the flaw. When you argue against a proposition of policy, you usually argue that the *status quo* is fine the way it is, so no change is called for, or the small flaws in the *status quo* call for a policy change other than the proposition.

In its clearest form, a policy proposition will state exactly who should take what specific action. So a proposition of policy might state, "The federal government should institute a comprehensive health care program for all U.S. citizens." It is better for a policy proposition to have such detail, because then both sides know specifically what they're arguing. In a conversation, someone might say, "Something should be done about health care," and the exact nature of "something" might become apparent as the people talk, but it may take quite some time. One person might mean, "Insurance companies should keep people covered instead of dropping them when they become sick," and the other might mean, "There should be national health insurance." If the policy being advocated isn't stated in fairly explicit terms, then it would be difficult to tell when the advocate has met her or his burden of proof, because there is so much room for disagreement over what that burden is.

The stock issues for a proposition of policy answer the following six questions:

1. What is the problem?
2. How big is the problem?
3. What's causing the problem?
4. What should be done to correct the problem?
5. How well will that action solve the problem?
6. Will the action create other benefits or harms?

The six stock issues for propositions of policy are harm, significance, inherency, plan, solvency, and advantages.

The first stock issue of a policy proposition is **harm** (also referred to as "need"). When arguing this issue, the advocate tries to demonstrate that something is wrong that needs to be fixed. The harm should be related to the policy called for in the proposition, even if the relationship isn't obvious, and it should be a harm that can be corrected by adopting the proposition. When dealing with this issue, the opponent tries to show that there really is nothing wrong. In the health care controversy, the advocate would probably say that the harm is that people are sick and dying.

Harms are not always things that are currently wrong. Sometimes they are problems that are likely to occur in the future. For example, if someone argued that you should brush and floss your teeth daily because you currently have dental problems, then that is a current harm. If she argued that you should brush and floss to avoid gingivitis in the future, then that is a future harm.

Most of the examples of harms in this text are direct harms to people. Harms may also refer to something that hurts animals, the environment, or organizations. In most argumentation, those kinds of harm ultimately cause some harm to people, but not always.

Closely associated with the need issue is **significance,** which shows how bad the harm is. Significance can be addressed in two ways. The first is referred to as *qualitative significance,* which shows that the harm has severe detrimental effects on whoever is harmed. It may include such characteristics as reduced quality of life, poor health, and death. When you make an argument about qualitative significance, you make a value argument. *Quantitative significance* is the second type, and it shows how many are harmed and how much they are harmed, usually using numbers. Arguing quantitative significance is making a factual argument. Remember, in this type of argument, you are advocating a change in policy, and the more people who are affected and the more they are affected by the problem caused by the *status quo,* the more reason there is to change. If you oppose the policy, you could argue that whatever harm there is isn't really that severe and doesn't affect enough people to call for the implementation of a new policy. An advocate of health care reform might argue that the lack of health care affects millions of people, causes thousands of unnecessary illnesses and deaths each year, and costs billions of dollars in lost productivity. An opponent might argue that it isn't as bad as claimed, so significant changes aren't needed.

The third stock issue of policy propositions is **inherency,** which refers to what is causing the harm in the *status quo,* or why the harm hasn't already been solved. An inherent cause would be something that is an integral part of the *status quo* and either forces the harm to come about or prevents it from being solved. **Structural inherency** refers to laws, regulations, and judicial decisions that either force or encourage people to do things that cause the harm. Structural elements of the *status quo* may also prevent individuals or the government from eliminating the problem, even though they want to. The lack of legislation to provide health care to everyone is structural inherency. **Attitudinal inherency** refers to attitudes people hold that cause the problem and that are unlikely to change without some kind of legislated encouragement.

Identifying the inherent causes of problems is crucial in solving them, because if we don't know what is causing harms, then we can't expect to eliminate them. The health care advocate would probably argue that people are sick and dying because they can't get decent health care, and the inherent cause is that insurance companies are allowed to exclude people from coverage (structural inherency), which they are motivated to do in the quest for profits (attitudinal inherency); without that coverage, those people can't get adequate health care, because doctors won't accept them (attitudinal inherency), and existing government programs won't pay for preventive medicine (structural inherency). An opponent might argue that the real causes of the illnesses and deaths are unhealthy lifestyles (smoking, driving recklessly, eating high-cholesterol foods, lack of exercise) and a shortage of general care physicians to treat sick people. The advocate identifies causes of the problem that can be solved by adopting the proposition, while the opponent identifies causes that will continue to exist even if the proposition is adopted. The opponent would strengthen his or her position by showing that curing the other causes will actually solve the harm more effectively, so there is no need to enact the policy called for in the proposition.

Once the cause of the problem is identified, you can move on to the next stock issue, which is the **plan.** The plan is what you propose be done to solve the problem. In most everyday argumentation, the plan is pretty vague. Something is advocated, but it is unclear what that "something" is. If you're just having a conversation with a friend about a current issue, then a vague plan isn't a problem, and it would probably be quite annoying if you kept pressing for details. But if you're trying to convince someone to actually change the *status quo*—whether through legislation or personal actions—then the details of the plan are more important. Often everyone agrees that a problem (such as health care or family debt) should be solved, but when actual plans are proposed, we realize they have their own problems. You can't tell if a plan is good or not until it is presented. Thus a critical thinker will not just agree that something should be done unless that "something" is spelled out. It just doesn't make sense to agree that something should be done if nothing that is proposed is worthwhile.

A well-formed plan generally identifies who will have the authority to act and what they are to do, a time frame for implementation of the plan, how the agents of action will get the money to do what they're supposed to, and how they will enforce the provisions of the plan. A fully formed plan not only removes the inherent barriers to solving the problem but also anticipates potential problems and addresses them. In our example, the advocate might say the following:

> The federal government will institute a system of national health insurance that will provide coverage for basic and catastrophic illnesses for all U.S. citizens. It will be administered by the Department of Health and Human Services and paid for by payroll and income taxes collected by the Internal Revenue Service. Doctors and hospitals will be required to treat all patients and will be paid by the federal government. Any doctors or hospitals who refuse to treat patients will be fined the full cost of treating that patient at another facility.

The plan could go into more detail, especially for a bill that is actually submitted in Congress, but this gives you a general idea of what could be proposed to develop the plan.

The existence of a plan is why definition and distinction is not a stock issue in policy arguments. The plan itself defines what the proposition means, and whatever is not in the plan is not considered part of the proposition by the person advocating it. Disputes can still arise over whether or not the plan actually does adequately define the proposition, however. Arguers on either side of a policy proposition may explicitly define the terms if they wish, and sometimes that's a good idea.

Someone opposing a plan, for example, could argue that the plan is inadequate because it fails to identify important provisions. Or, he could argue that this is not the best plan and suggest something different. For instance, in the health care example, he could argue that it isn't necessary to revise the entire system; we could simply change the laws so insurance companies can't drop coverage when people get sick. That strategy is referred to as a **minor repair,** because it acknowledges that some change is called for, but not a complete policy change, and not the policy called for by the proposition. The *status quo* is repaired but not significantly changed. The opponent of the proposition also could argue for something called a **counterplan,** agreeing that the harm exists and that major change is needed but that it would be better to solve the problem in a way that differs from that called for in the proposition. This would be especially useful if the opponent had already argued that the advocate was wrong about the inherent cause of the problem. For instance, a counterplan to the health care problem might be to subsidize medical education so that more physicians could be trained and available to treat patients. In any case, opponents of the proposition have the right to say that there's something wrong with the proposed plan of action.

The next stock issue for a policy proposition is **solvency,** which addresses the question "How much of the problem will be solved by the plan?" Too often people assume that if the inherent barriers to change are addressed in the plan, then that will automatically solve the entire problem, but that assumption is unrealistic. Problems have a way of hanging on despite attempts to eliminate them, and new actions rarely eliminate problems entirely. Moreover, as a critical thinker, you should not be satisfied that a particular plan, minor repair, or counterplan will solve the problem simply because the advocate asserts that it will. Instead, you should require evidence that the plan will have some effect and demand that proponents document the amount of the effect. So the advocate in our example would want to present evidence from well-conducted studies that will reveal the reduced number of illnesses and deaths it will lead to and the reduced costs resulting from the plan.

Someone who is opposed to the proposition would argue that the plan will not solve enough of the problem to be worthwhile. He could also argue that the plan is incapable of removing the harm and that even if it were implemented, the harm would continue. The opponent in our example might argue that if the plan were adopted, only 2 percent of those who do not receive care now would receive health care. You might think that even a 2 percent improvement would help, but once plans are implemented, we tend to think that we've done all that we should, and thus we forget about the problem for awhile. So a plan that only solves an insignificant portion of the problem usually has the effect of stopping us from trying to solve the rest of it.

An opponent of the proposition also could argue that the plan is unworkable, that there are provisions that simply cannot be carried out. The health care plan outlined earlier, for instance, could be unworkable because there aren't enough physicians and hospitals to treat all of the ill who would now be able to go to them. So even if it was a good idea, it simply can't be done. The advocate of the proposition, in a real-life situation, would argue that the plan is workable and would refute the objection, or would admit that it's correct and add money to train more physicians and build more hospitals. Such changes to a plan may improve it, but they open up the argument to questions of where the money will come from to implement the new provisions, whether the added physicians will be good enough to be worthwhile, and so on. These are the kinds of real-world concerns that arise regularly when major legislation is proposed at the national and state levels.

The final stock issue of policy argumentation is **advantages/disadvantages.** To address this issue, you answer the question, "What will be the benefits of adopting the plan?" At this point, you go beyond solving the problem, which was addressed during the solvency stock issue, and identify the *additional* positive outcomes of adopting the plan. Our health care advocate might argue that the health care plan would result in better relations among different races, as a perceived inequity is eliminated.

Disadvantages are brought up by those *opposing* the proposition as reasons the plan should not be carried out. The opponent would argue that whatever problems are solved and whatever advantages may come about will be outweighed by new problems the plan will create. So someone opposed to the health care plan might argue that it will lead to increased inflation of medical care costs, which taxes can't keep up with, and we'd end up with a worse medical system, with more illnesses, deaths, and costs than we have now. He could also argue that people would not want to become doctors under such a system, leading to even less opportunity for medical care and more illnesses, deaths, and costs. He might also argue that the increased demand for medical services would overwhelm the system, resulting in less care, more illness, and more deaths.

One thing the opponent to a plan should do is make the comparison between the current alleged harms, the proposed advantages, and the disadvantages. In other words, if the advocate says that the plan reduces deaths, then the opponent should say that it increases deaths. If the opponent says the plan will only increase the length of illnesses, then it still makes sense to do something that will save lives, so the advantages outweigh the disadvantages, and the plan ought to be adopted.

Using the Toulmin model of argumentation, a generic outline of a proposition of policy would be the following:

Claim: The *status quo* should be changed in a particular way.

Warrant: If a policy change would reduce a significant problem
          without creating more problems than it solves, then that
          change should be adopted.

Grounds: The *status quo* is creating a significant problem that would be
          reduced with the implementation of the plan proposed and
          would not result in additional problems.

An alternative way to address a policy proposition is to argue that implementation of the plan would lead to benefits, or a **comparative advantage approach.** With such an approach, you wouldn't try to prove that a significant problem exists but simply that the plan would create advantages that we do not have now, so it makes sense to change. In a way, missing out on whatever advantages we do not have now could be considered the harm, but you don't need to take the time to argue that as a harm. Using the comparative advantage approach, the advocate would present the plan, show why inherent barriers prevent enacting the plan now, and demonstrate that advantages would come about as a result of the plan. Thus the issues of a comparative advantage approach are plan, inherency, and advantages/disadvantages.

People can still be convinced that a proposition is correct even if all of the stock issues are not addressed, but addressing each helps the advocate make sure she has a strong argument. The strength of the argument also depends on how well she supports each stock issue. If some stock issues are not addressed at all, then the advocate's argument is easier to attack and less likely to prevail. On the other hand, the opponent of an argument is able to prepare better if he is aware of which stock issues should be addressed. If the advocate addresses all of them, then the opponent will have responses prepared for many of the stock issues, and, if the advocate does not, then the opponent can point out the oversight and explain how that weakens the case. Whenever you have time to prepare an argument, it's a good idea to organize your ideas to be sure you cover all of the stock issues.

As a critical thinker, you should be aware of the various types of arguments and the stock issues associated with each so that you can better evaluate the arguments you hear. If the argumentation doesn't address some of the stock issues relevant to a proposition, then you should consider carefully whether the proposition is truly well supported or if ideas are missing.

You should realize that each stock issue for a policy proposition, except the plan, is itself either a proposition of fact or a proposition of value, so the stock issues appropriate for each of those types of propositions will naturally arise for a policy proposition. For instance, whether or not a harm exists is a value question, whether a plan will or will not eliminate the harm, and whether the plan will create advantages or disadvantages are questions of future fact. Policy issues are usually not argued explicitly using the stock issues for propositions of fact or value, but those issues are still relevant.

ARGUMENT FIELDS

The stock issues just explained are the general stock issues for the three types of propositions. Different fields also have their own stock issues that are appropriate for various circumstances. For instance, there are issues that need to be addressed by a scientist to argue a scientific theory well. And there are particular issues that have to be addressed for a lawyer to successfully prosecute a criminal case. Stock issues for specific fields are learned during the process of education and training for each field.

Addressing the stock issues in select fields involves the use of the three types of stock issues described earlier. For instance, a lawyer prosecuting an accused criminal may have to address whether the accused had the motive to commit the crime, so he will address a question of past fact. A family deciding whether to spend money on a vacation or invest it for the children's education is addressing a policy proposition. A movie critic regularly addresses value propositions when she says whether films are good or poor. As individuals in various fields make their arguments, they may not address all of the stock issues of their propositions, and they may address stock issues in ways that don't make them very apparent.

EVALUATING ARGUMENTS
USING STOCK ISSUES

When you evaluate an argument based on stock issues, start by figuring out whether the arguer is proposing or opposing a proposition. For example, if you think someone is advocating a proposition when she is really opposing one, then you will misunderstand what she is doing, and her argument will look quite weak.

For example, newspaper and magazine columnists often write that a course of action should not be taken. Since you don't have the arguments in favor of the proposal, then it can seem as though they are advocating a proposition, when in fact they are opposing a change in the *status quo*.

Next, decide what the proposition is (even if it's not explicitly stated), and then what kind of proposition it is. The type of proposition will tell you which stock issues you should look for. As you do so, keep in mind that you may find a lot of rhetoric that has nothing to do with any of the stock issues; it may explain the background of a controversy, or it may just try to make the argument more interesting. Be careful that you don't try to force something to be a stock issue but also that you don't overlook something that does address one.

Also keep in mind that in most arguments the stock issues will not come in any particular order, and they will rarely be explicitly identified. Some stock issues may be addressed in different places throughout the argument. It's your job to look for the stock issues, wherever and however they're addressed.

After you've figured out how the stock issues are addressed, you must decide how well they were addressed. Remember, there is a burden of proof for *each* stock issue, whether the arguer supports the proposition or opposes it, so determine how well each issue is reasoned and supported. You may find yourself saying that a stock issue was addressed but had inadequate evidence, or that it was not sufficiently developed to be considered strong, which weakens the entire argument. Chapter 9 will further address how to evaluate an argument's evidence.

Finally, when you evaluate the use of stock issues, you make a judgment of how well the entire argument was done, thus supporting a value proposition. When you use stock issues you basically ask if the arguer fulfilled either the burden of proof or the burden of refutation. You analyze an argument using stock issues to decide how strong the argument is, so your overall evaluation should address that.

When you argue for your evaluation, your proposition is, "The argument is weak," or "The argument is strong." A generic outline of the argument using the Toulmin model follows:

Warrant: Strong arguments sufficiently address all stock issues.

Grounds: This argument sufficiently addressed all of the stock issues.

Claim: This argument is strong.

Most of your argument would provide evidence and reasoning that the stock issues were sufficiently addressed by describing what they are, quoting from the argument that you're evaluating, and explaining how the argument addresses the stock issues. Since some of the stock issues are likely to be implied, you will also evaluate how that affects the quality of the argument.

Making the evaluation is often not easy, because there are few absolute guidelines. If the argument includes virtually no evidence and was presented in a confusing manner, then it is easy to say that it is a poor argument. Or, if the argument clearly developed each stock issue, supporting each with strong evidence and clear reasoning, then it is easy to say it is a good argument. Most arguments fall somewhere in between, though, with ideas that are sometimes clear and sometimes not.

It's possible for someone to present a poor argument overall, even though some issues are addressed well, just as it is possible for someone to present a strong argument overall, even though some issues could have been better addressed. As you consider the argument, part of your judgment is how the strengths and weaknesses affect the entire argument. Avoid the temptation to say that the argument was strong because some parts were strong, or that it was poor because some parts were weak.

When you evaluate an argument using stock issues as your guide, also keep in mind the context of the argument. Arguments that are made in contexts that allow for unlimited time or space should be stronger than those made in contexts when time and space are limited. An argument made in a casual conversation, for instance, may not address some issues because they seem self-evident and because the arguer may not want to take too much time. A newspaper or magazine columnist has only a certain amount of space so may condense his reasoning.

USING STOCK ISSUES IN YOUR ARGUMENTS

When you present an argument orally or in writing, you have a chance to address stock issues for your proposition. You'll have to decide how explicitly you want to address them. Sometimes, because of the nature of the situation, you may want to address each issue but not be blatant about it; other times you'll want to be quite explicit.

Generally, it's up to you to make clear that you're addressing all of the stock issues; it's not the listener's or reader's responsibility to figure out when you address these issues. The best way to make your use of stock issues explicit is through sign-posting. This means that when you get to each stock issue in your speech or essay that you identify the stock issue that you're about to address. So if you're advocating a proposition of fact, you might say, "The criterion for determining the truth of this proposition is . . . " For a proposition of policy, you might say, "The significance of the problem is . . . " When you're writing, you can use section headings to identify the stock issues as you address them, but when delivering a speech, you obviously don't have that option.

This may sound awkward, but it gets easier with experience. It also helps you become more clear, and it makes your arguments stronger. As you address different audiences, you'll decide how explicit you ought to be, and you will adapt accordingly.

FALLACIES ASSOCIATED WITH TYPES OF ARGUMENTS AND STOCK ISSUES

APPEAL TO IGNORANCE (*ad ignorantium*, burden of proof, shifting burden of proof, evading burden of proof)—arguing that a claim must be true because there is no evidence that it is false.

People who commit the fallacy of appeal to ignorance essentially argue, "Since nobody has proven my claim to be untrue, it must be true." The idea they don't say out loud is "even though I haven't proven my claim to be true." If they have provided sufficient evidence and reasoning to overcome presumption, then they would point to their argumentation as reason for accepting the proposition instead of pointing to the lack of refutation. A common example of this fallacy is the argument, "Ghosts must exist, because nobody has been able to prove that they don't."

Argumentation is an appeal to ignorance if the lack of contradictory evidence is the only reason presented for accepting the claim, or if refutation has eliminated all of the proof offered by the claimant. It would not be a fallacy to say, "I have proven x, y, and z; there has been no refutation of anything I've said, and no evidence has been presented to contradict my claim, so my proposition stands."

The fallacy of appeal to ignorance has other names, such as "shifting burden of proof" and "evading burden of proof," because it is an attempt by an advocate to avoid taking on the responsibility of supporting the claim that he or she puts forth. The advocate arguing in favor of the proposition can commit the fallacy, but so can anyone arguing for any claim for or against the proposition. It can involve shifting either *a* burden of proof or *the* burden of proof.

Because of its name, people often think that appeal to ignorance means making an argument about something you don't really know about. That's why it is handy to remember that another name for the fallacy is "evading burden of proof." The alternative name can help you remember that the fallacy happens when you try to shift the burden to the other side by saying something such as, "If you can't prove my claim false, then it must be true."

COMPLEX QUESTION (many questions, fallacy of interrogation, compound question, *plurium interrogationum*)—asking a question that includes either an unproven assumption or more than one question, thus making a straightforward yes-or-no answer meaningless.

"Complex question" was one of Aristotle's original refutational fallacies. Remember, in the refutational "game" with which Aristotle was familiar, refutation consisted of asking the person in favor of the proposition a series of questions that could be answered yes or no. The person answering the questions had the responsibility to answer those questions directly, and once he answered a question, then he couldn't go back and change his answer. If the line of questioning could lead to inconsistencies and contradictions, or if the answerer was unable to answer the questions, then the proposition was successfully refuted. In addition, according to Aristotle, one of the purposes of using fallacies in asking questions was to reduce the opponent to babbling. Asking complex questions offered the questioner the opportunity to trap the other person in a position that he didn't want to take, or it would lead to contradictions if the answerer didn't notice the complexity of the question. If he did notice the complex question, then he could be reduced to babbling to try to escape the question and still abide by the rules of the dialogue.

We no longer abide by the rules of dialogue used in ancient Greece, so the complex question fallacy is generally less significant now, but it still does arise occasionally in everyday conversational argument. One way it happens is by asking a question that relies on an assumption that probably wouldn't be accepted if it were clearly stated. A common example of a complex question might be, "Are you still cheating on tests?" The unexpressed assumption in that question is that the person being questioned *did* cheat on tests. If not caught, this complex question allows the questioner to establish that claim without ever arguing for it, thus escaping a burden of proof.

The other way the complex question fallacy can happen is by explicitly asking two questions that may call for different answers at once and insisting on a single answer. So if someone asked "Did you cheat on tests and have you stopped? Yes or no!" then there is no hidden assumption, but a single answer still may not be appropriate. In either example, the answer "no" can mean "I've never cheated" but be used as "I haven't stopped."

Since we usually do not engage in dialogues that require adherence to yes-or-no answers, then the complex question is not a large problem outside of legal or political interrogations. People realize that if they are confronted with one, they may reply in a way that answers each part separately. However, sometimes they do not recognize that they have been asked a complex question. They give an answer that they believe honestly answers the question, and then they find themselves in a trap that they can't easily get out of. They may realize their mistake later, but when they try to explain their original answer, they seem to be shifting their position, because they're caught in a lie.

COMPLEX PROPOSITION (compound proposition)—including more than one claim in the proposition and treating proof for one claim as proof for all claims.

Sometimes people include more than one claim in their proposition without realizing it. Later, when they believe that they've proven one part of the proposition, they take credit for proving all parts. You should keep in mind that when the word "and" is in a proposition, you're likely to have a compound proposition and need to carefully think about what is needed to prove all parts of it.

For example, someone might argue the proposition that a particular movie "is a great film and will probably win the Academy Award." There is no problem if that person provides evidence that it is a great film and *also* provides evidence that it is likely to win the Academy Award. The problem arises if that person provides evidence that it is a great film and treats that as proof that it will win the award. The fact that it is a great film may be used as evidence that it will win the award, but you cannot assume that because one part of the proposition is proven that the other part also is.

This fallacy is common in everyday argumentation about policy propositions. A husband may say to his wife, "Our car costs too much in repairs, and we should get a new one." If his wife questions his statements, then he goes on to prove that the car costs a lot to repair and uses that as absolute proof that they should get a new one. There may be other ways to solve the problem of high repair costs without resorting to buying a new car. If the argumentation in favor of buying a new car is skipped, then no one should have much confidence in the conclusion.

Sometimes the wording of a proposition makes a big difference. "Our car costs too much in repairs, *and* we should get a new one" is a different proposition than "We should get a new car *because* our car costs too much in repairs." The first is a compound proposition; the second is a proposition of policy with an indication of the alleged harm.

Like many other fallacies, the conclusion may not be wrong even if the argument is fallacious. It may be true that a family's car does cost too much in repairs, and that they should get a new one, but if the argumentation commits the complex proposition fallacy, then you should take the time to test the conclusion by completing the rest of the argument.

APPEAL TO CONSEQUENCES (*ad consequentiam*)—arguing that something is or is not true because of the results expected from its truth.

When you argue whether something is true or not, the outcome of accepting that truth should not be a consideration. The outcome may be a legitimate concern when considering what to do with the information but doesn't have a bearing on the truth of the proposition. The fallacy of appeal to consequences happens when someone argues that the outcome does have some bearing on whether or not the subject is true.

This fallacy happens when an arguer confuses a proposition of fact with a proposition of value or policy. A proposition of fact is concerned with whether or not something is, was, or will be. A proposition of value is concerned with evaluating something favorably or unfavorably. A proposition of policy is concerned with what to do. The potential outcome of an evaluation can be relevant, because it makes sense to say that something is good because it will have good results. The potential outcome of a policy is relevant because it makes sense to avoid a policy that will result in significant harm. It doesn't make sense, though, to say that something isn't true because if it is true there will be negative results.

For example, the fallacy of appeal to consequences would happen if someone argued that there is no oil off the California coast because if there were it would lead to drilling and environmental degradation. Those results do not affect whether or not there is oil off the coast, only whether or not drilling should be allowed.

A PRIORI—reasoning that determines the conclusion one wants first, then accepts only evidence supporting that conclusion, or interprets all evidence as support for that conclusion.

Sometimes our prior beliefs and desires lead us to "know" what is true about a subject before we look into it. If they cause us to choose or interpret evidence to fit a predetermined conclusion, then we have committed the *a priori* fallacy.

For example, a high school principal confronts a student who has been caught fighting at school. The principal knows this student from past experiences and considers him a troublemaker. The issue is whether or not this student started the fight or was defending himself. If the principal only listens to the other party's account of what happened, without allowing the "troublemaker" to speak because the principal already is sure who started it, then the principal has committed the *a priori* fallacy. It may be true that this student did start the fight, but in the role of a fact finder, the principal should not make up his mind before considering the evidence.

The *a priori* fallacy has the effect of reversing presumption. The presumption becomes "the proposition must certainly be true" instead of "we don't know if the proposition is true or not."

When the discussion is about something you care about, or about something you have strong prior beliefs about, then it is difficult to avoid the *a priori* fallacy. People with strong religious beliefs, for instance, and those with strong scientific beliefs are likely to disregard evidence that conflicts with their beliefs. The *a priori* fallacy reminds us to be aware of how our beliefs affect our reasoning and to be open to evidence, even if it seems to contradict what we already "know."

In an advocacy situation, where there are two sides of the issue and each side will present its case, each advocate is expected to enter the argument with his or her mind made up. It is not an *a priori* fallacy for the advocate to only present evidence that supports her or his side or to interpret evidence presented by the other advocate to support her or his side. If a person listening to their arguments in order to render a decision came in with his or her mind already made up, though, that would lead to an *a priori* fallacy.

EXTENSION—a particular type of false criteria fallacy that argues that something is inferior just because it doesn't do something it was never intended to do.

Would it be fair to say that an art history class was a poor class because it didn't teach anything about the principles of higher mathematics? Most people would say no, because the art class isn't meant to teach math. That's the essence of the fallacy of extension. It happens when someone argues that something is flawed because it fails to meet a standard that it isn't supposed to meet.

The fallacy of extension happens in value argumentation because it is centered on how to evaluate something. It extends the evaluative criteria beyond those that are legitimate to apply to the object of evaluation. You can always find some standard that the subject of the argument doesn't meet, and if it's a standard it shouldn't be expected to meet, then you commit the fallacy of extension.

For example, sometimes arguments against ballot initiatives include statements such as, "It won't provide any more money for state schools." If one of the selling points for the initiative is that it will increase school funding, then that is a legitimate problem. However, if the initiative wasn't trying to increase school funding, then that is an irrelevant argument.

It is possible to apply additional criteria without committing the fallacy of extension if the argument is that something is better because it does something in addition to what it is designed to do. If an art history class somehow did teach higher math *and* the history of art, then you might argue that it's an outstanding class because it did what it should, and more. But it's wrong to say that it is a bad art class because it doesn't teach subjects other than art.

Suppose someone designed a fireplace for your house but didn't include any features that would prevent it from setting your house on fire. If the designer did not intend for the fireplace to be safe, would it still be the fallacy of extension to argue that the fireplace is flawed? No, because if a thing *should* have been designed to accomplish some purpose but was not designed with that intent, then you would not have a fallacy of extension. The question is whether or not those standards are relevant in making the evaluation.

SUMMARY

An advocate of a proposition assumes the burden of proof and tries to present a *prima facie* case to overcome the presumption against the proposition. An opponent of a proposition assumes the burden of refutation and tries to respond to the arguments made by the advocate. During the argument, each party has a burden of proof to provide evidence and reasoning in favor of each claim made.

The three general types of propositions are propositions of fact, propositions of value, and propositions of policy. Each has a set of stock issues that, if addressed, makes the argument more complete and stronger (see Sidebar 8.2). Understanding the stock issues for each type of proposition helps you make your own arguments, evaluate the arguments of others, and respond to arguments.

Sidebar 8.2 Stock Issues

Proposition of Fact
Definition and distinction
Criteria for factual determination
Application of criteria to subject

Proposition of Value
Definition and distinction
Value
Criteria for value determination
Application of criteria to subject

Proposition of Policy
Harm
Significance
Inherency
Plan
Solvency
Advantages/disadvantages

KEY CONCEPTS

a burden of proof   the responsibility of each person in an argument to provide evidence and reasoning for each claim put forth.

advantages/disadvantages   a stock issue of propositions of policy that argues what will happen beyond solving the harm. The advocate of the proposition argues that the plan will create benefits that make it even more desirable. The opponent to the proposition argues that the plan will create unexpected harms that make the plan less desirable.

application   a stock issue of propositions of fact and value that argues that the criteria are met, were met, or will be met, so the proposition is true.

assertion   a claim with no support to justify its acceptance.

attitudinal inherency   a type of inherency argument that claims that the cause of a problem is the attitudes and motives of the people who perpetuate it.

authoritative definition   identifying the meaning of a term in an argument by referring to authoritative sources such as a dictionary or textbook.

burden of refutation   the responsibility of those opposed to the proposition to dispute the claims, evidence, and reasoning that the advocate has presented.

comparative advantage approach   an approach to arguing propositions of policy in which the advocate of the proposition argues that adoption of a plan will lead to advantages over the *status quo,* without arguing that there currently are significant harms.

counterplan   a refutation strategy for propositions of policy that admits that the *status quo* problems are

significant but should be alleviated by making changes other than those called for by the proposition.

criteria   a stock issue of propositions of fact and value that seeks to establish how to determine whether the proposition is true or whether a value is being achieved.

definition and distinction   a stock issue of propositions of fact or value that establishes what the proposition does and does not mean.

harm (also referred to as "need")   a stock issue of propositions of policy that argues that something is wrong and calls for a policy change.

inherency   a stock issue of propositions of policy that identifies the cause of the harm.

minor repair   a refutation strategy for propositions of policy that argues that the *status quo* problems can be alleviated by making changes smaller than those called for by the proposition.

operational definition   identifying the meanings of the terms by the way they are used in an argument or explaining them as they arise.

plan   a stock issue of propositions of policy that identifies exactly what should be done to eliminate the harm in the *status quo,* and who should do it.

presumption   (1) the principle that a proposition or claim should not be accepted until sufficient evidence and reasoning have been provided to justify acceptance; (2) the recognition that the *status quo* will remain as it is until good reasons have been provided to change it.

***prima facie* case**   an argument that presents enough evidence and support that a person thinking critically ought to accept the proposition, at least until the argument is refuted.

proposition   the declarative statement that an advocate intends to support.

proposition of fact   a proposition that states that something is factually true, was factually true, or will be factually true.

proposition of policy   a proposition that argues in favor of a particular course of action.

proposition of value   a proposition that argues in favor of a positive or negative evaluation about something.

significance   a stock issue of propositions of policy that argues that the harm is qualitatively or quantitatively severe enough to call for a policy change.

solvency   a stock issue of propositions of policy that argues how much of the harm the plan will eliminate.

status quo   existing policies, attitudes, and beliefs.

stock issues   issues that typically arise for various types of propositions. Addressing all of the stock issues for a proposition generally leads to stronger arguments.

structural inherency   a type of inherency argument that claims that the cause of a problem is either the laws, regulations, and court decisions that force it to happen, or the lack of laws, regulations, and court decisions to eliminate it.

the burden of proof   the responsibility of the arguer in favor of the proposition to provide sufficient evidence and reasoning to justify acceptance of the proposition.

value   a stock issue of propositions of value that argues which value, or set of values, is the most important for drawing a conclusion about the subject of the proposition.

THINGS TO THINK ABOUT

1. Think of two different situations in which a proposition of fact might be argued. What might the propositions be? What might be propositions of value and policy about the same issues?

2. Think of an argument that you engaged in or observed (real or fictional). What was the proposition? What kind of proposition was it? Who had the burden of proof? Who had the burden of refutation? How were the stock issues addressed?

3. Think of a proposition of fact, a proposition of value, and a proposition of policy. How could you address the stock issues to support each proposition?

4. Find a proposition that Secretary of State Powell argues for in his speech in the Appendix. What is the proposition? How does he address the relevant stock issues?

5. Think of a time when your reasoning, or the reasoning of someone else, committed one of the fallacies described in this chapter. What made the reasoning fallacious?

TUTORIAL LINK

Go to *http://communication.wadsworth.com/Verlinden* and complete the tests for the Informal Fallacies, Set #3 tutorial.

9

Evidence

The truth of a proposition is simply an assertion until evidence is presented to support the claims. Without evidence leading to the conclusion for which you are arguing, all you have are the major premise and the conclusion. Of course, you can have an argument without presenting all three parts, but if you're challenged you should be ready to provide the missing part. As a critical thinker, you should be prepared to closely examine the evidence others present.

Charles Wilbanks and Russell T. Church define **evidence** as "supporting material known or discovered, but not created by the advocate" (81). When you present an argument, you support it with information that you've heard, read, seen, or have in your possession. If it's something that you've simply made up, however, it's not evidence but an assertion or a lie. How often do you hear people say something like "Ninety percent of college athletes don't care about their education"? Do they really know that statistic is correct, or did they just make it up to bolster their point? The answer to that question determines whether evidence should be accepted, and it is instrumental in determining the strength of arguments.

Evidence is the minor premise of the classical logical model and the grounds, or data, of the Toulmin model. Remember, the classical model could only determine the formal validity of an argument, assuming that the premises are accepted. To tell whether the argument is likely to be materially true, the premises ought to deserve acceptance.

As an arguer and a critical thinker, you should have some basic knowledge about evidence so you can recognize it, evaluate its use in arguments, and use it well yourself. This chapter will introduce you to

- forms that evidence may take.
- different classifications of evidence.
- ways to evaluate the quality of evidence.
- how to use evidence to make and evaluate arguments.

FORMS OF EVIDENCE

Evidence comes in several different forms, and you can use any of them to support your arguments. "Forms" means that the evidence has certain characteristics. Knowing the forms allows you to make choices about which to use to support your claims and will help you decide which *ought* to be used. To say that some evidence is of a certain form merely identifies the kind of evidence it is, but it doesn't indicate the quality of the evidence.

One form of evidence is **facts,** which are descriptions of events, objects, persons, or places that are empirically verifiable (Wilbanks and Church 82). "Empirically verifiable" means that they *could* be confirmed through observation. Ways to observe include simply looking, measuring, using scientific instruments to observe something that cannot be observed using unaided senses, reading historical artifacts, and so on.

Whether the observations *are* verified or not doesn't change the form of the evidence. If the observations *could be* verified, then the evidence is factual, even if verification would be so difficult that no one would actually do it. Remember, this only refers to the *form* that the evidence takes, not whether or not the content is correct. Thus evidence can take the form of facts, yet not be verified, and could turn out to be untrue. For example, a few years ago a couple of scientists said that they had created "cold fusion" in their laboratory, which was an amazing feat. Accounts of their experiment used in an argument would be factual evidence. Since that time, however, no one else has been able to duplicate their experiment with the same results, so their work has not been empirically verified. The general consensus is that reported results of the original experiment were false. It was still factual evidence, but it wasn't truthful. You must be careful not to confuse the term *fact* with *truth.* Calling evidence a "fact" refers to the form that it takes, and whether or not it is "factually true" refers to its quality.

A particular kind of factual evidence is **statistics,** which consists of quantified descriptions of events, objects, persons, places, or other phenomena (Wilbanks and Church, 83). In other words, it is using numbers to describe things. Statistics may simply indicate how much, how many, how big, or how often. They may also indicate relationships, trends, and changes. The quality of statistical evidence may

Figure 9.1 If you don't have adequate evidence, then it can be difficult to prove your claim.

be difficult to know unless you're very familiar with how statistics should be gathered and how they should be interpreted. Even simple statistics such as averages can mean different things depending on how the averages were determined. More complex statistics have their own rules for use, and if you're not familiar with those rules then you may not really know what the statistics mean or when they're being misused.

Statistics are commonly, and easily, misused, because most people do not know how they are gathered or interpreted or should be used. A letter to *U.S. News and World Report* (May 30, 1994, reprinted with permission from S. Robert Lichter) from S. Robert Lichter, codirector of the Center for Media and Public Affairs, points out a problem. He wrote

> As someone who has studied both Hollywood attitudes and TV violence, I turned eagerly to your survey of attitudes toward violence among what you call the "Hollywood elite." Unfortunately, the fine print reveals that this poll of "top-level Hollywood figures" and "entertainment industry leaders" consisted of a mass mailing to a whopping 6,333 people, a number equal to almost one-fifth of the total population of Beverly Hills. It's nice to know there's no lack of leadership in Hollywood. Of course, the fine print continues, 7 out of 8 recipients failed to respond. So we have no idea what 88 percent of these "leaders" think about violence, except that they presumably care less about it than the relative few who were motivated to reply.
>
> Before your next venture into elite surveys, I recommend consulting a major pollster on the niceties of sampling techniques and response bias. It might produce results that are less hyped but more meaningful.

As the letter implies, gathering statistics is not a simple task and requires the collectors to be knowledgeable about the way it should be done and what to look for in the results. A good understanding of statistics would require a more specialized text than this, but you should realize that using statistics well is more difficult than it may seem at first.

Sociologist Joel Best explains several common reasons the statistical evidence we often use may be weak, including the use of guesses and estimates as though they are statistics that were actually gathered, poor collection techniques, and the mangling of statistics by different arguers. Best also offers the following four ways to tell if statistical evidence is probably good:

1. Good statistics are based on more than guessing.
2. Good statistics are based on clear, reasonable definitions.
3. Good statistics are based on clear, reasonable measures.
4. Good statistics are based on good samples.

Another form of evidence is **examples,** which are descriptions of *individual* events, objects, persons, or places (Wilbanks and Church, 84). Sometimes **hypothetical examples,** which are examples that are made up, are used to help explain an idea, but they shouldn't be used as evidence to support a claim. Instead, **literal examples,** which are events that really happened, are used for evidence and subject to the criteria for reasoning by example, explained in Chapter 7. Examples usually come in the form of brief stories. For instance, a motivational speaker may present case histories of a few people who overcame adversity to support the claim "you should never give up."

The final form of evidence is **testimony,** which is authoritative opinion evidence that interprets or judges events, objects, persons, or places (Wilbanks and Church 85). Usually when you use testimony as evidence, it should come from someone considered an expert in that particular field. Testimony usually takes the form of direct quotations, although it also can be paraphrased, which means that the arguer summarizes what someone said in the arguer's own words. If the testimony is paraphrased, then the arguer must be careful to avoid distorting the meaning of what was originally said.

Testimony that *interprets* is evidence that describes, analyzes, or explains an event, an object, a person, or a place (Wilbanks and Church 85). Testimony from a State Department official explaining what is happening in Liberia is interpretive. Testimony that makes *judgments* is evidence that presents a determination of the value of the event, object, person, or place. So testimony from a State Department official that presents the administration's opinion of what should be done in Liberia would be a judgment.

One form of testimony that you should generally consider weak is **conclusionary evidence,** which is testimony in which only a conclusion is stated, with no indication of how the conclusion was arrived at. As a critical thinker, ask yourself if that testimony is really enough to justify accepting a claim. The use of conclusionary evidence usually commits the fallacy of appeal to authority, which is described at the end of this chapter.

You must also be careful not to simply state a claim and present testimony that says that an authority agrees with you. That by itself shouldn't mean much to a critical thinker, because there is no way that someone listening to your argument can know if you and the authority are actually talking about the same thing, or how the authority reached her conclusion. Using testimony that repeats your claim doesn't prove your claim; it only shows that others agree with you. Thus if the only evidence you have in favor of a proposition is that the governor is in favor of the proposition, then the evidence may sound good but doesn't really say anything that a critical thinker should accept. When you make an argument, you shouldn't just say, in effect, "Other people agree with me" but, "You ought to agree with me because . . . " Instead of using conclusionary evidence, try to use testimony that explains the reasoning behind the conclusion.

CLASSIFICATIONS OF EVIDENCE

Regardless of the form, evidence also fits into a variety of classifications that will help you evaluate the quality of the evidence. Higher-quality evidence makes stronger arguments. The quality of evidence also is important when you evaluate an argument, because it gives you reasons to accept or reject both the evidence and the argument. Evidence classifications come in three pairs, with one member of each pair considered better than the other.

The first pair is primary versus secondary evidence. **Primary evidence** comes from a source closest to the actual happening, a source with firsthand information. If the evidence describes an event, then primary evidence comes from someone who witnessed the event directly. If the evidence states the findings of a research project, then primary evidence comes from the people who actually did the research. **Secondary evidence** comes from a source that is at least one step removed from the actual happening, who has only secondhand information. An article in a newspaper that reports on someone's research findings is secondary evidence. Any source that is not a primary source of evidence is secondary, even if it is the third, tenth, or one hundredth person in the chain of retelling.

Since ideas tend to get distorted as they are transmitted from one person to another, secondary evidence is considered inferior to primary evidence. Even when people make every effort to report the information as accurately as possible, distortions still happen.

Best tells an amusing story that illustrates what can happen with secondary evidence, as well as how intelligent people can uncritically accept clearly poor evidence. A graduate student wanted to use an attention-getting statistic in the opening of his dissertation prospectus and wrote "Every year since 1950, the number of American children gunned down has doubled." Best questioned the statistic, looked it up in the academic journal the student cited, and found the exact same sentence. Best discovered that the author of the original article got the statistic from the Children's Defense Fund. When he looked it up, he found that the CDF's *The State of America's Children Yearbook—1994* stated, "The number of American children killed each year by guns has doubled since 1950." The journal author had changed that statement to say that the number doubled every year. To understand how different the meanings are, consider what the numbers would be if there were only one death in 1950. In 1994 there would be two deaths, according to the CDF statement. However, Best points out, as stated in the journal article, there would be a total of over 35 *trillion* deaths in 1994. No matter what the actual number was in 1950, the magnitude of the difference between the two figures for 1994 is astronomical. As a result, Best nominates the quotation as the worst social statistic ever (2).

Sometimes primary evidence is questionable because the source may have some motive to distort, or it may not be able to accurately recall what happened. In fact, eyewitness testimony is notoriously unreliable. Often five people who see the same event present five different versions of it. However, five people who read an account of an event also will present five different versions of what they read. So when everything else is equal, primary evidence is superior to secondary evidence, but that doesn't mean it is necessarily correct.

The second pair of evidence classifications is expert versus lay evidence. **Expert evidence** comes from a source who is experienced and knowledgeable in a subject. Some experts have credentials such as academic degrees or position titles that indicate their area of expertise. Other times, though, experts gain their expertise through working in a field long enough to know it very well.

Generally, you shouldn't consider journalists expert sources for anything outside of journalism, unless you are aware that they have some expert background. While some journalists do have specialized training in the fields about which they report, most do not, and thus they are not qualified to draw conclusions about the subjects on which they report, although they are qualified to report on conclusions that experts draw about the subjects. This is not meant to disparage journalists, but many students uncritically accept journalists' conclusions as expert opinions.

Lay evidence comes from a source who is neither experienced nor knowledgeable in the area of discussion. Everyone is entitled to an opinion, but every opinion doesn't have the same value. Expert evidence is considered superior to lay evidence because experts have the training and experience to know what to look for and what to ignore, when there are exceptions to general rules, what the consensus of opinion is in the field, and so on. Lay evidence may be well intentioned, and it may even reach the same conclusion as expert evidence, but all things considered, expert evidence makes an argument stronger.

Sometimes people make the mistake of thinking that a source who is an expert in one area is an expert in *all* areas, and thus they will give undue weight to the opinions of someone speaking outside of her field. Advertising is well known for taking advantage of that tendency, using celebrities as though they are all experts concerning the relative merits of products. Remember, though, that someone who is an expert in one field is a layperson in most other fields. Sometimes someone who is an expert in one part of a field may even be a layperson in another area of the same field.

While expert evidence is generally better than lay evidence, it isn't always *necessarily* good. Experts have been wrong and biased, and they have outright lied about their findings. Court psychologists, scientists, medical researchers, government agencies, and others have distorted their findings to achieve the results they wanted. The realization that experts can't always be trusted leads some people to decide never to trust them, which is also a mistake. If everything else is equal, then expert evidence is better than lay evidence, and if it's the best available evidence, then it should be given consideration. Expert evidence, however, could be proven wrong. If it is not better than lay evidence, then it is due to reasons other than that it comes from an expert source.

Lay and expert evidence should be considered two ends of a continuum. Some experts have more expertise than others, and some nonexperts have more expertise than other laypeople. Some laypeople may have developed more knowledge about a subject than some experts. For example, you can't just say that one person is believable because she has a Ph.D. and another should be disregarded because she didn't go to college. When using the expert/lay classification to evaluate the quality of evidence, carefully consider the sources.

The third pair of evidence classifications is casual versus created evidence. **Casual evidence** is evidence that naturally occurs without anyone trying to create it *as evidence*. Someone may still have created it, such as a photograph, but didn't create it intending to use it as evidence, especially for a particular argument. Casual evidence also may be something that wasn't created by humans, such as fossils or geological formations.

Created evidence is something purposely recorded for future use. It was meant to be evidence for something, such as a birth certificate, medical records, or the record of test scores for a class. Birth certificates, medical records, and grade records don't just spontaneously appear; they have to be created, and they are created to provide support for claims.

It is possible that a record created for one purpose could be used as evidence for a completely unintended purpose. For instance, a high school yearbook could be used as evidence that a school did or did not have minority students enrolled. The yearbook would not have been created for that purpose, however. In this case, is the yearbook casual or created evidence? An argument could be made for either classification, but since a school yearbook is not created to document the racial composition of a student body, then using it to do so would make it casual evidence.

You must know the circumstances of a particular argument to decide whether created or casual evidence is the best. Sometimes casual evidence will be best, because it is largely free of manipulation and is perceived as being more honest. Other times, though, created evidence is best, because it provides the most complete record of information needed to make an argument. For example, videotapes from surveillance cameras are created evidence, but they often are very good because they were set up to create a record of activity that wouldn't be available from casual sources.

TESTS OF EVIDENCE

Regardless of the form or classification, you must determine if evidence is good to use. When you make an argument, you don't want to be refuted because you used poor evidence, and when you evaluate an argument, you don't want to accept evidence that is poor. Six "tests of evidence" are commonly accepted in the field of argumentation. If you're familiar with all six, then you have a better chance of making and recognizing good arguments.

Lawyers use these tests to try to impeach the testimony of witnesses, so you may notice them in legal movies and television shows. The tests of evidence also are a foundation for scientific research. The scientific method is designed to produce the best evidence possible, and well-designed scientific studies attempt to eliminate weaknesses in gathering and interpreting evidence by making sure the results stand up to these tests.

The first test of evidence is **source credibility,** which examines whether the source of information has the background, knowledge, expertise, and opportunity to be relied upon. The source of evidence is whoever presented the information that the arguer uses as evidence. So when you read an argument that uses testimony to prove a point, the source of the testimony must pass the test of source credibility. When the person making the argument doesn't refer to another source of the evidence, then *she* should be considered the source. You should, however, consider her credibility. For most arguments, evaluate the credibility of several sources in addition to the credibility of the arguer.

The source of evidence may be a person or an organization, it may be either a primary or a secondary source, and it may be either an expert or a lay source. The *background, knowledge,* and *expertise* all relate to whether the source knows enough about the subject to be deemed an expert. *Opportunity* is a little different. It refers to whether or not the source knows enough about the particular subject being discussed. For instance, a psychiatrist may have the background, knowledge, and expertise to speak with authority about psychology in general; however, if he hasn't examined a particular person, then he could not discuss that particular person with any credibility.

Another trait associated with source credibility is trustworthiness. A source known to be honest is generally considered more credible than someone with a history of dishonesty. If the background of the source is unknown, then you must determine whether the source seems trustworthy. Most of the time, if there is no known reason to question a source's honesty, then we assume that the source is honest.

The second test of evidence is **source bias,** or whether the source of evidence has any self-interests that could distort perceptions or reports. A source may be biased for or against a particular person or issue, and that could distort what she says. That doesn't necessarily mean that the source is intentionally being dishonest, since most people have biases that affect their perceptions. The question is, does the bias affect the value of the evidence you get from that source?

Source bias has many roots. One could be any preconceived idea on the subject that could affect the source's judgment. For instance, someone who is strongly opposed to capital punishment may research the effects of capital punishment and unwittingly create the results he wants to find.

A source also may be biased if she will personally gain from others accepting a particular viewpoint. She may overemphasize information that would lead others to accept that viewpoint or underemphasize information that would favor the opposing view. For example, when the publisher of *Penthouse* magazine says,

"There is absolutely no scientific evidence that pornography has any negative effects," you should be at least a little skeptical of his biases. Any time someone will profit financially if you agree to do what he wants—such as trying to sell you something—you should at least scrutinize what he says.

Perhaps the most difficult origin of bias to recognize is a cultural bias that could influence observations. Such bias may be fairly easy to spot when considering evidence from a source who comes from a different culture, but it's much harder to recognize coming from someone from your own culture. We take much of what we learn from our own cultures for granted, so it's virtually invisible to us. Yet these taken-for-granted beliefs, attitudes, and values can significantly affect the perceptions of the sources of evidence.

The third test of evidence is **recency,** which considers whether the evidence came from an appropriate time period for the conclusion. In most cases, recent evidence is better than older evidence. Newer evidence is able to build on the knowledge of older evidence, extending and improving it. It also is able to correct the mistakes and biases of older sources. Moreover, it can take advantage of information that was not available to the sources of older evidence. So sometimes evidence may be legitimately rejected because it is too old to be valid.

Sometimes, though, older evidence is better than newer evidence, especially in matters such as history. If the older evidence is a primary source of information about what was happening at the time, then it is better than later evidence from secondary sources. Sometimes newer evidence simply repeats the errors of older evidence, so it doesn't always improve upon it. You can't simply look at the date of evidence to determine its relative quality.

The fourth test of evidence is **internal consistency,** which means that there are no overt or subtle contradictions in the source of evidence. In other words, the source doesn't say one thing at one time and the opposite at another. Of course, people do change their minds over time, so we're not talking about the difference between what someone said when she was eighteen and what she said when she was forty. But if the inconsistencies come within the same document, or the same political campaign, then the evidence becomes questionable.

For example, early in a book opposed to pornography, the author said that social science can't tell us anything, and that we should ignore social scientific findings that show that pornography isn't harmful. Later in the book, he used social scientific findings to try to show that pornography is harmful. If social science is invalid, then it should be invalid for both sides of the controversy.

Internal inconsistencies not only create contradictions that call for you, as a critical thinker, to question both contradictory statements from that source, but they also call into question all of the material from that source. When there are contradictory statements, you can't know which statement to accept. Moreover, if you use one of the statements in an argument, then an opponent may present the other, and your evidence will appear flawed. You should question all of the material from that source, because the internal inconsistency indicates sloppy thinking that may affect the rest of the information.

Remember, internal consistency is a test of the *source of evidence,* not the arguer. For example, while an arguer might contradict himself, that would weaken his argument but would not fail the evidence standard of internal consistency unless someone else used that person's arguments in his argument. Usually, you can only decide if there's been internal inconsistency if you look at the original source.

Completeness is the fifth test of evidence and refers to whether the source of evidence, or the evidence as presented in an argument, provides enough information for a critical thinker to accept. Generally, the more complete the evidence, the stronger it is. You can't reasonably demand that the source or the arguer present *all* of the information, because to do so would require every bit of evidence to contain all of the background on where it came from, from whom it came, its context, how it was obtained, and so forth. Instead of quoting a sentence or a statistic as evidence, people would have to present entire books for every bit of evidence if this test were carried to an extreme. Obviously, such a standard would be impossible.

Completeness does require that the original source provide some background to explain the origin of the information. If it's scientific research, then the scientist describes how the experiment was done in some detail. If statistical tests were applied to the data, then those tests should be named and their results indicated. Such completeness allows other knowledgeable people to determine whether the research was done correctly and if the results are valid.

For someone using the evidence, completeness means at least citing where the information came from and the qualifications of the source. It is more complete to provide a brief summary of how the source came up with the information, but time or space constraints may prevent that. Still, if asked, an advocate should be ready to explain how the conclusions were arrived at. Completeness also calls for the advocate to keep the evidence in context. You mustn't use one sentence out of a paragraph if the rest of the paragraph clearly indicates that the source disagrees with that sentence. Doing so would fail not only the test of completeness but also internal consistency and would be an ethical violation.

The test of completeness also is used to test the honesty of testimony. If, for instance, a teenager said he went to a movie the previous night, then his parents might ask the name of the movie, the plot, and who appeared in it. If he were able to provide accurate information about the movie, then there would be more reason to believe that he was telling the truth.

The final test of evidence is **corroboration,** which is sometimes referred to as "external consistency." Corroboration asks whether other qualified sources agree with this source of evidence. In general, such consensus among qualified people provides a reason to have more faith in what the source says. It doesn't have to be exact agreement in the wording of ideas, but it should be at least general agreement. Movie advertisers try to make use of this standard by quoting praise from several critics.

These tests of evidence all give you something to consider when evaluating evidence. Sometimes the failure of a single test will provide enough of a reason to reject the evidence, but usually it just casts some doubt on the evidence. The tests should be used in combination to decide whether the evidence is *probably* strong or weak.

Although these six tests of evidence should be applied to the evidence an arguer uses, you also can use them to evaluate what the arguer says, independent of his evidence. When you do so, keep in mind that you're evaluating not the evidence but the whole argument.

PERELLA'S HIERARCHY OF EVIDENCE

Another way to evaluate the quality of the evidence that you or others use is to determine where it fits in a hierarchy. Jack Perella points out the different kinds of evidence that people use, and some kinds are better than others. Starting with the weakest types of evidence, he discusses the different levels on which the evidence may be placed. This hierarchy provides a way to evaluate the quality of evidence.

Perella starts with level 1, **assertion.** When assertions are used as evidence, then the arguer says that some evidence is true, without providing any verification. Assertions can work to convince uncritical listeners for a variety of reasons. Sometimes an assertion agrees with what they already believe, or it comes from someone they think they should believe. Claiming that something is true without finding real evidence is weak, because it offers the listener no actual information on which to base acceptance of the claim.

In everyday argumentation, assertions are sometimes difficult to notice. Remember that any proposition will be supported by many subordinate claims that also need support. Arguers usually don't simply assert the main proposition, but they may assert the evidence for the subordinate claims. When they do, it seems as though evidence is presented, when really there is none. When evaluating an argument, continually ask yourself, "What evidence is really being presented?"

Level 2 consists of evidence that is **judicial notice** or **common knowledge.** *Judicial notice* is a term that comes from legal argumentation. In court, judicial notice is given when all parties agree to a fact, so there is no need to provide testimony to support it. For example, a prosecutor and the defense may agree that the defendant was in a certain place at a certain time. Judicial notice is weak, because the other side may not agree, so testimony would still be needed. However, if the other side does agree to it, then judicial notice eliminates the need to take the time to provide evidence. Although it is a legal term, judicial notice may take place in other argumentative contexts, when both sides of the controversy agree that certain facts are true.

Evidence that is *common knowledge* involves ideas that everyone is expected to believe, even though the ideas may not be true. For example, common knowledge may be that most welfare recipients are urban African Americans and an arguer may rely on that. However, the fact is, most people on welfare are European-Americans. Like judicial notice, common knowledge can eliminate the need to provide evidence of claims, but either another arguer or the audience may not accept it. If you rely on common knowledge, and the other arguer or a listener recognizes that it is incorrect, then it not only weakens your specific argument but also creates skepticism about the rest of what you say. To a certain extent, we have to rely on some common knowledge, or it would become too burdensome to engage in argumentation. You must exercise judgment when you rely on common knowledge, and make sure that the knowledge is both common and correct.

Lay opinion is Perella's third level of evidence. It includes using, as evidence, reasoned opinion by people outside of their areas of expertise. The opinions may be correct, but there is no reason to believe that the sources know more than anyone else. This can become especially problematic when someone is a recognized expert in one field but says something about a topic outside of that field. Lay opinion is different from common knowledge, because lay opinion consists of *reasoned* conclusions, whereas common knowledge is uncritical, taken-for-fact beliefs.

Level 4 is **expert opinion** or a **consensus of lay opinion.** *Expert opinion* is the reasoned opinion of someone about a subject within his or her field of expertise, and can be quite strong because of her background, knowledge, and so on. *Consensus of lay opinion* is the agreement of the reasoned opinion of many people outside of their fields of expertise. This has strength because through consensus errors may be eliminated, although that can't be assured. This also could be weak, because many uninformed people can support each other's mistaken beliefs. So, in Perella's hierarchy, the opinion of a single expert has about the same weight as the agreement of the opinion of many laypeople.

Level 5 consists of both an **empirical study** and the **consensus of expert opinion.** An *empirical study* is well-designed, observational research about the subject. It may be a scientific experiment, a survey, or some other type of study based on observable data. It is strong because if the study is well designed, then opinions and biases are reduced. *Consensus of expert opinion* is the agreement of several people who are experts in their field. Through both consensus and expertise, errors of opinion have a good chance of being eliminated. Consensus does not mean unanimous agreement among the experts though. Two arguers on opposite sides of a controversial issue may each use a consensus of experts to support their positions. In such a case, the consensus is not among all of the experts but is an agreement among some of them.

According to Perella, the highest level of evidence is level 6, the **consensus of studies.** This level is reached when there is agreement among several well-designed research studies. If they are all well designed, and they all have similar results, then you can be fairly confident that their results are true. This level is stronger than a consensus of experts because the studies eliminate interpretation as much as possible. The studies "speak for themselves" rather than rely on opinion and credentials. If most experts believe that watching television makes children healthier, but every study shows that children who watch television are less healthy, then we should put more faith in the studies than in the experts. Usually, however, the consensus of expert opinion will agree with the consensus of studies in the field. You should consider the credentials of the experts though. The consensus of experts regarding television may come from television executives, while the studies may be done by experts in health, psychology, and child development.

USING EVIDENCE

When you make an argument, don't just throw in evidence without giving some thought to how you present it. Naturally, in everyday conversation, when you generate ideas and arguments spontaneously, you're not expected to be able to present exact quotations or statistics to support your claims. When you have time to prepare your argument, though, you should be able to get specific information and present it effectively.

Generally speaking, especially in prepared arguments, you should *cite* the source of information. (Please note the spelling. "Cite" begins with a "C" and has no "g" or "h" in it. Don't confuse it with "site" or "sight.") Citing a source means stating where you got your information. When you write an academic paper, you generally cite sources by using footnotes, bibliographies, and "references cited." Nonacademic writers usually cite sources by identifying the source by name and title (if there is a title), such as, "Bill Hall, a spokesperson for the U.S. Department of Health and Human Services, said . . . " If you read good news magazines and newspapers, then you'll see this done regularly in the reporting, and you can use it as a model for citing sources. When you deliver a speech, do something similar to what journalists do when they attribute ideas in news stories—present more than just a name and title, but not as much as you'd find in a proper footnote or bibliography for a term paper.

You should cite sources of evidence for both direct quotations and for ideas that you paraphrase. Using ideas or data without citing the source is plagiarism. General knowledge does not need to be documented, however. Citing sources also helps enhance your credibility, by indicating that you have researched your subject.

The first time you introduce a source of evidence, state the source's name *and* qualifications *before* presenting the information. Also indicate when the evidence was made public. For example, you might say, "The July 18th issue of *Time* magazine quoted Secretary of Defense Donald Rumsfeld saying . . . ," or "Theodore H. White, author of *The Making of the President,* provides an example . . . ," or "The Bureau of Labor Statistics reported in October 2001 . . . " After the first citation, refer to the source by only the last name, prior to presenting the information. For example, "Rumsfeld says . . . ," or "According to White . . . " Of course, if subsequent citations come from different articles or books, you'll need to include the general dates of the new evidence.

Along with citing evidence, you should also interpret it for your listeners. From your point of view, the meaning of the evidence and the way it supports your claim may be perfectly clear, but remember that it might not be so clear for your audience. Do not just state a claim and present the evidence, but go on to explain what the evidence means, and show the connection to your claim.

You might think that doing all of this involves a lot of unnecessary work. However, as communication scholar Daniel O'Keefe (1998) found, "For two kinds of support explicitness—information-source citation and argument completeness—messages with more explicit argumentative support are significantly more credible and significantly more persuasive than their less explicit counterparts" (73). O'Keefe did a sophisticated statistical analysis, called a "metaanalysis," of forty-eight studies examining the effect of citing sources and completely explaining evidence, done between 1953 and 1994. The results of those studies, and his analysis, indicate that citing sources and explaining the meaning of evidence may take a little more time, but it will make your argument much stronger, especially when using high-quality evidence.

ANALYZING EVIDENCE

When analyzing evidence that someone else uses in an argument, begin by reviewing the argument and identifying each use of evidence as well as each time evidence wasn't provided but would have made the argument stronger if it were. For each bit of evidence used, ask "Where did that come from?" If there is no citation for the evidence, then you would have to decide whether the lack of a citation is important to a critical evaluation of the argument. If the information is known to you to be common knowledge, then no citation is needed, but the evidence has the weakness of common knowledge. If it's not common knowledge, however, you may take the lack of a citation to mean that the evidence is an assertion and then decide whether this source has the credibility to make such an assertion. Alternatively, the lack of a citation may be an attempt by the arguer to hide the nature of the source, which may be a sign that the source is not very good.

After identifying the use of evidence, you can evaluate how well it was used. When making a judgment about the quality of evidence used in an argument, the form of the evidence is not an important consideration. The classification of evidence used is more significant, because it can lead you to decisions concerning its quality. If the arguer used secondary sources then you would be justified in being suspicious about the quality, for instance. You also could apply the tests of evidence to each use of evidence to see if each stands up. If it doesn't, then you have to consider if failing to pass some of the tests is crucial.

In addition, you could determine where the evidence falls on the hierarchy of evidence. If the majority of evidence falls at the upper end of the hierarchy, then you could argue that the evidence was good, and if most of it fell at the lower end of the hierarchy, then you could argue that it wasn't very good. You'd still, however, have to use your judgment to decide whether it was good enough for what the arguer was trying to do and the context in which it was used.

FALLACIES ASSOCIATED
WITH EVIDENCE

SUPPRESSED EVIDENCE (overlooked evidence)—drawing a conclusion after purposely leaving out known evidence, or intentionally failing to look for likely evidence that might contradict a claim.

When someone knows of evidence that contradicts his or her position, or is aware that such evidence probably exists but ignores it when drawing a conclusion or making an argument, that person has committed the fallacy of suppressed evidence. The argument may appear sound, but it is based on the exclusion of some relevant evidence. For example, if a sales representative argues that a product is a good buy but conceals the actual cost compared to a competitive product or refuses to divulge known defects in the product, then that representative has made a fallacious argument about the merits of buying the product.

Whether or not someone's reasoning commits the fallacy of suppressed evidence is sometimes difficult to determine, since you may need background knowledge to know that the evidence exists. There are enough potential sources of evidence that someone may honestly be unaware of some. Moreover, since one must evaluate evidence to determine whether or not it's worthwhile, then one may decide that some evidence is not good enough, or relevant enough, to be important to the argument. If the evidence is good or relevant to the argument, then excluding it would still commit the fallacy of suppressed evidence, even though it would be unintentional.

Determining whether or not the fallacy of suppressed evidence has occurred also can be difficult in an advocacy situation, because each side has the responsibility to make its own case to whomever judges the dispute. Neither side has a responsibility to make the case for the other, so it's often unfair to say that someone commits the fallacy of suppressed evidence by not providing evidence to support the other side. On the other hand, if one side actively takes steps to prevent the other side from obtaining evidence, then that side would be suppressing evidence, leading to a fallacious argument. Also, if people judging the dispute fail to consider relevant evidence from either side when trying to reach a conclusion, then they would commit the fallacy in their reasoning.

Consider the folklore concerning sixteenth-century witch trials. The judges in the trials are commonly depicted as hearing evidence that the accused were witches but didn't allow the accused to present evidence and testimony in their own defense. By failing to consider potentially relevant evidence, the judges could not reason their way to a sound conclusion.

This fallacy reminds you to question whether you've been presented all the facts before accepting someone else's argument. It also reminds you to be careful about the way you use evidence when making your arguments.

POISONING THE WELL (no true Scotsman)—a way of suppressing evidence that eliminates a source of evidence from consideration by claiming that the source is flawed when there is no true relationship between the alleged flaw and the reliability of the source.

The source of evidence is an important consideration when determining the value of that evidence, and it is legitimate to question evidence that comes from unreliable sources. When an arguer attempts to exclude evidence from a particular source because of an alleged flaw, when that flaw really isn't true, or, if true, doesn't really matter, then he commits the fallacy of poisoning the well. The idea behind the name is, if someone poisons a well in the desert, it prevents others from drinking from that well. The analogy is, if an arguer "poisons" a source of information, then he or she prevents others from using evidence from that source.

A member of a hate group on a talk show once said that no one should pay attention to what the FBI says, because the FBI is a Zionist-run organization. By making that assertion, he had a ready answer for anyone who would present evidence from the FBI concerning hate crimes, or the rise of hate groups, thus poisoning that "well" of information. He did so without any evidence that the FBI is a Zionist organization or, if it is, that that necessarily makes its evidence unreliable.

Usually arguers poison the well in a more subtle manner. They say something to the effect of, "Nobody who really knows what they're talking about would disagree with my conclusions." If evidence is brought up from anyone who disagrees with the arguer, then they simply reply that it is obvious that that person doesn't know what she's talking about. This fallacy is sometimes called the "No true Scotsman" fallacy. Someone asserts that a Scotsman would not agree to a certain idea, and someone else points out that MacGregor has come out in favor of it. The response is, "Well, no *true* Scotsman would say that," thus poisoning the MacGregor well. The same poisoning is done if someone asserts, "No true patriot would . . . ," or "No respectable scientist would . . . ," or a similar assertion.

People who poison the well often attempt to eliminate evidence before it is brought up by attacking the credibility of *any* source that might advance such evidence, but it can also be done after the evidence is presented. People who commit this fallacy avoid the need to respond to the quality of particular evidence, or the credentials of particular sources, by branding all of the sources flawed and all of the evidence irrelevant.

When someone does attempt to poison the well, it is appropriate to call on him or her to prove the assertion that the source of evidence is flawed, or to argue that the source of the evidence is reliable. Those strategies often are not used, however, because people don't notice that their well has been poisoned when it happens, or they aren't prepared to prove that their sources are worthwhile because they didn't expect anyone to challenge them.

SLIPPERY SLOPE (thin entering wedge, camel's nose)—a type of causal reasoning in which it is argued that an apparently small cause will lead to a major effect when there is no evidence of such a causal relationship.

The slippery slope fallacy happens when one argues that a particular change will inevitably cause a more significant change to happen, and it is usually used to argue against the small change. The fallacy assumes that a chain of events will be set in motion, so there will be no way to avoid a significant problem, but the argument doesn't provide the evidence needed to make a convincing argument that the chain of events will really happen. The conclusion may be correct, but the argument is still weak.

Imagine that you have a pile of loose sand. If you take a single grain of sand away near the bottom, then it probably won't make much difference, but it is possible that it could cause the sand above it to slide down. Removing a grain of sand *might* create a slippery slope. The slippery slope fallacy argues that removing the grain *will* cause the slope to slide.

There is also the slippery slope *argument,* which argues against a change because making the change will result in significant disadvantages. The difference between the argument and the fallacy is that the argument provides evidence to show how the first event will lead to the second, how the second will lead to the third, and so on. There is enough argumentation to make the conclusion sound instead of just asserting the chain of events.

Examples of the slippery slope fallacy occurred almost every time women began to do more than their traditional roles called for. Opponents to women doing police work asserted that it would cause a rise in crime. Women in business would destroy the businesses. Women in college would diminish the colleges. And so on. Those arguments simply assumed that women were less capable than men, thus the slippery slope fallacy. When the arguments included more evidence, they may have still been wrong but were not the slippery slope fallacy.

An alternative name for this fallacy is the "thin entering wedge" fallacy. The idea behind that name is, if the thin edge of a wedge is inserted into a crack, then the rest of the wedge will follow, splitting apart whatever it was inserted into. Another name is the "camel's nose" fallacy, from the idea that if a camel is allowed to put its nose into a tent, then there will be no way to keep the rest of the camel from following. The implication is that neither the edge of the wedge nor the nose of the camel should be allowed to start the process.

SOLID SLOPE (spendthrift)—reasoning that an act, or a series of acts, should be carried out because it will have no significant consequences when there is no evidence for the lack of significant effects or there is reason to believe that there will be significant effects.

The solid slope fallacy is the opposite of the slippery slope fallacy. Where the slippery slope argues that slight changes will have a significant effect, the solid slope argues that slight changes will have no significant effect. The slippery slope fallacy assumes that taking away one grain of sand will cause the slope to collapse; the solid slope fallacy assumes that taking away many grains of sand will leave the slope intact.

For instance, someone trying to sell you a car may try to get you to add an option by telling you how handy it is, and that it will only cost five dollars a month more. You can afford an extra five dollars a month, can't you? When you say yes to that, the sales representative goes on to another option, then another, and so on. Each option, by itself, seems insignificant, but when added together they not only increase your monthly payment but also substantially increase the amount you'll pay in interest. As a buyer, you can eliminate some options when you realize the total cost, but many people are reluctant to do so, thus they just go along.

The solid slope fallacy also could be called the "spendthrift" fallacy. The idea behind that name is that someone who wastes money may justify it by saying that spending a little more won't matter, so goes on spending more and more money, refusing to acknowledge that all of the little costs add up.

SELF-EVIDENT TRUTHS (appeal to beliefs)—arguing that a claim should be accepted based on evidence that is not presented but is asserted to be well known or obvious when the information is either not well known or is incorrect.

Most people have had the experience of engaging in a conversational argument with someone else and supporting their position by saying "everybody knows" some information. To a certain extent, that can be acceptable, because people are not expected to always have specific information in their heads. Even so, it can be a fallacious argument when the facts that "everybody knows" aren't really universally known or aren't accurate even if they are widely accepted. The fallacy is more apparent in a situation where someone had the time to research and prepare an argument and thus the opportunity to provide better evidence than referring to what everyone supposedly knows.

The fallacy of self-evident truths has the potential to create another problem in an argument if it is used to deny better evidence. Sometimes arguments are initiated because widely held beliefs turn out to be incorrect, and better information leads to a different conclusion. If high-quality, accurate evidence is refuted by assertions that everyone knows what is true, then the outcome is determined before it can really begin. If facts that everyone knows really are true, then they can be substantiated with better reasoning than saying that they are widely believed.

An example of the fallacy of self-evident truths is when President Clinton claimed that he didn't consider the acts he committed with Monica Lewinsky to be "sex." Many outraged people argued that he had to be lying, because "everyone knows" that that was sex. However, some people pointed out that when they were growing up, those same acts were referred to as "heavy petting" and were considered stopping short of sex. While there could still be disagreement over definitions, it was clear that everyone did not "know" the same thing.

Another name for this fallacy is "appeal to beliefs," because the evidence used to support a position only consists of referring to what people believe to be true rather than evidence that is empirically verifiable.

ARGUMENT FROM AUTHORITY (appeal to authority, *ad vericundiam*)— arguing that a claim is true based only on evidence that an authority figure accepts the claim.

Relying on the reasoned conclusions of people who are experts in their fields makes a lot of sense. No one can have expertise in everything, and most of us do not have the time to thoroughly investigate every issue. Whether the subject is anthropology or zoology, finances or medicine, we often have to rely on the opinions of people who know a lot more about the subjects than we do. That reliance can be taken too far, though, and, when it is, we commit the fallacy of argument from authority.

In its simplest form, argument from authority happens when someone says "X is true because famous person A says it is true." There is no explanation of why the famous person says what is claimed, nor why we should believe that the famous person knows what he or she is talking about. A bit more credible is the argument, "X is true because expert B says it is true." In this case, the statement is at least attributed to an expert, but there is still no explanation of how the expert arrived at that conclusion, only that he or she agrees with the claim made by the arguer. In either case, there also may be some question whether the famous person or the expert really agrees with the claim or with a similar claim, or whether the authority's opinion is being distorted.

Note that it is not a fallacy if you say, "Authority B agrees with my claim and here is why . . . " The evidence and reasoning are presented, so one considering your claim can think critically about your argument and the expert's reasoning.

Making an argument from authority can be a problem, for several reasons. First, the authority may be wrong. Experts often disagree with each other. You don't decide who is correct in such cases by saying that one person is an expert because the other person is an expert too. You decide who is correct by examining the person's arguments and evidence. Your own arguments will also be stronger if you include the reasoning, even though you attribute it to someone else. Second, the authority may be biased. While explaining the authority's reasoning doesn't eliminate the bias, it does provide the basis of the authority's reasoning, so anyone can think critically about the arguments involved. Third, the authority may be uninformed about the particular subject. If an expert doesn't have appropriate information about the specific subject, then she can't be expected to have an accurate opinion, even though she's an expert about the general subject. Finally, the subject may be outside of the authority's field of expertise. This is particularly prevalent in advertising, when celebrities are used to promote products. An actor may have expertise in matters theatrical, but why should you trust one to recommend a pain reliever?

Sometimes the argument from authority will occur when the arguer is the authority referred to. For example, a student may question why he should do something a particular way, and his teacher may say, "Because I said so." That information, by itself, doesn't really present a good reason.

Argument from authority is also called "appeal to authority," because the evidence only provides the source's opinion instead of evidence and reasoning about the issue. It is also referred to as argument *ad vericundiam,* which means argument from revered authority.

When considering arguments that rely on the opinions of authorities, stop to think how much weight should be given to those opinions and how well they actually support the claim.

APPEAL TO TRADITION (*ad vericundiam*)—a particular type of appeal to authority that argues that something should be done based only on evidence that it has been done that way in the past, or should be believed only because it has been believed for a long time.

A tradition is an action that has been performed within a community for some time and has come to be expected without question. Traditions occur in communities as small as a couple and as large as a nation or culture. Sometimes people question traditions and argue that a tradition should end. Some traditions serve purposes that are helpful to a community, and some are continued just because they are traditions. The former can be defended from change based on their effects and the latter just because they are traditions.

The fact that something has been done, or has been believed, does not, by itself, warrant its continuation. An argument that only bases a conclusion on the preservation of a tradition provides an explanation for why the tradition continues, but it doesn't provide a sound argument. If the enactment of the tradition results in some benefit to the community, then the reasoning should address the stock issue of advantage, and the argument may justify the tradition.

An example of appeal to tradition would be if someone wanted to eliminate some pledge rituals performed by a fraternity or sorority. If the ritual is defended because "we've always done it," then that defense is an appeal to tradition. An appeal to tradition also can be about something that you might not normally consider a tradition, such as refusing to try a different recipe because one has always used a certain recipe.

Sometimes the fallacy of appeal to tradition is referred to as a type of *ad verecundiam,* or argument from authority. The tradition itself is considered the authority, and when questioned why the tradition continues, the answer is, "because that's the way it's done."

The reverse of appeal to tradition is also a fallacy, which would involve saying that something should not be done just because it is a tradition, such as when people argue that a procedure should be changed only because it has been used for a long time. Once again, whether or not it is a tradition does not indicate whether it is worthwhile by itself, and other attributes should be considered.

APPEAL TO ANONYMOUS AUTHORITY—a specific form of appeal to authority in which it is argued that a claim should be accepted based only on evidence that unidentified authorities accept it.

This fallacy occurs when someone might say, "Experts agree that . . . " The statement may sound quite strong, especially if said with conviction, but it really doesn't say much. Which experts agree? Are they experts in relevant fields? What is their expertise? Do all of the experts agree? A majority? Only a few? Do they agree with the specific claim, or a claim that is similar?

In a conversational argument, it is probably too much to ask that someone have specific information about the experts, but in a situation where the arguer had time to prepare, expectations can be higher, and the information on the authorities and what they actually said ought to be available.

A common example of this kind of fallacy is found in movie advertising, where ads often proclaim, "The critics agree! *Edgar's Plan* is the best film of the year!" The advertisers want to make it seem as though all of the film critics in the country have a unanimous opinion about the movie, but the statement could be true if only two critics could be found who agreed with it. In addition, you don't know who the critics are; they could represent tastes that don't coincide with yours, so even if the statement is true, you might hate the movie.

In addition to the authority being anonymous, the same problems that were found with argument from authority apply here. Not knowing the reasoning behind the authority's conclusion, there is no good way to consider the value of the evidence.

At times, statements such as "experts say" are not really a problem. For example, someone addressing other experts in a field may be able to say "research has shown . . . " because she knows that this audience is familiar with the relevant research and her statement has been well proven and is not controversial in that field, so there is no need to go into detail with that audience. That same arguer, though, may need to present a more developed argument to people who do not have the same background knowledge.

APPEAL TO THE PEOPLE (argument by consensus, bandwagon appeal, *ad populum, ad numerum*)—a form of appeal to authority in which it is argued that a claim should be accepted based only on evidence that a large number of people accept it or should be rejected because a large number of people reject it.

When someone makes an argument that is an appeal to the people, the arguer tries to support the claim with evidence indicating that many people already agree with the claim, reasoning that such large-scale agreement proves the claim valid. While it is true that often a large number of people hold correct beliefs, it is also true that sometimes they hold erroneous ones. Sometimes a large number of people will hold one opinion and an equal number will reject it. So the number of people who believe something to be true is usually not good support for a claim.

When thinking of the appeal to the people, the meaning of "large" may vary from one situation to another. In an office where twenty people work, someone may support a claim with "Everyone in the office agrees with me," and the meaning of large is nineteen people. Or someone may claim that her particular religion is the true one, because millions of people throughout the world practice it.

Those referred to in the appeal to the people also may be indicated in relative terms. For example, an advertisement claiming that a product is the most often purchased one of its type is a kind of appeal to the people. The implication is that you also should purchase it because so many others have done so. The argument itself may not claim that the product is the best, and the advertiser probably relies on the consumer inferring that since so many people buy the product, it is the best.

At times the beliefs of a number of people are relevant evidence, such as when the question is who will be elected to an office and thus polling evidence is referred to for support. On the other hand, often the opinions of people are not relevant, such as a poll asking people if they think that they will be better off in a year. As long as such a poll is used as evidence of people's attitudes, it is relevant evidence. If the poll is used as evidence of what the quality of living actually will be in a year, it is likely to be irrelevant.

The appeal to the people doesn't have to appear in the language of an argument—it may come nonverbally. An example of visual appeal to the people comes during political campaigns, particularly presidential elections. An advertisement for a candidate often shows him or her addressing apparently large, enthusiastic crowds, implying that there is substantial support for the candidate. The nominating conventions are held in huge buildings with thousands of excited supporters, giving the impression that everyone loves the party and its candidate, implying that that is a good reason to vote for the candidate.

Appeal to the people is also known as "argument by consensus" because the support for the claim consists of the assertion that the claim is the consensus of opinion. It is also referred to as the "bandwagon" appeal, because in earlier times candidates for offices would parade through town on a wagon, with a band playing on it to get attention. Supporters would literally jump on the bandwagon to show they were in favor of the candidate, so the number of people on or near the bandwagon was supposed to indicate the candidates' worth. The term *ad populum,* meaning the support for the claim is popular acceptance, is also used, and so is the term *ad numerum,* meaning that the support for the claim is that a large number of people accept it.

COMMON PERSON APPEAL (common man appeal)—a form of appeal to the people in which it is argued that a claim should be accepted based only on evidence that a regular person accepts it.

In the case of the common person appeal, a single individual, or a small group of people, seemingly possessing no special qualities, represents the "people." The arguer wants to bypass your critical thinking and hopes you will identify with the common person and be swayed by his or her presentation because he or she is so much like you. This appeal rests on an assumption that common people have some sort of intuitive sense that lets them see through fraud and recognize the truth. Since common people are so often the victims of fraud, that assumption is, at least, questionable.

The common person appeal also is regularly used by advertisers. Many commercials present the testimony of common people, extolling the virtues of the product being advertised. Usually there is no way to tell if those "common people" are really consumers stating their opinions or actors playing a role and following a script. Some advertisers have started to include disclaimers such as, "This is not an actor." You are expected to trust that person more and forget that his testimony would only be used if it is favorable, has been edited for time and effect, only represents one person's opinion, and is responding to the directions of the people producing the advertisement.

APPEAL TO PRIDE (flattery, apple polishing)—a particular type of appeal to the people that argues that one should accept a claim based only on evidence that he or she has the favorable characteristics needed to understand the truth of the claim.

The appeal to pride is exemplified by the fable "The Emperor's New Clothes." In that story, a ruler was tricked into paying phony tailors for clothes that were made of such fine material that only the wisest and most discerning people would see the cloth. While the tailors pretended to hold up invisible material, the emperor pretended to see it so he would be thought of as wise. As the tailors pretended to make the clothes, other members of the court pretended to see them, as did the public when the emperor went out. Their desire to be thought of as having special qualities made them agree to a claim that had no substance.

When one argues that his or her claim should be accepted solely because the recipient is smart enough, honest enough, perceptive enough, or has some other positive trait to recognize the truth of the claim, then one has made an appeal to pride. If the argument is partly an appeal to pride and includes other reasons for acceptance of the claim, then only the part that appeals to pride is fallacious. The rest may or may not be a fallacy, depending on the argument.

The appeal to pride is also known as the "fallacy of flattery," because the arguer is really only flattering someone to gain agreement for the claim. It is also known as "apple polishing," because that is a metaphor for flattery, based on an earlier practice of students bringing apples to their teachers and polishing them to make them look better, hoping to receive favorable treatment.

SNOB APPEAL—a form of appeal to the people in which it is argued that one should accept an idea or a product based only on evidence that prestigious people accept it or nonprestigious people reject it.

The snob appeal fallacy is similar to the appeal to pride, but it states that one should accept the claim because members of a prestigious group accept it. Both fallacies try to prey on people's wishes to be perceived as having desirable qualities, but they go about the argument a bit differently.

The snob appeal is pretty common among adolescents, who reason that they and their peers should do something, wear something, believe something, or be friends with someone because that's what the popular kids do. The popular kids are the prestigious group, and the argument is that others should follow their lead. The appeal is not limited to adolescents though. Advertisements targeted toward adults, showing only upper-class people using a product, can be considered a form of snob appeal.

APPEAL TO COMMON PRACTICE—a particular type of appeal to the people that argues that something is right or should be done based only on evidence that other people do it.

Sometimes when people make decisions about what to do, or when they try to justify their actions, they argue, in effect, "Everyone else is doing it." While that may be true, it is often not evidence that really leads to the conclusion that an individual should do it. The question should not be "Is everyone else doing it?" but "Should one person do it?" Are there actual benefits to the action? If nobody else did it, would it still be worth doing?

In this case, the "authority" in question is the authority of the group. If a large enough group is doing something, the reasoning goes, then it must be okay. Sometimes the group may be quite small in absolute terms, but the arguer still considers it large enough to justify his or her practices.

Children who want their parents to let them do something often use the appeal to common practice. When denied permission to go on an outing, for instance, the child may say, "Everyone else's parents are letting them go." The parents may point out the fallacy by responding with, "If everyone else jumped off a bridge, would you do that too?" The response is usually not satisfactory for the child, but it does indicate the weakness of the argument. Adults may justify cheating on their taxes in the same manner, reasoning that everyone else is cheating, so they might as well do the same. Students sometimes use the appeal to common practice in attempts to get course requirements and expectations changed. A student may argue against a policy by saying, "We don't have to do that in any of my other classes."

Like many other fallacies, the appeal to common practice tends to avoid presenting good reasons in favor of a claim. The person making the argument may believe that it should be compelling, but a critical thinker should demand better reasoning. If the reasoning is only "Everybody is doing it," then there really isn't an argument. If the reasoning is "Everybody is doing it, and they have good reasons for doing it," then the appeal to common practice is irrelevant, and the focus should be on the good reasons.

The reverse of the appeal to common practice also would be a fallacy. That is, if one argues that something should not be done just because everybody else is doing it, or should be done just because hardly anyone else is doing it. If there are reasons something should or should not be done, then the fact that others are doing it or not isn't relevant.

AD NAUSEUM—a form of appeal to the people that involves reasoning that a claim is true based only on evidence that it has been made so often.

If you hear a claim often enough, you may start to believe it, even if you don't hear any evidence to support the claim. This is especially true if you hear the same claim from several different sources. Advertisers count on that, which is one reason they repeat the same messages over and over. Political campaigns also count on that, which is one reason they not only repeat their message but try to make it seem as though it is coming from several different people.

The *ad nauseam* fallacy also can happen in an unplanned way. If you keep up with the news, you may notice that several different news organizations say the same thing, and you may decide that it must be true because you've heard it so often. You may not realize that all of those organizations got the story from the same wire service, or from the same press release, so you think they are presenting independent reports.

This fallacy reminds us that the truth of a claim should not be judged based on how often it is made but on the evidence and reasoning supporting it.

SIGNIFICANCE (misuse of statistics, questionable statistics, questionable use of statistics)—making an argument using statistical evidence when the basis of the statistic is not revealed, is distorted, or the statistics are misinterpreted, innocently or on purpose.

Many people find statistics difficult to deal with because they don't understand how they are generated or what they mean. For that reason, statistical evidence can be easily misused and lead to fallacious arguments.

For example, people often use statistical evidence to show that there is a trend, such as a 15 percent increase in the cost of something over a decade. Depending on the argument being made, if you don't know the initial price, the change in price of similar items, changes in the item itself over time, the definitions used over time, and the way the information was gathered over time then that statistic may not mean anything. When you hear trends discussed, as a critical thinker you should require enough evidence to understand the numbers.

Statistics also can be the source of a fallacy if they are questionable or false. Sometimes people use statistics to try to prove a point, but when you stop to think about it, it is unlikely that anyone could gather those statistics. For example, someone might use statistics about the value of marijuana growing to a local economy. Since the activity is illegal, it isn't possible to gather the data needed to provide accurate statistics. Estimates can be made extrapolating from certain assumptions, but definitive statistics are not available. If estimates are presented as estimates, and the assumptions are clear, then there usually isn't a problem. But if estimates are presented as highly accurate, then the argument is probably flawed.

The fallacy of significance also can come about when the numbers are distorted in some way. The street value of drugs confiscated in police raids is sometimes questioned as being highly inflated to make the police appear to score a major victory against crime. If those numbers are indeed distorted, then they may lead to a false conclusion.

As Joel Best points out in *Damned Lies and Statistics,* social advocates, corporate spokespeople, and government officials often estimate or guess at the size of a social problem before the actual data are gathered. Reporters and others then use those estimates as though they are the findings of properly conducted studies, and they are accepted as the truth. Then, when the actual data are collected, if they are different from the earlier guesses, then the guesses continue to be used. People who use such statistics may do so unwittingly, but they still commit the fallacy of significance.

SUMMARY

The strength of any argument is based, in part, on the evidence used to support the claim. Evidence can come in several forms, including facts, statistics, examples, and testimony (see Sidebar 9.1). Evidence also can be classified according to whether it is primary or secondary, from an expert or a lay source, and whether it was purposely created or is casual evidence (see Sidebar 9.2). Each form of evidence and classification of evidence has its own strengths and weaknesses.

Sidebar 9.1 Forms of Evidence

Facts
Statistics
Examples
Testimony

Sidebar 9.2 Classifications of Evidence

Primary or secondary
Expert or lay
Created or casual

Sidebar 9.3 Tests of Evidence

Source credibility
Source bias
Recency
Internal consistency
Completeness
Corroboration

Sidebar 9.4 Perella's Hierarchy of Evidence

Level 6	Consensus of empirical studies	BEST
Level 5	Empirical studies and consensus of expert opinion	
Level 4	Expert opinion and consensus of lay opinion	
Level 3	Lay opinion	
Level 2	Judicial notice and common knowledge	
Level 1	Assertion	WORST

You can apply several tests to determine the quality of evidence. These tests of evidence include source credibility, source bias, recency of the evidence, internal consistency, completeness, and corroboration (see Sidebar 9.3). Evidence that successfully meets all of the tests generally is better than evidence that fails some of the tests.

Jack Perella developed a hierarchy of evidence to help determine which evidence is the best (see Sidebar 9.4). His six levels do not guarantee that evidence will be absolutely accurate, but you can use them to evaluate the likely value of the evidence.

When using evidence to support a claim, you should cite the source and date of the evidence. You should also explain what the evidence means for the receivers so it is clear that the evidence is relevant and supports your claim. When confronted with an argument, you should consider the evidence to determine whether it is worthy of acceptance and actually does support the claim in the way the advocate says it does.

KEY CONCEPTS

assertion   (1) an unsupported claim; (2) the lowest (first) level on Perella's hierarchy of evidence.

casual evidence   evidence that naturally occurs without anyone trying to create it as evidence.

common knowledge   (1) using widely held beliefs as evidence for a claim; (2) the second lowest level on Perella's hierarchy of evidence, along with "judicial notice."

completeness   a test of evidence that refers to whether the source of evidence, or the evidence as presented in an argument, provides enough information so a critically thinking person can accept it.

conclusionary evidence   testimony in which only a conclusion is stated and does not provide any indication of how the conclusion was arrived at.

consensus of expert opinion (1) the agreement of several people who are experts in a field; (2) the fifth level on Perella's hierarchy of evidence, along with "empirical study."

consensus of lay opinion   (1) the agreement of the reasoned opinion of many people, outside of their fields of expertise; (2) the fourth level on Perella's hierarchy of evidence, along with "expert opinion."

consensus of studies   (1) agreement among several well-designed observational research studies; (2) the sixth and highest level on Perella's hierarchy of evidence.

corroboration   a test of evidence that asks if other qualified sources agree with the source of evidence, sometimes referred to as "external consistency."

created evidence   evidence that was purposely recorded for future use as evidence.

empirical study   (1) a well-designed observational research study about a subject; (2) the fifth level on Perella's hierarchy of evidence, along with "consensus of expert opinion."

evidence   supporting material known or discovered but not created by the advocate.

examples   a form of evidence that consists of descriptions of *individual* events, objects, persons, or places.

expert evidence   evidence that comes from a source who is experienced and knowledgeable in the subject of the evidence.

expert opinion   (1) the reasoned opinion of one within his or her field of expertise; (2) the fourth level on Perella's hierarchy of evidence.

facts   a form of evidence that consists of empirically verifiable descriptions of events, objects, persons, or places.

hypothetical examples   examples that are made up and should not be used as evidence in arguments but are useful to illustrate ideas.

internal consistency   a test of evidence that looks for overt or subtle contradictions within the source from which the evidence comes.

judicial notice   (1) accepting assertions as evidence without requiring proof; (2) the second lowest level on Perella's hierarchy of evidence, along with "common knowledge."

lay evidence   evidence that comes from a source who is neither experienced nor knowledgeable in the area of discussion.

lay opinion   (1) evidence that consists of a reasoned opinion by one outside of his or her area of expertise; (2) the third level on Perella's hierarchy of evidence.

literal examples   examples that are based in reality and are acceptable as evidence in arguments.

primary evidence   evidence that comes from a source that is closest to the actual happening; the source has firsthand information.

recency   a test of evidence that considers when the evidence was produced and if it was from an appropriate time period for the conclusion being drawn.

secondary evidence   evidence that comes from a source that is at least one step removed from the actual happening; one who has only secondhand information.

source bias   a test of evidence that asks whether the source of evidence has any self-interests that could distort perceptions.

source credibility   a test of evidence that examines whether the source of information is trustworthy and has the background, knowledge, expertise, and opportunity to be relied upon.

statistics   a particular type of factual evidence that consists of quantified descriptions of events, objects, persons, places, or other phenomena.

testimony   authoritative opinion evidence that interprets or judges events, objects, persons, or places.

THINGS TO THINK ABOUT

1. Find a written argument, such as an editorial, a letter to the editor, or an advertisement. What evidence does it include? What form does the evidence take? In which classification(s) does each fit?

2. Find a written argument and select one bit of the evidence in it. How well does it meet each test of evidence? After analyzing it, do you think it strengthens the argument? Why or why not?

3. Find a written argument and identify the evidence used to support the proposition. To which level does each bit of evidence belong on Perella's hierarchy? What are your reasons for placing each where you did?

4. Choose one of the arguments that Secretary of State Powell made in his speech in the Appendix. What is the evidence in that section? What form does the evidence take? How well does it meet the tests of evidence?

5. Think of how you would outline a brief argument about a significant

social issue, using the stock issues for the type of proposition that you'd support. What evidence would you need to make it a strong argument?

6. Think of a time when your reasoning, or the reasoning of someone else, committed one of the fallacies described in this chapter. What made the reasoning fallacious?

TUTORIAL LINK

Go to *http://communication.wadsworth.com/verlinden* and complete the tests for the Informal Fallacies, Set #4 tutorial.

10

Language and Argumentation

Language is the stuff of which arguments are made. No matter how sound your reasoning, how perfect your structure, how thorough your research, or how solid your evidence, you have to convert it all into language to share with others. Although we have been using language most of our lives, and it seems pretty natural, most of us can still learn more about how to use language well and what to watch out for in other people's use of it.

When we communicate with others, we can do so with or without using symbols. A **symbol** is something that a group of language users agrees stands for something else. We communicate nonsymbolically when what we do has a meaning that is independent of community agreement. So a person who is unusually pale, perspiring, and walks unsteadily, and whose eyes look unfocused, may communicate that she is sick without using symbols. She also can communicate that feeling by saying, "I am sick," which does use symbols. People who study nonverbal communication study the ways people communicate with each other without using symbols as well as how they use symbols without using language.

Symbols come in a variety of forms, some of which we do not usually think of as symbols. Words and numbers are clearly symbolic. To most people, pictographs and hieroglyphics do not seem symbolic, but they are, because the people who use them have agreed that certain pictures stand for particular meanings. Even less clear to many people is whether or not the use of sign language is symbolic. As its name implies, sign language is symbolic because people have agreed upon the meanings of specific gestures. Most facial expressions are nonsymbolic, because they are the natural result of the communicator's thoughts and feelings. However, when you consciously smile to convey a particular meaning, you use your face symbolically.

Symbolic and nonsymbolic communication usually, but not always, work together to convey meaning. In the general American culture, a person who sits close to another, looks into the other's eyes, and softly says "I love you" is using both symbolic and nonsymbolic communication to reinforce the message. The person who sits farther away, doesn't look up from the television, and says "I love you" with no vocal inflection is sending a contradictory message. Recipients of messages have to interpret both the symbolic and nonsymbolic content of every message.

Language and culture are inextricably related. In some cultures, and in some American co-cultures, it may well be that saying "I love you" while doing something else, and in what some might consider an expressionless tone, is expected, acceptable, and not at all contradictory.

This chapter will explain how language is used and how it can influence the way you think. It will

- describe some general characteristics of language.
- explain some ways of using language that a critical thinker should question.
- suggest some better ways to use language.
- identify argumentative fallacies associated with language.

CHARACTERISTICS OF LANGUAGE

Understanding that language is symbolic leads to a better understanding of several key characteristics of language that are important to know as an arguer and a critical thinker. Understanding the six characteristics that follow can help you present arguments that are clearer and stronger and can also help you understand why some arguments you hear are unclear.

Symbols Are Arbitrary

The sounds and shapes that groups of people agree stand for some meaning have no inherent connection to the things and concepts for which they stand. Over time, people may develop strong emotional reactions to the symbols, but the symbols themselves have no meaning other than those that people attribute to them. For instance, in the English language, we use the symbol "water" to refer to a particular natural substance. Each group of people on earth has experience with that same substance, but no other language uses the word "water" to refer to it. There is nothing about that substance that requires it to be called "water."

The arbitrary nature of language begins at the level of the word and extends to sentence structure. Different languages have different grammatical rules, so the order in which you string together words in English is different than in German, Russian, and Japanese languages, for instance. There is no intrinsic reason for different languages to have different sentence structures.

Don't think that because the symbols and usage are arbitrary anyone can refer to anything, using any symbol he or she wants, and be understood by others. Within a language community, there are "correct" and "incorrect" ways of identifying things and expressing yourself. As you grew up, for example, you probably learned your native language's rules pretty well, to the point that now they're second nature. The point is, what you learned was not learned universally, and what was correct in your community was not necessarily correct in others.

Language Is Imprecise

Actually, it is not language that is imprecise but the way people use it. We often use language that is not very specific when more specific language is available. Sometimes this happens because the precise term is not in our vocabularies, sometimes because we just can't think of the specific term at the time, and sometimes because we just don't want to put forth the effort to be more specific. Usually we can get away with that, either because precision isn't very important, or because the people we're talking with are able to fill in the gaps for us.

For example, what does the phrase "junk food" make you think of? What does "candy" bring to mind? How about the phrase "candy bar"? How about "Snickers"? These questions illustrate two ends of the continuum of types of language that we all use, which are abstract language and concrete language.

Abstract language is language that is vague or broad in its meaning, so it's more difficult to tell what the user really intends. **Concrete language** has more specific shared meanings, so it's easier to tell what the user really means. In the questions above, "junk food" is a pretty abstract use of language, because it could have such a wide variety of referents (things to which it refers). "Candy bar" is less abstract and more concrete, because it narrows the range of referents. There are still a lot of different kinds of candy bars, though, so it isn't very concrete. As long as you know what a Snickers candy bar is, then "Snickers" is the most concrete of the four terms, because it refers to a particular kind of candy bar. On a continuum from most abstract to most concrete, we could get even more abstract, with words such as "food" or even "physical matter." We could also be more concrete by referring to "the Snickers bar in the top left drawer of my desk." The more concrete the language, the more precise it is, as long as you don't use concrete terms to refer to objects and concepts to which they don't apply. "Snickers" is not a precise term to refer to a person who performs a wedding ceremony, for example, unless that's the slang term used by a particular group for that meaning.

Sometimes you may want to use relatively abstract language because you want to refer to more general classes of things. ("Things" is a pretty abstract word, but it fits here.) Other times you want to use more concrete language, so your specific idea is conveyed more effectively. Keep in mind, though, that your language is almost always going to seem more concrete to you than to other people, because you already know what you're thinking. Using words with higher levels of abstraction can lead to arguments because of misunderstandings and can keep arguments going, because people end up talking about different ideas when they think that they're talking about the same thing. That's one reason a stock issue for two types of propositions is definition and distinction—to avoid using different meanings of the terms of the proposition during the argument.

Language Is Ambiguous

If someone told you "The teachers at this college are good," what would that mean? Would it mean that every teacher at this college is good, or most of the teachers, or would it mean some of the teachers at this college are good? Does "good" mean that teachers get students to learn the material, that they are entertaining, or that they are morally upstanding? Does it mean that they are good today but were not good yesterday, or that they are good today and will be good tomorrow? Does it mean that they are good in all of their classes? Does it mean that they are held in high esteem by students, get along with administrators, or do research that is respected by others in their fields? The statement seems quite simple, but there are many different ways to understand it.

The previous paragraph illustrates the third characteristic of language, that language is ambiguous, which means that there are often multiple possible interpretations of utterances. A lot of words have multiple correct definitions; the way in which words are strung together in phrases usually can be interpreted in more than one way; the context in which ideas are expressed can lead to different interpretations; and the emphasis on different words or syllables can change interpretations.

Most people think of words as having meanings, so when we use a word we expect others to understand. There's a saying in the communication discipline, though, that states, "Words don't have meaning, people do." If you remember any of the misunderstandings that you've had because of differences in meanings of words, then you should recognize how true that saying is. Often people do share the meaning of words, so communication usually works pretty well. Sometimes, though, your meaning for a word is different than someone else's, which could pose trouble. A better understanding of language can help you make arguments more effectively, avoid some misunderstandings that can harm relationships, and repair other misunderstandings without trying to blame the other person.

One reason language is ambiguous is because words and phrases have both denotative and connotative meanings. **Denotative meanings** are meanings such as those you would find in a dictionary. They are similar to what you might find in a dictionary, because a denotative meaning that you believe applies to a word may not be found in any dictionary, but it's still what you believe the word is "supposed to mean." For instance, think of the definition of the word "chair." Now look up the definition of "chair" in a dictionary. The two meanings are probably similar, but they're not likely to be exactly the same. They're both denotative meanings though. You may be the only person in the world who has a particular meaning for a word, but it is still a denotative meaning. Most of the time, however, denotative meanings are close enough so that they're shared among communicators.

Denotative meanings can be influenced by culture in many ways. Age differences can profoundly affect them. Think, for example, of the differences in the denotative meanings between you and your grandparents for the word "lame." To your grandparents, this might be "a person or an animal with a bad leg." To you, it might mean "someone or something that is stupid." Even among people from the same general area and age, language differences will occur. Language used by surfers may have a different meaning to nonsurfers, for instance, even when they're using words familiar to everyone.

If someone uses a word that you're totally unfamiliar with—such as a foreign or technical word—then it's very confusing because you have no denotative meaning for that word. When that happens, you're aware that you have no denotative meaning, so you're likely to be conscious of the need to try to figure out what the other person means. Sometimes, however, someone will use a word that you *do* have a denotative meaning for, so you may incorrectly think that you understand and act based on that understanding. A great deal of trouble could result until you realize the differences in your meanings. Arguments can be created through differences in denotative meanings, and arguments can be harder to resolve because of those differences. Some language scholars refer to such trouble as **bypassing,** which occurs when two people think that they're talking about the same thing, but they really aren't.

For instance, a friend says, "Meet me at Wendy's tomorrow at 4 o'clock." The language is fairly straightforward, so, at 4 o'clock the next day, you wait for your friend at Wendy's restaurant. As time passes, you become irritated, because your friend didn't show up. The next day you see her and ask, "Where were you? I waited for an hour at Wendy's!" She responds, "Where was *I*? Where were *you*? I was there from 3:30 to 5:00 and you *never* showed up!" After a while, it turns out that you were at a restaurant near the mall, and your friend was at a mutual friend's house. You each had a denotative meaning for the word "Wendy's," but you each had a *different* one.

Along with denotative meanings, the language we use also has **connotative meanings,** which are the personal, emotional reactions that we associate with words and phrases. While denotative meanings can be personal, they are intellectual reactions, not emotional. Your connotative meanings for words fall on an emotional continuum ranging from strongly positive to strongly negative. In the middle of the continuum is indifference, or words for which you have no real emotional reaction. Depending on the word, the continuum may range from happy to sad, excited to bored, relaxed to tense, angry to calm, and so on. Remember, having a different definition of a word doesn't make that a connotative meaning. It is your *emotional* reaction that is the connotative meaning.

Connotative meanings are based on your personal and cultural reactions to words. For example, for someone who had a cocker spaniel as a child, and loved that dog, the term *cocker spaniel* probably has positive emotional associations. However, if every day on your way to school you had to walk by a house with a vicious cocker spaniel who lunged at you, barking and growling, so the trip to school became a terrifying experience, then you probably have negative emotional associations with the term. Your denotative meanings for "cocker spaniel" would probably be similar, although the other person might say that they're friendly dogs, and you might say that they're vicious. Your connotative meaning would be quite different, though. The other person probably would have very pleasant feelings, while you might be fearful.

When people engage in arguments, they commonly use emotionally charged language, intentionally or unintentionally, which is one reason arguing can be so unpleasant. If someone uses language that you find emotionally troubling, then you will dislike interacting with that person. On the other hand, if the language you use emotionally upsets someone when you don't intend it to be upsetting, then you will be more reluctant to talk to that person.

Words that members of one cultural group think are harmless may upset members of another group due to their connotative meanings. For example, a lot of people see nothing wrong with saying, "I'm not prejudiced. I treat everyone the same, whether they're white, black, red, yellow, or green." Some African Americans find such statements very objectionable, though, because they feel it puts them in a group with green people, who don't exist, and it makes it sound as though they and their problems are imaginary. Some African Americans, however, don't object to the phrase, just as some women don't object to being called "girls." The point is not whether anyone is right or wrong to become upset by the language but to recognize that they *do* become upset and *why* they do. Once you're aware of it, then you'll have to decide whether to use language in a way that you know bothers other people. On the other hand, some language has positive connotations for people, and arguers may want to decide whether they'll use language that they know is pleasant for their audience or co-arguers.

Keep in mind that people attribute *both* denotative and connotative meanings to words and phrases *at the same time,* and the meanings may be fairly elaborate. What, for instance, does the phrase "cigarette drawer" mean? In the past, when I've asked that question, students have said that it means a drawer containing cigarettes. Such a denotative meaning fairly accurately represents how I use the phrase, but it is quite incomplete. For me, "cigarette drawer" refers to a specific drawer in the kitchen of the house in which I grew up, right next to the door to the backyard. When I think of the cigarette drawer, I also think of the room, the lighting it normally had, the color of the walls, the brand of cigarettes (Raleigh), the smell of tobacco when the drawer was opened, some of the events that took place in the kitchen, and about my father, whose cigarettes were in the drawer. So far, that's a personal denotative meaning. But I also think about my feelings regarding the events that took place in the room and about my father, so I react to the term emotionally. That emotional reaction is my connotative meaning. Even though other people have a denotative meaning for "cigarette drawer," their meanings can't include the same detail or the emotional reaction to the phrase. Other people's definition for the phrase is not incorrect, but it is far from complete, at least regarding my meaning of the phrase.

While the ambiguity of language is something to try to control when you make arguments, it is not something you should expect to eliminate, or expect others to eliminate. It is something to be aware of and try to deal with. Try to recognize when you could be misunderstood because of multiple meanings, and strive to make clear what you do and do not mean. Also, try to recognize when you could misunderstand someone else, and attempt to get a clear and an accurate understanding before evaluating his or her reasoning.

When using language in argumentation or other communication, several ideas must be kept in mind relating to denotative and connotative meanings. First, your meaning may not be the other person's meaning, so don't take language for granted. Always be ready to deal with differences in meanings, instead of assuming that people will always understand you the way you intend, or that the way you understand them is what they meant by the words they say. Second, consider the effect your language may have on the other person, and adjust accordingly. The words you use may be accurate, but they may still be offensive. You may have a constitutional right to use whatever language you want, but that doesn't mean that others can't be offended by the language and be upset with you for using it. When you engage in true argumentation, your purpose should not be to upset people— it's a good idea to learn to think about what you say. Third, recognize that sometimes you'll end up having an argument with someone and won't know why you're arguing until you realize that it's because of differences in meanings. It won't necessarily be anyone's fault that the argument happened, but it might be both people's fault for letting it continue and escalate. Finally, not all interpersonal problems are caused by the use of language. Problems may be more related to other interpersonal and individual needs or incompatible goals. However, the way language is used can make a big difference in resolving or continuing the problems.

Language Is Figurative

Psycholinguist P. N. Johnson-Laird writes, "If natural language had been designed by a logician, idioms would not exist" (viii). Idioms and other figures of speech, such as metaphor and irony, are characteristics of natural language that make it more interesting and lively but can also make what is said harder to interpret. That leads to the fourth characteristic of language: language is figurative, which means that the way people naturally use language is often not literal.

Literal language is language in which the agreed-upon denotative meanings correspond exactly to what the communicator intends to communicate. Scientific writers usually strive to be as literal as possible. Mathematics is probably the purest example of literal language. Figurative language is less exact and more creative. Words are used in ways that if translated by a non-native speaker using a dictionary wouldn't make sense. Most figurative language is quite understandable to competent speakers of the language, however, since speakers are free to create their own figures of speech, figurative language also can lead to misunderstandings.

Several different kinds of figurative language are relevant to argumentation. One of the most common is **metaphor,** which is language that characterizes one subject with terms that literally apply to another subject, making an implicit comparison between the two. The terms do not literally apply to the subject of the statement, but the metaphor leads to a different understanding. When the metaphor works really well, it becomes such an accepted part of the language that people forget that it's a metaphor. For instance, the phrase "love is a rose" is a metaphor that love is something beautiful and desirable but also can be dangerous (thorny) and can die. Literally, love is not a rose but an emotional attachment to another person. The metaphor, though, is a much richer way of characterizing the experience.

In time, we get so used to a metaphor that we accept it without explicitly expressing it, using *underlying metaphors* in our language. George Lakoff and Mark Johnson use the example "argument is war," commonly accepted in American English. When discussing arguments, people commonly use phrases such as "*standing* your ground," "*attacking* his position," "*defending* her claim," and "*winning* the argument." As I write this, I am aware of using an underlying labor metaphor as I discuss language, writing phrases such as "language *uses* metaphors," and "when a metaphor *works* really well." In both cases, and in many others, the metaphors are so common that they no longer seem figurative, until it is pointed out.

An important aspect of metaphors is their "entailments," or the characteristics of the subjects, and the appropriate actions, implied by the metaphors. For example, when people are opposed to something, they often use a health metaphor, saying that the undesired subject is "infecting" the community. When that metaphor is accepted, the entailments include that it will make the community sick. What do we do with something that will make us sick? We try to eliminate it, isolate it from the community. We try to "cleanse" the community of the "disease." Sometimes the people presenting the arguments continue the metaphor and talk about the entailments, but sometimes they just develop the metaphor and let the audience develop the entailments in their own minds. If, for example, love is a rose, what are the entailments for that metaphor?

Idioms are similar to metaphors, but they are phrases that refer to one thing or event in terms of something unrelated, but there is no implied comparison. Once again, a non-native language user who tried to interpret an idiom word for word by using a dictionary to understand the meaning of each individual word would have trouble understanding what is meant. Experienced language users usually understand the meaning though.

An example of an idiom is saying "He kicked the bucket" instead of "He died." Most people understand what is meant by kicking the bucket, but a literal translation has a completely different meaning. Table 10.1 lists a few common idioms used in American English.

New idioms are constantly introduced to the language and are spread by popular culture, sometimes replacing older ones. Those who are unfamiliar with the new idioms may have trouble understanding those who are familiar with them. For instance, an older person may not know what is meant by "He went postal" or "She went off" until the phrases are explained.

Irony is figurative language that says something that is literally the opposite of what is meant. Someone who trips and falls and says "Oh, I am so graceful" is using irony, as is someone reluctantly going to the dentist who says "I'm really looking forward to this." Sarcasm is similar to irony but is directed to someone else and is usually mean-spirited, such as saying to someone who just tripped, "Oh, you are so graceful."

Table 10.1 Common American Idioms

Back to the salt mines	Bow and scrape
Dry behind the ears	The fat is in the fire
Have kittens	Stick in your throat
Take the stump	Be behind the eight ball
Pay cash on the barrelhead	Explode a bombshell
Feel one's oats	Grease someone's palm
Lick someone's boots	Have your ears pinned back
Straw in the wind	Take to the woods
Throw your hat in the ring	Be asleep at the switch
Darken someone's door	Fall down on the job
Grease the wheels	Make the feathers fly
Polish the apple	Trip the light fantastic
The shoe is on the other foot	Pour oil on troubled waters
Take the starch out of someone	Be under the gun
Break the ice	Have your head in the clouds

Adapted from Cristina Cacciari, "The Place of Idioms in a Literal and Metaphorical World," in C. Cacciari and P. Tabossi (eds.), *Idioms: Processing, Structure, and Interpretation* (Hillsdale, NJ: Lawrence Erlbaum, 1993, 53–54), with permission.

Irony is difficult for a non-native speaker to understand, and it also is often difficult for native speakers to recognize. For example, even people who know that their friend has an ironic sense of humor often aren't sure when that friend is saying something truthfully and when he is being ironic or sarcastic.

We often hear people say that something is "totally awesome" when it is something they like. In this media- and advertising-saturated age, we often hear products referred to as "outstanding" or a film as "a masterpiece." Often those phrases are examples of **hyperbole** (pronounced hi-*per*-bo-lee), which is figurative language that uses gross exaggeration to make a point. As with other figurative language, hyperbole happens when the speaker doesn't really mean that the subject was as great or as awful as the words literally mean. Sometimes hyperbole is used to make the discourse more exciting and interesting, and sometimes it is used as an attempt to fool people into thinking that the subject is something that it is not.

You may think, given that figurative language can be difficult to interpret and understand, that you should use only literal language in argumentation. That isn't possible though, since figurative language is so common and well accepted. Discourse also would be quite boring if only literal language were used. Arguers and critical thinkers should be aware of figurative language in argumentation and be prepared to deal with it. You should be ready to recognize metaphors and think critically about how appropriate they are and what their acceptance entails. You should be ready to recognize idioms and irony and how they can create misunderstanding. And you should be ready to recognize hyperbole and not accept unwarranted exaggeration in arguments.

Language Frames Experience

The way we speak about something affects the way we think about it and what we expect from it. That is the idea behind language framing experience. Any experience is rich in things we could say about it, but usually we distill our description to only a few words. The words we use inevitably emphasize some features of the experience and deemphasize, or hide, other features. The framing that language does is similar to the framing done by a motion picture camera. When an event is happening, the camera shows what is in the frame but not what is just outside of it. The camera also focuses on some elements, blurring others. The language we use for a past event frames it in a way that influences what we remember, or what we know about it. The language we use for a future event frames what we expect, and our expectations influence how we experience the event. Sometimes it becomes important to remember that what is said about something is not all that could be said, and that what is left unsaid could be important.

The word choices we make is one way that language frames. A dwelling that is a "run-down shack and an eyesore" to a neighbor might be a "quaint cottage" or a "handyman's delight" to a real estate agent. A shirt that is "colorful" to the person wearing it might be "gaudy" to someone else. Writing that is "precise" to the writer may be "drab and lifeless" to the reader. One group's "terrorist" is another group's "freedom fighter." Referring to tattoos and piercings as "mutilation" creates a very different image than referring to them as "body art." Politicians commonly name legislative acts in a way that frames them in a positive way. When encountering arguments as a critical thinker, it is important to remember that the terms used are often not neutral, thus do not be unduly influenced by them.

Language also can frame experience by the kind of statements being made. Generally, three types of statements might be made about something: reports, inferences, and judgments. **Reports** are statements of fact that are capable of being verified. A statement that is a report may be incorrect, but it is still a report. **Inferences** are statements that are conclusions about something based on information the person making the statement knows. The person making the inference does not *know* if it is correct, she only knows the information upon which it is based. The person making the inference may act as though it is a known fact, but it is still an uncertain conclusion. **Judgments** are statements that express a personal opinion, usually explicitly or implicitly evaluating something. Saying "The temperature is 98 degrees" is a report, because the temperature can be checked. Saying "It's hot" is a judgment, because it's a subjective opinion; what is hot to one person may be comfortable to another. Saying "You must be hot" is an inference, because it calls for a conclusion about the other person based on what is known.

One thing that makes distinguishing between reports, inferences, and judgments tricky is that they all have the same sentence structure. As a result, it is easy to think that an inference or a judgment is a report when you make, or someone else makes, an argument. That becomes important, because an argument that uses reports usually is stronger than one that uses inferences or judgments as evidence.

Language Creates and Separates Communities

Creating and separating communities means that the way language is used helps people think of themselves as sharing membership in a group and helps them think of others as being outside of their group. You can probably think of words and phrases that people in groups you are in use and that people outside of the groups do not use. The vocabulary of different professions not only provides precise meaning but also creates language barriers that say, in effect, "I'm a member of this professional community, and if you don't understand me, you're not." The same is true for language used by cultural groups and different socioeconomic, age, and social groups.

One of the clearest examples of this is the language differences between teenagers and their parents. Both groups may speak English, but the way they speak it can be significantly different. Teenagers create and use slang and jargon that causes a separation between them and their parents. When their parents start using the slang of their teenagers, the teenagers quickly stop using it.

QUESTIONABLE LANGUAGE USE

The general characteristics of language described above should give you some ideas about what to try to do or not do generally when communicating and specifically when arguing. The following, in no particular order, are some types of language use that are, at best, questionable. These are ways of using language that you should avoid to be the most effective, ethical, and credible arguer that you can be. They are also ways of using language that you should be aware of when receiving other people's arguments so that you're not fooled into thinking that they're better than they are. The following are "questionable" uses of language, because none are always wrong. Consider each situation to determine whether the language is somehow a problem.

The first questionable use of language is **weasel words,** or using language to make it appear as though more is being claimed than is literally said. A fairly typical advertisement might say, "The Amazing Grapefruit Diet Pill *can help* you lose *up to* 10 pounds a week!!!" The italicized words are the weasel words in that sentence. To say the pills "can help" you is the same as saying they might, or might not, help you. So if you don't lose weight, you can't blame the diet pills, because the advertisers only claim that they *can* help, not that they *will*. When they say you could lose "up to" ten pounds a week, you should realize that the lower end of that range is zero pounds a week. So while people looking for a way to lose weight could easily read more into the ad, and the advertisers certainly want them to, the advertisement literally says, "You may, or may not, lose weight at the same time that you use the Amazing Grapefruit Diet Pill."

When encountering arguments that you think use weasel words, it is important to consider them in context and be fair. Sometimes people use similar language when they try to be precise and make a conscious attempt to *not* mislead anyone into thinking that they're making absolute statements. So don't think that people are misusing language just because their claims are qualified. For example, when asking for clarification on assignments, students often ask, "*Exactly* what do you want?" A teacher can't say *exactly* what she wants, because most assignments can be done correctly several different ways. If she did say *exactly* what she wants, then the student would turn in the teacher's work instead of his or her own, and that's exactly what the teacher does not want. So the teacher says you "might" do a variety of things. In such cases, "might" isn't a weasel word, because you do have many options, and the teacher isn't being vague to trick you. Medical research reports are another example, because they often say that findings *may* lead to a cure for a disease, because the researchers can't yet be sure what the outcome will be. They are not, in that case, using weasel words, because they are trying to avoid appearing to claim more than the research supports. You can probably think of other examples when arguers legitimately qualify their statements, thus they do not really try to trick others.

A second questionable use of language is **jargon,** or using language that can only be understood by experts in the field or members of a particular group to hide meaning or intimidate others. For instance, if you heard somebody say, "You must comprehend the ontological and axiological ramifications of this theory before you can even consider the epistemological effects," then you would likely wonder what he meant. If he said it to make you appear ignorant, then that would be using jargon in a questionable manner. In some contexts, where listeners could be expected to understand that language, there would be no problem. In other contexts, where most listeners couldn't reasonably be expected to understand that language, the speaker may be more interested in impressing everyone with his intelligence and vocabulary than in making sense and presenting a clear argument. While the use of an expanded vocabulary can make communication more precise, some people use jargon as a way to make other arguers or listeners feel inferior and stop questioning, or as a way to make it seem as though they have stronger evidence or reasoning than they really do.

Puffery, the third questionable use of language, occurs when people use language to overinflate their claims, to "puff up" what they say to make it sound more important than it really is. For instance, I once heard someone on television say, "Current advertising practices will be *disastrous* for this country. It is the *worst thing to happen* to this nation *in history.*" While it isn't difficult to think of problems with advertising, it also isn't difficult to think of some historical events that make current advertising practices seem quite benign. A couple of world wars, a few major economic depressions, a civil war, slavery, and the death of a significant portion of the indigenous population come to mind fairly easily. When people's ideas must compete for attention with all of the other ideas out there, and when individuals try to get on talk shows to get their books sold, they may feel a need to resort to puffery to be perceived as important. Something that could cause some inconvenience isn't very newsworthy; something that is potentially catastrophic will get attention. That doesn't mean that you should simply accept such statements as being untrue, however. If there is enough support to show that the

Figure 10.1 Jargon can be used to make it seem as though something is more important than it really is.

Dilbert reprinted by permission of United Media Syndicate, Inc.

inflated language is justified, then there's no real problem, but if that support is lacking, then you would be wise to remain skeptical.

Sometimes when people can't really make sound arguments themselves, they'll resort to **asking questions to replace statements,** which is the fourth questionable use of language. This technique usually seems to work when the tone of the question implies what the answer *should* be, and accepting that answer implies that there is support that doesn't exist.

For example, when I was in college, I sold Bible books door to door in southern Missouri one summer. The company I worked for taught us all a standard sales pitch and ways to handle people who were reluctant to buy. We were taught to start off the presentation by asking, "The Bible's really a wonderful book, isn't it? Wouldn't you like to be able to understand your Bible better?" Almost everyone would reply yes to both questions, especially in that part of the country. Later on, if they didn't want to buy, we were supposed to ask, "Do you see how buying this book would really help your children? You do want to help your children, don't you?" Once again, few people would say anything but yes. The answers to all of the questions were strongly implied, and only very strong-willed people would give an unexpected answer. At the same time, when people gave the expected answer, we wouldn't have to provide support for the idea that buying these books really would help the children. Later on, it was harder for the potential customers to say that they didn't want to buy the books, since they said all along that the books would be a good idea.

It's been a long time since I sold Bible books, but I've heard others use those kinds of questions, both as a conscious strategy in sales and as a habit in interpersonal arguments. Keep in mind that sometimes questions are used to sincerely elicit responses, and that's usually a good idea. In addition, some people come from backgrounds where it is considered rude to come right out and state arguments, so asking questions is a more polite method of engaging in argumentation. It's only when someone tries to escape her burden of proof that using questions to replace statements becomes a problem.

Another common characteristic of language use that can lead to problems is **bipolar thinking,** which has nothing to do with a mental disorder and occurs when we use language in a way that leads people to think in either-or dichotomies instead of recognizing a continuum of choices or a range of options. For instance, a neo-Nazi on a television talk show once said, "The Aryan race is supreme, and if you're not working for the supremacy of the race, you're a race traitor." The way he phrased his statement allowed for only two options—when a critical thinker would be able to identify other possibilities and question the first part of his statement. (By the way, the only thing bipolar thinking has in common with "bipolar disorder" is a word. They're completely different concepts.)

The English language has a lot of bipolar extremes that are even more common than the example above. Good/bad, strong/weak, beautiful/ugly, light/dark, healthy/unhealthy, and ethical/unethical are only a few. Usually an arguer doesn't have to explicitly use both ends of the continuum; saying that one idea is good is enough for listeners to infer that all opposing ideas are bad, or saying that a proposal is strong implies that other ideas on the subject are weak. When you stop to think about it, though, just because one idea is good doesn't mean that a competing idea also cannot be good, and just because one proposal is strong, doesn't mean that another proposal also cannot be strong.

The sixth questionable use of language is **sloganeering,** which happens when an arguer uses catchphrases to substitute for the content of an argument. Sometimes people call this "bumper sticker arguing," and it's quite popular in advertising and political campaigns. For instance, when Ronald Reagan ran for president, his campaign used slogans such as "Go ahead, make my day," "There you go again," and "Tax and spend." More recently, the complex issue of appropriate ways to lessen crime was reduced to "Three strikes, you're out." Slogans serve a purpose as memorable phrases that sum up arguments. Their intent, though, should not be to replace thorough reasoning and argumentation about the issues. When issues are reduced to little more than slogans, a critical thinker should question whether there's enough information on which to base a decision.

SUGGESTED LANGUAGE USE

There are also uses of language that promote clearer thinking and better argumentation. The first is to use the *active voice* whenever you can. When you do this, you simply use sentence structure that says "Someone *did* something" instead of "something *was done* by someone." For instance, saying "A good argument was made in your speech" uses the passive voice. You could turn that into the active voice by saying "You made a good argument in your speech." The difference may seem slight, but the active voice is more direct and clear.

A second suggestion is to use *concrete language* as much as you can. Earlier you read about the difference between abstract and concrete language, so you should realize that you make your ideas more clear when you use concrete terms, which helps you think through your ideas to clarify them and also helps others better understand your ideas.

You can make your arguments stronger as well by using *declarative statements* when you speak or write. When doing so you use relatively short sentences that come right to the point. Don't ramble. (Did you notice that was a declarative statement?) People have gotten so used to beating around the bush so they don't offend anyone, or so they don't say anything that can be contradicted, that they too often end up saying things that are quite confusing.

Students often won't directly state a claim and present evidence when they write papers and deliver speeches, perhaps because they think a less direct style is preferable, don't really know what they're talking about, don't know how to clearly say what they mean, or aren't willing to take a stand. The problem is more significant in oral communication, because by the time the speaker finishes the sentence, audience members can't remember what the speaker started with. Often people aren't direct because they don't want to say something with which someone else might disagree but that still makes their claims and reasoning unclear.

Using declarative statements doesn't mean that all of your statements need to be short. After you state a claim, you can explain what you do or don't mean and what the exceptions to your claim might be, but avoid doing all of that in the same sentence.

Another suggested use of language is to use **"I statements"** in your discourse to distinguish your opinions from claims or facts. For instance, instead of saying, "*The Simpsons* is the best show on television," you would say, "I think *The Simpsons* is the best show on television." I statements are good to use, especially in conversational argument, when making statements of judgment, and when reporting on your perceptions of an event. Others generally accept reports of your opinions or perceptions, but they may dispute the same statements if you seem to mean them as incontrovertible facts. Such disputes can be disturbing, because it can appear that you are attacked for your opinions or perceptions. You realize the underlying intent of your statements, while the other person does not. Using I statements can diffuse unnecessary arguments before they begin.

The final suggested use of language in argumentation is to simply *strive for clarity*. Try to say or write everything as clearly as you can. Think from your audience's point of view rather than just from your own. Do not merely express yourself in whatever way your ideas come easiest, but consider what your audience does and does not know about your subject. Ask yourself what you need to tell the audience first to make later ideas more clear. While planning your communication, make sure that your proposition is stated early enough so your listeners or readers know what you're trying to prove. Explain the connection of your evidence to your claims. While clarity doesn't guarantee that your arguments will be correct, or that they will convince your audience, it does give you a better chance of communicating your intended message.

These suggested uses of language also apply when evaluating other people's arguments. If the argument is unclear to the audience for which it was intended, then it is legitimate to consider the argument weaker than one that is clear.

FALLACIES ASSOCIATED WITH LANGUAGE

The following fallacies often arise in arguments because of the way people use language. Remember, if you notice language use that you think is fallacious, then that is an indication that you should think further about the argument, not that there is necessarily something wrong with it or that the conclusion is necessarily false.

EQUIVOCATION—changing the meaning of a word or phrase from one part of the argument to another.

Many words in our language have more than one meaning, and as competent language users, we regularly determine which meaning applies in a particular context. Sometimes people will shift from one meaning to another during an argument, either accidentally or on purpose, and treat a statement that is acceptable in one sense as acceptable in a different sense.

The following explanation of why fire engines should be red is an example of several instances of equivocation. It's not a real argument, and there are other problems in the reasoning, but it illustrates how equivocation can work.

> To understand why fire engines are red we start with the fact that there are twelve inches in a ruler. It is a fact that Queen Elizabeth was a ruler. Queen Elizabeth was also a ship. Ships sail in the ocean. Fish swim in the ocean. Fish have fins. The Finns fought the Russians. The Russians are (or were) reds. And fire engines should be red because they go rushin' to fires.

In the example, you can see that equivocation can happen when a term has multiple meanings (such as "ruler"), and when there are homonyms involved (such as "fins" and "Finns").

In an argument made by one person, the meaning of terms may change as the argument is made. In an argument between two people, one arguer may believe that a meaning is appropriate, while the other arguer may believe that another meaning is, so confusion may result.

LOADED LANGUAGE—using emotionally charged language to create an impression about the subject of a claim without making an argument that the language fits the subject.

When people engage in loaded language, they use terms that are either positive or negative to create an emotional reaction to a subject. Protesters may be referred to as "terrorists" or "filthy hippies," corporate executives as "greedy" or "murderers," politicians as "liars" and "bureaucrats," and liberals as "traitors" who "hate America." The intent is to taint the subject of the argument by name-calling, so the recipient of the argument is more likely to accept other negative claims about the subject without considering the strength of the evidence for those claims.

Loaded language does not have to be about people. It can involve acts or objects as well. If we don't like the way someone drives, then we might say his driving is "reckless" or "aggressive." A billboard may be called an "eyesore."

Loaded language also can be positive. Those who don't want to cut down a tree call it "majestic," for example.

Discourse would be quite drab if loaded language were never used, so don't expect it to be missing entirely. But when you do encounter it, consider how it affects the argument. Step back from the emotional thrust, and ask what the evidence is for the claim.

QUESTION-BEGGING EPITHETS—a form of loaded language that uses an emotionally charged restatement of the claim, often in the form of name-calling, in place of support for the claim.

The fallacy of question-begging epithets is a combination of begging the question and loaded language. It begs the question by restating the claim as support for the claim, and it uses loaded language by the way the claim is restated.

For example, if someone said a movie they saw was bad, a friend might ask what was wrong with it. If the reply is, "It sucked!" then you have a question-begging epithet.

AMPHIBOLY (unclearness, misusing ambiguity, ambiguity)—using language and punctuation in a way that can have multiple interpretations, so it's not really clear what is meant.

Amphiboly is a fallacy not seen very often in arguments, but it can be a source of confusion that leads to an argument or makes an argument hard to follow. Amphiboly also can be used to trick someone into agreeing to a claim because they think it means something else.

For example, someone is writing a letter of recommendation and doesn't want to come right out and say that the person is a poor employee. To get around the problem, the individual writing the recommendation might write, "To say he did a fine job doesn't come close to describing this employee." That statement could mean either that the employee greatly exceeded expectations or failed to meet expectations.

This is a case of amphiboly, but it isn't an example of the *fallacy* of amphiboly, because it isn't in the context of an argument. The following example is in the context of an argument, and it does illustrate how the fallacy can fit into everyday life. It's a letter to the editor of a college newspaper, a response to an earlier article written by a reporter, Austin, regarding a resolution made at a student government meeting. The letter states:

> Austin writes, "The resolution was conceived shortly after the Sept. 11 attacks by the Student Environmental Action Coalition and sponsored by Brian Godwin and Charles Roehr."
>
> The Student Environmental Action Coalition did not commit the attacks on Sept. 11. And as far as I know, Brian Godwin and Charles Roehr did not sponsor them.

Note how the quoted sentence could be taken to have two different meanings because of the way it was written. The letter writer chose the meaning that was easiest to respond to in order to make his opponent appear weaker.

FIGURE OF SPEECH—Confusing figurative language with literal language.

Like the fallacy of amphiboly, the figure of speech fallacy isn't seen very often within arguments$_1$, because the fallacy is dependent on someone failing to understand what is meant. Such a failure may lead to confusion among those receiving the message, an argument because of the misunderstanding, or an unintended admission when people are engaged in a question-and-answer type of argumentation, but it is rarely a real problem in modern argumentation.

An example of the confusion generated by a figure of speech would be a misunderstanding over the meaning of "bad." Some people use the word "bad" figuratively, to mean "good," and others, who are unfamiliar with that meaning, take it to mean "bad," and then act accordingly, when they are expected to act as though "bad" means "good." It's fairly easy to see why that would lead to a misunderstanding, and how an argument might arise from that misunderstanding, but it's harder to think of cases where such confusion would help someone make an argument that shouldn't be accepted.

SPECIAL PLEADING—referring to an act committed by an opponent in negative terms, while referring to the same act committed by the arguer or supporters in favorable terms.

The language we use to refer to someone, something, or some act makes a difference in how we think of the referent. By carefully choosing our wording, we are able to make ourselves and the people we like seem good and noble and people we don't like seem bad, even when there's no real difference in the things we and they do.

An example of special pleading would be to say that someone else who doesn't tell the entire truth is a liar, but when you don't tell the entire truth, you're being tactful. Or when someone else says something to hurt someone else's feelings, he is being rude, but when you do the same thing, you're being honest.

Special pleading seems especially prevalent in political campaigns. Any candidate with a record in office has voted in ways that some people will not like. For example, one candidate may say that her vote took a stand against special-interest groups, while her opponent's votes, which were the same, are out of step with his constituents.

HYPOSTATIZATION (reification)—treating something that exists only as a concept as though it were a tangible object.

The modern world in which we live is populated by many entities that are legal fictions, or labels with no specific referent. Sometimes we talk about such fictions as though they are real, and when we do so, we may commit the fallacy of hypostatization.

For example, we may talk about "the government" doing something, as though we could go out and point at the government and watch it do things. In reality, people do things, not "the government." They may do what they do with the authority of the government, and in the name of the government, but it is still people acting, not "the government." We talk about "society," "the patriarchy," and a variety of other concepts as though they are physical entities that exist, when in reality they aren't. We also speak of abstract terms such as *justice* and *democracy* as though they are concrete.

The fallacy of hypostatization reminds us that sometimes the language we use is a shortened version of what we really mean. When we say "the government" did something, we are really thinking "people who are working in the name of the government" did something. That's pretty unwieldy, so we shorten it to "the government." There's no harm in that, as long as we remember that that is what we're doing. The same is true of abstract concepts. Some people justify an action because "love" made them do it, forgetting that love is not a concrete entity that "makes" anyone do anything. Realizing that takes some of the romance out of love, but it also avoids excusing actions for which that the individual should be responsible.

STYLE OVER SUBSTANCE—reasoning that ideas presented in an appealing manner are correct, regardless of the content.

People who are able to present their ideas in a confident, an entertaining, and an enthusiastic way have an advantage over those who aren't able, or willing, to generate such stylish messages. Many people won't pay attention if a message isn't highly interesting, and many people base their evaluation of the quality of an argument on how well it was presented. When they do so, they place style over substance, instead of judging the argument on the basis of how well the claim is supported by evidence and reasoning. Arguers who take advantage of style to hide weaknesses in their arguments commit the fallacy in their arguing.

Style over substance is included with fallacies associated with language, because one way of committing the fallacy is to use entertaining or powerful language to gain agreement. Swaying opinion by style instead of substance is not limited to the language used, however. The style in question can be physical style, such as attributing correct ideas to people who are physically appealing or well dressed. The style involved in the fallacy doesn't have to be positively received style either. Someone may try to disparage an idea by presenting it in a negative style and attributing that style to those in favor of the idea.

This fallacy does not mean that style is irrelevant to argumentation. Good arguments will have both style *and* substance, so strong reasoning is presented in a way that gets people to pay attention. It's only when style replaces strong reasoning, or hides poor reasoning, that the fallacy of style over substance occurs.

SUMMARY

Language is important to argumentation and critical thinking, because we use the symbol system of language to construct, and to think about, arguments. People often take language for granted and think of it as a naturally occurring part of existence. They don't realize that the symbols used in any language are arbitrary, that language is imprecise, that language is naturally ambiguous, that much of language is figurative instead of literal, that the language we use affects our interpretations of what we experience, and that language can create or separate communities.

Language can be used in a questionable manner in several ways when engaging in argumentation. The use of weasel words, jargon, puffery, replacing statements with questions, bipolar thinking, and sloganeering can all make discourse less productive. On the other hand, using the active voice, concrete language, and declarative sentences and striving for clarity are ways to use language to better express ideas.

KEY CONCEPTS

abstract language   language that is more vague or broad in its meaning, so it is harder to tell what is meant.

asking questions to replace statements   a questionable use of language in which an arguer asks questions to get the audience to supply evidence instead of providing the evidence for a claim.

bipolar thinking   a questionable use of language that uses language in a way that leads people to think in either-or dichotomies instead of

recognizing a continuum of choices or a range of options.

bypassing   a communication problem that happens when two people think that they are talking about the same thing but really are not.

concrete language   language that is more specific in what it refers to, so it is easier to tell what is meant.

connotative meanings   the personal, emotional reactions that individuals associate with words and phrases.

denotative meanings dictionary-like meanings that people have for words and phrases.

hyperbole figurative language that uses gross exaggeration to make a point.

idioms language that uses phrases that refer to one thing or event in terms of something unrelated, with no implied comparison between the two.

inferences statements that are conclusions about something based on information that the person making the statement knows.

irony using language that says something that is literally the opposite of what is meant.

I statements statements that identify ideas as personal opinions or perceptions rather than as undisputed facts or claims needing support.

jargon a questionable use of language that uses language that can only be understood by experts in the field or members of a particular group to hide meaning or intimidate others.

judgments statements that express a personal opinion, usually explicitly or implicitly evaluating something.

language creates and separates communities a characteristic of language that means that the way language is used helps people think of themselves as sharing membership in a group and helps them think of others as being outside of their group.

language frames experience a characteristic of language that means that the way we talk about things affects the way we think about them and what we expect.

language is ambiguous a characteristic of language that means that there are often multiple possible interpretations of utterances.

language is figurative a characteristic of language that means that the way people naturally use language is often not literal.

language is imprecise a characteristic of language that means that people often use language that is not very specific when more specific language is available.

metaphor language that characterizes one subject with terms that literally apply to another subject, making an implicit comparison between the two.

puffery a questionable use of language in which a claim is made to sound more important than it really is.

reports statements of fact that are capable of being verified.

sloganeering a questionable use of language that happens when an arguer uses catchphrases to substitute for the content of an argument.

symbol something that a group of language users agrees stands for something else.

symbols are arbitrary the sounds and shapes that groups of people agree stand for meanings have no inherent connection to the things and concepts for which they stand.

weasel words a questionable use of language that uses language to make it appear as though more is being claimed than literally is.

THINGS TO THINK ABOUT

1. What are two idioms that you are familiar with that other people might not understand? What does each idiom mean?

2. What is an example of a word or phrase that would have a connotative meaning that is different from the denotative meaning? In what ways are the meanings different?

3. Think of an example of weasel words or puffery. What makes some of the language weasel words or puffery?

4. Think of an example of jargon. How could you change it so someone unfamiliar with the jargon could understand it?

5. Think of a statement that is an example of a report about a significant subject. Then think of a statement that would be an inference about the same subject, and another that would be a judgment about that subject.

6. Think of a disagreement that you've had that was influenced by the use of language. Which principles of language are illustrated by your experience?

7. Find an example of a written argument. Evaluate the quality of the use of language using the ideas in this chapter.

8. Think of a time when your reasoning, or the reasoning of someone else, committed one of the fallacies from this chapter. What made the reasoning fallacious?

TUTORIAL LINK

Go to *http://communication.wadsworth.com/verlinden* and complete the tutorials for the Language and Informal Fallacies, Set #5.

11

✳

Refutation

When there is argumentation, usually there will be two sides to the issue. Whether the situation involves two friends arguing over the quality of a film, spouses discussing how to spend a tax refund, opposing counsels in a legal trial, scientists arguing about what caused the extinction of the dinosaurs, politicians arguing over the best policy to address poverty, environmentalists and loggers arguing over forest management practices, or any of thousands of other propositions, each side not only makes its own argument in favor of its position, but also makes arguments denying the others side's argument.

Refutation is the act of responding to the other person's argument, denying what she said. After the advocate in favor of the proposition presents her argument, the opponent tries to refute it by casting doubt on what she said and making independent arguments against her proposition. Then the original advocate responds by reaffirming the initial arguments and refuting the independent arguments against it. **Direct refutation** directly contradicts what was said. **Indirect refutation** tries to deny the proposition, without speaking directly to what the other advocate said.

Chapter 8 already discussed some general ideas for refutation. For instance, in policy argumentation, when the person opposed to the proposition argues that there is no problem, that whatever problem there is isn't significant, that the cause has been misidentified, or that what the advocate said about solvency and advantages is wrong, that is all direct refutation. When the opponent argues for minor repairs in the *status quo* or for independent reasons why the plan won't solve the problem, won't work, or will create disadvantages that outweigh any advantages, that is all indirect refutation. When propositions of fact or value are argued, direct refutation would involve disputing the definitions, arguing that there is a more important value to use for judgment, or that the criteria are flawed, don't apply to the subject, or the application of criteria to the issue is incorrect. Indirect argumentation would involve presenting independent reasons to reject the proposition.

Refutation is an important part of the process of argumentation, and not just to try to win arguments. Refutation helps to test ideas, to ensure that flaws are detected, and to come to the best decisions. Some people do not like to engage in refutation, because they feel that they're attacking the other person, or they feel that the other person is attacking them. Refutation done well, however, tests ideas and does not attack people.

Knowledge of refutation can help your own reasoning, either prior to presenting your argument or when you make a decision on your own. It helps you prepare for arguments by predicting what others might say against your position. It also helps you examine your own thinking by considering ideas that you probably wouldn't otherwise think of because you're in favor of your conclusion.

Knowledge of refutation also is important in critical thinking. First, it helps you understand what another arguer does by helping you recognize arguments opposing a proposition. Second, it helps you evaluate refutational arguments by better understanding what should go into refutation. Finally, it helps you evaluate arguments in favor of a proposition by making you aware of what could be said in response. Knowledge of refutation not only helps you recognize when arguments are weak but also helps you better recognize strong arguments.

When responding to another person's arguments, you should use both direct and indirect refutation. The following pages will describe some of these basic methods of refuting arguments to both reinforce your position and avoid attacking the other person. You won't always be able to use all of the methods, so think of them as a menu of options from which you may choose. This chapter

- explains direct refutation.
- explains indirect refutation.
- provides suggestions for doing refutation.
- describes how to analyze someone else's refutation.
- identifies fallacies that can be associated with refutation.

DIRECT REFUTATION

When you do direct refutation, you attempt to show that the advocate's arguments inadequately support his or her proposition. You do that by attempting to respond to every claim the advocate made to support the proposition. If you can't object to every claim, respond to as many as you can and explain why the others don't matter. Remember, when you're the advocate in favor of a proposition, you will also refute claims made by those opposed to the proposition, so both sides in a controversy use techniques of direct refutation. Some choices that you have to refute claims follow.

First, you could argue that any claim is **not relevant** to the proposition. When you make this argument, you say that no matter how true the claim or evidence is, it has no bearing on the proposition. If you were arguing with someone advocating handgun control, for example, and he claimed the number of handgun sales increases each year, then you might say that that's not relevant, because simply buying or selling handguns doesn't mean anything by itself. If you're sensitive to the fact that sometimes things are said in arguments that aren't relevant, you might be surprised at how much is said in everyday argumentation that isn't really relevant to what people are trying to prove. As a critical thinker, it's good to become more sensitive to what is relevant and what is not. This is where a good knowledge of fallacies can be very helpful, because most of the fallacies identify ways in which grounds are not relevant to the claim.

Second, you could argue that the claim is **not proven.** Remember, each advocate has a burden of proof for each claim, and, if that claim isn't proven then a critical thinker shouldn't consider it when judging the proposition. If some of the advocate's claims aren't considered, the entire argument becomes much weaker. There are three ways that you can argue a claim isn't proven. First, you can show that the claim is just an *assertion,* which means that no evidence was presented for the claim. If the advocate is a recognized expert on the subject, then asserting claims may be enough, but you can challenge the experts. For example, in an argument about health care, a politician may assert the number of people who don't have health insurance. While he might have expertise because of the committees he serves on, the source of his numbers is still important, and you could respond to him by pointing out his assertion.

You also could show that a claim is not proven by arguing that the evidence is simply *not relevant* to the claim. If you listen carefully, you'll find that people often make claims and present evidence that you can't deny, but when you think about it, the evidence does not support the claims. For example, a friend may argue that *Titanic* is the best film ever made, and he may support that claim with evidence that it made more money than any other film. You could admit that his evidence is correct but refute him by arguing that ticket sales are not a relevant measure of film quality.

A final way to show that a claim hasn't been proven is to point out that the evidence supporting the claim comes from an *inadequate source.* Evidence was discussed earlier, and several tests of evidence were explained. Your refutation could argue that evidence that fails any of the tests should not be considered as support.

A third method to directly refute specific claims is to argue that the claim is **not true.** This is usually the strongest form of direct refutation and does the most to weaken the advocate's argument. To make this argument, present evidence that clearly contradicts the claim or the evidence used in support of it, and be sure to use good evidence. For example, an advocate for a proposition about global warming might claim that particular computer models are good to predict global warming. The opponent might present evidence that says those computer models that predicted global warming would already have occurred, and it hasn't, so those models are not good predictors. To sustain her argument, the advocate would then need to bring in evidence that shows that those models have been accurate, or that the objection itself isn't relevant. The more often you can directly contradict the accuracy of the other arguer's claims with high-quality evidence of your own, the weaker those claims will be.

The fourth way to directly refute a claim would be to **turn arguments** against the other arguer, which uses the arguer's own evidence, reasoning, or claim against him. To turn an argument, you accept what the arguer said as being correct but show how it actually argues against his position rather than for it. For example, I once saw a student deliver a speech arguing that athletic departments do not provide equal treatment to women athletes, in violation of Title IX. When the departments are sued, the student said, they fight the lawsuits with the support of the universities and are slow to comply, even when ordered by the courts to do so. The plan she advocated was for students and faculty to tell the athletic departments at their schools to be more fair. Considering that this student had documented how difficult it is to get athletic departments to comply with federal law and court orders, her own evidence seemed to argue against the adequacy of her proposed solution. An opponent could argue that her own evidence proves that her plan will not solve the problem and should be rejected.

Another time, I saw a college debate team argue that the government of Sudan was brutally persecuting a minority group, killing thousands of unarmed women, children, and men. Their plan was for the United Nations to send women into the country to conduct peace conferences. Given the brutality documented by those debaters, it was hard to see why that government would be influenced by uninvited peace conferences. Their own evidence for harm could be turned against them to show that the plan would not solve the problem.

A final way to directly argue against a specific claim would be to **point out contradictions** with other claims. To do this, read, or listen to, the entire argument, noticing if there are claims or evidence that contradict each other. If so, point out the contradiction and the fact that both claims cannot be true. Accepting either would require rejecting the other, and rejecting either would call for rejecting the entire argument. While this method can be effective if the person making the decision is willing to think critically, it often does not change people's minds very well in everyday argument, because many people feel that it just picks on minor details. To be effective, the contradictions ought to be fairly major.

INDIRECT REFUTATION

In addition to the elements of indirect refutation, already discussed in Chapter 8, five main approaches can be used to indirectly refute an advocate's proposition. Depending on the argument refuted, you may use multiple methods or none of them.

Figure 11.1 It can be difficult to respond to contradictions when they're pointed out.

Dilbert reprinted by permission of United Media Syndicate, Inc.

First, you could argue that the other's argument is **not *prima facie,*** which was explained in Chapter 8. This type of refutation says that the advocate didn't meet his burden of proof and didn't present a *prima facie* case, and it shows how he failed. You would argue that regardless of what the advocate did say, he left out enough important lines of reasoning that the proposition shouldn't be accepted. For instance, if it is a proposition of fact, you could argue that the advocate hasn't presented any way to determine if the fact is true (that is, she hasn't established the criteria), so a reasonable person can't accept the proposition. If it's a policy proposition, you might argue that since the advocate hasn't presented any plan, we have no idea if what she suggests can be done, so we have no idea if the problem can be solved or not, thus a reasonable person can't accept the proposition. This type of argument focuses on the other person's deficiencies in argumentation and can weaken his position. However, by itself, lay audiences generally perceive it to be a weak defense, because they aren't often aware of what constitutes a *prima facie* case.

In some contexts, such as educational debate and court trials, the advocate of a proposition has to present a *prima facie* case by a certain point in the proceedings, so this method of refutation can be effective in those contexts if the advocate's case is clearly not *prima facie.* In other contexts, though, when the inadequacies of an argument are pointed out, the advocate has the opportunity to add them, so this form of refutation is less effective for defeating the argument. It is still valuable, though, for arriving at better decisions, because it points out the need to consider additional issues. Also, when argumentation is considered as a means to determine truth, examining whether an argument is *prima facie* helps identify the underlying assumptions that the argument relies upon.

The second way to indirectly refute an argument is to argue that what the advocate said is **nonpropositional.** A nonpropositional argument says that the advocate's argument doesn't really support the proposition but supports something that is slightly different from the proposition. During informal argumentation, this usually isn't that important, because the proposition normally isn't explicitly stated, and people generally let it shift a little during the argument. But in judicial, legislative, and educational argumentation, the proposition is a more important issue. In judicial argumentation, for example, the prosecution has the responsibility to prove that the defendant committed the crime he is accused of, not that he just did something people don't like. In legislative argumentation, advocates for policy change have the responsibility to argue that a particular law should be passed, although they may shift somewhat if they believe that amendments improve the law. And, in educational argumentation, students have the responsibility to stick to the point and to not go off on tangents. In academic debate, this idea is referred to as "topicality," because it argues that the affirmative side is not really arguing about the topic agreed upon. One ability that skillful arguers and critical thinkers develop is to really listen to what is being argued and to determine whether it actually supports the proposition as stated.

There are two specific ways to argue nonpropositionality. First, you could say that the advocate's argument is *nontopical,* which means that she's talking about something entirely different from the proposition. For example, if a proposition calls for more control of handguns, but the advocate argues for control of all "firearms," then you could argue that your opponent is nontopical, because the evidence and plan are not specific to handguns. When arguing policy propositions, you might argue that the advocate's plan is subtopical, which is a particular way to be nontopical. When an argument is subtopical, the plan doesn't do everything that the proposition calls for, so it doesn't really support the proposition. For example, a husband may propose that the family finances be used to buy a new SUV and put away money for their child's education. If his plan for budgeting the family's money only pays for the SUV, then his wife could argue that it doesn't do everything his proposition calls for, and thus should be rejected.

Second, you can say that the advocate's argument is *extratopical,* which means that she's going beyond the proposition to justify the plan. For example, if her proposition calls for government control of handguns, and her plan not only calls for control of handguns but for more severe prison sentences for everyone convicted of a violent crime, then she is going beyond the proposition. For the proposition to be upheld, as stated, you can't add anything to the plan to create advantages. If you add to the proposition, you really argue for a different proposition and don't fulfill your burden of proof. The idea is, if you need to go beyond the proposition to gain advantages, then those advantages may only be coming from the additions to the proposition, not from implementing the proposition itself. While nontopicality can be argued for any type of proposition, extratopicality generally is limited to propositions of policy, since the other types of propositions don't involve plans. Remember, though, topicality requirements usually are only effective in formal argumentative situations such as academic debate and courts of law. In everyday argument, the actual proposition may be so vague that it is hard to say if someone's argument is nontopical, subtopical, extratopical, or topical. However, when you recognize that an argument is nonproposiitonal, you can question it, which may lead to revising the proposition, and that helps lead to improved decisions.

The third way to indirectly refute is to argue in favor of the **counterproposition.** This involves creating arguments supporting the position that the proposition is *not* true. Regardless of what the advocate says, you argue against the proposition. Sometimes you find that some of your counterpropositional arguments directly refute the advocate's argument. If so, then present them as direct refutation. More likely, though, your counterarguments raise issues that the advocate didn't want to address at all. In policy arguments, independent solvency arguments and disadvantages would argue against the proposition without directly refuting what the advocate said.

For instance, I've seen several advertisements for methods of Internet access. At first, the ads only touted the benefits of DSL or cable access. Then, some of the DSL ads argued that cable is only worthwhile if you want to use the Internet in the middle of the night, and the cable ads argued that DSL isn't available to most customers. Neither group wanted the shortcomings of its system brought up, so neither mentioned them. When the other company presented those shortcomings, it was indirect refutation. In this case, the ads made counterpropositional arguments, because the original propositions were, "Buy our type of Internet access." In the subsequent ads, the unstated claims were, "Don't buy the other type of Internet access."

When you present counterpropositional arguments, point out how they're related to the advocate's arguments to make your arguments more effective. Explain how your arguments make a better case against the proposition than the advocate's arguments make in favor of the proposition. If you don't explicitly explain how your refutation overcomes the advocate's arguments, then it may seem as though you're talking about two different propositions. If that happens, it will appear that you failed to assume your burden of refutation. So in a policy argument, take the time to explain that the disadvantages that the plan will create outweigh the advantages claimed. For a value proposition, argue that by using the advocate's own value or criteria, the proposition isn't true. And in arguments over propositions of fact, present evidence and reasoning that the proposition probably isn't true. Those are only three possibilities, of course, and there are many other ways you can argue counterpropositionally.

Making counterpropositional arguments can be very important when trying to convince others that your position is the best. Without them, all you can do is find fault with the advocate's arguments. Technically, that should be enough, because the advocate has the burden or proof, and that burden is not fulfilled if there are flaws in the reasoning. Many listeners, however, will be bothered if they perceive that you are only pointing out flaws, so you should have your own position to advocate.

The fourth method of indirect refutation is to **question underlying assumptions** in the opponent's case. For example, if someone presented an argument in favor of a plan to increase the wages of middle-class workers in the United States, then an opposing arguer might question the underlying assumption that greater wealth is necessarily good for individuals or for society. Questioning assumptions can lead to arguments either denying a value or identifying the disadvantages of a policy.

A final method of doing indirect refutation in a policy argument would be to present minor repairs or a counterplan, as described in Chapter 8.

DOING REFUTATION

The context in which you refute arguments will make a difference in how you approach it. If you're having a friendly conversation with someone, then the expectations for each of you will be less than if you're involved in a formal situation and you're both expected to be well prepared. Some general guidelines follow for engaging in refutation.

First, keep in mind the purpose of engaging in the argument and the place that refutation has in achieving that purpose. If you think of the process of argumentation as doing the best you can to determine the truth of an issue, then you can see that refutation is an important part of that process. Refutation helps test ideas by exposing them to scrutiny, and, if they deserve support, refutation will help show that the support is deserved. On the other hand, if they do not deserve support, then refutation will expose their weaknesses. Refutation should not be thought of as an opportunity to overwhelm or embarrass someone with whom you disagree.

Second, be aware that refutation begins in the preparation process, particularly for formal arguments. When you have a chance to prepare for an argument, while you do research, look for arguments your opponent might use, take notes on them, and look for evidence against them. Later, as you're thinking about what you'll do in your oral or written presentation, formulate mini-arguments that respond to the various arguments you expect. Then when your opponent presents arguments, you are prepared to respond to them instead of being caught off guard.

When you argue in favor of a proposition, sometimes it is a good idea to present the opposing arguments you expect to hear and refute them in your original presentation. That takes more time or space, so you'll have to decide if it is worth it given whatever limitations you have. If you do so, though, you can enhance your credibility and reduce the effectiveness of your opponent's future refutation.

Third, if you are engaged in oral argumentation and the situation allows for it, really listen and take notes. Write down your opposition's arguments in the order in which they come. As you take notes, listen critically to determine whether the speaker covers all of the stock issues, evidence is provided to support the claims, problems are associated with the evidence used, the reasoning is sound, any of the arguments incorporate fallacies, and so on. If the argument you refute is written, then you can still take notes, but you will usually have more time to read and think about what the other arguer wrote.

Fourth, when you present your refutation, take each argument in turn, following the other speaker's organization the best you can. Your arguments will be confusing, and less effective, if you skip around. As you arrive at each of the other arguer's claims, state the claim (but not the reasoning or evidence used, unless doing so would help you refute the claim), state your response, and then support your response with evidence and reasoning. Explain the effect of your response on the claim. Sometimes you might have more than one response for a single claim. If so, it helps to state the number of responses you have when making an oral argument so the audience can more easily follow your train of thought. After finishing your first response, state your next one, support it, and explain the effect. After you've finished your responses to one claim, go to the next and repeat the procedure.

You're not expected to refute every claim. If you don't want to refute some, identify each when you get to it, so the audience can more easily follow your organization. Say something like, "I'll grant that," or "That doesn't matter because . . . " For instance, you might say, "Jennifer said the unemployment rate has gone down for the past four years, and I'll accept that assertion. Then she said . . . " In addition to helping your audience follow the arguments, granting some of your opponent's claims helps you appear more reasonable and less adversarial.

At the end of your refutation, summarize the effect that it has on the advocate's argument. Don't just stop, but tell the audience or reader why you should win the overall argument.

The suggestions just discussed are general guidelines that you'll have to adapt to different situations. For instance, if your argument is part of a two-person conversation, then you probably won't take notes and you'll try to respond to claims soon after they've been presented. If your refutation is written, then you may not be able to expect your reader to have read the argument that you're responding to, so you'd have to pay more attention to explaining what it said in a fair manner.

ANALYZING REFUTATION

As a consumer of other people's arguments, you will be called on to render a decision about them. Sometimes that decision will only affect your reasoned opinion about a subject, sometimes what you spend your money on, sometimes who or what you vote for, and sometimes other actions you take. There will be times when you present support for a proposition and later need to respond to refutation presented against your ideas. Following are some steps you can take to analyze refutation you encounter. Keep in mind that these are general steps, and in different contexts, you may skip some.

First, decide whether the argument supports an original proposition or responds to someone else's position. That is a crucial decision, because if you interpret an argument as supporting a proposition when the arguer was really refuting someone else's ideas, then the argument may seem confusing and weak when actually it is quite acceptable. Newspaper and magazine editorials and columns often take issue with someone else's arguments and should be considered refutation rather than the original argument, but it's not always immediately apparent that that's what they're doing.

After you recognize that some argumentation is refutation, to evaluate the quality determine what the initial proposition was. If the refutation comes immediately, as in a conversation, then the proposition and claims may be clear. If the refutation is separated from the original argument, which often happens with newspaper and magazine columns or editorials, then the original proposition usually is not stated in any detail. After reading the entire argument, you should be able to figure it out. If you can't tell which proposition was refuted, that could be a reason to decide that the refutation wasn't done very well.

Next, identify what the author did to refute the opposing argument. Ask yourself if the author adequately summarized the advocate's arguments so you, the reader or listener, have a good idea what was refuted. If so, you'll have a better chance of telling whether the author addresses those arguments well. If the author leaves you guessing at what was said in favor of the proposition, then you may conclude that such lack of clarity weakens the refutation. When someone refutes your argument, think carefully about what they say to ensure that the person characterizes your arguments accurately and fairly. A common strategy when doing refutation is to characterize an opponent's arguments in a way that is easier to refute. Be aware of that possibility in both the arguments you make and the arguments made to you.

Also, ask yourself which forms of direct and indirect refutation the arguer used. In everyday argumentation, people do not signpost their refutation clearly, so you have to figure out whether they are arguing that the source of evidence is inadequate, the original argument is not *prima facie,* and so on. That is important, because the nature of what the arguer is trying to do during refutation helps you determine whether the argument accomplishes that purpose.

Evaluate next how well the arguer fulfilled a burden of proof for each claim. Remember, people refuting arguments have a burden to prove each of their claims, so you should examine how well they use evidence and reasoning. Fulfilling a burden of proof involves different standards, for different claims, in different situations. For example, when claiming that the original arguer didn't present adequate evidence in support of the proposition, the refuter may only need to explain that the evidence was all assertions. When claiming that the facts presented by the original arguer are not true, the refuter probably needs to use good evidence of her own.

Finally, after evaluating the arguments used in the refutation, you can reach a general conclusion about the overall argument. Given the refutation that was presented, was it enough to retain presumption and deny the proposition?

FALLACIES ASSOCIATED
WITH REFUTATION

Several fallacies that may arise when people are involved in refutation follow. They are not exclusive to refutation but do have a tendency to show up during that process because of the arguers' involvement with each other when engaged in an argument. Noticing any of the fallacies does not necessarily mean that the argument is actually flawed or that the conclusion is false, but slow down and consider the argument carefully. Also, remember that you can better consider arguments when you're aware of the common ways that they may go astray.

APPEAL TO EMOTIONS—an attempt to gain agreement based solely on the feelings aroused in the message.

Emotions are difficult to avoid when you're arguing about something that you really care about. They are a natural part of human interaction and are not something that you necessarily ought to avoid. Emotional appeals are the parts of argumentative messages that attempt to get the other party to feel the same way you feel. Emotional appeals usually are intertwined with logical arguments, so the task of the critical thinker is to distinguish between the relevant support and reasoning leading to a conclusion and emotional appeals that seem relevant but really aren't. Making that distinction can be difficult, because the emotions often appear to be a proper way to feel about a subject and seem relevant to drawing conclusions about it. Sometimes they are, but if they appear appropriate and upon further reflection aren't, then the appeal is fallacious.

Identifying appeals to emotion as a type of fallacy does not mean that they have no place in argumentative communication. Emotional appeals can stir up more interest in a subject and can make the discourse much more interesting than unemotional, purely logical appeals. On the other hand, their value in making messages interesting does not mean that they necessarily contribute to sound arguments. The task of the critical thinker is to question whether the emotional appeals really are relevant, and if they are not, then how strong the argumentation is when the emotional appeals are disregarded.

While it's important to be able to recognize when emotional appeals are irrelevant, it is also important to know when they are relevant. Remember, just because emotions are involved doesn't mean that the argument is fallacious. Sometimes the feelings aroused by a subject are a legitimate reason to act, so you really have to stop and think about the argument, and the issue, before you decide that the argument is a fallacy. For instance, it is probably legitimate to say that it is worthwhile to spend time with friends because you will feel happier, while it probably is not legitimate to say that you should steal something you want because having it will make you feel happier. Emotionalism is a signal that you shouldn't take what is said at face value but should stop and think about it.

Appeals to emotions can relate to any emotion you might have, from sadness to joy and everything in between. They are commonly used because they are so persuasive, which is also why you should beware of them. A few specific emotional appeals that can be fallacies follow, but an arguer might try to appeal to other emotions as well.

APPEAL TO FEAR (scare tactics)—an appeal to emotion that argues that actions should be taken to avoid negative results when the negative results are exaggerated, unlikely, or irrelevant.

When there are legitimate concerns about the potential negative results of existing or proposed policies, then it is reasonable to take steps to avoid them, and arguments in favor of such steps are not necessarily fallacious. However, when the arguments distort the real problems to make them seem more urgent, more widespread, or more severe than they really are, and scare people into agreeing to the actions proposed by the arguer, then the argument is flawed. The hard part is determining whether the problems are presented accurately, because that may require information to which you don't have easy access.

Modern political campaigns frequently make use of fear appeals, including the fear of crime, losing Social Security benefits, immigrants, terrorism, jobs, and a variety of other subjects. Each side tries to make it seem as though the other party is unconcerned about dire threats facing our country. The threat of communism was used to enhance fear appeals about a variety of subjects for decades. Anti-drug campaigns often try to scare people away from drugs, as do anti-smoking campaigns. Commercial advertisers are usually subtler but sometimes use the fear of being unpopular to market products.

APPEAL TO COMPASSION (appeal to pity, *ad misericordiam*)—an appeal to emotion that argues that a conclusion should be made based on feeling sorry for someone when that feeling is irrelevant to the conclusion.

The appeal to compassion is one of the oldest recognized appeals to emotion. It typically consists of a "sob story" used to justify a position. Compassion is generally a positive trait, but sometimes it just isn't relevant to what is asked. For instance, an employee may argue for a promotion based on the needs of her family—the children need better clothes, the house needs repairs, the car needs to be replaced, and so on. Since promotions are generally supposed to be based on qualifications and past performance, the needs of the employee's family are irrelevant and are a fallacious appeal to compassion. The employee may be motivated to seek the promotion based on her family's needs, but she should present to her supervisor better reasons for deserving one.

Another example of the fallacy would be a student who appeals to the instructor's compassion by arguing that he should get a higher grade in a class because he's had a hard time during the semester. Since a grade should be based on performance in the class, the student's personal difficulties should not be considered, although the instructor may still feel insensitive or mean when rejecting the appeal. The student's circumstances may not be entirely irrelevant, though, because they may be a legitimate reason for withdrawing from the course or for taking an incomplete and finishing the course later. So the compassion may justify a different proposition than the one the student favors.

The appeal to compassion presents an interesting problem when applied to criminal defense. The question is whether or not someone should be found guilty of a crime if he or she had problems during childhood. If guilt is based only on whether the person did an act, then the accused's background isn't relevant. If, however, guilt is based both on whether the person did the act and on whether the person is to blame for committing it, then the person's background can be relevant. In such a case, whether an appeal to compassion is really fallacious may depend on how the law defines guilt.

APPEAL TO INDIGNATION—an appeal to emotion that argues against a position based only on negative personal feelings toward it.

When someone is accused of doing something wrong, it is common to hear that person respond by saying that he is insulted by the charges or won't dignify them with a response. Such a response doesn't answer the charges, except to say that the person is indignant that they were brought up, and it is an example of a way the appeal to indignation works. For example, an officer of a company who is accused of wrongdoing by a superior might say, "I can't believe you'd accuse me of such a thing. After all the years I've worked here, and all I've done for this company, it's offensive that you'd accuse me of anything like this." Notice that these stastements do not deny the charge.

I once dealt with a student who wanted to add a course to her schedule several weeks after the university deadline for adding courses. The deadline is important, because the university does not receive any funding for courses added after the deadline. Her reasons were based on her desire to withdraw from another course in which she was not doing well, and she wasn't doing well because it conflicted with the schedule for a job she accepted long after she enrolled in the class. Withdrawing from the course would drop her below the minimum required by her financial aid, so she would be placed on financial aid "probation." She felt she needed to add a different course because, she believed, financial aid probation would jeopardize her chance to be accepted to graduate school. When I pointed out that she was in this situation because she didn't pay proper attention to the consequences of the choices she made, she responded by angrily asserting that she does pay attention and she didn't appreciate that I would suggest otherwise. In other words, she got indignant. She didn't provide any reasons to believe I was incorrect, though, and certainly no reasons that countered the evidence she already provided that lead to my conclusion. (By checking with the financial aid office, I also discovered that she was completely incorrect about the effect of being put on financial aid probation.)

Another way someone may commit the appeal to indignation is to attempt to get others to take a negative stand on an issue by emphasizing that she and others are outraged or repulsed by some aspect of the issue. For instance, people who are opposed to pornography often argue that it should be suppressed because it is "disgusting." Such personal feelings may describe why the individual expressing them dislikes pornography, but they don't provide a relevant reason for material to be kept from others who are not disgusted by it.

Please note that the fallacy is due to the arguer's personal indignation. If the argument is that a practice is horrific because it causes unnecessary harm that the arguer finds outrageous, then the harm is the reason to accept the claim, not the arguer's indignation.

APPEAL TO LOYALTY—an appeal to emotion that argues that an action should be taken based only on the need to be loyal to someone or to a group.

Sometimes people try to get their friends to do something by saying something like, "Come on, if you don't do it you'll let everyone down," or "I was here when you needed help, now it's your turn to do something for me." Their arguments don't focus on the merits of taking the action but on the need to be loyal and to demonstrate that loyalty by doing something that the friend wouldn't otherwise do. If there are good reasons to do something, separate from the issue of loyalty, then those reasons ought to be the basis of the argument, and the appeal to loyalty is irrelevant. For instance, an alcoholic might say, "Keep this a secret. You're my friend, and that's what friends do."

There may be times when the action called for is easy to do, is harmless, and the only reason to do it is to show loyalty. In such cases the appeal to loyalty is probably not a fallacy. Often, however, the appeal to loyalty is used to try to get someone to do something that he or she really does not want to do and may actually be something the person thinks is wrong. In such cases, it becomes important to call for better reasons than loyalty.

APPEAL TO SPITE—an appeal to emotion that argues that someone should do something only because of ill will toward someone else.

When we do something for spite, we do it because we don't like someone and want to do something to harm him or her. The harm may be physical or emotional, as when we hurt someone's feelings on purpose. Some people making arguments know it can be easy to motivate others to harm someone that they don't like, so they use the appeal to spite. Someone may say that you should do something harmful to another person, and you say you won't because you think it would be wrong. The arguer may then refute you by arguing that doing what he says will get even with the person he wants harmed. He'll bring up instances of what the other person did to you to try to arouse your emotions and act spitefully.

If you're really angry with someone, it may be tempting to do something to get back at him or her, and that's when you should beware of appeal to spite in your own reasoning and in arguments from others.

APPEAL TO POPULARITY—an appeal to emotion that argues that someone should do something only because it will make that person better liked by others.

People rarely come out and say, "Do this and I'll be your friend," or "If you don't do this nobody will like you," but they have ways to convey such messages even if they don't state them explicitly. Even when others don't communicate those thoughts, some individuals may reason to themselves that they should or should not do something because of the effects it will have on their popularity. Almost any advertisement showing someone using a particular product, surrounded by happy, smiling people, is an appeal to popularity.

There are probably times when doing something because it's likely to make someone else like you more is quite appropriate, but there are other times when it is not. Something we all have to do on a regular basis is figure out when popularity is a legitimate reason and when there needs to be other reasons to justify thoughts and actions.

APPEAL TO JOY—an appeal to emotion that argues that something should be done only because it will make the person doing it feel happier.

We all like to feel joyful and happy, so messages that create the impression that accepting a proposition will help us feel that way can be quite persuasive. As with many other fallacies, there are times when the feeling is a legitimate reason to do or believe something, but other times it is quite irrelevant. For instance, an acquaintance might try to talk you into going to a party instead of studying, because the party will be a lot of fun. The emphasis on the joy you would experience by going to the party might distract you from the fact that there is a second issue that needs to be addressed in the argument: the consequences of not studying. Once that issue is addressed, it may turn out that partying is a better choice than studying, but until it is addressed, the only reasoning in the argument is irrelevant.

APPEAL TO FORCE (*ad baculum*)—using threats of harm instead of good evidence and sound reasoning to gain agreement.

An appeal to force basically says, "Agree with me or I'll hurt you." If credible, it is reasonable for the recipient to comply, but the argument is still a fallacy. If agreement is called for, then the threats are an irrelevant appeal, and if there are not good reasons for agreement, then the threats do not substitute for them. An appeal to force is usually used after other arguments have been reasonably responded to and it is the only refutation that the arguer has left.

An appeal to force occurs when an arguer directly says, or strongly implies, that he will cause the harm if agreement is not forthcoming. So a school bully who says "If you don't give me your lunch money, I'm going to beat you up" appeals to force. So does a vice president of a company, who says to a division manager, "You may not agree with me now, but I think you'll change your mind when the budget revision comes out." The vice president is less direct but is no less the bully.

The fallacy of appeal to force also can occur when someone reasons that something was done voluntarily when it was really the result of coercion. For example, a parent may say, "My child loves to practice the piano. The first few times I had to show him what would happen if he didn't, and since then I don't have to tell him more than once." If the "first few times" involved some threat or punishment, then this parent fails to understand that the perceived love of practicing the piano may really be compliance to avoid punishment.

An argument is not an appeal to force if the arguer describes the natural results of failure to comply. So someone who argues that you should brush and floss your teeth because if you don't you'll probably get dental cavities and gum disease does not make an appeal to force. The arguer isn't saying that she will cause you to have cavities, only that they are the likely result of neglecting your dental health.

Some people think that the appeal to force is not really a fallacy, because it is reasonable to change your behavior to avoid being harmed. That is true of the reasoning of the person who is threatened. The person who makies the threat, though, still commits a fallacy.

***IGNORATIO ELENCHI* (ignorance of refutation)**—causing confusion during refutation because of a real or feigned lack of ability to engage in refutation.

This is one of Aristotle's original types of fallacious arguing. Remember, the sophistical refutations that he wrote about were a kind of intellectual game. If someone didn't know how to engage in the game, then he could cause confusion and reduce the opponent—who was still trying to follow the rules—to babbling. Thus the arguer could appear to "win" the refutation, even though he didn't really do refutation.

Since we don't play the game of sophistical refutation any more, this fallacy may seem obsolete. However, we do regularly engage in refutation, and when we do we expect the other person to follow the train of thought, to present claims and support them, and to reasonably engage in discourse. So if someone violates those informal rules of the communication situation by going off on tangents, refusing to answer questions, refusing to accept facts that he himself introduced, repeating irrelevant statements, or a variety of other acts, then we could still say that he commits commit this fallacy. If, in his own mind, he believes that he is making good argument, then what he is doing is fallacious, even if others do not accept the argument. Also, if his actions cause enough confusion and frustration so that the other arguer's ideas are lost and observers believe the refutation has been successful, then the actions "appear to be sound arguments but are not."

Some contemporary authors have equated *ignoratio elenchi* with "appeal to ignorance." The fallacy of appeal to ignorance, however, is sufficiently different so that the two remain distinct. Just be aware that the term is used in a different way sometimes.

EVADING THE ISSUE (red herring, irrelevant conclusion)—supporting a claim with evidence or reasoning that is not relevant to the proposition, or responding to another's argument by changing the subject.

Suppose you were engaging in an argument with someone and made a point you thought was quite good. As you waited for the other person to respond, you are surprised that he virtually ignores what you said and changes the subject while pretending to respond to your point. Or, suppose during an argument you ask the other person a question and instead of answering it directly she launches into a long explanation that never really addresses your question. Or, suppose you try to support a claim with evidence that doesn't really have anything to do with the claim.

All of those examples are ways that people evade issues in argumentation. Evading the issue happens when people appear to make relevant arguments, but what they say isn't really relevant when you stop and think about it. Many other fallacies, such as appeal to emotion, could be categorized as "evading the issue," because they take the argument off on a tangent.

Keeping arguments from going off on tangents is often difficult. Usually the person who evades the issue believes that he or she is making a relevant point and will resist the suggestion that it is not central to the discussion. Some people, though, don't want to make their ideas or answers clear, and thus they purposely evade the issue.

It may help to understand this fallacy if you understand the reference to "red herring." The idea is, if an escaped criminal rubbed a particularly smelly fish on his clothes and body, then the dogs tracking him would be thrown off his scent, and he would get away. The phrase is a metaphor for people in an argument who throw other arguers off track.

TU QUOQUE ("you too" fallacy, two wrongs make a right, common practice)—responding to charges of wrongdoing by saying that the accuser or others do something equally bad.

A story was told during the 1980s of a diplomat from the Soviet Union who was trying to defend his nation's treatment of Jews to diplomats from the United States. Instead of arguing that his country treated Jews in a reasonable manner, his answer was something to the effect of, "Well, look at the way you treated the Indians."

Whether or not that really happened, it illustrates the essence of the *tu quoque* fallacy. *Tu quoque* means "you too" or "so are you." The fallacy occurs when an arguer's response to charges is to say that the accuser does the same thing. While that counteraccusation may be correct, it doesn't prove that the accused is innocent, or that what either party did is justified. It is a form of evading the issue and, if it's not caught, then the argument turns into one of whether the accuser is guilty rather than the accused. Such an argument may ultimately be correct, but if it is used to respond to charges, it comes at the wrong time.

Some people consider the common practice fallacy a variation of *tu quoque.* The common practice fallacy involves responding to charges of wrongdoing by saying that other people are doing the same thing. A motorist pulled over for speeding who says that other people are driving as fast or faster is an example. The argument is fallacious, because it doesn't deny that the motorist was breaking the law or argue that the circumstances are such that speeding was a legitimate choice, only that others also broke the law. Sometimes "everybody is doing it" is a reasonable argument, but often it doesn't really address the issue. The common practice fallacy as a way to respond to charges of wrongdoing also is often considered a variation of the appeal to the people fallacy, described earlier.

STRAW PERSON (straw man)—falsely asserting that an opponent made an argument that is easy to defeat, defeating it, and acting as though that does significant damage to that person's actual argument.

If you were going to fight someone, which would you rather fight, a strong, well-armed opponent or an opponent who is literally made out of straw, bundled together to resemble a human being, holding a wooden weapon in its hand? Most people would prefer to fight the "straw person," because the chances of winning are very good, and the chances of being hurt are very small. That imaginary situation is where the name for the "straw man" argument originates.

When people make straw person arguments, they set themselves up for easy success by distorting their opponents' arguments in the process of refuting them. They may exaggerate those arguments so that they seem more extreme than they really are. They may depict their rivals as taking certain actions to portray them as uncaring or insensitive. And they may rephrase their opponents' arguments to make them seem silly or outlandish. In any case, when someone commits the straw person fallacy, he or she unfairly depicts other people's actions or ideas.

Sometimes advertising makes use of the straw person fallacy, even when the advertiser doesn't appear to make an argument. A local pharmacy once ran an ad that began with a customer approaching three different employees of a large chain drug store for help and being met with indifference and incompetence. Then the ad extolled the service that a customer would receive at the local pharmacy and denigrated the service at the chain. The kind of indifference and incompetence dramatized in the ad seemed to be an exaggerated, unfair depiction of the competition. It helped make the local pharmacy look better but didn't make a very good argument.

REDUCING TO AN ABSURDITY (*reductio ad absurdum*)—characterizing an opponent's position in such a way as to make it, or its consequences, appear ridiculous.

Part of the process of refutation is summarizing the opposing argument so you can respond to it appropriately. When you refute well, you summarize the opposing argument accurately and fairly. The reducing to an absurdity fallacy summarizes the opposing argument inaccurately, and unfairly, by stretching it to something that wasn't at all intended. Arguers who commit this fallacy avoid their responsibility to respond to what was really said, and they try to respond to a distortion of the argument.

For instance, if someone argues in favor of using hemp for products such as paper and lubricating oil, then the opposing arguer might respond by saying that the advocate is in favor of elementary school children having unlimited access to addictive narcotics. Such a position would be absurd for anyone to take, so the refutation can make the hemp advocate's argument appear dangerous and poorly thought out.

Reducing an argument to absurdity is similar to the slippery slope fallacy, because the argument may consist of claiming that the opponent's argument will lead to some unwanted effects. However, the slippery slope fallacy argues that an act will inevitably lead to some unwanted effect that even the advocate doesn't favor, while *reductio ad absurdum* characterizes the opponent's position as something absurd that the advocate does favor.

Reducing to an absurdity also is similar to the straw person fallacy, because it distorts the opponent's position into something easily defeated. The straw person fallacy happens when an arguer claims an opponent is in favor of a position when that opponent never supported it. *Reductio ad absurdum,* on the other hand, takes something the other person actually did say, mischaracterizes it, and lets the absurdity speak for itself.

HORSE LAUGH—responding to an argument with an expression of derision instead of a counterargument.

If you make an argument and somebody responds to it by saying "Oh please" or "That's ridiculous" or rolls his eyes or just laughs at what you said, then he is committing the horse laugh fallacy. A horse laugh is an exaggerated and a phony laugh that expresses contempt for something. Thus it is committed when someone derides an idea without really responding to it. That may lead others to think that there is a problem with the original argument, without any actual refutation presented. As with many other fallacies, if the "horse laugh" is accompanied by reasons the argument is wrong, then it is still a fallacy, but it can be disregarded, and you can focus your attention on the other aspects of the refutation. So if someone's response to a claim is only "That is so ridiculous," then it is a fallacy. If the response is "That is so ridiculous, because . . . " then the reasoning that follows should be considered.

GENETIC FALLACY—arguing that an idea should be accepted or rejected only because of its origin.

An example of the genetic fallacy is if a conservative politician argued that a policy proposal should be disregarded because it was suggested by a liberal group, or vice versa. Labeling the source of the idea as "liberal" may persuade a particular audience to reject it, but as an argument it is quite weak. If there are flaws in the proposal, then those flaws should be addressed, and if the proposal is rejected, then it should be rejected because of the flaws, not because of the source.

The genetic fallacy also can be committed in a reverse way. That is, instead of saying that an idea should be rejected *only* because of its source, someone could say that an idea should be accepted *solely* because of its source. Thus one could say that a proposal from a respected environmental group should be accepted just because it came from that group. Once again, the proposal should be accepted if the argumentative support is strong, not because of who favors it.

The genetic fallacy is not limited to policy proposals either. In addition, scientific ideas, moral principles, economic predictions, and the like are subject to acceptance or rejection because of who presents them. If an individual or a group has a past history of presenting good ideas, then that is a reason to take seriously the ideas presented later, and if an individual or a group has a past history of presenting poor ideas, then that is a reason for skepticism about future ideas. Those past histories, however, do not mean that ideas should necessarily be accepted or rejected.

The name of this fallacy comes from the argumentation's focus on the genesis, or origin, of the ideas rather than on the support for the claim.

ARGUMENT AGAINST THE PERSON (*ad hominem*)—attacking the character or background of the person making an argument instead of responding to that person's claim, evidence, and reasoning.

The argument against the person fallacy occurs when one party in an argument disparages the other arguer rather than pointing out weaknesses in the argument. This tactic often involves name-calling, such as when environmental activists are referred to as "a bunch of dirty hippies on welfare" or business executives are referred to as "old, white, capitalist pigs" instead of responding to the arguments of either group. It also can be done more subtly, such as when someone mentions that an opposing arguer means well but doesn't have the background to really understand the issues involved.

There are times when focusing on the background of an arguer is relevant, so an argument against the person isn't really a fallacy. If support for a claim is based on the credibility of the person making the argument, then undermining that credibility is probably reasonable. Often, though, the argument against the person is made because the person who does it doesn't have anything else to say to refute an argument.

The *ad hominem* fallacy is similar to the genetic fallacy. The difference is the *ad hominem* fallacy typically involves personal attacks on the person engaged in the argument, while the latter calls attention to the person or group who originated the idea in the argument.

FALSE CONSOLATION—arguing that someone is not really harmed because things could be worse, or pointing out what one has to be thankful for.

When people have trouble, it seems there are always others who want to deny it by saying that they are well off in some way, or that things could be worse. They may say, "It's too bad you lost your job, but you still have your health." Such people usually mean well, and usually don't know what else to say, because they can't really argue that the other doesn't have any troubles. Nevertheless, it is still a fallacy, because it avoids the issue at hand. The argument would be especially fallacious if someone did something harmful to you, you objected, and he responded that he could have done much worse.

SUMMARY

Refutation is responding to the arguments made by the advocate for the opposing side of the issue. Direct refutation responds directly to the other person's claims, evidence, and reasoning, and indirect refutation responds to the other person's general position on the proposition but doesn't respond directly to what he or she said.

The general types of direct refutation argue that what the other person said isn't relevant to the proposition; that the other person didn't prove his or her claim, because it was just an assertion without support, because the evidence used is not relevant to the claim, or because the evidence comes from an inadequate source; or that the claim made by the other isn't true. Also, one might turn the other's argument against him or her or call attention to contradictions in the other's argument.

To argue indirectly you could argue that the other's argument in favor of the proposition is not *prima facie;* that the other's argument does not really address the proposition; that the counterproposition better addresses the issue; that underlying assumptions of the opponent's arguments shouldn't be accepted; or that, in policy argument, minor repairs of the *status quo* or a counterplan would be better policies.

When doing refutation, you should keep your purpose for engaging in the argument in mind, and understand that refutation begins in the preparation process. During the argument, pay close attention to what the other arguer says, keeping notes if you can. When it's your turn, take each part of the other's argument in order, summarizing what was said and then responding to it. After dealing with the other's arguments, refuting them directly and indirectly, summarize how your refutation affects the other person's argument.

KEY CONCEPTS

counterpropositional (argument) an indirect refutation technique in which the arguer presents arguments that the proposition is *not* true.

direct refutation an argument that directly contradicts what was said in favor of a proposition.

indirect refutation an argument that denies the proposition without speaking directly to what was said in favor of the proposition.

nonpropositional (argument) an indirect refutation technique that argues that the advocate's argument doesn't really support the proposition but supports something that's at least slightly different from the proposition.

not *prima facie* an indirect refutation technique that argues that regardless of what the advocate did say, he or she left out enough important lines of reasoning that the argument, as presented, shouldn't be accepted.

not proven (argument) a direct refutation technique in which the arguer says that the advocate has failed to prove a claim because the evidence was asserted, is not relevant to the claim, or comes from an inadequate source.

not relevant (argument) a direct refutation technique in which the arguer says that no matter how true the claim or evidence is, it has no real bearing on the proposition being argued.

not true (argument) a direct refutation technique in which the arguer presents high-quality evidence that clearly contradicts the opponent's claim or the evidence used in support of the claim.

point out contradictions a direct refutation technique in which the arguer shows that the opponent's claims are contradictory.

questioning underlying assumptions an indirect refutation technique in which an arguer identifies, and argues against, unstated assumptions in an advocate's argument.

refutation the act of responding to the other person's argument, trying to deny what he or she said.

turn arguments a direct refutation technique in which the arguer accepts what the opponent says as being correct but shows that it actually argues against his or her position rather than for it.

THINGS TO THINK ABOUT

1. Find an example of an argument in favor of a proposition. How might it be refuted using the direct refutation techniques described in this chapter? How might it be refuted using the indirect refutation techniques described in this chapter?

2. Find an example of an argument that contains support that isn't really relevant to the proposition or claim being argued. Why isn't the support relevant?

3. Find an example of an editorial that refutes a position. Evaluate it according to the ideas presented in this chapter.

4. Choose a section of Secretary of State Powell's speech in the Appendix. Identify what an arguer might say about his argument using the direct and indirect techniques described in this chapter.

TUTORIAL LINK

Go to *http://communication.wadsworth.com/verlinden* and complete the tutorials for the Language and Informal Fallacies, Set #6.

PART III

Contexts and Applications

The previous section addressed some fundamental ideas involved in making strong arguments. Those fundamentals are applicable to any argument done in any context. In addition to knowing the fundamentals, it is helpful to understand how to apply argumentation and critical thinking skills in various contexts. Each of the following chapters looks at a different general communication context and explains some considerations that are particularly relevant to that context.

Each chapter is only meant to be an overview of that context specifically related to argumentation. Don't expect to learn as much about communicating in any context as you would by taking a full course devoted to it.

12

✻

Persuasive Public Speaking

Erin is worried. Developers have asked the city council where she lives to allow them to build a new shopping center in her neighborhood. The developers want to convert land currently used as a park and playground near her home, and Erin is concerned that would change her neighborhood for the worse. Although she's never considered herself an activist, she knows that she must speak out to her neighbors and the city council to have any hope of stopping the proposal. She realizes the time has come to become a persuasive speaker.

Erin is not alone. Every day, people are faced with situations that call on them to use persuasive speaking skills. Those who thought that they would never speak in public become advocates for causes due to unexpected events. Many people's jobs call for them to deliver persuasive speeches, and their career advancement depends on their ability to present convincing messages. You're likely to face many occasions that call for you to speak persuasively, and you'll need to know how to do it effectively.

Public speaking is a skill that you can develop, but it is fairly complex. This chapter cannot address every aspect of public speaking, so it will focus on ideas that are most related to the content of persuasive speeches, understanding that the ability to effectively deliver content is also important. This chapter will

- explain persuasive public speaking.
- describe the basic components of persuasive speaking.
- offer suggestions for speakers.

As you read the following, be aware that most of what is said also applies to interpersonal and written persuasion.

WHAT IS
PERSUASIVE PUBLIC SPEAKING?

Persuasive public speaking is oral communication designed to influence the attitudes, beliefs, or behaviors of others in a setting where one person talks to many others at one time. As with other forms of oral communication, the speaker and the listeners mutually influence each other, but the speaker is the primary agent of influence in public speaking contexts.

Public speaking traditionally has been classified as persuasive, informative, or entertaining. Informative speaking and entertaining speaking also are persuasive, though, because they influence listeners. The primary purpose of informative speaking is to educate the audience, which will inevitably influence beliefs and may also change attitudes and behaviors. For example, an informative presentation about tornados could change your belief about how likely you are to experience a tornado, might make your attitude toward tornado safety more favorable, and may result in changing the way you react to storm warnings. Speakers who entertain may not intend to influence their audiences, but they do. So, in some ways, all public speaking is persuasive.

Effective persuasive public speaking fulfills all three purposes. As Cicero said almost 2,000 years ago, in order to persuade, you must educate the audience, and to keep the audience listening, you must entertain them. That doesn't mean that you must entertain the way a comedian does but that you make the speech interesting enough to hold the audience's attention.

Persuasive speaking has a natural connection to critical thinking and argumentation. A significant part of preparing to speak persuasively is to think critically about your subject, situation, and audience. Also, the major way to persuade an audience is to make sound, convincing arguments.

ELEMENTS OF
PERSUASIVE SPEAKING

The ancient Greeks, with whom most Western ideas about public speaking originated, studied rhetoric, which Aristotle (1991) defined as the study, in all cases, of the available means of persuasion. They identified five **"canons" of rhetoric,** or lesser arts, that constitute the greater art of rhetoric.

The first canon is **invention,** which helps the speaker discover what to say in the speech. Effective speakers do not simply say whatever happens to come to mind on the spur of the moment. They systematically search for content and consciously decide what should be included for the audiences they address. The canon of invention is most related to critical thinking and argumentation and will be discussed later in the suggestions for speakers.

The second canon is **disposition,** or the arrangement of ideas. After you decide on the ideas to include in your speech, you must determine which should come first, second, and so on. Effective arrangement helps the audience understand the relationship of the ideas to each other to follow your train of thought to avoid confusion. Arrangement also affects the persuasiveness of your message by allowing each idea to build on what was presented previously, making the argument more compelling.

Style is the third canon of rhetoric and refers to the way language is used to express ideas. Effective use of style can help make your message more clear, interesting, and powerful. Language also can hide ideas and trick people into thinking that you're saying something that you're really not. As an ethical persuader, you should use language to effectively express sound arguments. As a critical thinker, you should be aware of the language that persuaders use.

The fourth classical canon of rhetoric is **memory,** which relates to how to remember to say what you want. In ancient times this meant learning ways to remember ideas in the order that you wanted to present them, using the language you planned. Today it has more to do with how to use notes or a manuscript instead of relying completely on memorization.

Delivery is the final canon of rhetoric. As the name implies, it involves the way you vocally and physically present your speech. Delivery is important, because people pay more attention to ideas presented in interesting and powerful ways. On the other hand, delivery should be used in the service of the ideas and not to make weak ideas appear stronger.

All of the canons influence each other in the final speech. For instance, the ideas that you include affect the language that you choose, and your language choices make a difference in how you use your voice as you deliver your speech. So while there are five distinct canons of rhetoric, you cannot apply them separately.

While all of the canons of rhetoric are important in persuasive public speaking, learning about all would be too much, so this chapter will focus on the canon of invention and will provide suggestions for how it can be used by both speakers and the audience.

SUGGESTIONS FOR SPEAKERS

As a persuasive public speaker, you must be aware of certain things. Most of the suggestions that follow focus on the critical thinking you might do when preparing your speeches and the arguments you might include. There is no particular order to the suggestions, so don't think of any as necessarily more important than others.

1. *When you can choose your topic, speak about something worthwhile.*

Whenever you deliver a speech, you are competing for your audience's attention. Everyone in your audience could be thinking of many other things that are important to them, so your subject should be worth their time and attention.

Part of what makes a speech topic worthwhile is its intrinsic importance. The standards of harm and significance described for propositions of policy in Chapter 8 are good guidelines in deciding whether a topic is intrinsically worthwhile. Another part of what makes a speech topic worthwhile is its connection to the audience. Some people pay attention to topics that have little to do with them, but most lose interest if they don't see the connection. That doesn't mean that you should avoid topics that your audience isn't already interested in, because sometimes the most important topics are those that the audience isn't even aware of yet. It does mean that part of the invention process is to discover how the topic affects the audience. A third part of what makes a topic worthwhile is whether or not you ask the audience to take actions that they actually can. For example, it would not be appropriate to ask an audience of everyday citizens to pass a law, because these people are not legislators and do not pass legislation. However, it would be appropriate to ask them to contact their representatives to support the passage of a law, or to vote in a particular way on a referendum. If your message is only that a law should be passed, then your audience may agree with you, but nothing is likely to happen, thus your speech would not be worthwhile to them.

2. *Know your subject.*

Many authors of public speaking texts suggest that you choose your topic based on subjects you know something about. When you have a choice, that's good advice, especially if you also ensure that your subject is worthwhile. Sometimes, however, you may have to deliver a persuasive message on a subject you can't choose. That often happens when you make speeches as part of your job, when you get involved in an advocacy movement, or when a speech is part of a class requirement.

Knowing your subject means that you shouldn't necessarily speak on what you already know, but that you should make an effort to know as much as you can about the topic. This will not only help you think of ideas to include in a speech but also will help you decide which ideas are most important. Knowing your subject well helps you deliver the speech effectively, because you have the confidence to look up from your notes and speak to the audience.

You will probably need to do some research in order to know your subject well. If it's something with which you're already familiar, you've probably already done a lot of the research, but it would help to do more to make sure that you're up to date. If it's a new subject to you, then consult a variety of sources to get a good background and specific evidence to support your arguments.

Most college libraries now have online resources for looking up facts and background material about any subject. You'll find it helpful to be able to find such information, both for classes and for future occasions when you need to know more about a variety of subjects. You'll want to do a thorough job, but remember, you will always be able to find more, so at some point, you have to stop researching.

3. *Know what you want from your audience.*

Students who have persuasive speaking assignments often want to present information to the audience and let them make up their own minds. That's appropriate during an investigation of a subject when you're trying to decide on the best course of action, but when you've critically thought about the issue and reached a sound conclusion about what should be done, then it is time to try to convince others to agree with you and to take action. If you don't know what you want from your audience and make your arguments with that in mind, then there's no telling what your audience may think you want from them. Even if you're reluctant to convince the audience to agree with you, you can bet that those who want something else will try to convince others to agree with them.

Knowing what you want from your audience doesn't mean that it should be something with which they already agree. Sometimes your intent will be to reinforce what the audience already believes or does, but don't base your choice of topics on that. Decide what your audience can do to improve something that is wrong, and then try to ethically convince them to do it.

4. *Make the best arguments you can.*

Although there is more to persuasion than arguments, arguments are the foundation. The stronger your arguments are, the more reason your audience has to accept your message, and the more difficult it is to find reasons to reject it.

Earlier chapters discussed how to make strong arguments. Chapters 5 and 6 showed you how to structure arguments to make them valid. Chapter 7 showed you how to ensure that your reasoning is strong, depending on the kind of reasoning you use. Chapter 8 explained how to discover the common issues for the type of proposition you support or refute so you can address those issues. Chapter 9 described how to select and use evidence to support your claims. And Chapter 10 explained how to use language more effectively. Don't think of these as separate. Good arguments are a combination of sound reasoning, good evidence, and appropriate language. Keep in mind the principles presented earlier as you create the substance of your speech.

5. *Analyze your audience.*

From the time Aristotle wrote *The Art of Rhetoric,* persuasive speakers have been advised to think about what their audiences are like. Different people respond to different ideas, and if you haven't thought about your audience, then you're less likely to use arguments that work for them. For instance, most twenty-year-old students are not interested in the same things as are thirty-five-year-old parents or sixty-four-year-old business owners.

One way to analyze your audience is to do a **demographic analysis,** which uses categories into which people with similar characteristics can be grouped to try to determine the appeals that are likely to influence them. Demographic categories include such things as age, sex, race, religion, political affiliation, occupation, hobbies, and education. The idea is that people with similar demographic characteristics often have similar beliefs and attitudes. That doesn't mean that they all think exactly alike, but the analysis helps predict some of the ways people respond to ideas.

Another way to analyze an audience is to consider their psychological characteristics. A **psychographic analysis** considers what members of the audience think and feel rather than the categories they fit into. You try to figure out what they want, already know, believe, are interested in, fear, and so on. That information can then be used to choose persuasive appeals that fit the particular audience. For instance, a psychographic analysis of a particular teenage audience might discover that they don't like feeling misunderstood by adults, fear being ridiculed by their peers, and think that they have little to offer anyone. That wouldn't necessarily mean that all teenagers think and feel that way, but the group to which you're going to speak does. Knowing that information can help you with the next suggestion.

6. *Tailor the speech to the audience.*

The reason to analyze the audience is to fit your speech to that audience instead of making generic arguments. You'll be more effective if you use premises that your audience will most likely accept, and if you use examples to which they can relate. For instance, references to the Vietnam War and the events of the 1960s may resonate well with people who are fifty years old, but they are much less effective with audience members who recently graduated from high school. The examples may be quite relevant to the topic but not to the audience. If you know that your audience doesn't like being misunderstood by adults, then you might argue that doing what you call for will help adults understand them better.

Tailoring your speech to the audience does not mean deceiving them. Everything you say must still be honest and ethical. Making up facts, altering evidence, or presenting hypothetical examples as literal is not tailoring, it is lying. Tailoring also does not mean that you change your proposition to reflect what your audience already believes but that you use your audience's beliefs as starting points to develop arguments for your proposition.

7. *Make sure your audience knows that the subject is worthwhile.*

Even when the subject is worthwhile, your audience may not recognize its importance. If they don't perceive it as important, then they're less likely to pay attention, you're less likely to persuade them, and they're unlikely to do what you want. So it's a good idea to tell your audience why the topic is important early on and continue to emphasize its importance during the rest of your speech.

When expressing the importance of your topic, try to tell the audience why it's important to *them.* Some people are interested in subjects that are globally important, but many will lose interest if they don't see the relevance to their lives. So look for ways to make your subject appear important, both generally and specifically to your audience.

8. *Use high-quality evidence.*

Chapter 9 indicated ways to help determine the quality of your evidence. Assume that your audience will apply many of those same standards to your speech. You don't want them to reject your arguments because they don't accept your evidence, so you're better off using the best evidence you can. Even if your audience doesn't think about your evidence very critically, you can take pride in knowing you used the best evidence you could find.

For a persuasive speech, high-quality evidence has two traits. The first is that it has the characteristics of good evidence, described in Chapter 9. That is, it meets the tests of evidence and is high on Perella's hierarchy of evidence. The second trait is that the evidence comes from sources your audience will accept. Often, audience members will be neutral toward your sources, but sometimes their preconceived ideas may lead them to reject particular sources of information. For example, individuals opposed to the power of corporations are not likely to accept what the CEO of a Fortune 500 company has to say, because they believe that he or she would be biased. There is an exception though. If the source who is generally not accepted says something contrary to his or her interests, then the evidence will probably be more acceptable. So evidence from a Fortune 500 CEO who says that corporations have too much power is more likely to be accepted by the audience just described.

9. *Cite the sources of your evidence.*

In terms of persuading your audience, it doesn't do much good to use high-quality sources if the audience is unaware of them. Chapter 9 explained how to cite sources, and it explained that research has shown that citations make persuasive arguments more effective.

Another practical result of citing sources is that it makes you more credible to the audience. As noted in Chapter 1, Aristotle (1991) identified three general types of appeals that a speaker might use to persuade an audience: *ethos, pathos,* and *logos. Pathos* includes emotional appeals, *logos* includes arguments in favor of a position, and *ethos* is equivalent to credibility. **Credibility** is the audience's perception that the speaker is someone to be believed. Credibility has long been recognized as being generally the most influential of the appeals. Aristotle said that *ethos* had three general components—sagacity, which is a combination of knowledge and wisdom, honesty, and goodwill.

Credibility has been studied for a long time, and different researchers have grouped its components in various ways. Two characteristics have been recognized since the time of the first-century Roman rhetorician Quintilian: expertise and trustworthiness (Rhoads and Cialdini, 2002). **Expertise** is the audience's perception that the speaker is knowledgeable about the subject, which is similar to Aristotle's sagacity. **Trustworthiness** is the audience's perception that the speaker is honest and unbiased, much like Aristotle's component of honesty. When citing your sources of evidence, you prove to your audience that you've done your research and have some expertise, and at the same time you indicate that you're honest about where the evidence came from.

In addition to the practical reasons for citing sources of evidence, there is also a moral reason: citing your sources is simply more ethical. Since your evidence came from someone else, you are using her or his ideas. By crediting your sources, you avoid plagiarism (using others' ideas without giving them credit).

10. *Be organized.*

There are several different ways to organize your speech, and audiences don't show much preference for one way over another. They do, however, want to have a sense of where your ideas are headed and how they relate to each other, and if your speech seems disorganized, the audience will pay less attention. As the speaker, you can help them by both having a clear organizational pattern, and by helping them recognize the pattern.

At a minimum, any speech should have an introduction, a body, and a conclusion. The introduction prepares the audience for the content of the body, the body presents the reasons and evidence for the proposition, and the conclusion reminds the audience of what they've heard, so they will better remember the important ideas. In addition, the introduction begins the speech in a way that gains the audience's attention and shows that you're prepared to deliver the speech. The conclusion ends the speech in a way that makes it clear that the speech is over and that you've put some thought into how to finish it. The conclusion also provides a final opportunity to say something that could convince the audience to accept your proposition.

One of the most common organizational patterns for persuasive speeches is the problem-solution arrangement. When using this arrangement, begin by detailing the problem and then describing what ought to be done to fix it. The stock issues for a proposition of policy described in Chapter 8 are a more elaborate version of the problem-solution arrangement. The stock issues of harm, significance, and inherency describe the problem in detail, and the issues of plan, solvency, and advantages are the solution. You also can use the stock issues for propositions of fact and value to organize speeches that do not advocate a policy change.

Clear organization is the first step. It also is a good idea to help your audience follow your organization, and there are three ways to do that. The first is to preview the main points of the body during your introduction, so your audience knows what to expect. The second is to use signposting, or using numbers or phrases to signal when you move from one idea to the next. In this paragraph, "first" and "second" are signposts to help you recognize where one item on the list ends and the next begins. Third is to use internal summaries between the main parts of your speech to signal more significant shifts in your thoughts. For example, if the body of your speech has three main points, then you'd have an internal summary at the end of the first and second points. In each internal summary, you'd briefly remind the audience of what you covered in the point you're ending and introduce them to the point you're moving to next. Internal summaries are similar to transitions, but they're more elaborate.

The use of those three techniques is generally more important in oral communication than in written communication. When writing, you can use punctuation, paragraph breaks, and section headings to give the reader cues that you're moving to another point. In oral communication, you must help your audience follow you by using your voice, movement, gestures, and visual aids to signal changes.

Another consideration in your organization is the order in which you present ideas. Many different factors are involved in making that decision, and an important one is whether or not your audience is initially sympathetic to your proposition. In general, if your audience is already likely to agree with your position, then you should present your proposition early, followed by the reasoning and evidence to support it. If your audience is likely to initially disagree with your position, then you should present reasoning and evidence leading up to the proposition, and you should use ideas that they already agree with at the start and gradually move to those with which they don't initially agree.

11. *Respond to potential objections.*

Whenever you take a side on an important issue, be aware that others disagree with you and that they are likely to try to persuade your audience to their side. You might be inclined to simply ignore their arguments and hope that your audience will not hear them, but that is not the best idea, because people who are not exposed to the opposing ideas are more susceptible to being persuaded by them.

Persuasion theorists refer to inoculation theory, which states that when a speaker presents arguments opposing the proposition and presents good arguments refuting them, audience members are less likely to be persuaded by the opposing arguments when they hear them from other sources. If the audience is not exposed to the arguments, then they have no responses available, but if they have, then they're more likely to reject the opposing ideas because they remember that there are reasons to reject them. This is especially true if they've also been motivated to remember the arguments by establishing the possibility of future attacks on their attitudes and beliefs (Szabo and Pfau).

Sometimes, though, you'll try to persuade people who initially disagree with your position because they've already heard arguments against it. In those cases, as you present your side, the audience may think of the responses they've heard and reject your proposition. By presenting the other side, you respond to what they're thinking and have a better chance to persuade them. Either way, it's a good idea to present opposing arguments and refute them.

When you do so, though, make sure that you present the opposing ideas fairly, which is both more ethical and more effective. It's ethical because you don't distort the ideas and deceive your audience. It's more effective because the people you're trying to persuade either already know the opposing arguments or may hear them in the future. If they realize that you've distorted them, then they're likely to find you lacking in expertise, trustworthiness, or both.

12. *Adapt to the constraints you face.*

Rhetorical scholar Lloyd Bitzer argues that situations calling for rhetorical responses include an urgent problem that can be addressed by rhetoric, an audience capable of bringing about change, and constraints or limitations on the speaker. The urgent problem and the need for the topic to fit the audience have already been discussed. Now it's time to discuss the constraints.

Constraints on the speaker are anything that will prevent him from saying whatever he wants. Most speakers, especially in a classroom setting, face the constraint of time. You only have so much time available, so you may not be able to develop your arguments as completely as you could if your time were unlimited.

Another constraint is what your audience considers acceptable language. Some audiences will accept a wider range of language than others. Generally speaking, if your language goes beyond what they find acceptable, or understandable, then they will either stop listening or more actively reject your message.

All audiences also have expectations of speakers, and those expectations act as a constraint. If you meet their expectations, then you're more likely to be persuasive. Those expectations can include which topics are acceptable, how to begin a speech, the place of humor in a speech, what constitutes good evidence, and so on.

The list of constraints on a speaker is endless. Remember to think about the constraints as you prepare your speeches, and adapt accordingly.

SUGGESTIONS FOR
THE AUDIENCE

You'll probably be a *member* of an audience for persuasive speeches much more often than you'll deliver them, so it's important to have some ideas regarding the role of a critical listener. In general, apply the principles of argumentation and critical thinking discussed earlier in this text. Seven specific suggestions follow, in no particular order, for listening to the persuasive speeches, or other persuasive messages, to which you'll be exposed. They apply as much to written as they do to oral communication, and as much to conversational attempts to persuade as they do to public speeches.

1. *Consider substance over style.*

The substance of a persuasive speech consists of the evidence and reasoning supporting the proposition and claims. Style consists of the language, as

Figure 12.1 Good content is important in effective public speaking.

Dilbert reprinted by permission of United Feature Syndicate, Inc.

discussed in Chapter 10. It also includes delivery techniques that the speaker uses, such as vocal variety, eye contact, gestures, and movement. Substance and style are both important to excellent persuasive speaking, but each needs to be given the appropriate respect.

Style that is used to augment the content of a speech, to make sound arguments clearer and more interesting and powerful, deserves to be admired as much as the arguments. Style that is used in place of sound content, to make weak arguments appear strong or to camouflage the absence of good evidence and reasoning, is something to be recognized and resisted. Beware of speakers who seem charming but who don't have good arguments.

Unfortunately, unscrupulous speakers are adept at using their ability with language and delivery to persuade. They use rhetorical questions, loaded language, repetition, and other devices to make it appear as though they have a case, when they really do not. They use their voices, faces, and body language to give the impression that they are absolutely sure that what they say is true, and they get their audiences to believe them. As a critical thinker, make sure that they do not fool you.

2. *Think critically in the "strong sense."*

You'll remember from Chapter 2 that critical thinking in the strong sense means to apply your skills as a critical thinker both to those arguments you favor and those with which you disagree. Speakers with whom you agree may have arguments as weak as those with whom you disagree. This doesn't mean that you should necessarily change your mind about an issue because a speaker with whom you agree presented a weak argument, but that you should be willing to recognize that his or her argument is not worth accepting. By the same token, when speakers with whom you disagree make sound arguments, then you should be willing to admit it and reexamine your position.

3. *Consider the evidence.*

As a critical thinker, ask yourself if the speaker is presenting a series of assertions or claims that she supports with evidence. It wouldn't be reasonable to expect every claim to be fully supported in any speech, because that would take too much time and would be quite tedious. So expect some assertions. The question is, how many?

Recognizing that some assertions are inevitable, the next question is whether the assertions are acceptable. Does your background knowledge indicate that they are sufficiently accepted or proven that evidence isn't necessary? If so, they are acceptable and don't present a problem. If not, then don't accept them as being necessarily correct. That doesn't mean that you should automatically reject the message, but you should have some uncertainty about the conclusions.

Some claims will be supported with evidence, and that should lead you to consider the quality of the evidence. The material in Chapter 9 will help you decide whether the evidence is good enough to deserve acceptance. If it doesn't meet the standards, then that doesn't necessarily mean that the evidence is false, but it does mean that you shouldn't accept it without question.

4. *Consider the speaker's credibility.*

Since persuasive speakers can't provide evidence for every assertion, much of what they say must be based on their credibility. Evaluate the speaker's credibility using the same principles to evaluate the credibility of sources of evidence, described in Chapter 9 and earlier in this chapter. Ask yourself whether the person shows evidence of having the expertise to know what he or she is talking about. If you think critically, you won't just accept that person's assurance of his or her expertise but will look for other signs such as how well the speaker appears to know what he or she is talking about, or background information from other sources that you can trust.

Also ask yourself whether the speaker is someone you can trust. If you're familiar with the person, you can answer that question based on what she or he has done in the past; if you're not, then you may want to withhold judgment until you have some evidence that the speaker is trustworthy. Keep in mind that many public speakers, as well as many other persuaders, know how to appear trustworthy even as they deceive.

Also be aware that many public speakers who have a great deal of expertise and are quite trustworthy don't appear so because they're apprehensive about public speaking. That apprehension often presents itself in delivery styles that can give the impression that the speakers don't know what they're talking about, or that they're trying to hide something. As a critical thinker, consider alternative explanations for apparent lack of credibility, and look for other evidence that you should or should not believe the speaker.

5. *Make an independent judgment.*

Part of being a critical thinker is drawing a conclusion based on your own judgment of evidence and reasoning rather than simply agreeing with what others believe. Sometimes that will mean you're pretty much alone, that others will think that there's something wrong with you because you don't agree with them.

You're probably already aware that your judgment might be that the speaker is correct or incorrect. There are other possible judgments, though, that people often don't consider. The first is that the speaker is not wholly correct or incorrect but is somewhat correct and somewhat incorrect. The other is that it is too early to tell whether the speaker is correct. Perhaps you've only heard one side of an issue, or you question evidence that was presented, or you simply need more time to think about what was presented. Whatever the reason, you don't always have to reach a firm conclusion immediately after a speech is finished.

6. *Recognize that there will always be some uncertainty.*

The issues about which people make persuasive speeches are ones that have not yet been decided upon. If they were certain, then there would no longer be the need for persuasion. The nature of persuasion is to provide guidance for people in an uncertain world. Do not expect a persuasive speech to remove all doubt from your mind. You may accept or reject a speaker's proposition provisionally, understanding that you might change your mind later when you have more information.

SUMMARY

When Erin became a public speaker to advocate for the retention of the park in her neighborhood, she had to use her knowledge of various principles of persuasive speaking. She had to think about the people to whom she would present her speeches so that she could tailor the speeches to them. She considered the demographic categories into which they fit to get some ideas of what they were like, and she considered the psychographic characteristics so that she could talk about her issue in terms of what motivated the audience (see Sidebars 12.1, 12.2, and 12.3).

Erin used all of the classical canons of rhetoric, even if she didn't know the names of all of them. As she analyzed her audiences, decided which evidence to use, and determined which stories to tell, she used invention. As she decided on the order in which to present her idea and created an introduction and conclusion, she was involved with disposition. When she considered what language to use for the best effect, she was considering style. When she worked on remembering what to say and wrote her notes and outline, she was engaged in the canon of memory. And when she rehearsed her speeches to most effectively use her voice and body to communicate her ideas, she was involved with delivery.

Erin's speeches weren't perfect, and your speeches won't be either. But by putting thought and effort into it, Erin was able to create messages that were far more influential than if she had done nothing, just as you can do for subjects that you care about.

Sidebar 12.1 Canons of Rhetoric

Invention
Disposition
Style
Memory
Delivery

Sidebar 12.2 Suggestions for Speakers

Speak about something worthwhile.
Know your subject.
Know what you want from your audience.
Make the best arguments you can.
Analyze your audience.
Tailor the speech to your audience.
Make sure your audience knows that the subject is worthwhile.
Use high-quality evidence.
Cite the sources of your evidence.
Be organized.
Respond to potential objections.
Adapt to the constraints you face.

Sidebar 12.3 Suggestions for the Audience

Consider substance over style.
Think critically in the "strong sense."
Consider the evidence.
Consider the speaker's credibility.
Make an independent judgment.
Recognize that there will always be some uncertainty.

KEY CONCEPTS

canons of rhetoric   lesser arts that make up the greater art of rhetoric, including invention, disposition, style, memory, and delivery.

credibility   the perception of the audience that the speaker is someone to be believed.

delivery   the classical canon of rhetoric that helps the speaker use his or her voice and body to effectively deliver a persuasive message.

demographic analysis   the use of categories into which people with similar characteristics can be grouped to try to determine which appeals are likely to influence an audience.

disposition   the classical canon of rhetoric that helps the speaker decide the order to present ideas in a speech.

expertise   the audience's perception that the speaker is knowledgeable about a subject, giving the speaker more credibility.

invention   the classical canon of rhetoric that helps the speaker discover the ideas that might be included in a speech and choose those that he or she will actually use.

memory   the classical canon of rhetoric that helps the speaker remember the ideas, order, and

language choices planned for the speech.

persuasive public speaking   oral communication designed to influence the attitudes, beliefs, or behaviors of others in a setting where one person talks to many others at once.

psychographic analysis   analysis of the audience's thoughts and feelings to try to determine which appeals are likely to influence them.

style   the classical canon of rhetoric that helps the speaker decide how to use language to express ideas in a speech.

trustworthiness   the audience's perception that the speaker is honest and unbiased, giving the speaker more credibility.

THINGS TO THINK ABOUT

1. Consider the story about Erin that begins this chapter. What arguments might she use to convince her neighbors to oppose the project? What arguments might she make to the city council to prevent the approval of the project?

2. Identify an important current problem that calls for persuasive speaking. Identify the following for that issue:

   a. What is the appropriate audience to address to correct the problem?

   b. What are the demographic and psychographic characteristics of the audience?

   c. What would you ask the audience to do to correct the problem?

   d. What are the reasons you would argue for the audience to do what you want?

   e. What evidence would you need to support your reasoning?

3. Think of an appropriate persuasive speech subject. What sources does your school's library have that you could use to create a bibliography of evidence and other background material for your subject?

13

❖

Critical Listening

Imagine you're in a class, and your instructor gives you an assignment. You hear part of what your instructor says but not all of it because you have other things on your mind and it's almost time for class to end. You think you understand the assignment, but you're not really sure you have it all correct. You want to remember to do the assignment, so you make a mental note to yourself about what is expected and when it is due. You consider writing it down but you're sure you'll remember. You notice that the instructor is pretty emotionless as she says what you're supposed to do and interpret that as meaning she doesn't really care about it very much. You evaluate what the instructor says, your past experience with this instructor and others, and what you know about this particular course, and you decide that the assignment isn't very important to your success in this class. You consider asking the instructor a question to clarify what is expected, but you decide that you might seem foolish, so you give as little of an overt response as you can.

What part of your actions involved listening? As you will see in the rest of this chapter, the listening process includes everything described in the previous paragraph.

Listening is the most common communication activity that you do. Although the ratio may vary from one day to another, over time you probably listen much more than you talk, read, or write. You listen to teachers lecture, to supervisors give instructions, to TV, to radio, to movies, to friends in conversations, and to relatives on the phone. Sometimes all you do is listen, and other times you listen while you read, watch TV, drive a car, or prepare supper.

Although it is a very common activity, most people haven't had any instruction in listening. Most of us have had to learn to do it on our own, and for most of us that self-learning has led to some misconceptions and poor habits. You can change poor habits, though, especially when you have an idea of why they are poor and how to change them.

This chapter will

- introduce you to listening.

- make you aware of some common barriers to listening.

- give you some ideas about how to improve one very important type of listening: critical listening.

LISTENING

Many definitions of listening are quite similar. Communication scholars Melvin DeFleur, Patricia Kearney, and Timothy Plax define **listening** as

> an active form of behavior in which individuals attempt to maximize their attention to, and comprehension of, what is being communicated to them through the use of words, actions, and things by one or more people in their immediate environment. (102)

Several parts of that definition deserve closer examination to understand what listening involves.

First, listening is an "active form of behavior," not passive. In other words, listening is something people *do,* not something that just happens. This is an important idea regarding listening well or improving your listening, because it emphasizes that listening requires your active involvement. Most people see no difference between hearing and listening, but as we shall see later, there is a significant one. For now, remember that when you listen, you take control of what you do.

Second, the definition says that listening involves an "attempt to maximize . . . attention to, and comprehension of, what is being communicated." This part of the definition emphasizes both attention and comprehension. That means that listening does not stop at just hearing but also involves working at understanding what is meant. Also, when we listen, we try to pay attention and understand the best we can. Obviously there are times when people don't pay attention very well and don't comprehend what is communicated very well. If that happens because they don't know how to listen well, then they're still attempting to maximize attention and comprehension, but they don't have the skills to do it well. If that lack of attention and comprehension happens because they don't want to try to pay attention or comprehend, then they haven't made the choice to listen, so they listen poorly.

The definition goes on to say that individuals attempt to pay attention and comprehend "what is being communicated to them through the use of words, actions, and things." Most people understand that we listen to words, but the idea that actions and things are involved in listening may be new. When you stop to think about it, a person's facial expression, posture, gestures, movement, and the use of objects while he or she speaks make a lot of difference in the way a message is interpreted. Good listeners realize that we listen with our eyes as well as our ears and pay attention to both aural and visual content.

THE LISTENING PROCESS

Understanding what listening is also involves understanding what happens as we listen. Remember, most people conceive of listening as being equivalent to hearing, so they're unaware of the complexities involved. Listening experts have devised different models of the process to help describe what happens when we listen. Judi Brownell's **HURIER model** of listening is a model that captures the full complexity of the behavior.

HURIER is an acronym for the steps in the listening process, which include

Hearing

Understanding

Remembering

Interpreting

Evaluating

Responding

The **hearing** portion of the listening process involves the act of receiving the auditory and visual stimuli. Hearing may seem like an automatic process, but it really isn't. Each of us constantly makes choices of the stimuli that we attend to, and different people will hear different sounds even when they're right next to each other. If you try to listen to a favorite song while there are people talking nearby, you know that you can focus your attention to block out some sounds and attend to others. Skillful listeners make use of that ability to focus their attention on what the people they are listening to are saying. The same is true of what listeners look at. At any moment, you can look at a wide variety of visual stimuli, and you can choose to focus your attention on any of them. The skillful listener, for example, will focus his attention on those that help him attend to and comprehend the messages he is listening to.

The **understanding** step is the part of the listening process in which you figure out what the speaker means. At this point, you make sense of individual words, phrases, and sentences, determine if the meaning is literal or figurative, and decide whether there is anything you don't comprehend. Understanding may seem automatic, because most of the time we make sense of messages quickly, and we usually get by just fine. Sometimes, however, we need to give more careful consideration to understanding messages, and then understanding is clearly not automatic. For instance, if a supervisor tells you how to do something you've never done before, then as a good listener you would do more to think about how well you understand those instructions than you would if given instructions about something already familiar.

The ease with which we understand many messages can cause trouble when listening. Sometimes messages seem easy, so we miss important details because we don't concentrate on understanding. Unscrupulous people rely on that lack of concentration to cheat people, so it's good to get into the habit of thinking a little more about what people say. Even when people don't try to cheat us, treating understanding as automatic can lead us to think that we understand others when really we don't.

If you've ever tried to learn the lyrics to a song you hear on the radio, then you've probably had the experience of the effort needed to remember what you hear. To learn the lyrics, you focus your attention on the song, and you concentrate on retaining the words in sequence. This is an example of the third step in the listening process, **remembering,** in which the listener stores the meaning in memory so it can be retrieved later. Depending on the situation, that later retrieval may be immediate—as in a conversation—or in the future—such as when you listen to someone explain employee benefits. Sometimes we remember what we've heard with so little effort that it can seem automatic, but it is also something we do actively. You have to put more effort into remembering when it is more important to remember something, or when you have to remember the information more precisely.

Interpreting is the next part of the listening process. It is deciding what the speaker feels as he or she is talking. The emotional content of messages is often as important to full comprehension as the intellectual content, and determining the emotional content also takes some effort. Interpreting feelings requires the listener to pay attention not only to what is said but to how it is said and what accompanies the words. When you interpret feelings, you listen for meaningful use of vocal tone, pitch, force, rate, and quality. You also use your eyes to gather information from facial expressions, gestures, posture, movement, and involuntary physical responses, such as flushing skin, blinking, perspiration, and pupil dilation. As a listener, you take all of this information, interpret it, and draw conclusions about what it means. Some people are extremely skillful at interpreting others' feelings and pay attention to emotional cues without realizing that they are. Others virtually ignore the emotional cues, thinking that the intellectual content of messages is all that matters. Certainly there are plenty of times when the speaker's feelings are neutral or don't really matter, but there are also lots of times when the feelings are the more important part of the message.

The fifth step in the listening process is **evaluating.** This is the part of the listening process in which you decide how much weight to put on what is said. You determine, based on everything you hear, understand, and interpret, as well as using other information that you have, whether or not to believe what the speaker says, and whether or not other information is important. At this point, you put everything together, comparing what is said to your background knowledge, identifying the type of argument, evaluating whether there is a *prima facie* case, noting discrepancies between what the speaker said and her behavior, etc. Some listening contexts call for more attention to evaluation than do others, but evaluation is not automatic, it's something you have to actively do.

The final step in the listening process is **responding,** which is letting the speaker know you're listening and how you understand. There are a variety of ways to respond, including nodding your head, smiling, frowning, saying "uh huh," and explicitly stating what you think the speaker means, among many others. It's important to understand that as long as you're within the speaker's perception, you are going to respond. Looking around the room, staring ahead blankly, and doodling are as much responses as saying "I understand." The question is not *whether* you respond, but *how* you respond.

Good listeners monitor their behavior so that their responses more accurately convey their understanding. They are aware that listening is not just passively letting sound waves hit their eardrums but also involves thinking and providing feedback to the speaker. Many listeners are so practiced at responding that they are often not consciously aware that they are doing it, yet they consistently provide responses. Those responses tell the speaker whether he or she can go on, should back up and try again, should clarify an idea, and so forth.

By now it should be clear that a lot happens when you listen. As you listen, you are constantly making decisions and drawing conclusions. All of the steps happen quickly, though, so it can seem that listening is quite automatic and not a problem. When listening becomes difficult or important, however, you may realize that it's harder to do than you thought.

TYPES OF LISTENING

All listening is not alike. Listening to a lecture in class is different from listening to a friend talk about troubles, which is different from listening to someone trying to sell you something, which is different from listening to dialogue in a movie. Listening experts categorize listening into four different types: discriminative, evaluative, appreciative, and empathic (Wolff, Marsnik, Tacey, and Nichols).

Discriminative listening is listening for understanding, the kind of listening you do when you intentionally listen to a lecture in class or to someone giving you directions in an unfamiliar town. When you engage in discriminative listening, you actively search for new information, information that may confirm or contradict what you already know, and information that may be useful to you in the future.

When you listen responsibly to messages that "attempt to influence [your] attitudes, beliefs, or actions," you engage in **evaluative listening** (Wolff, Marsnik, Tacey, and Nichols, 54). In other words, when you listen to people who try to persuade you, evaluate what they have to say.

Appreciative listening is the kind of listening you do when you listen for pleasure. When you listen to radio, TV, or movies, you do so for entertainment. Appreciative listening may seem to take the least amount of conscious effort, but often when we listen for pleasure, we put more effort into concentrating on what we want to hear than we do in other types of listening. In addition, sometimes appreciative listening is enhanced when we know more about what we're listening to and can think about it as we experience it. For instance, someone who's taken a music appreciation class may think about the style of music as she listens to it.

The final type of listening is **empathic listening,** which is listening you do to help the speaker. It involves letting the speaker know that you care about him or her, understanding what the speaker means and feels, and showing him or her that you understand. Empathic listening can be very light, such as when you just chat with another student between classes. It also can be very serious, such as when someone close to you tells you about a serious problem in her life. Therapists and counselors do empathic listening professionally, but most of us have opportunities to do empathic listening in our everyday life. Empathic listening not only deals with the precise content of the conversation but also with everyone's underlying need to be heard, to be understood, and to matter to someone else.

Regardless of the type of listening you do, you engage in all of the steps of the HURIER model. The different types of listening emphasize one or more of the steps, however. Discriminative listening emphasizes understanding and remembering, evaluative listening understanding and evaluating, appreciative listening hearing, and empathic listening hearing, interpreting, and responding. Keep in mind that during any particular listening situation, you may shift from one type of listening to another.

When you consciously become actively involved in the listening process, focusing your attention on engaging in the full range of listening behavior instead of passively letting listening happen, you listen effectively. Such effective listening is most apparent in a face-to-face conversation when you can orally and physically respond to the speaker, but it also can be done in a situation where you cannot directly respond but can still concentrate on hearing, understanding, remembering, interpreting, evaluating, and responding internally. You also can actively do any of the four types of listening, because the important part of active listening is getting involved in the listening process.

CRITICAL LISTENING

Critical listening is active listening in which the listener applies principles of critical thinking. When you're critically listening, you think about what the speaker is saying, what the claims are, how well the claims are supported, what kind of reasoning is being used, and so on. Moreover, critical listening asks what is unsaid as well as what is said, and the listener considers alternative explanations and conclusions to those explicitly or implicitly presented by the speaker.

Critical listening is most clearly related to evaluative listening, because evaluative listening is specifically directed to persuasive messages, and considers whether the arguments presented warrant acceptance. Critical listening also can be done in the other categories as well.

Discriminative listening lends itself to critical thinking when you make decisions about attending to the message, the probable truth of the information presented (asking how well it conforms to other known information, how well it is verified, if the information is based on fallacious reasoning, etc.), whether there is something missing, and whether there are alternative explanations. A critical thinker won't simply accept information as being true and complete but will consider it carefully. In addition, as a critical listener, you should question your own understanding regarding whether you really comprehend what is being said instead of simply assuming that you're being accurate.

Appreciative listening may not seem like it calls for any critical thinking, but it can. While you can watch a movie or listen to a story without thinking about either, you can also be aware of how well the stories hold together, both within the world created by the movie and the world as you know it. For instance, in police dramas, why do so many officers race across town to stop a murderer instead of calling for nearby patrol units to go to the scene? How accurately are physical laws portrayed in films such as *Armageddon* or *Godzilla*? Asking such questions may seem picky, but they can lead to a better appreciation of films that do not depend on violating common sense or science. Someone who is knowledgeable about music can apply critical skills to music to better appreciate what composers and musicians do. This does not mean that you cannot derive pleasure from uncritically accepting entertainment, but critical thinking allows you to have a richer experience at times.

Finally, critical thinking can be applied to empathic listening, which involves helping the speaker, and that can be done by being attentive, by trying to understand, and by showing that you understand. Trying to understand a speaker can involve the same critical thinking skills discussed earlier regarding discriminative listening. Showing that you understand can involve making reasoned choices about the best way to respond, and how to best help the speaker. Helping a speaker also can involve assisting him or her to sort through ideas, notice alternative explanations of situations, and conceive of a variety of options to respond to the situation and make an intelligent choice among those options. Sometimes simply listening and agreeing are all that is needed, and sometimes questioning and suggestion are called for.

BARRIERS TO LISTENING

Regardless of the type of listening you may do, several barriers can prevent you from listening as well as you might. An awareness of those barriers can help you avoid them in the first place and overcome them if you can't avoid them, thus helping you think critically about the content.

DeFleur, Kearney, and Plax cite *physical conditions* as one barrier to listening. It's harder to listen well if you're uncomfortable or if it's noisy around you, for instance. They also note that *personal problems* impair listening, because it's harder to concentrate on what is said when you're preoccupied with other matters. *Prejudging the speaker or the message* can lead to poor listening, because we tend to dismiss ideas before we really know what they are or hear what we expect to hear from a speaker. Prejudgment can include agreement or disagreement with what

Figure 13.1 Deciding that a message is unimportant can be a barrier to listening and can harm relationships.

Arlo and Janis reprinted by permission of Newspaper Enterprise Association, Inc.

will be said, positive and negative evaluations of the value of listening to the speaker, and positive or negative evaluations of how the speaker will present the message. Finally, they say that the *personal meanings* we have for words and phrases can hamper our ability to comprehend others.

Joseph De Vito identifies five other barriers to listening. He says that *preoccupation with other issues* can distract our attention, so we don't really hear or think about what the other person says. Some of that preoccupation can be with personal problems, as mentioned earlier, but it can also be with other issues that aren't relevant to the listening situation and are not personal problems. Second, he says that *assimilation,* or the tendency to reconstruct messages to reflect your own attitudes, prejudices, needs, and values can be a barrier to good listening. When you assimilate a message, you change it from what it was meant to be to something that better fits what you already believe. De Vito also discusses the *"friend-or-foe factor,"* which is the tendency to listen for positive qualities about friends and negative qualities about enemies. Thus instead of listening to the entire message, we listen only to selected parts. *Rehearsing your own responses* is another common barrier to listening, according to De Vito. As we mentally rehearse responses, our attention is distracted, and we can't really listen to what the other person says. His other barrier to listening is the tendency we have to *filter out unpleasant messages.* If there is something that we don't want to hear, then we find ways to ignore it, distort it, or forget it instead of listening to it, understanding it, and appropriately responding to it.

Julia T. Wood adds four other distinct barriers to listening. The first is *message overload,* or having too much to listen to in our daily lives to effectively listen to everything. The parent who is trying to talk on the phone while a television set blares nearby and several children noisily play is one example of message overload. The student who goes to class after class of lectures that call for intense listening is also faced with message overload, because even though she is listening to only one source at a time, the demands are so great that it is very difficult to sustain her attention over time. Another barrier is *message complexity,* which acknowledges that detailed and complicated ideas are more difficult to follow than simpler ones. The third barrier that Wood notes is *lack of effort,* or the fact that when we don't have or use enough energy, we usually don't listen as well. The final barrier to listening is *not recognizing diverse listening styles.* Wood explains that different cultures have different "rules" of listening. Eye contact may be prized or avoided, other activities while listening may be accepted or inappropriate, and so forth. For instance, she says that in Nepal, it is considered disrespectful to make sounds when someone else is talking, so the responding behavior of saying "uh huh" and "I see" during a conversation may lead to problems in that culture. While this barrier may not prevent the listener from listening to what is said, it may negatively affect the communication situation, lead to misunderstanding, and create disputes.

In addition to those barriers to listening, Wood also describes six forms of "nonlistening," or behavior that can prevent people from fully listening. She refers to **pseudolistening** as pretending to listen when you're not. The stereotypical spouse who says "Uh huh," and "Yes, dear" while continuing to read the newspaper is an example of this. You can probably remember times when as a student you pretended to listen to a lecture while you daydreamed about something else. Many of the barriers just listed can lead to pseudolistening, because people don't want to listen for some reason but know they are expected to do so.

A standard joke about first dates is the idea that one of the parties only wants to talk about himself, to the extent that his responses to his date do not really follow the conversation. Even though his date says only a sentence or two to interrupt his monologue, he ends up saying something to the effect of, "Enough about you. What about me?" Dominating a conversation by continually focusing on yourself instead of the other person is **monopolizing.** Of course, such behavior is not restricted to men. In most conversations, you are expected to talk about yourself somewhat, but it's expected that the conversational time will be shared somewhat equally. Monopolizing takes talking about yourself to an extreme, to the extent that the other person gets little chance to talk. Obviously if you're doing almost all of the talking then you don't have much opportunity to listen. You end up listening to the other person only to jump on opportunities to bring the subject back to yourself and not to try to understand the other person. Certainly there are situations when you or the other person ought to monopolize the conversation, such as when you're talking to someone else about your troubles, but even then monopolizing can keep you from listening to ideas the other person might have to contribute.

Another form of nonlistening is **selective listening,** which is focusing only on particular parts of the communication. It's like the joke about the employee who is reprimanded by his supervisor, who says the employee is remarkably incompetent. When he leaves, a coworker asks how it went, and the employee says, "She said I'm remarkable." Selective attention and selective perception are natural and unavoidable; there is just too much going on around you at any moment to fully attend to everything, so you have to be selective. Even when you do concentrate on what the other person says, to hear it, to understand it, to interpret it, and to evaluate it is a fairly large task, and you may miss something. If you listen only for certain ideas, you'll miss even more. To listen well, you need to be open to as much of the message as possible.

Sometimes when you're in a conversation with someone, you may perceive that you're being personally attacked, even though the other person has no intention of attacking you. If so, you are engaging in **defensive listening.** When you are defensive, you are more likely to understand messages as being more critical than intended, and you can end up being hurt and angry. If you really are being attacked, then you aren't listening defensively, but sometimes when you're in the situation, it's difficult to tell the difference. The psychodynamics of defensiveness are far too complicated to go into here, but at this point you should remember that defensiveness impairs your ability to listen well.

If you've ever spoken to someone who seems to just wait for you to say something wrong, who picks at what you say, and who makes demands for evidence that are unreasonable given the situation, you've experienced ambushing. **Ambushing** happens when the listener listens very carefully but only for the purpose of attacking the speaker. Ambushing is pseudolistening, because the listener doesn't really want to understand the speaker but instead wants to point out the speaker's weaknesses, often to appear superior. Good listening does involve critically listening to the speaker's ideas, but one must also recognize both the weaknesses and strengths in the information and arguments.

Wood also says that **literal listening** is a form of nonlistening. Literal listening is listening only for the content level of meaning and ignoring the relationship meaning. Sometimes the content meaning is what is important, but there are times when the most important part of the message concerns the kind of relationship the communicators have with each other. Often the relationship meaning is expressed indirectly; the listener has to be sensitive to cues in language, voice, and body. Remember that listening involves both understanding ideas and interpreting feelings, so listening only to ideas is not fully listening. For many of us, listening for both is difficult, because we've been trained to listen only for content, so it may take awhile to learn to listen for both.

This should make it clear that listening is not necessarily easy to do. It may seem like it should be easy, because we are in a position to listen so often, and we often don't recognize the struggle to listen well. Many potential difficulties are associated with good listening though.

IMPROVING LISTENING

Skillful listening is important to both good argumentation and critical thinking, since so much argumentation and so much of what we think about is communicated orally. Improving listening does start with an awareness of the listening process and the variety of ways people listen poorly. If you think listening only involves hearing, then there's not much you can do to improve. If you don't know what assimilation is, or that it leads to poor listening, then you can't be expected to deal with it.

The next step is to be more aware of what you do as you listen. You need to monitor your own listening to see which barriers you commonly face. You may not have a problem with ambushing or monopolizing, for instance, but you may discover that you often let personal problems distract you from listening to others. Since the majority of the listening process is internal, most of the information you need to improve has to come from yourself. You should reflect on what happened as you listened soon after you do it, because there's too much to think about to do so when you're already trying to listen. It can be helpful to get information from others though. Ask people with whom you interact regularly to honestly tell you how they perceive your listening ability. You may find that the aspects of listening that you think are your weaknesses are really not, and that what you feel are strengths are really not. At this point, it's a good idea to make a list of those barriers you commonly face and those that don't seem to be a problem for you to realize that you're already doing some things well and to know what to work on. It's also a good idea to determine which barriers are most important to work on, so you can tackle those first.

The third step in improving listening is to work on reducing barriers. You probably can't entirely eliminate any of the barriers, so it's better to think in terms of reducing them as much as you can. Exactly how you do so depends on the barriers you face. If you are trying to listen to someone in an environment that is too noisy, you can either move to a better place or concentrate more on the other person. If you regularly rehearse your own responses while you should be listening, then you can mentally remind yourself to concentrate on understanding and interpreting the messages and to hold off formulating responses until you fully understand the other person.

When you work on reducing barriers, it is best to work on them one at a time. If you try to work on them all at once, the task can be overwhelming. Pick the barrier that you think is most important in your listening and work to reduce it for a few weeks, then move to another. Keep in mind that most of the barriers to listening are habits that you've developed throughout your life, so you need to replace them with new habits. Change doesn't happen easily or quickly, so give yourself enough time.

As you work to improve your listening, you're developing new skills, which can seem awkward at first, especially when you're aware of what you're doing. In fact, until you create new listening habits, sometimes your listening may actually be worse, because your attention is focused on what you're doing as a listener rather than on what the other person says. Over time, though, you'll think about what you're doing less and less, and you'll reap the benefits of improved listening.

ACTIVE LISTENING

In addition to reducing the barriers to listening that you face you also can improve your listening by developing the skill of active listening. Judi Brownell states: "An important part of effective listening, then, is to respond in a manner that will facilitate shared meanings, contribute to accomplishing tasks, and develop satisfying relationships" (266). Active listening is a style of communication that enhances the responding phase of the listening process, letting the other person know that you are listening.

Active listening is, according to DeFleur, Kearney, and Plax, the act of exerting substantial effort to intentionally listen well *and* show the other person that you are listening. You can listen actively during a conversation and when you're in an audience for an oral presentation. Active listening helps you better understand by encouraging the other person to say more if that is needed, or to continue on to the next point. By letting the other person know that what he or she says is important, you increase the chance that that person will share ideas and feelings, as well as the chance that he or she will find the relationship rewarding.

Active listening involves several types of behavior. First, active listeners show that they are paying attention. Brownell cites research that identifies attentive behavior as including "eye contact, forward trunk lean, physical proximity, and verbal following" (90). Exceptions to those generalizations will be discussed later, but most Americans feel that they're being listened to when the listener looks right at them instead of around the room or at other objects, leans toward the speaker slightly, stays close by when possible, and when the listener's comments are directly related to what the speaker just said. You also can show your attention by nodding or shaking your head, by changing facial expressions, and vocally by saying "uh huh," "I see," or a variety of other appropriate responses.

Giving the other person the floor is the second active listening behavior, which means letting the other person talk about what she or he wants to talk about. The ways people take away the floor (which ought to be avoided) include unannounced subject changes, monopolizing the conversation, and interrupting. Announced subject changes, during which someone says something like "I need to talk about something else now," don't seem to be as much of a problem, because they acknowledge that what will be said is a different subject, which shows that the listener knew what was just said. Interruptions include breaking in before the speaker is finished talking and not letting the speaker regain the floor. The times you incorrectly think the other person is through so you start talking do not count as interruptions, unless you refuse to let the speaker continue.

A third aspect of active listening is focusing your attention on listening to the other person. Mentally you focus your attention by concentrating on listening, knowing that it takes some effort on your part to listen well. Physically, you focus your attention on the other person by orienting your body toward him, looking at him, and refraining from looking around the room. This is quite similar to showing the speaker that you're paying attention, but your purpose is to help yourself listen rather than help the other person recognize that you're listening.

Another part of active listening is thinking about what the other person says. The actual thinking will not be apparent to the speaker, of course, but you'll make it apparent with your overt responses. This means that you don't engage in pseudolistening and you don't spend time thinking of responses until you understand the other, but in some cases you do think critically about what is said.

Even when you're trying hard to listen well, sometimes your attention lapses and you don't really hear what the other person said. When that happens, a skillful, active listener will acknowledge the lapse by saying something like, "I'm sorry, I didn't get that," or "Could you repeat what you just said?" For many people, overtly acknowledging that they missed something is very hard to do, so they pretend that they heard when they didn't. Most speakers appreciate the effort to really understand them and are not offended if you admit that your mind wandered.

Asking questions of the speaker also is part of active listening. There are a variety of types of questions, but three that are common to listening well are **clarifiers, confirmers,** and **probes.** Clarifiers are questions that ask for more information to better explain ideas that are unclear. An example would be a student who says to a teacher, "I don't understand. Could you explain that again?" Confirmers are questions that ask whether the listener's understanding is accurate, such as, "Do you mean you would never consider going to Hawaii for a vacation?" Probes are questions that ask for more information so the listener can more fully understand the speaker, such as, "How did you feel when your sister got married?" Those types of questions both show that you're paying attention to what the speaker says and that you're thinking about it.

A final way to listen actively is to use **mirroring, paraphrasing,** and **interpreting.** Mirroring is a listening technique in which you repeat back what the other person said word for word. Paraphrasing is similar to mirroring, but you summarize what the speaker said in your own words, attempting to accurately capture his or her meaning. Interpreting involves saying what you understand the speaker to mean or feel, going beyond what was just said. If someone said "I can't believe Jerry got a raise," responding with "You can't believe Jerry got a raise?" would be mirroring. Paraphrasing would be, "You were surprised when Jerry got a raise." Interpreting might be, "You're angry that Jerry got the raise that you deserve." The three techniques explicitly indicate that you listened to what the speaker said, and they are invitations to say more. They're also helpful in achieving a more complete understanding of what is said.

People from different backgrounds generally have different rules to show that they're listening. Those rules are culturally based, and what seems natural and appropriate to show interest in one culture may convey a different meaning in another. (Remember, as with any description of cultural practices, some members of the cultural group will not engage in the practice. These generalizations don't necessarily apply to everyone.) Kearney and Plax identify a few of the cultural differences:

> African American and European American listeners may lean forward, nod in agreement, and show a variety of facial expressions.
>
> Native Americans show deference and attentiveness by avoiding sustained and direct eye contact.
>
> Asian Americans are likely to avoid eye contact and exhibit little overt expression in their facial or bodily movements, which communicate respect for the speaker.
>
> Latino and Middle Eastern American audience members are likely to show active listening behaviors similar to African and Euro-Americans, and show pleasure and agreement even when they may not agree with what they hear. (187–88)

There may be times when you are speaking and don't get the response you expect because you are speaking to someone with a different listening pattern.

Active listing is like critical thinking in the sense that you probably cannot do it all of the time. Both behaviors require concentration and energy, and sometimes the situation doesn't call for the effort. It is helpful to be able to do either when called for, however.

LISTENING AND READING

Listening is related to oral communication in the way that reading is related to written communication. Both involve the reception and understanding of messages. Critical listening and critical reading both call on you to carefully consider what is said or written, to determine what the message means by deciphering the codes used, to revise your understanding based on added information, and to consider possible meanings. When reading, you control the pace at which you read, and you can reread difficult passages as often as you want, while oral messages quickly disappear. On the other hand, oral messages provide vocal and visual information not usually available with written messages, and you often have the opportunity to provide feedback about your understanding so that the speaker can adjust the message.

The critical thinking skills involved in listening and reading are the same. With each you have to figure out what is claimed, what supports the claims, and the quality of the reasoning. You also may ask yourself what isn't being said and what the underlying assumptions are in the messages.

It would be a mistake to think of listening and reading as being the same, just as it would be a mistake to think of them as being totally different. Both are ways to get ideas from others, however.

SUMMARY

Listening is the most common of communication activities, but it should not be taken for granted. Although most people believe that listening just happens, it is really an active process that requires effort on the part of the listener to do well. We listen not only with our ears but also with our eyes and the rest of our bodies.

The HURIER model of listening (see Sidebar 13.1) identifies the steps in the listening process and shows that listening involves more than simply hearing. The four general types of listening are discriminative, evaluative, appreciative, and empathic. Each type calls for different skills and emphasizes various parts of the HURIER model. Critical listening can be done as part of any of the four general types.

There are several barriers to listening (see Sidebar 13.2) and forms of nonlistening (see Sidebar 13.3) that must be overcome to improve listening. It *can* be improved, though, and working to become a more active listener is one method to do so (see Sidebar 13.4).

Sidebar 13.1 HURIER Model of Listening

Hearing
Understanding
Remembering
Interpreting
Evaluating
Responding

Sidebar 13.2 Barriers to Listening

Physical conditions	Rehearsing responses
Personal problems	Filtering out unpleasant messages
Prejudging speaker or message	Message overload
Personal meanings	Message complexity
Preoccupation with other issues	Lack of effort
Assimilation	Not recognizing diverse listening styles
Friend-or-foe factor	

Sidebar 13.3 Forms of Nonlistening

Pseudolistening
Monopolizing
Selective listening
Defensive listening
Ambushing
Literal listening

Sidebar 13.4 Active Listening Responses

Clarifiers
Confirmers
Probes
Mirroring
Paraphrasing
Interpreting

KEY CONCEPTS

active listening   the act of exerting substantial effort to intentionally listen well and show the other person that you are listening.

ambushing   a form of nonlistening in which the listener listens very carefully to the speaker, but only for the purpose of attacking the speaker.

appreciative listening   listening done for the listener's pleasure.

clarifiers   questions that an active listener asks to get more information to better explain ideas that are unclear.

confirmers   questions that an active listener asks to see whether the listener's understanding of the speaker is accurate.

critical listening   active listening in which the listener applies the principles of critical thinking.

defensive listening   a form of nonlistening that involves the listener perceiving that he or she is being personally attacked and acting accordingly, when really there is no attack.

discriminative listening   listening to understand the speaker's meaning.

empathic listening   listening done to help the speaker.

evaluating   the part of the listening process in which the listener decides how much weight to put on what is said.

evaluative listening   listening responsibly to messages that attempt to influence the listener's attitudes, beliefs, or actions.

hearing   the step in the listening process in which the listener receives the auditory and visual stimuli.

HURIER model   a model of the listening process that includes Hearing, Understanding, Remembering, Interpreting, Evaluating, and Responding.

interpreting   (1) the step in the listening process during which the listener decides what the speaker feels; (2) an active listening technique that involves the listener saying what he or she understands the speaker to mean or feel, going beyond what was just said to confirm impressions and encourage further talking.

listening   an active form of behavior in which individuals attempt to maximize their attention to, and comprehension of, what is being communicated to them through words, actions, and things by one or more people in their immediate environment.

literal listening   a form of non-listening that involves listening only for the content level of meaning and ignoring the relationship meaning.

mirroring   an active listening technique in which the listener repeats back what the other person said word for word to confirm understanding and to encourage continued talking.

monopolizing   a form of nonlistening that involves dominating the conversation by continually focusing on oneself rather than the other person.

paraphrasing   an active listening technique in which the listener summarizes what the speaker said in the listener's own words, attempting to accurately capture the speaker's meaning to confirm understanding and to encourage further talking.

probes   questions that an active listener asks to get more information so the listener can more fully understand the speaker.

pseudolistening   a form of non-listening that involves pretending to listen when the listener is really not paying attention.

remembering   the step in the listening process in which the listener stores the meaning in memory so it can be retrieved later.

responding   the part of the listening process in which the listener lets the speaker know that the listener is listening and how the listener is understanding the message.

selective listening   a form of nonlistening that involves focusing only on particular parts of the communication being listened to.

understanding   the step in the listening process in which the listener decides what the speaker means.

THINGS TO THINK ABOUT

1. Pay attention to an example of your own listening. What did you do that involved each part of the HURIER model?

2. Think of a recent example of doing critical listening. Evaluate how well you listened using the principles from this chapter.

3. Take an opportunity to listen actively. What did you do, specifically, to enact the principles from this chapter? What could you have done to be a better active listener?

4. Choose five of the barriers to listening described in this chapter and explain how each can also be a barrier to critical thinking.

5. Think of an example of a time when you experienced one or more of the barriers to listening. What could you have done to listen better?

6. Pay attention to your own listening behavior for a few days. What are your strengths as a listener, based on the principles in this chapter? What are your weaknesses? What could you do to improve?

7. Choose three of the barriers to listening described in this chapter. How could each also be a barrier to critical thinking?

14

✻

Dyadic Argumentation

One context in which we most commonly argue is in a one-to-one conversation with another person. Such arguments are marked by a free flow of taking turns talking, the absence of a third party who decides which side will prevail, each party directing their arguments to the other person, and, too often, hurt feelings and damaged relationships. Such argumentation is a common part of everyday communication, so it is important to develop an understanding of how to do it better, both to be able to convince others and to maintain good relationships. This chapter will

- explain dyadic argumentation.
- identify the purposes of dyadic argumentation.
- explain some differences between positive and negative ways of arguing with another individual.
- suggest ways to manage relationships when arguing.

WHAT IS DYADIC ARGUMENTATION?

A **dyad** is simply two people engaging in some activity together. Dyadic communication, then, is two people communicating with each other, and **dyadic argumentation** is two people arguing together.

The phrase "dyadic argumentation" encompasses any two people arguing, regardless of their relationship. If they have an ongoing, personal relationship, then they engage in interpersonal argumentation, which is an important type of dyadic argumentation. However, a great deal of argumentation is done in dyads where the parties have an ongoing relationship but it isn't really personal, such as in a work situation. In addition, people often argue with others in a fleeting, impersonal relationship, such as a customer arguing that she should receive a refund from a company's customer service representative whom she has never met before, and is unlikely to meet again. The argumentation done in each of those types of dyads will be similar because only two people are involved, but it will have some different characteristics because of how well the people know each other and their differing desires to maintain a good relationship.

PURPOSES OF
DYADIC ARGUMENTATION

Dyadic arguments have several purposes, and they're not always intended to persuade the other person to accept a proposition. For some people, engaging in an argument with another is a type of pleasurable interaction. The give-and-take of ideas, the challenge of being able to make and respond to arguments on the spur of the moment, and the opportunity to test skills with an equally matched co-arguer are as fun and exciting to them as dancing and snowboarding are to others. For such people, the position they take on an issue may not matter, and the outcome may be no more important than that of a tennis match with a friend. They enjoy arguing in a friendly way, and they believe that other people do too.

Sometimes people use dyadic argumentation to test ideas. One person expresses an idea to another, implicitly or explicitly asking for an opinion. The second person responds, and the argument begins. The second person may disagree with the first and present her reasons, to which the first person responds. The second person also may agree with the first person and present her reasons. The first person may accept some of those reasons and dispute others. Such argumentation allows both parties to examine the problem from different perspectives and determine which ideas have merit and which cannot be supported. Although both parties start out believing that their opinions should be accepted, they are willing to yield to better arguments, because the goal is not to win the argument but to create better ideas. Using argumentation to test ideas in this way is common when two people work together on a project.

People also commonly use dyadic argumentation to resolve disputes. Two people have some sort of a conflict, and each believes he or she is right. At some point, the conflict becomes uncomfortable enough so that one of them starts talking about it. Each person presents, supports, and refutes claims and counterclaims. Often the parties involved in the conflict try to ignore or avoid it for a while, so when it is explicitly brought up, tension and feelings may be quite high. Depending on the people involved, the argumentation may remain calm and stick to

Figure 14.1 The give-and-take of claims and counterclaims is a characteristic of dyadic argument.

the issues, or it may become heated and move to irrelevant personal attacks and unrelated issues. Dispute-resolving argumentation does not have to degenerate into a fight, but often it does.

Argumentation also is used to maintain and improve relationships. For example, one member of an interpersonal or a work dyad may express inferences about the other's behavior and present the evidence that led him to those inferences. The other party may then confirm that those inferences are correct, or respond with arguments about why they are incorrect. Such argumentation can improve understanding between the two. Dyadic relationships are inevitably subject to change, and the parties can negotiate that change through argumentation, presenting different options, arguing for them, and reaching agreement. Finally, argumentation can be used to vent feelings, so they are out in the open, and the parties can deal with them before they become destructive to the relationship.

Some people also use dyadic argumentation to achieve goals that aren't so noble or positive. One of those goals is to satisfy the ego of one of the participants, by proving that he or she can make better arguments than the other. In such cases, the ideas and the relationship are not as important as proving self-worth. To some extent, ego satisfaction can be good for a person, but when it becomes the overriding goal of dyadic argumentation, then it tends to create unpleasant situations.

Even more unpleasant situations are created when one's purpose is to dominate another. Argumentation can be used to dominate by using personal attacks, fallacious reasoning, and other strategies to make the other person feel bad. Such argumentation is used to exert power over others rather than to reach true understanding and agreements.

These purposes are not mutually exclusive. A particular situation may involve one or more of them for either person in the dyad. Keep in mind that people engage in argumentation for a variety of reasons, and those reasons are not always apparent to them or others.

ARGUMENTATIVENESS AND
VERBAL AGGRESSIVENESS

Communication theorist Dominic Infante identified two general personality facets that are especially important in thinking about dyadic argumentation. The facets explain why some argumentative behavior is destructive and hurtful and other behaviors are constructive and productive. He calls the two facets "argumentativeness" and "verbal aggressiveness."

Argumentativeness is associated with assertive communication behavior, which Infante describes as

> a general tendency to be interpersonally dominant, ascendant, and forceful. Behavior of this type takes many forms, e.g., a defense of your rights such as asking someone not to smoke, taking leadership responsibilities in group situations, initiating a conversation with a stranger, resisting pressure to conform to a group opinion. Argumentativeness includes the ability to recognize controversial issues in communication situations, to present and defend positions on the issues, and to attack the positions which other people take. Assertiveness is a broad trait which includes argumentativeness, a more specific trait. Thus, all arguing is assertive behavior, but not all assertiveness involves arguing. (7)

It may seem odd to think of argumentativeness as a positive behavior, because we usually describe people who are quarrelsome, rude, and unpleasant as "argumentative." It's important to realize that our use of the term is different from the everyday meaning. When we refer to **argumentativeness,** we mean a positive personality facet exhibited by the willingness to engage in argumentation when appropriate and to argue in a manner that focuses on issues and reasoning and avoids attacking other people's self-concepts.

Verbal aggressiveness, on the other hand, is a negative personality facet exhibited by "the inclination to attack the self-concepts of individuals instead of, or in addition to, their positions on particular issues" (Infante, 7). Verbal aggressiveness is not true argumentation, because the verbally aggressive individual does not stick to the issues but also says things that are meant to hurt or silence the other person and to shift the topic away from the issues. Thus in addition to being socially unpleasant, verbal aggressiveness involves *ad hominem* attacks, evading the issue, and, often, implied or explicit appeals to force.

People who are argumentative, in Infante's sense, engage in constructive argumentation, which he says involves five skills related to argumentative competence. Those skills include the ability to (1) state the controversy in propositional form, (2) analyze the proposition and invent arguments, (3) present and defend your position, (4) refute other positions, and (5) manage interpersonal relations. The first four skills have been discussed in earlier chapters. This chapter discusses some strategies involved in the fifth skill.

What can you do when faced with verbal aggression in others? Rather than feel too threatened to to respond at all, or to respond with verbal aggressiveness of your own, Infante suggests five ways that you can respond constructively (93–98). To make these responses work, you have to do them calmly and sincerely. If it appears that you are responding with another form of verbal aggression, or if you say them in a way that seems sarcastic or patronizing, then you are likely to escalate verbal aggressiveness rather than reduce it.

Infante's first suggestion is *leave taking,* and it consists of simply leaving. He suggests that if you do leave, it's best to say something about why you're doing so, such as, "Now you're attacking me personally, and I am not going to accept that kind of behavior. We can continue this discussion when there will be no more personal attacks." Having said that, you leave. This response calls attention to the inappropriate behavior and makes it clear that it will not be accepted, but it also leaves open the possibility to continue the discussion later. Importantly, it does not blame or belittle the other person.

Infante also that says you can *explicitly make the distinction between an argument and verbal aggression.* You might say, "Now you're making personal attacks on me instead of discussing the issue. Our discussion will be more productive if any attacks are made on ideas rather than on people." This response helps keep the argumentation focused on where it should be by describing the inappropriate behavior and identifying the preferred behavior. Again, it does not say that something is wrong with the other arguer but with his behavior.

The third suggestion is to *ask the person to justify using verbal aggression.* If the verbal aggression takes the form of denigrating your character, then you can call attention to the fact that the argument has shifted from the issues to your character and that the claim hasn't been supported, and then ask for evidence that the claim is true.

This also might be accomplished by saying, "Why are you attacking me instead of responding to my ideas?" This calls attention to the verbal aggression, and most people will say that they didn't mean to attack you and will be more careful to stick to the issues as the discussion proceeds. If they do say why they are resorting to verbal aggression, then they will provide valuable information about how they feel about the situation. For instance, someone might respond with verbal aggressiveness because she felt that you attacked her earlier, and you may need to adjust your behavior if the discussion is to be productive.

Another tactic that Infante suggests is to *appeal to the other person's rationality.* That is, point out that verbal aggressiveness has been introduced into the dialogue, and explain that the consequences of verbal aggressiveness will be to change a rational conversation into irrational communication. Since most people want to be perceived as rational, they will try to avoid appearing irrational to others.

Infante's final suggestion is actually a combination of the others, which is to *refuse to reciprocate the use of verbal aggression.* If the other person yells and insults, that doesn't mean that you have to yell and insult back. To diffuse the situation, it is almost always more effective to remain calm when the other person starts to lose control. You may have to let her vent her feelings for a while, and it might take a lot of self-discipline to remain calm when you're being attacked, but it usually works better.

All of these suggestions are probably easier to understand than to do, unless you already do them. To learn to do them when you engage in arguments, rehearse the responses mentally when you're not in a difficult situation, so you don't have to come up with what to say in the heat of the moment. Since you're learning a new skill, it will seem awkward to actually do this at first, and you probably won't always successfully achieve the results you want. Over time, though, you'll become more comfortable using the strategies, and you'll avoid being the target of verbal aggressiveness.

On the other hand, if you're someone who tends to be verbally aggressive, then you should reflect on what you've said in arguments, identify what is verbally aggressive, and think of other things that you could have said to make your point without attacking the other person. Then you can mentally rehearse making arguments without becoming aggressive and start to incorporate the new behavior in your actual arguments.

People learn their argumentative styles as they grow up, partly by observing how others argue. Those who have observed a lot of verbal aggressiveness will think that it is normal behavior and will engage in it without really thinking about what they're doing. It's a behavior that can be changed, though, even if it isn't easy. Like any other habit, it takes some work to break out of the old pattern and establish a new one that then becomes second nature. It helps if you have an idea of what productive new patterns could be.

SUPPORTIVE AND THREATENING COMMUNICATION

Responding to verbal aggressiveness is a way to manage interpersonal relations when the other person starts to attack you, but you don't have to wait for that situation to act in ways that create a better argumentative climate. You also can manage interpersonal relations during an argument, or any other encounter, by using supportive rather than threatening communication. **Supportive communication** is verbal and nonverbal messages presented in ways that are unlikely to be perceived as an ego threat. **Threatening communication** is verbal and nonverbal messages presented in ways that are likely to be perceived as an ego threat. Threatening communication can lead to, or escalate, verbal aggression from another and is itself a form of verbal aggressiveness, while supportive communication can prevent or reduce verbal aggression.

An ego threat is behavior that is perceived to imply that the receiver is incompetent, stupid, or has some other personal defects. Ego threats attack people's self-worth and lead them to react in ways intended to protect their sense of self. It is probably impossible to remove ego threats entirely, because sometimes their source is within the receiver. For instance, some students are perfectionists, and it is very important to them that everything they do is praised and rewarded. Such students can be psychologically devastated if they earn anything less than the highest grade for their work, so even when they receive high grades accompanied by suggestions for improvement, the idea that their work wasn't perfect is ego threatening. Even when there is, objectively, no personal attack on them, they perceive that there is.

On the other hand, most people are able to accept criticism when it involves what they did rather than who they are. However, almost anyone would begin to feel defensive when criticism is presented in the form of personal attacks or perceived as personal attacks. When we're defensive, we do what we can to avoid, escape, or eliminate personal attacks. Some ways in which we act defensively are to withdraw and cease to listen, to become hostile and lash back, to procrastinate and otherwise avoid doing things that could be evaluated, and to rationalize our behavior and avoid making productive changes. Defensiveness creates barriers to communication, meaning that unnecessary conflicts arise, differences are not resolved, and relationships are impaired.

Communication theorist Jack Gibb identified a set of behaviors that tend to be threatening to many people and a corresponding set of behaviors that tend to be supportive. The threatening behaviors are similar to Infante's verbal aggressiveness, and the supportive behaviors help to better manage interpersonal relations. In dyadic arguments, and in other communication encounters, it is helpful to avoid the threatening behaviors and try to be more supportive. If you can incorporate the supportive styles into your communication repertoire and reduce the threatening styles, then you're likely to create a better communication climate for arguing about issues, or any other type of conversation you might have.

One communication style that arouses defensiveness is presenting messages that indicate you believe you are somehow better than, or superior to, the other person. The superiority may involve intelligence, looks, wealth, ability, or a variety of other attributes. **Superiority** can be shown by tone of voice, facial expression, posture, and silence, as well as by the things you say. Sometimes superiority isn't shown by directly saying that you're somehow better than someone else but can be indicated by name-dropping and bragging about accomplishments or possessions. You also might show superiority by pointing out that others are deficient in some way, implying that you're not. The supportive style opposed to superiority is **equality,** which is communication showing you believe that others are as important and worthy as you are. Inevitably, there will be differences between people, but those differences don't have to be emphasized in a divisive way. In addition, feelings of equality can be generated by sincerely emphasizing the other person's strengths. Doing so helps the person become more receptive to suggestions for change.

A second way of creating a defensive climate is to communicate in a controlling way. **Control** is a threatening communication behavior that focuses on telling others what to do. Controlling statements include "Do it this way" and "Do it my way, or else." Messages of control imply that the other person is incapable of making his or her own decisions, even when the message is presented with the most helpful intentions, which often happens, for example, when parents tell their teenagers what to do. Controlling messages also are often are made without fully understanding the circumstances, so they may be premature, which can be frustrating to those who feel controlled. If you've ever worked on a group project with someone who is "bossy," then you've encountered controlling communication. A more supportive form of communication is **problem orientation,** which focuses attention on mutually determining how to solve a problem rather than controlling one's behavior. When you ask for information, opinions, and suggestions rather than immediately give orders, you exhibit a problem orientation that is more likely to result in continued interaction and cooperation. This doesn't mean that you can't also give your opinions and make suggestions but that you should make an effort to have them perceived as opinions and suggestions, not commands. A project member who asks others how they think the group should proceed exhibits a problem orientation. People who are used to giving orders and working in a controlling environment may defend controlling communication on the basis that it takes less time, and in the short term, it does. However, a problem orientation better allows people to learn to solve problems on their own, generates more commitment to solutions, and creates an environment in which people share ideas with others. In the long run, the problem orientation saves time.

Neutrality is a threatening communication that indicates that you don't care about the other person. You don't care about his welfare, what is happening to him, or problems he might have. Neutrality can convey the impression that the other person is not worth caring about, leading to defensiveness. It is important to note that Gibb uses the term *neutrality* differently than most people do in everyday life, and he doesn't use it to identify positive behavior. He does not mean an unbiased or a fair-minded attitude. Perhaps "indifference" would be a better word for this threatening type of communication, but it's not the term Gibb used. A more supportive style is **empathy,** which shows the other person that you care about her and that she is valued. Empathy is accepting the other person's feelings as legitimate, rather than discounting them by saying things like "You shouldn't feel that way." Many times small talk and empathic listening will show another person you care about him or her and establish the supportive climate.

You've probably been in a situation where someone has accused you of doing something wrong when there's a perfectly legitimate explanation for what you did, but the other person won't listen to it because he is so sure that his perception is correct. That is an example of the threatening communication style of certainty. **Certainty** is communication that gives the impression that you know everything and that you're always right. Through language, voice, and physical communication, you let the other person know that if her idea is different from yours, then she must be wrong. People who show this kind of certainty may jump to conclusions without getting all of the necessary information, and they may cut people off who try to provide the information. Later, if they turn out to be wrong, they may say, with certainty, that it is someone else's fault. Typically, self-assurance in arguments is seen as a positive quality, but certainty goes beyond being confident. A better approach is **provisionalism,** which is operating from the assumption that you don't know everything, that you're not always right, and that you can learn important information by listening to others. The provisional style allows you to draw tentative conclusions but leaves you open to gaining more facts and revising your position. If you use the provisional style, then you are more likely to ask, "What happened?" "Why?" and "How can we do what you suggest?" before reaching a final conclusion. People showing certainty try to justify their conclusions and win arguments; people showing provisionalism try to reach the best conclusions.

Most people feel nervous when someone else judges them. Even when the judgment turns out to be positive, the process can be intimidating. That's why evaluation is Gibb's fifth category of threatening communication behavior. **Evaluation** is communication that lets the other person know that you've judged him in some way. Usually, when the judgment is positive, there isn't much of a problem, although such a judgment carries the possibility of taking away the positive evaluation in the future. Negative evaluations are a more immediate problem. Our language is full of evaluative terms, and you probably can't avoid them entirely, but you can think before you speak and try to eliminate statements that are most likely to produce defensiveness. For example, a parent may try to motivate a child to clean his room by saying, "You are such a pig," but that sort of evaluative name-calling is likely to lead to a worse outcome than a dirty room. The supportive equivalent to evaluation is **description,** which is communication that describes situations or behaviors and how they affect you. Rather than saying "You are such a pig," the parent could say, "When your room looks like it does now, I feel like you're showing a lack of respect for our house. I'd really appreciate it if you'd clean it up." Such a statement describes the situation, describes the parent's reaction, and describes what the parent wants done. In a situation where you're arguing with someone over an issue, instead of saying "That's a ridiculous suggestion," you could say, "I don't agree," and then go on to state your reasons.

Gibb's final category of threatening communication behavior is **strategy,** which is communication that appears to be rehearsed and manipulative rather than open and honest. If you've ever received a direct marketing call during which the caller tries to seem friendly while stiffly reading from a prepared script and mispronounces your name, then you know what it's like to be confronted with strategy. You can't take what is said at face value, and you strongly suspect that you're being trapped into agreeing to something. Often people bring up the most sensitive issues in a strategic way, because they want to avoid prompting defensiveness. Ironically, that brings about the defensiveness that they tried to avoid. The supportive counterpart to strategy is **spontaneity,** or communication behavior that appears to be a natural, unprepared response to the moment. If you follow the thread of conversation where it goes rather than try to steer it in a particular direction, then you are more likely to create a feeling of spontaneity. Generally speaking, if you want to steer the conversation in some direction, it is better to come right out and say so instead of attempting to manipulate it.

By now you may have noticed that the same communication may involve more than one category of threatening or supportive behavior. A parent who says, "Clean up your filthy room. Quit being such a pig!" shows superiority (calling someone a pig implies that the speaker is not), control (there's no discussion of how to solve the problem, only a command), certainty (the parent is certain that her perception and solution are the only possibilities), and evaluation (judging the room as filthy and the child as piggish), all at the same time. Conversely, substituting one kind of threatening communication with a supportive style may effectively replace other threats.

You also may have noticed that in some situations it is quite difficult to eliminate all threatening communication, because of the nature of the parties involved.

For instance, when a supervisor wants an employee to complete a normal, everyday task, a command is probably more appropriate than a discussion, even though it indicates control. The way the command is presented, however, can make a lot of difference. A command that directs action in a businesslike way, in language and nonverbal communication that indicate respect for the employee, is unlikely to raise defenses. If the employee raises a concern about the command, then rather than respond with control ("Just do it!") or certainty ("Don't question my orders!"), the supervisor can respond with provisionalism and problem orientation ("This seems like the best way to proceed to me. Why do you think it won't work?"). The employee's concerns might be well founded and based on information that the supervisor didn't have. By listening to them, a better course of action would result. Of course, if the supervisor has already established a threatening communication climate, then asking the employee why he thinks the idea won't work can easily be perceived as a veiled threat rather than as a legitimate request for ideas.

You also might realize that some people simply do not appreciate efforts to create a supportive communication climate. They are not interested in being treated as an equal. They want to be controlled, and they expect others to show no doubt about their conclusions. They can make it harder to create a supportive climate, because they resist it. If you get into the habit of being more supportive than threatening, then it will become a natural part of your style, and it will be easier to deal with such people, although it probably won't become pleasant.

Like other changes in communication styles, becoming a more supportive communicator isn't quick or easy, especially in the context of arguments. If you've learned habits of threatening communication, then you have to learn new habits, which takes time. And until you've firmly established a new style, you're likely to revert to the old habits when under the stress of an argument. In addition, as you establish a new style, you'll probably be less comfortable and spontaneous in your communication. Paradoxically, as you incorporate more supportive communication in your everyday argumentation, you may seem more strategic than usual. As the new habits are established, though, they become more natural and spontaneous.

MANAGING RELATIONS
AND ARGUMENTATION

Creating supportive communication climates can be combined with other specific suggestions for improving dyadic argumentation. Infante has nine recommendations for improving the way you manage relationships while arguing. Combining them with knowledge of how to make strong arguments can help you present your arguments and avoid causing interpersonal problems. Infante's strategies for managing relations are not only pragmatically sound, but they also meet the ethical standards for interpersonal argumentation, addressed earlier. If you're able to follow his suggestions, then you're much more likely to be the "arguer as lover."

First, Infante suggests that you *use the principles of argumentation with compassion*. As a result of studying argumentation, you should have some argumentative skills that others don't. You can use those skills as a tool for productive conversations or as weapons to threaten or humiliate others. For example, by now you have an idea of how to use evidence in an argument and how to refute other people's arguments. In an informal conversation, you might point out that the other arguer hasn't presented any evidence for a claim but not emphasize that because you know that the information isn't readily available. That uses a principle with compassion. On the other hand, you might continually pressure the other person for the evidence, demanding to know the source, the source's qualifications, how he or she came to a conclusion, and so on. You may "win" the argument with such tactics, but the cost may not be worth the benefit. As a skillful arguer, you should adapt your behavior to the context. Do not treat every argument as though it were a murder trial.

Infante also suggests that you *reaffirm your opponent's sense of competence* during an argument. When she makes a good point, say so. When there's a flaw in her argument, address it in a manner that recognizes that perfect arguments are uncommon. Show respect for the other person's argumentative skills, and she will be more likely to engage you in conversation rather than avoid you.

Allowing your opponents to finish what they're saying is a very good way to create better relations with another. Doing so avoids the impression that what others have to say is unimportant, or that you know what they will say before they say it. Interruptions invite interruptions in response, which encourages argument by volume; whoever talks the loudest gets to have her or his say. Interrupting also leads to frustration, defensiveness, and, ultimately, lack of participation.

You can manage relations in a positive way by *emphasizing equality* through your communication. This is the same idea that was discussed as a supportive communication style: recognize the ways in which you are equal to the other person, and avoid emphasizing ways in which you consider yourself superior.

Infante further suggests that you *emphasize shared attitudes*. People tend to be attracted to others who share similar attitudes, beliefs, and values and are more likely to try to maintain good relations with them. You can emphasize shared attitudes by reminding the other person of ideas you agree upon and by minimizing your differences. This does not mean that you should pretend that there are no differences, or make them smaller than they really are. When people engage in arguments, they tend to make their differences seem larger, however, making it more difficult to bridge the gaps.

Infante's sixth suggestion is to *show your opponents that you are interested in their views*. This is another way of demonstrating respect for the other person, which leads to better relations. Some ways of showing interest have already been mentioned: good listening behavior, including giving responses that show you're listening; allowing the other person to finish what she's saying; and following the conversation instead of changing the subject. Another way is to directly ask for opinions and feelings about the subject. When people believe you are interested in their views, they feel less of a need to resort to verbal aggressiveness to be heard and taken seriously.

Infante also suggests that you *use a somewhat subdued, calm delivery* as a way to manage relations with others while arguing. Heated, loud, and overly forceful delivery presents a threat similar to the barking and growling of dogs, and people respond to it reflexively by withdrawal or counterattack. A calmer delivery promotes a calmer response from the other.

Sometimes, when we're engaged in an argument with another, we want to go straight to the solution without discussing the nature of the problem and what's causing it. Infante believes that that leads to argumentation that jumps around without adequately dealing with issues and also leads to worse relations. He suggests that you *control the pace of the argument.* That means you should make sure that you take the argument step-by-step and discuss the appropriate stock issues. Instead of quickly looking for a victor, he suggests that you take your time to reach the best conclusion. That doesn't mean that an argument should go on forever, but that you ensure that you don't leave out any considerations.

Finally, he suggests that you make sure you *allow your opponent to save face* during the argument. Saving face means that a person is able to retain a sense of dignity and worth. In many ways, this goes back to the issues of respect, equality, and affirming a sense of competence. It goes beyond that, though, because it says that you should give your opponent a chance to accept your argument without being humiliated or totally defeated. When there is a chance to save face, it is much easier for people to modify their positions and argue cooperatively instead of trying to protect their position to the end.

I would add two more suggestions for managing relations when arguing with another individual. First, *stick to the issue.* Too often, when people argue with one another, they start off on one subject but shift to another unrelated issue. A couple may start arguing about how to best handle household finances, and, part way through, one person condemns the other's behavior at a party some weeks ago, and the second person talks about the other's poor cooking skills. Both of those issues may be important to discuss at some time, but they are irrelevant to the initial question and constitute red herrings. Such arguments are sometimes called "kitchen sink" arguments, because they include everything in a relationship, including the kitchen sink. Too often, the irrelevant issues are brought up to hurt the other person's feelings, and that damages relationships.

Second, during a dyadic argument, *accept the other person's feelings.* Whatever the other person feels is his or her reality, and should be accepted as such. Whether he or she is hurt, angry, scared, frustrated, or a variety of other emotions, accept these feelings as legitimate. That doesn't mean that you have to agree that those emotions are the most appropriate, but you shouldn't question the validity of them *for that person.* During arguments, people often say things like, "You're not really angry," "Don't be mad," or "You shouldn't be upset." Sometimes they say such things because they're truly trying to be helpful, but sometimes they are said to diminish the other person's experience and to get out of dealing with the consequences of their own actions. Whatever the reason for the sayings, they have the effect of discounting the other person and may evade the real issue in the argument.

SUMMARY

Dyadic communication takes place between two people. The two people involved may or may not have an ongoing relationship, and their relationship may or may not be personal. Dyadic argumentation takes place between two people and may be used to accomplish several purposes. People use it to try to persuade the other person, as a pleasurable type of interaction, to test ideas, to resolve disputes, and to improve relationships. Sometimes dyadic argumentation is used to boost an arguer's ego or to dominate the other person though.

People who have the personality trait of argumentativeness tend to readily engage in argumentation, stick to issues, and use argumentative skills advocated in this text. People with the personality trait of verbal aggressiveness tend to use arguments as opportunities to attack the self-concepts of the people with whom they argue. Argumentativeness is a positive trait, while verbal aggressiveness is a negative trait. Dominic Infante recommends several ways to deal with verbal aggressiveness when you encounter it (see Sidebar 14.1).

Managing relationships is an important part of dyadic argumentation, because if the relationship is not managed, then negative feelings, retribution, and disengagement may result. Communication in dyads can be more or less supportive, and supportive communication usually results in better relationships. Jack Gibb identified six categories of ego-threatening communication and six alternative categories

Sidebar 14.1   Dominic Infante's Suggestions for Responding to Verbal Aggressiveness

Leave-taking
Explicitly make the distinction between argument and verbal aggression
Ask the other to justify using verbal aggression
Appeal to the other's rationality
Refuse to reciprocate verbal aggression

Sidebar 14.2   Jack Gibb's Categories of Communication Behaviors Characteristic of Supportive and Defensive Communication Climates

Defensive Climates	Supportive Climates
Superiority	Equality
Control	Problem orientation
Neutrality	Empathy
Certainty	Provisionalism
Evaluation	Description
Strategy	Spontaneity

Sidebar 14.3   Dominic Infante's Strategies for Managing Relations

Use the principles of argumentation with compassion.
Reaffirm your opponent's sense of competence.
Allow opponents to finish what they're saying.
Emphasize equality.
Emphasize shared attitudes.
Show opponents that you are interested in their views.
Use a somewhat subdued, calm delivery.
Control the pace of the argument.
Allow your opponent to save face.

VerLinden's Additional Strategies

Stick to the point.
Accept the other person's feelings.

of supportive communication (see Sidebar 14.2). The more supportive communication behaviors are used during arguments, the less likely people are to become defensive, and the argument is more likely to be productive and worthwhile. In addition, Infante suggests nine ways to manage relationships during arguments (see Sidebar 14.3). Those suggestions, along with the two added, help manage relationships, whether they are close, personal relationships, working relationships, or impersonal relationships.

KEY CONCEPTS

argumentativeness   a positive personality facet exhibited by the willingness to engage in argumentation when appropriate and to argue in a manner that focuses on issues and reasoning and avoids attacking other people's self-concepts.

certainty   a threatening communication behavior that gives the impression that the communicator knows everything and is always right.

control   a threatening communication style in which the communicator tells others what to do.

description   a supportive communication style in which the communicator describes situations or behaviors and how they affect him or her.

dyad   two people engaged in an activity together.

dyadic argumentation   two people arguing together.

empathy   a supportive communication style in which the communicator exhibits a caring attitude toward the other person.

equality   a supportive communication style in which the communicator shows that he or she believes that others are important and worthy.

evaluation   a threatening communication style in which the communicator lets the other person know that he or she is being judged in some way.

neutrality   a threatening communication style in which the communicator indicates that he or she doesn't care about the other person.

problem orientation   a supportive communication style in which the communicator focuses attention on mutually determining how to solve a problem rather than controlling anyone's behavior.

provisionalism   a supportive communication style in which the communicator operates from the assumption that he or she doesn't know everything, is not always right, and can gain important information by listening to others.

spontaneity   a supportive communication style in which communication appears to be a natural, unprepared response to the moment.

strategy   a threatening communication style in which what is said appears to be rehearsed and manipulative.

superiority   a threatening communication style in which the communicator indicates that he or she is somehow better than others.

supportive communication   verbal and nonverbal messages presented in ways that are unlikely to be perceived as an ego threat.

threatening communication   verbal and nonverbal messages presented in ways that are likely to be perceived as an ego threat.

verbal aggressiveness   a negative personality facet exhibited by the inclination to attack the self-concepts of individuals instead of, or in addition to, their positions on particular issues.

THINGS TO THINK ABOUT

1. Think of different dyadic arguments you engaged in or observed that which were used to (1) test ideas, (2) maintain or improve a relationship, and (3) achieve ego satisfaction or establish dominance over another person. What were the characteristics of each?

2. Think of a time when you were the target of verbal aggressiveness. What was the situation, and what was said that was verbally aggressive? How did it make you feel? How did you react? How did it affect your relationship?

3. When you engage in argumentation, are you more likely to be argumentative or verbally aggressive? What do you do that makes you believe that you are that style of arguer?

4. Think of a dyadic argument you engaged in or observed. How were threatening and supportive

communication behaviors used? Remember that even a brief encounter may exhibit several of the types of communication behavior, and that sometimes the behaviors are exhibited nonverbally.

5. Evaluate your own dyadic argumentation style. Which threatening communication styles do you tend to use? Which supportive styles do you tend to use? What steps could you specifically take to improve the way you manage relationships in dyadic arguments?

15

✱

Argumentation and Small Groups

Most of us will spend a good portion of our personal and professional lives communicating in small groups. Classes often call on students to work together on group projects. People often socialize in small groups. Businesses often accomplish tasks through small groups. When you're with your family, you're probably in a small group.

In any of these groups, there is a likelihood that argumentation will occur. Students working on group projects have to make decisions regarding how they will proceed, and it's uncommon for each person to immediately agree that the first suggestion is the best. People who are socializing may engage in argumentation as they discuss controversial issues or decide what to do together. Business committees regularly engage in argumentation as they try to determine causes of situations and plans for future action. And arguments are a regular part of family life, especially when some members of the family are adolescents. You are extremely likely to engage in small group argumentation quite often throughout your life.

The arguments that groups engage in can be a good thing. As explained in Chapter 1, argumentation can be used to reach the best decisions. That's a major reason groups are formed: to reach better decisions by considering multiple ideas and perspectives. Chapter 1 also identified the value of argumentation in educating others about issues, seeing both sides of issues, and assisting in the search for truth.

The *way* people engage in small group argumentation can make the experience productive and positive or fruitless and damaging.

A **small group** consists of more than two people, but not so many that they cannot all engage in the interaction. The minimum number of people in a small group is three, but the upper limit is unclear. As groups get larger, fewer members become involved in the discussions, and the context seems more like public speaking than group interaction. This may occur with more than eight people, sometimes with more than twelve, but by the time you reach twenty people, the group can hardly be considered small. Communication scholars Steven A. Beebe and John Masterson define **small group communication** as "interaction among a small group of people who share a common purpose or goal, who feel a sense of belonging to the group, and who exert influence on one another" (6). Argumentation is one type of communication done in small groups and is a major way members influence each other.

This chapter will

- describe some differences between small groups and dyads.
- identify some advantages and disadvantages of making decisions in small groups.
- describe three discussion techniques that lead to better decision making.
- suggest ways to better participate in groups.

SMALL GROUPS VERSUS DYADS

Almost everything said in the previous two chapters is also true about argumentation that takes place in a small group context. Listening is much better than not listening, interrupting, or pseudolistening. Supportive communication styles are much better than threatening styles. Argumentativeness is better than verbal aggressiveness. You must manage your own self-presentation and relations with others in groups just as you must in dyads or public speaking.

Even though small groups share many characteristics with dyads, they have dynamics not found in dyads. One of those dynamics has to do with the number of people involved. In a sense, a group consists of multiple dyads. As the number of people in the group increases, so does the number of people with whom you must manage relationships. However, it isn't as simple as that, because everyone is managing relationships with many others at the same time. The number of dyads in a group increases more than the number of people increases. When there are two people, there is one dyad (person A and person B). Add one more person and you have two more dyads, so when there are three people, there are three dyads (AB, AC, and BC). When there are four people there are six dyads (AB, AC, AD, BC, BD, and CD), when there are five people there are ten dyads (AB, AC, AD, AE, BC, BD, BE, CD, CE, and DE), and so on.

In a group, however, you do not communicate with just one other person at a time but with everyone in the group. The lines of communication among people are increased, and instead of tailoring messages for only one person, you have to consider how several people may interpret the same message. The dynamics become even more complicated over time, as group members have dyadic interactions away from the group that influence perceptions of group members and affect the communication within the group.

Another different dynamic is **peer pressure,** which is the influence exerted by a group to get members to conform to a group's norms. **Norms** are the expectations of the attitudes, values, and behaviors that members have for everyone in a group. One type of group norm is the group's **communication rules,** or the procedures members of a group follow as they communicate with each other. For instance, in some groups, communication rules include not interrupting others and raising your hand when you want to speak. Other groups do not have those same rules though. Once norms are established, they become very important to a group, and members will often go to great lengths to maintain them.

Communication rules and other norms are enforced by rewards given by other members of a group when the rules are followed and punishment when the rules are violated. People rarely come out and say "You violated one of our communication rules." Instead, they show approval or displeasure vocally and through other nonverbal means, or they express their emotional response to the event without talking about the rule itself. Because communication rules and other norms usually are not thought about consciously, other members of a group may not even notice when they enforce the rules with their responses.

Families are a special kind of small group within which communication rules are established. For example, when I was growing up, one of the communication rules in my family was "Don't talk while my parents were watching a television show." The reward for following that rule was getting attention from my parents during commercials. The punishment for violation could range from being ignored if we talked at the wrong time, to angry glares, to being told in a threatening voice "Shut up! I can't hear the show!" to being banned from the room with the television. Another communication rule was to call and let our parents know if we were going to come home from some event later than expected. The reward for following the rule was being thanked for being considerate and being allowed to go where we wanted on future occasions. The punishments included being told, upon arriving home, that our parents were worried sick and thought we were dead, usually spoken in loud, angry tones. That might be followed by being ignored for a while and not being allowed to go to one or more events in the future.

When you first become a member of a group, you learn the norms and communication rules through observation and participation. Sometimes some of the norms and rules are explicitly presented, but you learn most of them by paying attention to what others do, by receiving rewards for following the rules, and by sanctions for breaking the rules. Those rewards and sanctions constitute the peer pressure to conform. Once you are fully integrated into a group, the norms and communication rules become so well understood that they seem natural, and violating them seems difficult and strange. If the group is not well established when you join, then it will go through a process of establishing the norms and communication rules.

For example, over time a group of college men living together may establish a value that having fun and partying together is more important than anything other than their families. The corresponding attitudinal norm is that doing well in classes is not very desirable, and the behavioral norms are members will drink excessively and not do schoolwork on weekends. If a member of the group decides to do better in school and passes on going to a party so he can study on a Saturday night, then the other members may ask him repeatedly to go, tell him he needs to go, tease him about becoming a nerd, ridicule his efforts, and ostracize him until he follows the norms again. If he does conform to the group's expectations, then other members will then pay a lot of attention to him, tell him what a great guy he is, and find other ways to reward that conformity. If he does not conform, though, either the group norms will change in some way or the nonconforming member will leave the group. As the other group members see how the nonconforming member is treated, the norms are also reinforced for them.

As you go through your daily life, you probably are a member of several different groups, each with at least slightly different norms. You have to monitor your own thoughts and behavior as you move from group to group, adjusting the assumptions you take for granted and adjusting the way you act to meet expectations. If the norms and communication rules for the groups are very different, then it becomes harder to make the adjustments, because the habits developed to fit into one group are not appropriate for another group. So you have to either expend more effort to monitor your behavior or face the sanctions of at least one of the groups. Students who go away to college often experience this vividly when they go home for a break. While living in their residence halls, they adjust to the norms and communication rules of the hall and fall into the habit of using language of which their parents do not approve. When they go home, at some time they stop monitoring themselves carefully and say something that's appropriate for the residence hall but not for their family. At that point, their parents remind them where they are and to whom they are speaking, encouraging them to adapt to the norms of the group they are in at home. In other words, the students swear in front of their parents, and their parents tell them to watch their mouths.

So what does this have to do with argumentation? First, the norms and communication rules may be established, maintained, and changed through argumentation, as various group members present reasons for or against them. Second, and more important, the norms and rules affect the argumentation done within a group. Some of the norms and rules are directed toward argumentation, so in some groups engaging in arguments is a valued way to address issues, while in other groups, arguments are considered too aggressive and are avoided. When members do engage in arguments, communication rules help determine how they are done: whether voices are raised, whether certain subjects are taboo, whether certain ideas are assumed by a group, whether personal attacks are acceptable, and whether discussion can become physically violent.

All of this is important to realize as you deal with other people in groups, whether it is part of argumentation or not. What you expect from other members of the group is constructed from your experiences, and they may or may not be reasonable expectations. If the members of the group have been together for some

Figure 15.1 Peer pressure comes in a variety of forms and affects us throughout our lives.

Reprinted with special permission of King Features Syndicate.

time, then the norms have probably been pretty well established, and it is reasonable to expect members to abide by them. If the group has not been together long, or if an individual is new to the group, then it is reasonable to expect that some people do not know what the norms are, so violations are probably inadvertent. Often behavior that seems quite rude is a result of someone acting according to the norms of one group while he's in another group that does not share those norms.

BENEFITS OF SMALL-GROUP DECISION MAKING

Although small group communication is more complex than working with only one other person, there are benefits to working in groups to reach decisions or accomplish tasks, especially compared to doing either alone. Generally speaking, groups accomplish more and do better work than do individuals.

The first benefit is that working in groups allows for a *division of responsibilities.* One or two people don't have to do everything. Several people can put less effort into the task and get much more accomplished than one person can alone. If a decision is to be made, then each person can be responsible for getting different information, so the group has more information on which to base its decision. If different tasks need to be done, then they can each be taken on by a person who is best suited for that task, rather than by people who don't really know what they're doing.

The second benefit of working in groups is that it creates *more ideas* from which to choose. One reason this happens is simply because more people are generating ideas. If you have a group of five people, and each person has only one idea on a subject that other members don't, then you have five more ideas from which to choose. That increases the chances that the best idea will be considered. The other reason you get more ideas in groups is that people think of new ideas as they hear what others have to say. Perhaps what one person says is not very good, but it stimulates someone else to think of an idea that will work really well.

A third advantage to working in groups is that it allows *better criticism of ideas.* As an individual, when you're working on something you can get "too close" to it and fail to see its weaknesses. When others look at your work, they notice things that you missed, and you can then correct those problems before it's too late. This usually works best when members of a group think critically, express themselves, and manage relationships, as described in Chapter 14. If members feel threatened by others' communication, then they are less likely to criticize ideas or express themselves and more likely to criticize people and withdraw.

A fourth and very important reason for working in groups is that it can lead to *more satisfaction* with the outcome. It also leads to an increased commitment to the outcome by group members than when decisions are made and people do not have the opportunity to be involved. When decisions will affect people, it is usually best to involve them rather than to impose decisions on them. Even when individuals don't prefer the final decision, their attitudes are more favorable because they were involved in the process.

DISADVANTAGES OF
GROUP DECISION MAKING

While there are significant advantages to working in groups, there are also some potential problems that should be addressed. None of the problems are insurmountable, and an awareness of them allows you to avoid them so that they don't outweigh the positive benefits of group discussion.

One potential weakness of working in groups is the *dilution of good ideas.* If an individual has a great idea, there is the chance that as others work with it it will be modified so it isn't as good as it once was. There is always the chance that genius will be unrecognized, but this problem can largely be avoided if group members participate in the argumentation process to test the ideas. If the idea truly is good, then it will stand up to scrutiny.

A second potential problem of working in groups is the *avoidance of responsibilities.* It is not uncommon that members of groups assume that someone else will do the work, so they don't take on their fair share. Students often dislike working in groups, because they can't rely on all of the other students to do what they should. It is important to the group process that each member does what is expected of her or him.

Working in small groups *takes more time* to reach decisions and accomplish other tasks than working individually usually does. When group members take their job seriously, they present their ideas and support them, challenge the ideas of others, and try to reach the best decision. When they're doing other tasks, they have to schedule meetings, work between meetings, reconvene, work at the meeting, then schedule the next meeting, and so on. The time spent in group work is important, though, since it does tend to lead to better decisions and better outcomes than working alone. Each person who works in a group is faced with the question, "Is the improved outcome likely to be worth the time and effort of working in a group?" If it is, then the time is well spent. If it is not, then alternatives to group work should be chosen.

Dominance by one member is a fourth potential problem when working in groups. Since advantages to group efforts are improved decision making and increased commitment to the decisions, then all members of a group should be encouraged to get involved. When one person dominates a discussion, then other ideas cannot be heard, and the purpose of working as a group is frustrated. Those people who dominate group discussions may not know they're doing it, or think their ideas are so good that they ought to dominate, but dominance by one member usually creates problems. Everyone working in groups should participate by expressing themselves, listening to others, and monitoring their own behavior to allow others to participate as well.

On the other hand, *trying to please* everyone can also be a problem. In any group decision-making process, some people's ideas will be accepted and some rejected. If the group tries to make sure that everyone's ideas are incorporated, it is not likely to end up with the best decisions, because some ideas may be weak or contradict others. Each group member should decide from the outset that his or her purpose is to work with others, be willing to accept group decisions, and not always insist on having his or her idea accepted. This does not mean that members should not vigorously argue for their ideas; in fact, that's what members in groups should do. It also does not mean that individual needs and feelings should not be considered. But in trying to please everyone, members are inviting failure, and no one person should always expect that his or her ideas will be those accepted by the group.

The sixth problem with working in groups is having *a group that is too large.* The larger a group, the less opportunity there is for each member to participate, and the greater the chance that a few people will actively participate and the rest will either watch, withdraw their attention, or drop out altogether. In addition, the larger the group, the more difficult it is to schedule meetings and have everyone attend.

The final potential problem with group decision making is *groupthink,* a concept developed by sociologist Irving Janis. Beebe and Masterson say groupthink

> occurs when a group strives to minimize conflict and reach a consensus
> without critically testing, analyzing, and evaluating ideas. When a group
> reaches decisions too quickly, it does not properly consider the implications
> of its decisions. Groupthink results in an ineffective consensus; too little
> conflict often lowers the quality of group decisions. When a group does not
> take time to examine the positive and negative consequences of alternative
> decisions, the quality of its decision is likely to suffer. (262)

Groupthink happens when the group places more value on harmony than on making good decisions, and when there is a persuasive leader to whom members look for guidance. Harmony and good decisions can both be achieved, though, if the argumentation focuses on ideas rather than on people, and if group members recognize the value of engaging in critical discussions.

The way to avoid groupthink is to consciously think critically about whatever the group is considering. That means that group members should question ideas, especially those of the leader, even when they think they agree with the ideas; it also means analyzing and refuting arguments made in favor of decisions rather than simply accepting a decision, because doing so would be quick and easy. Avoiding groupthink requires patience and calls for a group to establish a norm that challenging ideas is acceptable. When ideas related to routine matters are critically evaluated, this leads to better decisions and makes it easier to critically evaluate ideas for more serious matters.

SMALL-GROUP DISCUSSION TECHNIQUES

One reason many people dislike working in groups is that they don't really know how to do so. They've been forced to work in groups and they've probably had both good and bad experiences in groups, but they haven't had any guidance about how to make decisions in a group. This section describes three techniques that can be used to guide groups as they make decisions.

Brainstorming

Brainstorming is a technique intended to generate ideas that can be evaluated later by having a group invent as many ideas as it can in a short period of time. The purpose of brainstorming is to generate the largest quantity of ideas possible.

Brainstorming requires someone to lead the group during the session, so the group can follow the procedure. Brainstorming starts by getting group members to identify their specific task, so that everyone knows what the group is trying to accomplish. The task may be to do a group project for a class, to create a new policy for an organization, to eliminate an environmental problem in the community, or to create a new public relations campaign.

Once the task is clarified, group members try to come up with as many possible ways of doing the task as they can, and they share them with the group. Any possible idea, no matter how outrageous or silly it seems, should be welcome at this point in the discussion. The whole point is to create the longest list possible, so ideas should not be censored, even if the person who thinks of them feels that they won't work. Group members also should be encouraged to use other people's ideas as springboards for new ideas. Outrageous ideas are welcome, because they can lead to a style of thinking that is more creative and can lead others to think of solutions that haven't been thought of before.

As ideas are generated, someone should record them for future use. Generally it is best if they are recorded in a way such that all group members can see them while they're brainstorming, but that isn't always possible. Recording the ideas ensures that they won't be lost while more are generated, and it confirms the participation of each member, which encourages each to continue participating.

It is important to remember that ideas are not evaluated at this point. Keeping people from declaring ideas good or bad prematurely may be the hardest part of brainstorming. Whoever is leading the brainstorming has to be sure to stop members from evaluating, and to do it in a way that doesn't create negative feelings. The time to evaluate will come, but it's premature to do so while ideas are still being generated.

Obvious ideas usually are generated fairly quickly. Then there is a lull while people try to think of something new. When that happens, everyone should remain patient and try to keep coming up with more ideas. The most creative ideas often come after the obvious ideas have been exhausted. When there is a lull, it is often followed by people making silly suggestions, which opens the gate for a flood of different ideas. It is a mistake to think that because there is a pause, all of the ideas have been expressed and it's necessarily time to move on.

After the group has generated numerous ideas, it will be time to evaluate them and eliminate some. One way to do that is to ask group members which ideas they think should be struck from the list, eliminating those that members unanimously agree should go. The remaining ideas can be discussed one by one, identifying the strengths and weaknesses of each. The weakest ones can be eliminated, and the discussion can continue about those remaining, until one is accepted as the idea to use. At this time, group members should argue about the ideas, using the suggestions in Part 2 of this text.

During the process of evaluation, more ideas may emerge, and they can be added to the list. Also, those on the list can be modified, with members responding to the criticisms raised in the discussion. One way to modify them is to merge different ideas, combining the strongest parts. Remember, the ultimate goal is to develop the best way to complete the task, not to ensure that any one idea wins, so no one should feel that he or she needs to defend a particular idea.

Nominal Group Technique

Some people in groups don't feel very comfortable speaking up, for a variety of reasons. Their ideas may be lost in a freewheeling brainstorming session or in other discussions where ideas are only proposed by those willing to take the risk of stating them. People who are shy, who feel that it is impolite to interrupt others, and who don't have loud voices may have the best ideas but may find it too difficult to break into the discussion to present them. The **nominal group technique** provides a structure that allows voices to be heard and makes it harder for one person to dominate a discussion.

The nominal group technique also needs a leader to direct the procedure, and it begins by identifying the task. People are asked to generate a list of ideas for accomplishing the task on their own. As with brainstorming, the goal is to get as many ideas as possible, but the difference is that they are not shared yet. After all members have had time to generate ideas, the leader explains that each will be asked to take turns sharing them, and each is to share one idea each turn. The turn taking will continue until everyone's ideas are shared. As with brainstorming, the ideas are recorded, preferably where everyone can see them. During the sharing process, the ideas are only recorded, not evaluated. Group members are encouraged to add to their lists during the process, so if someone else's idea sparks a new one, then it can be shared later. If more than one person comes up with the same idea, then after it is shared the first time the others simply share a different idea when it is their turn. For example, when one has shared all of the items on her list, then she passes when her turn comes, but if she thinks of something else later, she can then present it at her next turn.

After all of the ideas are presented, it is time to evaluate and argue about them in a way similar to that described for brainstorming.

Reflective Thought Pattern

The **reflective thought pattern** is a traditional way of organizing a problem-solving group discussion and has been shown to be very useful over time. The pattern explicitly calls for users to employ critical thinking and argumentative skills, and it increases the likelihood that relevant issues will be addressed instead of being skipped over in favor of a quick solution. The reflective thought pattern, which is also useful for individual and dyadic problem solving, involves six basic steps.

The first step is to *identify the problem*. Depending on the nature of the group, you should think of "problem" in very broad terms. Sometimes the problem is something bad that is happening that needs to be eliminated. Other times it is a goal that your group wants to achieve. For instance, a group of students working on a project doesn't have a problem in the sense that it needs to eliminate a harm, but it does have a goal to achieve. In this step of the reflective thought pattern, the group discusses its goal.

Identifying the problem may seem easy and obvious, but often it isn't, for a variety of reasons. Sometimes what appears to be a problem to one person may not be to another, so a discussion may ensue over whether an idea is really a problem (or should be a goal). Also, even when two people agree that there is a problem, each may have a different conception of it. Another reason identifying the problem is difficult is that so often we see the surface of a problem without recognizing its underlying nature, or we think of the problem as being much more complex than it really is.

For example, imagine that you're in the management group of a business that is solvent but is going to face increased competition in the near future and is unlikely to survive if there isn't some change. If the problem is identified as "How do we decide who to lay off?" then the ensuing discussion is likely to be quite different than if the problem is identified as "How can we increase profits?" or even "What should we do to ensure the continued survival of this business?" Laying off employees ultimately may be the best solution but shouldn't be the starting point of the discussion. Often when time is spent identifying the problem, people realize that it is quite different from what they originally had thought.

Identifying the problem is quite similar to addressing the stock issue of harm when arguing a policy proposition. The difference is, in a small group discussion, you try to figure out what the problem is rather than convince others that a problem exists. When working to identify the problem, group members should regularly ask "Is that *really* the problem?" so that they can avoid simply accepting the first plausible definition of the problem that they're trying to solve.

The second step in the reflective thought pattern is to *identify the cause(s) of the problem*. At this point, you have to distinguish between symptoms of the problem and causes, which often isn't easy. You also have to try to determine whether a cause is, in turn, a result of another cause, so you can get to the ultimate cause that must be dealt with to eliminate the problem. If you were trying to achieve a goal rather than solve a problem, you'd identify the specific characteristics of successfully meeting that goal.

Identifying the causes of the problem is similar to addressing the stock issue of inherency in a policy argument. When using the reflective thought pattern, however, the point is to discover the causes by arguing about the many possibilities rather than to argue that one particular cause is responsible for the problem.

Identifying possible solutions is the third step in the process. This is the time when you and the other members of the group think of a variety of ways to deal with the problem. At this point, do not determine how good the solutions are but try to generate possibilities. This is a time in the discussion when creative thinking should be encouraged, so various approaches can be considered. It also is a time when brainstorming or the nominal group technique could be used productively within the reflective thought pattern.

Those possibilities are studied in more detail in the fourth phase, which is to *evaluate the possible solutions*. Each possible solution must be examined carefully to determine what it would involve, how likely it is to solve the problem, if it would result in any additional benefits, and if it would result in any new problems. The argumentation done at this time is similar to that done for the plan, solvency, and advantages-disadvantages stock issues of a policy proposition.

You may be tempted to reject some possible solutions immediately, but you should be careful about doing so. The whole point of the reflective thought pattern is to make sure that the group takes the time to thoroughly examine issues. Sometimes an idea that seems unworkable at first turns out to either be the best idea or can be modified to be the best.

Fifth, after the solutions are evaluated, it is time to *pick the best solution*. Sometimes the best solution may be very clear after the evaluation, but often there are multiple possible solutions that are all good in different ways and all have different weaknesses. When picking the best solution, the group will most likely engage in value argumentation and reasoning by criteria, even though those criteria haven't been explicitly stated. During this part of the process, it is usually a good idea to try to identify those criteria and make them more explicit so the group can decide whether they are really the best to use.

When picking the best solution, it is helpful to try to reach a consensus among the group. **Consensus** is reached when all of the members of a group agree that a particular proposal is acceptable and that they will support it, even if the proposal is not each individual's preferred choice. There does not have to be unanimous agreement that the proposal is the best, but it must be at least acceptable to everyone, so they can all support it. If some members of the group cannot accept the proposal because of legitimate concerns, then the group needs to continue refining it until it is acceptable. If there is no consensus, then some members of the group will not support the decision as it is implemented, and the group misses the opportunity to create a better solution. Reaching consensus is slower than making decisions by simple voting, but it has long-term benefits that make it worthwhile.

Please note that consensus is different from compromise. When consensus is reached, the group members agree that the decision meets their needs, and each member supports it. Compromise happens when some members "give in" on some issues, so a decision can be reached, even though that decision doesn't meet their needs. When members are tempted to compromise, that is an opportunity to try to think creatively so a better solution that addresses everyone's needs can be reached.

The sixth and final stage in the reflective thought pattern is to *implement the solution*. At this point, decisions are made as to how to go about carrying out the proposal. Usually there are procedural matters that someone must attend to: people to contact, policies to write, legal requirements to fulfill, and so on. If the group just disbands after agreeing to the proposal, everyone may assume that someone else is going to do the implementation, so nothing really gets done. A discussion should occur to identify what must be done, to establish a time line for the completion of each task, and to assign each task to a specific person. During follow-up meetings, progress reports should be made to ensure that everything gets done.

The reflective thought pattern does not have to be limited to problem-solving discussions. The steps can be used to make future plans, even if no current "problem" has to be addressed. In fact, the reflective thought pattern does not have to be done in a group. You can do it individually, whether thinking critically about your own plans or solving your own problems. The strength of the technique is in taking the time to really examine ideas and having a clearly defined procedure for making sure that important issues are considered.

Argumentation, reasoning, and critical thinking are done at every step of the reflective thought pattern. Whether individually or in a group, claims are made and reasons are given about the nature of the problem, what is causing it, which solutions could work, which solution is the best, and what should be done to implement the preferred solution. In the group setting, members usually present their arguments and refute the arguments others make.

The reflective thought pattern is not necessarily done independently of brainstorming or the nominal group techniques either. The other two techniques can be used productively when identifying the problem, the causes, and the possible solutions.

All three techniques call for someone to guide the group through the process. That can be a member of the group, but often that doesn't work well. If the person guiding the group also participates in the discussion, then that person may steer the group to the decisions that he or she wants, either purposefully or without knowing it. Even if the leader doesn't do so, other members of the group may feel that he or she is and may consider the process unfair. Participating leaders also may become so involved in the discussion that they lose track of the process, so they don't really do a good job of guiding the group. If the person guiding the group is the group's leader, then members may defer to that person's opinions or pick up on real or imagined cues from that leader. When possible, it is helpful to have a facilitator who is not a member of the group to guide the group through the process. The facilitator has no stake in the final outcome and no opinion about what should be done, so doesn't get involved in the arguments. His or her only purpose is to ensure that the group doesn't skip over steps in the process and that it thoroughly considers ideas. Having an impartial facilitator doesn't guarantee that group members won't be unduly influenced by someone in the group, but it does reduce the likelihood.

PARTICIPATING IN GROUPS

Regardless of the technique used to work in groups, several things can be done by each member to improve the experience. Some suggestions follow for participating in group communication.

1. *Take responsibility.* When people come together for a group meeting, they usually take time that they could use for other things, they want the meetings to be efficient, and they appreciate people who are responsible group members. Taking responsibility includes simply showing up to meetings, arriving on time, and doing everything expected in preparation for each meeting.

2. *Participate.* The whole purpose of working in groups is to use the talents and expertise of everyone, and that cannot be done if people show up but don't participate in the discussions. That doesn't mean that you need to say something about every issue, but when you do have a relevant idea, share it.

3. *Give others a chance.* While participation should be encouraged, it can be taken too far. No one should dominate group discussions, and no one needs to respond to every statement made by others. When participating in discussions to the extent that others have little opportunity to share their ideas, the purpose of working in a group setting is thwarted.

4. *Listen.* Sometimes people in group discussions blatantly ignore what others say, and later they do things such as raise the same issues that have already been discussed, object to what was never said, or fail to do what is expected of them. If the purpose of working in a group is to be fulfilled, then members must listen to what others say.

5. *Think.* One strength of working in groups is the chance to consider ideas from different perspectives. If ideas are simply accepted when they're presented, then the members of the group are not taking advantage of the opportunity they have. You, and others, should think critically about what is said so the group can correct, add to, refine, and improve its ideas.

6. *Adapt.* Some people come to group discussions feeling as though they have to be right about everything. Then, if someone points out a flaw in their ideas, they feel attacked and turn the discussion into an adversarial situation in which they try to defend their ideas at all costs. Group members should

realize that they don't always have to be right, and that others in the group don't always have to do things their way. Developing ideas in groups does involve argumentation, but it is used to test ideas and lead to the best decision, which often involves modifying the ideas that people originally come up with.

7. *Clarify expectations.* When people join groups, they're usually not really sure what is expected of them, and members learn as they go along. Sometimes that process leads to misconceptions of what is expected, which can lead to ill feelings among members. Even when people do understand the basic norms and communication rules, they often don't know that they were expected to carry out particular tasks in preparation for meetings. Clearly talking about both kinds of expectations rather than relying on indirect messages can help the group operate more smoothly.

8. *Balance needs.* Every group has two types of needs: task needs and socio-emotional needs. Task needs are the things needed to accomplish the task at hand—the information and resources to do the group's job. Socio-emotional needs are the things needed for members to feel good about being in the group—the greetings, small talk, and confirming responses. Sometimes groups are so focused on the task that members hate being part of the group, which means that the task suffers too. Other times, groups are so focused on meeting socio-emotional needs that while members like the people they're with, the tasks don't get done, and people perceive the group as a waste of valuable time. Task needs and socio-emotional needs are both important for groups to function well, and they need to be balanced.

9. *Include others.* Many times, people who don't feel comfortable inserting their ideas into the discussion have excellent ideas that would be valuable for the group to hear. If you notice that someone in the group isn't talking much, it can be helpful to directly ask him what he thinks. Doing so can establish the fact that you value that person's participation to make it easier for him to participate in the future and to add more ideas to the discussion.

SUMMARY

Interacting in groups is a common form of communication, and it presents many opportunities to engage in argumentation. The skills described in earlier chapters are useful in groups, and additional considerations arise when communicating in small groups. In addition to more people being involved in small groups creating more relationships to manage, peer pressure, norms, and communication rules must also be kept in mind. Working on projects in small groups has both advantages and disadvantages (see Sidebars 15.1 and 15.2).

Working in small groups can be better if people in those groups have an idea of how to make group discussions and arguments about ideas proceed. Brainstorming, the nominal group technique, and the reflective thought pattern are all ways to help small groups better discuss ideas (see Sidebars 15.3 and 15.4).

Sidebar 15.1   Advantages of Working in Groups

More ideas
Division of responsibility
Better criticism of ideas
More support for decisions

Sidebar 15.2   Disadvantages of Working in Groups

Dilution of good ideas
Avoidance of responsibilities
Time
Dominance by some members
Trying to please everyone
Too large
Groupthink

Sidebar 15.3   Reflective Thought Pattern

Identify the problem.
Identify the cause(s) of the problem.
Identify possible solutions.
Evaluate possible solutions.
Pick the best solution.
Implement the solution.

Sidebar 15.4   Participating Better in Small Groups

Take responsibility.
Participate.
Give others a chance.
Listen.
Think.
Adapt.
Clarify expectations.
Balance task needs and socio-emotional needs.
Include others.

KEY CONCEPTS

brainstorming   a small group discussion technique intended to generate ideas that can be evaluated later by having the group invent as many ideas as it can in a short period of time.

communication rules   the procedures that members of a group follow as they communicate with each other.

consensus   the agreement by all of the members of a group that a particular proposal is acceptable and one that all will support, even if the proposal is not each individual's preferred choice.

nominal group technique   a small group discussion technique intended to generate ideas that can be evaluated later by having the individuals invent as many ideas as they can and take turns sharing them with the group, one at a time.

norms   the expectations of the attitudes, values, and behaviors that group members have for all members of a group.

peer pressure   the influence exerted by a group to get members to conform to that group's norms and rules.

reflective thought pattern   a small group discussion technique that establishes a process that helps ensure that a group considers major relevant issues in problem solving.

small group   a gathering of more than two people, but not so many that they cannot all interact with all other members of the group.

small group communication   interaction among a small group of people who share a common purpose or goal, who feel a sense of belonging to the group, and who exert influence on one another.

THINGS TO THINK ABOUT

1. Think of a group of which you are a member. What are some of the communication rules of the group? What rewards and sanctions are used by the group to enforce those rules?

2. Think of a small group of which you have been a member. What

were the strengths and weaknesses of that group?

3. Think of a situation in which you were a member of a group and it did not work out well. What could various group members have done to make it work better?

16

The Scientific Method and Critical Thinking

In your everyday life, you act as a kind of scientist. You observe and draw conclusions about the world around you. You make predictions about how one event will affect another. You develop explanations for what happens around you. When something unexpected happens, you try to figure out why. This is often referred to as acting as a "naïve scientist."

For example, when you meet a new person, you pay attention to the way she responds to what you say and do. Based on those observations, you predict how she will respond to something you are about to say. If the response is what you expect, your prediction is confirmed. If the response is unexpected, then you think of an explanation. If you continue to interact with that person, you continue to observe behaviors and reactions, compare them to past experiences, make more predictions, and develop a better understanding of how that individual will react to various actions.

Or you might have a job that calls for you to determine how to best accomplish a task. Based on what you've learned in classes and on your personal experience, you may decide that one procedure is more likely to have a positive outcome than another. If someone were to ask you why you believe that, then you'd provide an explanation of how the different procedures work, and why you predict that one would be better than the other.

Both examples are similar to scientific methods of thinking. Most of us are not very systematic as we do our everyday science though. We don't do our observations as carefully as practicing scientists should. We fail to recognize the differences between one set of conditions and another. We make rather vague predictions, so a wide range of results can confirm what we expect. Our explanations often don't account for all of the factors that may be involved. Most of the time we do well enough to get by day to day, but we also commonly jump to conclusions supported by questionable evidence, without realizing that that's what we're doing.

Over time, scientists and philosophers have developed procedures designed to overcome common problems in gathering evidence and drawing conclusions. Those procedures are referred to as the "scientific method." Understanding the basics of the scientific method helps you understand how principles of critical thinking, reasoning, and argumentation can be applied. While most of us will rarely have the opportunity to take the time to fully use the scientific method in our everyday lives, knowledge of the method can help us improve our daily reasoning.

Understanding basic scientific methodology also helps you as a critical thinker, because you will be confronted with scientific findings throughout your life. You'll read or listen to news reports about health and medical discoveries, environmental findings, social and psychological conclusions, and information from various areas of the physical and social sciences. You'll also hear all sorts of claims about things that could be verified using scientific techniques but haven't been examined, and you'll have to decide whether the support for the claims is adequate to justify your acceptance in the absence of empirical verification. There will probably be times when you make personal decisions, such as changing your diet or supporting some cause, based on news reports, and you'll have to decide how much you can believe about them. You also may find yourself in a career that calls on you to make decisions based on information that is gathered scientifically, and you'll have to evaluate such information even if you yourself are not a scientist.

This chapter describes the fundamentals of the scientific method and how the procedures are connected to critical thinking and argumentation. Describing the scientific method in depth is far beyond the scope of this chapter, so you may notice some discrepancies with specific scientific procedures of which you are already aware. Physicists do their work differently than psychologists, who work differently than astronomers, who work differently than anthropologists, who work differently than chemists, who work differently than sociologists, and so on. The basic principles and methods are shared by different disciplines, but the specific ways in which they are applied vary. As you read the following pages, keep in mind that this is only an overview of the scientific method, and that it would take several classes for you to be exposed to all of the complexities.

The following is meant to help you better understand scientific thinking and help you make the connection between scientific and critical thinking. It is not necessarily meant to develop your skill at "doing" science but to begin to demystify it. This chapter also is not meant to give the impression that scientific thinking is the only legitimate way to do critical thinking. It is important though, and as an educated person and a critical thinker, you ought to be aware of the

Figure 16.1 We often use a version of the scientific method without even knowing it.

basic principles it follows. You also should be aware that it is suitable for some subjects and issues but inappropriate for others.

This chapter will

- describe ten principles that are basic to the scientific method.
- describe the basic procedures of both descriptive and experimental research.
- explain the difference between scientific hypotheses and theory.

PRINCIPLES OF THE SCIENTIFIC METHOD

The scientific method is designed to overcome common problems in reasoning by devising procedures to take into account those common problems. The basis of those procedures can be summed up by the following ten principles, which are not listed in any particular order because they are all equally important. They are goals that the scientific method attempts to achieve, although all scientific endeavors are not equally successful.

To put them into context, imagine a situation that might call for the use of the scientific method, in this case using social scientific techniques rather than those of the physical sciences. Let's say that Lewis created a way of teaching critical thinking that he believes is the best way it could possibly be taught. He thinks that his method of teaching is fantastic for helping any student become the best possible critical thinker. He's used it before, and he's seen lots of students become better critical thinkers. His way of teaching will revolutionize the way critical thinking is taught, if only everyone else would recognize how wonderful it is and start using it. That's his opinion, based on his experience, and he wants others to agree with him. What can Lewis do? He can use the scientific method to provide evidence of the worth of his way of teaching, and then he can use that evidence to persuade others to change their ways.

Now let's look at the principles of the scientific method to see how they relate to Lewis's need for evidence.

Principle 1: Objectivity

As we go through our everyday lives, we think we encounter the world the way it is. However, the way in which we perceive the world is influenced by our expectations of what we will experience, our biases, our wishful thinking, our individual and cultural beliefs, our states of mind, what we're paying attention to at the time, the language that we and others use, and a variety of other factors. All of those influences can cause anyone to perceive the world in an individual, subjective way that does not correspond to what actually happens. It doesn't matter whether a person is highly intelligent and honest and has the best intentions. He or she can still be swayed by his or her subjective perceptions.

The principle of objectivity means that people following the scientific method attempt to overcome biases, so different people who encounter the same phenomenon will report the same experience and draw the same conclusion. If they follow the proper procedures, then they can avoid being swayed by their own subjectivity. They describe what they did and what they observed in the neutral language of reports instead of judgments. The criteria for what "counts" as an incident of a particular phenomenon are clearly defined before making observations, so different observers will note them. Methods of recording phenomena are devised so that there is no question whether something happened or not.

You may have already heard the idea that objectivity is impossible to achieve, because people cannot eliminate their own subjectivity. While that is true, it doesn't mean that steps cannot be taken to be *more* objective and minimize the effects of subjectivity.

When Lewis looks for evidence that his way of teaching critical thinking is the best, he wants to believe in it. He'll feel good because he's created something so worthwhile. He'll feel even better because he'll become famous for his teaching method. Maybe he'll even make money from it. Lewis doesn't want to doubt himself, so he's motivated to believe in his method. Because he has reasons for wanting to believe in his way of teaching, when he compares it to other methods he may come up with reasons his is the best by using *a priori* reasoning and subjective judgments. Of course, he would never intentionally favor some evidence over other, but he can come up with reasons to disregard evidence that isn't favorable to his way of teaching. He will be, at least, unintentionally biased.

If Lewis follows the scientific method to test his opinion, though, he needs to create procedures to make sure that his study isn't biased in his favor. He should determine ahead of time which criteria would be used to decide which way of teaching is the best. He might decide that the best method is determined by whether or not his students score higher on a standardized test than students taught by another method. At the end of the study, an individual, regardless of his or her biases, can determine which method best met the criteria. Lewis may not reach the conclusion he had hoped for, but he's more likely to reach the conclusion that is closest to the truth. He's done that by trying to be as objective as possible.

Notice that in trying to be objective Lewis would follow the stock issues for a proposition of fact, described in Chapter 8. He'd define what he means by his method and other methods. He'd establish criteria to determine the best way of teaching, making sure that those criteria could be applied to any treatment, not just the one he favors. Then he would apply the criteria by discovering whether one way of teaching meets the criteria better than another.

The principle of objectivity is something to be aware of in your everyday arguing and critical thinking. You may not be able to set up conditions so that you can be as objective as possible, but you can recognize the potential for you or others to be biased and try to avoid it, or you can consider the effects of the bias on the arguments. If you can recognize your own biases and set them aside as you consider evidence and reasoning, then you are more likely to come to better conclusions.

Principle 2: Observation

The principle of observation means that scientists do the best they can to actually examine the phenomenon they're studying, so the conclusions they draw are based on more than speculation. Rather than decide what the conclusion must be, based on what they already know, they try to determine what "is" by doing observations. Sometimes this is referred to as gathering *empirical* evidence, because empirical means "observable."

When you think of observation, you may think of looking at something, and some scientific endeavors do involve sight. But sight is not the only method of observing. You can make observations using sound, touch, smell, and taste, or by using instruments that extend and replace human senses. The key is that good scientists don't reach conclusions based on what they *think* they'd observe if they took the trouble to do so, but they draw their conclusions based on actually making the observations.

Sometimes direct observation is impossible. The phenomenon under investigation may be something that is either too difficult to observe directly or cannot really be directly observed. For instance, in the social sciences, human attitudes are often studied, but an attitude cannot be directly observed. So researchers have to observe behaviors associated with attitudes, and those behaviors are often the responses to items on a questionnaire. The associated behaviors are signs of the attitude, but they aren't the attitude itself. When the phenomenon cannot be directly observed, the question arises whether the signs are really accurate indicators of the phenomenon.

In the study of ways of teaching critical thinking, Lewis cannot really observe critical thinking, because that's done in his students' minds. He can only observe signs of critical thinking—in this case, the students' performances on the test. But if he wanted to have the strongest evidence possible, he shouldn't just say, "I'm sure my students are better critical thinkers now, so there's no need to test them to find out." Instead, he would administer the test to them.

Sometimes you'll need to make decisions under circumstances where you cannot make observations, and you'll have to do the best you can. However, when the opportunity presents itself, you can have more faith in your conclusions if you gather empirical evidence. You also can consider other people's arguments stronger if they are based on empirical evidence.

Principle 3: Measurement

When observing a phenomenon, it becomes important to accurately measure it, especially if you're going to make comparisons. You can't, for example, really tell if the size of something has changed unless you know how big it was to begin with. And you can't tell how much it has changed unless you accurately measure it. Some things are simple to measure, and some are quite difficult, but most scientific investigations involve some kind of measurement. In your everyday life, it may be enough to say that something looks like it got bigger, but scientific endeavors attempt to be more precise, so great care is taken to measure well.

If Lewis is going to test how his way of teaching critical thinking compares to others, then he should first find out how well his students, and students who are taught by other methods, critically think to begin with. Later he should find out how well they all think after they're taught. Assuming that everything else is equal, if Lewis's students' scores improve more than other students' scores, then he has grounds to conclude that his method is superior.

Principle 4: Controlling Variables

Almost any event you can think of could be affected by a variety of different factors. How well you feel on a particular day, for instance, can be influenced by how much sleep you got the night before, what you ate and drank the previous day, whether you have a cold, the kind of exercise you did the previous day, whether you've been under psychological stress, and so forth. If you wanted to reach a conclusion about why you feel the way you do, then you should consider all of the things that could affect your physical state, not just the most obvious.

The same is true when answering scientific questions. A scientist may have an idea of the way one event affects another, but if other factors are involved, then she can't be sure which one makes the difference. So she attempts to control the variables, either by eliminating their influence or by making sure that they influence everything being studied equally.

In testing Lewis's teaching method, there are a lot of variables to consider. The backgrounds of the students could make a difference in how well they think or respond to teaching, because students from better schools or students with certain majors may have an advantage over others. Their ages could make a difference, because perhaps people become better critical thinkers just because they grow older and gain more experience. The length of time that each class runs might have an effect, because Lewis can teach more in a semester than someone else can in a quarter. The length of time the different teachers in the study have been teaching could make a difference, as could many other factors. If Lewis doesn't somehow account for all of them, then he can't really say that it was his method of teaching, and not some other factor, that made the difference.

Controlling variables aids in causal reasoning about whatever is studied using the scientific method. Alternative potential causes are accounted for, and the chances of arguing for a false cause are reduced. Even when you don't do actual scientific studies, your thinking can improve by becoming aware of different factors that might cause an effect besides the cause argued for.

Principle 5: Replication

If a researcher's findings are really true, then other researchers ought to be able to reproduce them. That's the idea behind the principle of replication. Experiments and descriptive studies should be explained in sufficient detail so that others could do the same study to see whether they get the same results. The more times the research finds the same results, the more confidence there can be that the results are correct. Replication repeats the procedures to see whether they consistently lead to the same results.

If Lewis does his study only one time, then that provides some evidence for his claim (if it turns out the way he expects). But those results might just be an accident, so the study should be repeated. The original results could be due to Lewis's enthusiasm about his way of teaching the class, so someone else should repeat the study.

Replication of studies creates multiple examples, so reasoning by example can be sounder, and there can be more confidence in the generalizations. It also provides corroborating evidence, so the facts can be used to make more cogent arguments.

Principle 6: Generalization

When scientists generalize, they draw conclusions about members of a group who are not observed, based on what is observed about some members of a group. Usually they cannot observe all of the members of the group, because there are too many, and studying all of them would be too costly, both in terms of time and money.

To make generalizations, scientists strive to ensure that the sample, which consists of the members of the group who are actually studied, is adequate. Remember, you generalize by reasoning by example, and each member of the sample is one example of the larger population to which the generalization will be made. So the standards for reasoning by example apply here. One standard is that the sample has to be reasonably large enough to make the generalization. Statisticians have determined how many members of a large population need to be studied to draw a reasonably accurate conclusion. For very large populations, the number in the sample may be a lot smaller than you might think, because at a certain point as you increase the sample size, the increase in accuracy is so small that increasing the size isn't worth the benefit.

To make sound generalizations, the sample studied also needs to be representative of the larger population. That means that all of the segments of the population are represented. In some cases, the researchers may select the members of the sample to ensure that all types of members of the population are included. Another way to achieve a representative sample is to choose it randomly, which means that every member of the larger population has an equal chance of being selected. If the sample size is large enough, and the selection is truly random, then the chances are quite good that the sample will be representative.

Finally, generalizations can be made with more confidence if either the same researcher repeats the study or others repeat the study. That may be done by repeating exactly the same procedures or by studying the same phenomenon using different methods. If the same results are found by different studies, then the researchers can be more certain that their conclusions are correct and apply to the entire population. On the other hand, if the results are not consistent, then it is doubtful that the outcome applies to the entire population, and more studies would be called for.

So in Lewis's study of his teaching methods, the population may consist of all college students in the United States, which would be too many people to test, so he selects some of those students to be part of his study, making sure that he selects enough and that they are representative of all college students. That may mean that Lewis needs to include students from different regions of the country and those attending different kinds of schools. After doing the study, he then argues that because the study was conducted properly, the findings about the students in the sample apply to all college students in the United States. If Lewis hadn't proceeded in a way to allow him to make that generalization, then his teaching approach may still be fabulous, but he may be the only person who cares, because only his students are affected by it.

Principle 7: Sharing Findings

In general, the scientific method values sharing findings of studies. That means that researchers communicate what was done and what the results are with others, usually by publishing their studies in journals or presenting them at conferences. Sharing findings is important, for three primary reasons. First, researchers can identify unrecognized errors in their methods, in their analysis, and in the conclusions they come to. When the findings are widely distributed, many other experts can look at what was done and note whether any errors occurred. The people who did the study, and who want it to be successful, may inadvertently overlook errors that others who are not as involved may catch. On the other hand, if no errors are noted, then there can be greater confidence in the findings.

Second, sharing findings allows the study to be repeated and the results confirmed by others. If researchers don't share the results of their studies, then others will not know what was found, and they cannot use the conclusions. If the results are shared but the methods are not, others cannot know whether they should really accept the conclusions.

The third reason for sharing findings is simply to add to the body of knowledge about the subject. Researchers usually are interested in advancing knowledge, and they know that the body of knowledge is not enlarged unless they and others are willing to share what they've done, as well as the results.

If Lewis did the study about his method of teaching, then he would share his findings by identifying the best journals to publish the report. He would then write the report, following the guidelines for that journal, and include the information needed to make it complete: an explanation of how the research was conducted, the results, how the data were analyzed, and so on. Like other journal authors, Lewis would work on it until he was satisfied and then send it to the editor. The editor would send it to a few reviewers, who would give the editor advice about whether the article was worth publishing in that journal. If the article is good enough, then it will be published, probably with some changes. If it's not good enough for that journal, and the reviewers' comments indicate that it is still worthwhile, then Lewis would revise it and send it to an editor of a different journal.

In some cases, research is not shared. When businesses do research to improve their products or services, they may not want to share their findings, because they would lose the competitive advantage they sought by doing the research.

When doing scientific thinking in your everyday life, you're not likely to try to publish your findings, unless you are a practicing scientist. You might, however, as part of a normal, everyday conversation, share your thoughts with others to let them know what you "discovered." The people you talk to may then comment on your thinking and question your methods of collecting your data. They might then observe some similar phenomenon and let you know that they found something different, or that they can confirm your conclusions. So even though you may not publish in journals, you will still probably share your findings with others.

Principle 8: Peer Review

Peer review involves letting others who are knowledgeable about the subject and research methods examine the study to make sure that it was done properly and analyzed correctly. Studies that undergo peer review are generally considered better than those that are not reviewed.

The process of doing peer review usually happens prior to the wide distribution of the study. Well-respected journals use peer review to decide whether a study should be published, and they may reject more than 90 percent of the studies submitted. Peer review is a method to both determine whether a particular study was done properly and to ensure that only the best studies are published.

Research projects often go through peer review at two different stages. The first stage occurs prior to doing the research. Universities and laboratories funded by the government have committees that are supposed to look at proposed studies and approve them before they are done. The primary purpose of that examination is to make sure that no humans or animals are mistreated or endangered by the study, but the committees usually also comment on how appropriate the procedures are. Many private institutions have similar review boards. The second stage of peer review happens when the researcher sends the findings to be published. Editors send copies of submissions to experts to review, usually without identifying who did the research, so that that doesn't bias the reviewers. The reviewers send their comments to the editor either supporting publication or supporting publication if changes are made, or rejecting the submission. One of the prime reasons for rejecting a report is that the proper procedures weren't followed. So the peer review helps weed out those studies that weren't done well enough to draw sound conclusions.

Another stage of peer review occurs after publication. As other scholars in a field read studies, they also consider whether they are well done and the conclusions are sound. Responding to published studies and pointing out their flaws is relatively common.

Thus if Lewis did a scientific study of his approach to teaching, then when it was over he'd write an article detailing why the study is important, how it was done, what the results were, and his conclusions. Then he'd send it to a reputable journal that publishes studies about educational methods or critical thinking. The editor would have people who are knowledgeable about the subject read the article and provide suggestions about whether the study was done well, whether the article should be published, and whether revisions should be made before publishing. If the article is good enough, then other critical thinking teachers will read it, realize the superiority of Lewis's teaching approach, adopt it themselves, and Lewis will become famous. That's an exaggeration, but other teachers could read it and decide whether they want to adopt the approach or replicate the study.

The "peer review" that you might go through as a naïve scientist is likely to be much more informal. It would consist of talking with other people about what you observe and the conclusions you come to. When others indicate that they agree or disagree with you, they serve the same function as peer reviewers in the more formal process.

Principle 9: Falsification

A hypothesis that cannot be proven false cannot be studied using scientific methods. A hypothesis is a statement of what the expected results of the study will be. If the subject being studied is such that the hypothesis cannot be proven untrue, then it is not something that can be studied by the scientific method.

A type of hypothesis that cannot be falsified is one that proposes that something does not exist. It cannot be falsified, because no matter what evidence there is for its nonexistence, someone can always say that the researcher just didn't look in the right place. Another hypothesis that cannot be falsified is one that says that something does exist but cannot be proven because we don't have the means to prove its existence.

The hypothesis of Lewis's study—that his teaching method will result in an improvement in critical thinking test scores more than other methods of teaching—is capable of being proven false, so it can be studied using the scientific method. If the results of the study show that other methods result in more, or equal, improvement, then the hypothesis is falsified.

The issue of falsification probably is not going to be raised often in your everyday life. However, it is still important to know, because as a critical thinker, it helps determine which kinds of claims you can actually prove by gathering empirical evidence.

Principle 10: Provisional Conclusions

Conclusions drawn from studies are never the final word on the subject. Future studies can always alter them or prove them incorrect. When you read about studies, it may seem as through the findings are absolutely true and cannot be doubted, but what they really reveal is what the study found and how those findings relate to other knowledge about the subject.

So after doing all of the work to complete his study and publish his findings, and assuming that his students did show more improvement in their test scores than students taught by other methods, all Lewis might say is, "The results indicate that my method of teaching critical thinking is probably superior to other methods."

As a naïve scientist, the importance of provisional conclusions relates to making claims that you can actually support rather than making claims that go beyond the evidence you have for them. As a fallible human being, there is little you can know with absolute certainty. Most claims you make should be either explicitly or implicitly qualified (as described in the Toulmin model). Also, making provisional claims helps you avoid the threatening communication behaviors of certainty and superiority, described in Chapter 14.

PROCEDURES OF THE
SCIENTIFIC METHOD

Studies done using the scientific method generally follow a common set of procedures. Knowing these procedures can both help you think critically about the studies you read and help you design your own studies so that they can better stand up to critical scrutiny. All studies do not use every step in the following description, and some disciplines commonly use variations of the basic procedure.

If your field of study or occupation calls for you to use the scientific method, then you will learn far more about scientific procedures than can be described here. However, if you are not in a scientific field, you may still find yourself making decisions that would be better made if you were familiar with scientific thinking and procedures. The following is also a simplified version of what researchers really do; actual scientific studies usually are much more complicated.

Scientific studies begin with a problem statement, which is a general statement of what the researcher wants to find out. The problem statement helps the researcher focus his or her attention to ensure that everything done later is designed to fit it. A problem statement might be, "I want to find the best way to teach critical thinking."

From the problem statement comes a research question, which is a specific question that the research is intended to answer. It might be, "Is Lewis's method of teaching critical thinking better than other methods?" The specific research question is important, because everything else in the process should be done to answer it rather than a more general or similar question. For instance, "Does Lewis's method of teaching critical thinking affect students' performances in college?" is much more vague. It can still be studied, but it's a different question.

The study that is actually done may be either descriptive or experimental. A **descriptive study** is designed to report on what "is," without attempting to draw causal conclusions. An **experimental study** is designed to draw a causal conclusion about how one variable affects another. The study in the example would be an experimental study. A descriptive study on the same general subject might be, "Which process do students use when analyzing the believability of a persuasive essay?"

Based on the research question and everything else that the researcher already knows about the subject, the researcher then devises a **hypothesis,** which is a prediction of what he or she expects to find. In everyday life, we regularly make vague predictions without establishing the problem statement or research question. In a more rigorous scientific procedure, you would state your hypothesis more carefully to account for the variables and exactly what is studied. The hypothesis in the example might be, "American college students who are taught critical thinking using Lewis's method will score higher on the Cartman test of critical thinking than students taught using other methods."

Two types of variables are involved in the hypothesis. The **independent variable** is what the researchers control and predict to be the cause of a particular effect. The **dependent variable** is what the researchers expect to be affected by the independent variable. They're called variables because each can vary in some way, even if it is as simple as existing or not existing. In the example, the method of teaching critical thinking would be the independent variable, and the dependent variable would be the score on the Cartman test of critical thinking. The researchers can control the way students are taught, when they are taught, where they are taught, and so on. They cannot control how well the students score on the test.

One of the first things a researcher does when conducting a study is to identify the population that he or she will study. The **population** is the entire group to which a scientific study is intended to apply. It may be everyone in the United States, women over age forty-five, redwood trees within fifty miles of the California coast, television sets sold in the United States, or any number of other groups. In most cases, when researchers want to draw a conclusion about a group, it would be too expensive and difficult to study all of its members, so they study a sample. The **sample** consists of members of the larger population that are actually studied. The researchers try to make sure that they get a sample of adequate size, one that represents the population as a whole. In the example, we've already identified the population as "all college students in the United States." The sample might be "six hundred randomly selected American college students."

When designing the study, researchers also have to figure out how to measure whatever they are studying. Measurement transforms observations into numbers to allow for statistical analysis. One way to do that is to actually count the phenomenon, whether it's the number of times something happens, how long something is, or how heavy something is. Another way is to turn something into a numerical form. For example, someone's attitude may be measured by a survey that allows for answers such as "Strongly Agree" and "Disagree." The answer "Strongly Agree" may be counted as a value of 5, while "Disagree" may be counted as 2. Turning non-numerical concepts into numbers allows statistical analysis that wouldn't be possible otherwise.

In deciding which kind of measurements to use, researchers have to be concerned with two different ideas: reliability and validity. **Reliability** is the ability of the measurement device to consistently give the same results when measuring the same phenomenon. For instance, a weight scale is said to be reliable if it gives the same reading whenever the same item is placed on it. If the measurement device is unreliable, then the conclusions of the study can't be as confident. **Validity** is the ability of the measurement device to actually measure what it is supposed to measure. A scale, for instance, would be an appropriate device for measuring weight but not distance.

So if variations of the Cartman test of critical thinking were properly administered, and if the same people kept getting the same scores, then it would be considered reliable. If the test actually discovers how well people think critically, then it would be considered valid.

At this point, the general procedures become different for descriptive and experimental studies, thus I'll explain what is done in the design of descriptive studies first and then turn to the experimental design.

Descriptive Design

The design of descriptive research is generally simpler than that for comparable experimental research. Researchers develop procedures to make enough observations so that a generalization can be made. That doesn't mean that descriptive research is necessarily easy though. If surveys are used, for example, they have to be designed in a way that the questions are not likely to be interpreted in multiple ways, do not identify a "desired" answer, do not ask compound questions, and account for other concerns. Physical observations have to be done in ways that account for potentially different perspectives and biases, and for the possibility that the observers may affect what they observe.

For a typical descriptive study, the researcher generally does the following:

- Identifies the population
- Selects the sample
- Identifies, or devises, a reliable and valid measurement instrument
- Gathers data by using the measurement instrument
- Analyzes the data statistically
- Draws conclusions

Experimental Design

The design for experiments is more complicated than for descriptive studies, because the researcher is manipulating variables to find out what would happen if certain changes were made.

As with descriptive studies, the design begins by identifying the population and the sample. The sample is then divided into two or more groups. One is the treatment group (also called the "experimental group"), and the other is the control group. In a relatively simple experiment, there is one treatment group and one control group. In a more complex experiment, there are multiple experimental groups.

The **treatment group** consists of the members of the sample who are exposed to the experimental treatment. Remember, the experimental treatment is the administration of the independent variable. That means that the independent variable (cause) that the researcher hypothesizes will change the dependent variable (create an effect) is applied to the treatment group. In the example, since the hypothesis is that students in the sample who are taught using Lewis's approach will improve their test scores more than those who were taught using another method, then the treatment group consists of those who are taught using Lewis's approach.

The **control group** consists of the members of the sample who are exposed to all of the same conditions as the treatment group, except for the experimental treatment. If, for instance, researchers want to know how well a fertilizer improves the growth of grass, then they will set up at least two plots of grass. One plot will be fertilized, and the other won't. They'll make sure both plots have the same soil, amount of light, amount of water, temperatures, and so on, so the only difference in growth rates will be due to the fertilizer. When working with humans, it is more difficult to control all of the variables, but researchers do the best they can. In the example, the assumption may be that by choosing a large enough random sample and by randomly assigning participants to the treatment and control groups, then the overall experiences will be the same in the treatment and control groups. Of course, it would be difficult to randomly assign students from throughout the United States to the different classes, because you'd have to get some of them to move to places they didn't want to go. Thus this experiment would have a problem that casts doubt on the results. The experimental group is taught using Lewis's approach, and the control group is taught using another approach. Since there are lots of different approaches to teaching critical thinking, Lewis may need several different control groups. And since not teaching the students critical thinking at all may have an effect, then Lewis should have a control group that is taught something, but not critical thinking.

In medical studies, patients in the control group are often given a placebo. A placebo is something given to the control group that is similar to the independent variable but has no known effect on the dependent variable. It is used because just doing something that the patient *thinks* will help sometimes does help, and the research should control for that. So if an experimental medicine were administered in the form of a pill taken three times a day, then the patients in the control group would take a placebo pill three times a day.

Many experiments use a pre-test, treatment, post-test design. The **pre-test** measures the dependent variable in the entire sample, prior to doing any treatment. The **post-test** measures the dependent variable in the entire sample, after the treatment is done. If the post-test shows that there is more change in the treatment group than in the control group, and if everything else is done correctly, then it is reasonable to conclude that the independent variable caused the difference in the change. If no difference occurred in the change between the two groups, then you would have to conclude that the independent variable had no real effect.

In the example, the results of the pre-test are everyone's score on the Cartman test of critical thinking prior to being taught. The results of the post-test are everyone's score on the Cartman test of critical thinking at the end of the courses. (By the way, I made up the title of the test for this example. I don't think there is really a "Cartman Test of Critical Thinking.") Real experiments are likely to be much more sophisticated, though, and they might measure other effects as well. For example, an experiment on a treatment for heart disease may test for the effect on patient mortality as well as the effect on other symptoms of heart disease. So all of the subjects might be given a complete physical with blood tests and a stress test as the pre-test, and then again as the post-test. The researchers would determine the change in a variety of variables as measured by the tests.

When the data are collected, a statistical analysis is done and the conclusions are drawn based on the results of the experiment. If the data show that there is more change in the treatment group than in the control group, and that the change can be shown, statistically, unlikely to be due to chance, then the hypothesis is confirmed.

HYPOTHESIS VERSUS THEORY

Among people who are not scientists, often there is some confusion about the difference between a hypothesis and a theory. We often hear people who don't want to accept a scientific theory say something like, "Oh, that's *just* a theory," as though that is proof that the idea shouldn't be taken seriously.

A scientific **theory** is an explanation of a phenomenon and a prediction of what will happen in the future, based on the accumulation of well-collected data. Scientific theories, especially those that are accepted in the scientific community, are not just speculation. They have a great deal of evidence supporting them. Hypotheses, on the other hand, are speculations of how one variable will affect another, based on what is known before an experiment is conducted. When people say, "Oh, that's just a theory," they are likely thinking of a theory as having no more support than a hypothesis.

Theories are accepted because they provide a cogent explanation for what happens. They don't just say that one variable affects another but how and why that variable has the effect that it does. They also are accepted because they accurately predict how one variable will affect another. If there's a reasonable explanation but the predictions are inaccurate, then the theory is rejected. If there are competing theories, then they are tested with more experiments to identify the strengths and weaknesses of each. The best one is accepted, or both are rejected, and then another theory is proposed. Whichever theory is accepted is subject to more research, which may strengthen or cast doubt on it.

Theories do come and go, but that happens because a better theory supplants an earlier one. New ways of making measurements are devised, which will generate new data, which will create better understanding and expose inaccuracies, and a new theory is developed and tested to account for the new information. The experiments and theorizing are shared with others and undergo peer reviews to expose weaknesses. Theories are revised and refined until they appear to make the best explanations and predictions.

So if you hear something presented as an accepted scientific theory, and if you can trust the person presenting it, then you can be pretty sure that it has received a great deal of scrutiny by people who are very good at examining the subject. And if you hear a theory dismissed because it is "just a theory," then you should question whether the person making the charge knows what he or she is talking about.

OPPOSITION TO THE SCIENTIFIC METHOD

Some people dislike the scientific method and reject it for all purposes, often because it doesn't answer the kind of questions that they think are the most important. There is some truth to that position, because the scientific method can only answer questions of fact. It can help us understand what "is" and how one event affects another, but it can't answer questions of value or policy. The scientific method can't answer what is good or just, and it can't tell us what to do with the knowledge we have gained. It's unfair, though, to reject the scientific method entirely because it doesn't do what it's not intended to do. You may remember that that's the fallacy of extension.

Another reason some people reject the scientific method is because sometimes scientists don't follow it very well. Highly publicized cases have revealed some scientists skipping steps or telling outright lies about the data they collected. That is reason to reject those studies and to be suspicious of anything else that those scientists produce, but it's not a very sound reason to reject the method as a whole. That would be a hasty generalization. The vast majority of scientists will collect their data the best way they can and will report it accurately. They may not follow the method as well as it would ideally be followed, but usually that's because the resource expense would be too great, or following the entire procedure would create ethical problems that are more important than the scientific method. Studies should be examined on an individual basis to determine how well they should be accepted, but all studies should not be rejected just because some are flawed.

Sometimes people reject the scientific method because they find some research unethical. There are examples of humans being harmed by unethical scientific procedures, and there are many people who find the use of animals in experiments unethical. While those are reasons to advocate changing the way specific experiments are done, they are not sound arguments for dismissing the scientific method altogether.

Some people also are opposed to science and the scientific method because they don't like what is found. The results of research are contrary to some people's beliefs, or they provide evidence favorable to policy changes to which they are opposed, so they reject science. Sometimes there are reasonable arguments against a particular line of research because of what will be done with it, but once again that doesn't make a good argument against the scientific method in general. It is better to understand how the scientific method works and to recognize when it is used correctly rather than to decide that all scientific research is worthless.

SUMMARY

Knowledge of the scientific method can help you make better arguments and better think critically. It is meant to overcome common flaws in thinking and can be applied to everyday thinking as well as to scientific studies. The scientific method is based on ten principles and a set of procedures designed for descriptive and experimental studies. It employs both hypotheses and theories, but the terms are not interchangeable. Some people are opposed to the scientific method for reasons that are legitimate objections to individual studies but are not reasonable indictments of the method as a whole.

KEY TERMS

control group   the members of the sample who are exposed to all of the same conditions as the treatment group except for the experimental treatment.

dependent variable   what the researchers expect to be affected by the independent variable.

descriptive study   research designed to report on what "is," without attempting to draw causal conclusions.

experimental study   research designed to draw a causal conclusion about how one variable affects another by controlling and manipulating variables.

hypothesis   a prediction of what the researcher expects to find based on what is already known about the subject.

independent variable   an act that researchers have control over and predict will be the cause of a particular effect.

population   the entire group to which a specific study is intended to apply.

post-test   measure of the dependent variable in the entire sample after the treatment.

pre-test   measure of the dependent variable in the entire sample prior to any treatment being done.

reliability   the ability of the measurement device to consistently give the same results when measuring the same phenomenon.

sample   in the scientific method, members of the population that are actually studied.

theory   an explanation of a phenomenon and a prediction of what will happen in the future, based on the accumulation of well-collected data.

treatment group   members of the sample who are exposed to the experimental treatment. Also known as the "experimental group."

validity   the ability of a measurement device to actually measure what it is supposed to measure.

THINGS TO THINK ABOUT

1. Find a news report about a scientific discovery. Which principles of the scientific method are described in the article? Which principles are left out?

2. Think of a recent conclusion you drew about a factual subject. How did your reasoning make use of the principles and procedures of the scientific method? Which principles and procedures did you not use but might have?

3. Think of something about which you'll someday need to make a decision. How might your objectivity about the subject be compromised?

4. Imagine that you're trying to decide whether two of your friends are dating each other secretly. How could your decision-making process follow the principles and procedures of the scientific method described in this chapter?

Appendix

Secretary of State Colin Powell's Speech to the United Nations Security Council, February 5, 2003

Secretary of State Colin Powell presented the following speech to the United Nations Security Council as part of the Bush administration's efforts to persuade the United Nations to support the military invasion of Iraq. The speech is reproduced as it appeared on the Secretary's Web Site (http://www.state.gov/secretary/rm/2003/17300pf.htm). The only changes are the addition of paragraph numbers so you and your instructor can easily refer to specific parts of the speech.

Remarks to the United Nations Security Council
Secretary Colin L. Powell
New York City
February 5, 2003

1   **SECRETARY POWELL:** Thank you, Mr. President. Mr. President and Mr. Secretary General, distinguished colleagues, I would like to begin by expressing my thanks for the special effort that each of you made to be here today. This is an important day for us all as we review the situation with respect to Iraq and its disarmament obligations under UN Security Council Resolution 1441.

2   Last November 8, this Council passed Resolution 1441 by a unanimous vote. The purpose of that resolution was to disarm Iraq of its weapons of mass destruction. Iraq had already been found guilty of material breach of its obligations stretching back over 16 previous resolutions and 12 years.

3   Resolution 1441 was not dealing with an innocent party, but a regime this Council has repeatedly convicted over the years.

4   Resolution 1441 gave Iraq one last chance, one last chance to come into compliance or to face serious consequences. No Council member present and voting on that day had any illusions about the nature and intent of the resolution or what serious consequences meant if Iraq did not comply.

5   And to assist in its disarmament, we called on Iraq to cooperate with returning inspectors from UNMOVIC and IAEA. We laid down tough standards for Iraq to meet to allow the inspectors to do their job.

6   This Council placed the burden on Iraq to comply and disarm, and not on the inspectors to find that which Iraq has gone out of its way to conceal for so long. Inspectors are inspectors; they are not detectives.

7   I asked for this session today for two purposes. First, to support the core assessments made by Dr. Blix and Dr. ElBaradei. As Dr. Blix reported to this Council on January 27, "Iraq appears not to have come to a genuine acceptance, not even today, of the disarmament which was demanded of it."

8   And as Dr. ElBaradei reported, Iraq's declaration of December 7 "did not provide any new information relevant to certain questions that have been outstanding since 1998."

9   My second purpose today is to provide you with additional information, to share with you what the United States knows about Iraq's weapons of mass destruction, as well as Iraq's involvement in terrorism, which is also the subject of Resolution 1441 and other earlier resolutions.

10   I might add at this point that we are providing all relevant information we can to the inspection teams for them to do their work.

11   The material I will present to you comes from a variety of sources. Some are U.S. sources and some are those of other countries. Some [of] the sources are technical, such as intercepted telephone conversations and photos taken by satellites. Other sources are people who have risked their lives to let the world know what Saddam Hussein is really up to.

12   I cannot tell you everything that we know, but what I can share with you, when combined with what all of us have learned over the years, is deeply troubling. What you will see is an accumulation of facts and disturbing patterns of behavior. The facts and Iraqis' behavior, Iraq's behavior, demonstrate that Saddam Hussein and his regime have made no effort, no effort, to disarm, as required by the international community.

13   Indeed, the facts and Iraq's behavior show that Saddam Hussein and his regime are concealing their efforts to produce more weapons of mass destruction.

14   Let me begin by playing a tape for you. What you're about to hear is a conversation that my government monitored. It takes place on November 26th of last year, on the day before United Nations teams resumed

inspections in Iraq. The conversation involves two senior officers, a colonel and a brigadier general from Iraq's elite military unit, the Republican Guard.

[The tape was played.]

15   **SECRETARY POWELL:** Let me pause and review some of the key elements of this conversation that you just heard between these two officers.

16   First, they acknowledge that our colleague, Mohammed ElBaradei is coming, and they know what he's coming for and they know he's coming the next day. He's coming to look for things that are prohibited. He is expecting these gentlemen to cooperate with him and not hide things.

17   But they're worried. We have this modified vehicle. What do we say if one of them sees it? What is their concern? Their concern is that it's something they should not have, something that should not be seen.

18   The general was incredulous: "You didn't get it modified. You don't have one of those, do you?"

19   "I have one."

20   "Which? From where?"

21   "From the workshop. From the Al-Kindi Company."

22   "What?"

23   "From Al-Kindi."

24   "I'll come to see you in the morning. I'm worried you all have something left."

25   "We evacuated everything. We don't have anything left."

26   Note what he says: "We evacuated everything." We didn't destroy it. We didn't line it up for inspection. We didn't turn it into the inspectors. We evacuated it to make sure it was not around when the inspectors showed up. "I will come to you tomorrow."

27   The Al-Kindi Company. This is a company that is well known to have been involved in prohibited weapons systems activity.

28   Let me play another tape for you. As you will recall, the inspectors found 12 empty chemical warheads on January 16th. On January 20th, four days later, Iraq promised the inspectors it would search for more. You will now hear an officer from Republican Guard headquarters issuing an instruction to an officer in the field. Their conversation took place just last week, on January 30.

[The tape was played.]

29   **SECRETARY POWELL:** Let me pause again and review the elements of this message.

30   "They are inspecting the ammunition you have, yes?"

31   "Yes. For the possibility there are forbidden ammo."

32   "For the possibility there is, by chance, forbidden ammo?"

33   "Yes."

34   "And we sent you a message yesterday to clean out all the areas, the scrap areas, the abandoned areas. Make sure there is nothing there. Remember the first message: evacuate it."

35   This is all part of a system of hiding things and moving things out of the way and making sure they have left nothing behind.

36   You go a little further into this message and you see the specific instructions from headquarters: "After you have carried out what is contained in this message, destroy the message because I don't want anyone to see this message."

37   "Okay."

38   "Okay."

39   Why? Why? This message would have verified to the inspectors that they have been trying to turn over things. They were looking for things, but they don't want that message seen because they were trying to clean up the area, to leave no evidence behind of the presence of weapons of mass destruction. And they can claim that nothing was there and the inspectors can look all they want and they will find nothing.

40   This effort to hide things from the inspectors is not one or two isolated events. Quite the contrary, this is part and parcel of a policy of evasion and deception that goes back 12 years, a policy set at the highest levels of the Iraqi regime.

41   We know that Saddam Hussein has what is called "a Higher Committee for Monitoring the Inspection Teams." Think about that. Iraq has a high-level committee to monitor the inspectors who were sent in to monitor Iraq's disarmament—not to cooperate with them, not to assist them, but to spy on them and keep them from doing their jobs.

42   The committee reports directly to Saddam Hussein. It is headed by Iraq's Vice President, Taha Yasin Ramadan. Its members include Saddam Hussein's son, Qusay.

43   This committee also includes Lieutenant General Amir al-Sa'di, an advisor to Saddam. In case that name isn't immediately familiar to you, General Sa'di has been the Iraqi regime's primary point of contact for Dr. Blix and Dr. ElBaradei. It was General Sa'di who last fall publicly pledged that Iraq was prepared to cooperate unconditionally with inspectors. Quite the contrary, Sa'di's job is not to cooperate; it is to deceive, not to disarm, but to undermine the inspectors; not to support them, but to frustrate them and to make sure they learn nothing.

44   We have learned a lot about the work of this special committee. We learned that just prior to the return of inspectors last November, the regime had decided to resume what we heard called "the old game of cat-and-mouse."

45   For example, let me focus on the now famous declaration that Iraq submitted to this Council on December 7th. Iraq never had any intention of complying with this Council's mandate. Instead, Iraq planned to use the declaration to overwhelm us and to overwhelm the inspectors with useless information about Iraq's permitted weapons so that we would not have time to pursue Iraq's prohibited weapons. Iraq's goal was to give us in this room, to give those of us on this Council, the false impression that the inspection process was working.

46   You saw the result. Dr. Blix pronounced the 12,200-page declaration "rich in volume" but "poor in information and practically devoid of new evidence." Could any member of this Council honestly rise in defense of this false declaration?

47   Everything we have seen and heard indicates that instead of cooperating actively with the inspectors to ensure the success of their mission, Saddam Hussein and his regime are busy doing all they possibly can to ensure that inspectors succeed in finding absolutely nothing.

48   My colleagues, every statement I make today is backed up by sources, solid sources. These are not assertions. What we are giving you are facts and conclusions based on solid intelligence. I will cite some examples, and these are from human sources.

49   Orders were issued to Iraq's security organizations, as well as to Saddam Hussein's own office, to hide all correspondence with the Organization of Military Industrialization. This is the organization that oversees Iraq's weapons of mass destruction activities. Make sure there are no documents left which would connect you to the OMI.

50   We know that Saddam's son, Qusay, ordered the removal of all prohibited weapons from Saddam's numerous palace complexes. We know that Iraqi government officials, members of the ruling Ba'ath Party and scientists have hidden prohibited items in their homes. Other key files from military and scientific establishments have been placed in cars that are being driven around the countryside by Iraqi intelligence agents to avoid detection.

51   Thanks to intelligence they were provided, the inspectors recently found dramatic confirmation of these reports. When they searched the homes of an Iraqi nuclear scientist, they uncovered roughly 2,000 pages of documents. You see them here being brought out of the home and placed in UN hands. Some of the material is classified and related to Iraq's nuclear program.

52   Tell me, answer me: Are the inspectors to search the house of every government official, every Ba'ath Party member and every scientist in the country to find the truth, to get the information they need to satisfy the demands of our Council?

53   Our sources tell us that in some cases the hard drives of computers at Iraqi weapons facilities were replaced. Who took the hard drives? Where did they go? What is being hidden? Why?

54   There is only one answer to the why: to deceive, to hide, to keep from the inspectors.

55   Numerous human sources tell us that the Iraqis are moving not just documents and hard drives, but weapons of mass destruction, to keep them from being found by inspectors. While we were here in this Council chamber debating Resolution 1441 last fall, we know, we know from sources that a missile brigade outside Baghdad was dispersing rocket launchers and warheads containing biological warfare agent to various locations, distributing them to various locations in western Iraq.

56   Most of the launchers and warheads had been hidden in large groves of palm trees and were to be moved every one to four weeks to escape detection.

57   We also have satellite photos that indicate that banned materials have recently been moved from a number of Iraqi weapons of mass destruction facilities.

58   Let me say a word about satellite images before I show a couple. The photos that I am about to show you are sometimes hard for the average person to interpret, hard for me. The painstaking work of photo analysis takes experts with years and years of experience, poring for hours and hours over light tables. But as I show you these images, I will try to capture and explain what they mean, what they indicate, to our imagery specialists.

59   Let's look at one. This one is about a weapons munition facility, a facility that holds ammunition at a place called Taji. This is one of about 65 such facilities in Iraq. We know that this one has housed chemical munitions. In fact, this is where the Iraqis recently came up with the additional four chemical weapons shells.

60   Here you see 15 munitions bunkers in yellow and red outlines. The four that are in red squares represent active chemical munitions bunkers.

61   How do I know that? How can I say that? Let me give you a closer look. Look at the image on the left. On the left is a close-up of one of the four chemical bunkers. The two arrows indicate the presence of sure signs that the bunkers are storing chemical munitions. The arrow at the top that says "security" points to a facility that is a signature item for this kind of bunker. Inside that facility are special guards and special equipment to monitor any leakage that might come out of the bunker. The truck you also see is a signature item. It's a decontamination vehicle in case something goes wrong. This is characteristic of those four bunkers. The special security facility and the decontamination vehicle will be in the area, if not at any one of them or one of the other, it is moving around those four and it moves as needed to move as people are working in the different bunkers.

62   Now look at the picture on the right. You are now looking at two of those sanitized bunkers. The signature vehicles are gone, the tents are

gone. It's been cleaned up. And it was done on the 22nd of December as the UN inspection team is arriving, and you can see the inspection vehicles arriving in the lower portion of the picture on the right.

63   The bunkers are clean when the inspectors get there. They found nothing.

64   This sequence of events raises the worrisome suspicion that Iraq had been tipped off to the forthcoming inspections at Taji. As it did throughout the 1990s, we know that Iraq today is actively using its considerable intelligence capabilities to hide its illicit activities. From our sources, we know that inspectors are under constant surveillance by an army of Iraqi intelligence operatives. Iraq is relentlessly attempting to tap all of their communications, both voice and electronics. I would call my colleagues' attention to the fine paper that the United Kingdom distributed yesterday which describes in exquisite detail Iraqi deception activities.

65   In this next example, you will see the type of concealment activity Iraq has undertaken in response to the resumption of inspections. Indeed, in November of 2002, just when the inspections were about to resume, this type of activity spiked. Here are three examples.

66   At this ballistic missile site on November 10th, we saw a cargo truck preparing to move ballistic missile components.

67   At this biological weapons–related facility on November 25th, just two days before inspections resumed, this truck caravan appeared—something we almost never see at this facility and we monitor it carefully and regularly.

68   At this ballistic missile facility, again, two days before inspections began, five large cargo trucks appeared, along with a truck-mounted crane, to move missiles.

69   We saw this kind of housecleaning at close to 30 sites. Days after this activity, the vehicles and the equipment that I've just highlighted disappear and the site returns to patterns of normalcy. We don't know precisely what Iraq was moving, but the inspectors already knew about these sites so Iraq knew that they would be coming.

70   We must ask ourselves: Why would Iraq suddenly move equipment of this nature before inspections if they were anxious to demonstrate what they had or did not have?

71   Remember the first intercept in which two Iraqis talked about the need to hide a modified vehicle from the inspectors. Where did Iraq take all of this equipment? Why wasn't it presented to the inspectors?

72   Iraq also has refused to permit any U-2 reconnaissance flights that would give the inspectors a better sense of what's being moved before, during and after inspections. This refusal to allow this kind of reconnaissance is in direct, specific violation of operative paragraph seven of our Resolution 1441.

73   Saddam Hussein and his regime are not just trying to conceal weapons; they are also trying to hide people. You know the basic facts. Iraq has not complied with its obligation to allow immediate, unimpeded, unrestricted and private access to all officials and other persons, as required by Resolution 1441. The regime only allows interviews with inspectors in the presence of an Iraqi official, a minder. The official Iraqi organization charged with facilitating inspections announced publicly and announced ominously, that, "Nobody is ready" to leave Iraq to be interviewed.

74   Iraqi Vice President Ramadan accused the inspectors of conducting espionage, a veiled threat that anyone cooperating with UN inspectors was committing treason.

75   Iraq did not meet its obligations under 1441 to provide a comprehensive list of scientists associated with its weapons of mass destruction programs. Iraq's list was out of date and contained only about 500 names despite the fact that UNSCOM had earlier put together a list of about 3,500 names.

76   Let me just tell you what a number of human sources have told us. Saddam Hussein has directly participated in the effort to prevent interviews. In early December, Saddam Hussein had all Iraqi scientists warned of the serious consequences that they and their families would face if they revealed any sensitive information to the inspectors. They were forced to sign documents acknowledging that divulging information is punishable by death.

77   Saddam Hussein also said that scientists should be told not to agree to leave Iraq; anyone who agreed to be interviewed outside Iraq would be treated as a spy. This violates 1441.

78   In mid-November, just before the inspectors returned, Iraqi experts were ordered to report to the headquarters of the Special Security Organization to receive counter-intelligence training. The training focused on evasion methods, interrogation resistance techniques, and how to mislead inspectors.

79   Ladies and gentlemen, these are not assertions. These are facts corroborated by many sources, some of them sources of the intelligence services of other countries.

80   For example, in mid-December, weapons experts at one facility were replaced by Iraqi intelligence agents who were to deceive inspectors about the work that was being done there. On orders from Saddam Hussein, Iraqi officials issued a false death certificate for one scientist and he was sent into hiding.

81   In the middle of January, experts at one facility that was related to weapons of mass destruction, those experts had been ordered to stay home from work to avoid the inspectors. Workers from other Iraqi military facilities not engaged in illicit weapons projects were to replace the workers who had been sent home. A dozen experts have been placed

under house arrest—not in their own houses, but as a group at one of Saddam Hussein's guest houses.

82   It goes on and on and on. As the examples I have just presented show, the information and intelligence we have gathered point to an active and systematic effort on the part of the Iraqi regime to keep key materials and people from the inspectors, in direct violation of Resolution 1441.

83   The pattern is not just one of reluctant cooperation, nor is it merely a lack of cooperation. What we see is a deliberate campaign to prevent any meaningful inspection work.

84   My colleagues, Operative Paragraph 4 of UN Resolution 1441, which we lingered over so long last fall, clearly states that false statements and omissions in the declaration and a failure by Iraq at any time to comply with and cooperate fully in the implementation of this resolution shall constitute—the facts speak for themselves—shall constitute a further material breach of its obligation.

85   We wrote it this way to give Iraq an early test, to give Iraq an early test. Would they give an honest declaration and would they, early on, indicate a willingness to cooperate with the inspectors? It was designed to be an early test. They failed that test.

86   By this standard, the standard of this Operative Paragraph, I believe that Iraq is now in further material breach of its obligations. I believe this conclusion is irrefutable and undeniable.

87   Iraq has now placed itself in danger of the serious consequences called for in UN Resolution 1441. And this body places itself in danger of irrelevance if it allows Iraq to continue to defy its will without responding effectively and immediately.

88   This issue before us is not how much time we are willing to give the inspectors to be frustrated by Iraqi obstruction. But how much longer are we willing to put up with Iraq's non-compliance before we, as a Council, we as the United Nations say, "Enough. Enough."

89   The gravity of this moment is matched by the gravity of the threat that Iraq's weapons of mass destruction pose to the world. Let me now turn to those deadly weapons programs and describe why they are real and present dangers to the region and to the world.

90   First, biological weapons. We have talked frequently here about biological weapons. By way of introduction and history, I think there are just three quick points I need to make. First, you will recall that it took UNSCOM four long and frustrating years to pry, to pry an admission out of Iraq that it had biological weapons. Second, when Iraq finally admitted having these weapons in 1995, the quantities were vast. Less than a teaspoon of dry anthrax, a little bit—about this amount. This is just about the amount of a teaspoon. Less than a teaspoonful of dry anthrax in an envelope shut down the United States Senate in the fall of 2001.

91   This forced several hundred people to undergo emergency medical treatment and killed two postal workers just from an amount, just about this quantity that was inside of an envelope.

92   Iraq declared 8500 liters of anthrax. But UNSCOM estimates that Saddam Hussein could have produced 25,000 liters. If concentrated into this dry form, this amount would be enough to fill tens upon tens upon tens of thousands of teaspoons. And Saddam Hussein has not verifiably accounted for even one teaspoonful of this deadly material. And that is my third point. And it is key. The Iraqis have never accounted for all of the biological weapons they admitted they had and we know they had.

93   They have never accounted for all the organic material used to make them. And they have not accounted for many of the weapons filled with these agents such as their R–400 bombs. This is evidence, not conjecture. This is true. This is all well documented.

94   Dr. Blix told this Council that Iraq has provided little evidence to verify anthrax production and no convincing evidence of its destruction. It should come as no shock then that since Saddam Hussein forced out the last inspectors in 1998, we have amassed much intelligence indicating that Iraq is continuing to make these weapons.

95   One of the most worrisome things that emerges from the thick intelligence file we have on Iraq's biological weapons is the existence of mobile production facilities used to make biological agents.

96   Let me take you inside that intelligence file and share with you what we know from eyewitness accounts. We have first-hand descriptions of biological weapons factories on wheels and on rails.

97   The trucks and train cars are easily moved and are designed to evade detection by inspectors. In a matter of months, they can produce a quantity of biological poison equal to the entire amount that Iraq claimed to have produced in the years prior to the Gulf War.

98   Although Iraq's mobile production program began in the mid-1990s, UN inspectors at the time only had vague hints of such programs. Confirmation came later, in the year 2000. The source was an eyewitness, an Iraqi chemical engineer who supervised one of these facilities. He actually was present during biological agent production runs. He was also at the site when an accident occurred in 1998. 12 technicians died from exposure to biological agents.

99   He reported that when UNSCOM was in country and inspecting, the biological weapons agent production always began on Thursdays at midnight, because Iraq thought UNSCOM would not inspect on the Muslim holy day, Thursday night through Friday.

100   He added that this was important because the units could not be broken down in the middle of a production run, which had to be completed by Friday evening before the inspectors might arrive again.

101   This defector is currently hiding in another country with the certain knowledge that Saddam Hussein will kill him if he finds him. His eyewitness account of these mobile production facilities has been corroborated by other sources.

102   A second source. An Iraqi civil engineer in a position to know the details of the program confirmed the existence of transportable facilities moving on trailers.

103   A third source, also in a position to know, reported in summer, 2002, that Iraq had manufactured mobile production systems mounted on road-trailer units and on rail cars.

104   Finally, a fourth source. An Iraqi major who defected confirmed that Iraq has mobile biological research laboratories in addition to the production facilities I mentioned earlier.

105   We have diagrammed what our sources reported about these mobile facilities. Here you see both truck and rail-car mounted mobile factories. The description our sources gave us of the technical features required by such facilities is highly detailed and extremely accurate.

106   As these drawings, based on their description show, we know what the fermentors look like. We know what the tanks, pumps, compressors and other parts look like. We know how they fit together, we know how they work, and we know a great deal about the platforms on which they are mounted.

107   As shown in this diagram, these factories can be concealed easily—either by moving ordinary looking trucks and rail-cars along Iraq's thousands of miles of highway or track or by parking them in a garage or a warehouse or somewhere in Iraq's extensive system of underground tunnels and bunkers.

108   We know that Iraq has at least seven of these mobile, biological agent factories. The truck-mounted ones have at least two or three trucks each. That means that the mobile production facilities are very few—perhaps 18 trucks that we know of. There may be more. But perhaps 18 that we know of. Just imagine trying to find 18 trucks among the thousands and thousands of trucks that travel the roads of Iraq every single day.

109   It took the inspectors four years to find out that Iraq was making biological agents. How long do you think it will take the inspectors to find even one of these 18 trucks without Iraq coming forward as they are supposed to with the information about these kinds of capabilities.

110   Ladies and gentlemen, these are sophisticated facilities. For example, they can produce anthrax and botulinum toxin. In fact, they can produce enough dry, biological agent in a single month to kill thousands upon thousands of people. A dry agent of this type is the most lethal form for human beings.

111   By 1998, UN experts agreed that the Iraqis had perfected drying techniques for their biological weapons programs. Now Iraq has incorporated this drying expertise into these mobile production facilities.

112   We know from Iraq's past admissions that it has successfully weaponized not only anthrax, but also other biological agents including botulinum toxin, aflatoxin and ricin. But Iraq's research efforts did not stop there.

113   Saddam Hussein has investigated dozens of biological agents causing diseases such as gas gangrene, plague, typhus, tetanus, cholera, camelpox, and hemorrhagic fever. And he also has the wherewithal to develop smallpox.

114   The Iraqi regime has also developed ways to disperse lethal biological agents widely, indiscriminately into the water supply, into the air. For example, Iraq had a program to modify aerial fuel tanks for Mirage jets. This video of an Iraqi test flight obtained by UNSCOM some years ago shows an Iraqi F-1 Mirage jet aircraft. Note the spray coming from beneath the Mirage. That is 2,000 liters of simulated anthrax that a jet is spraying.

(Video.)

115   In 1995, an Iraqi military officer, Mujahid Saleh Abdul Latif told inspectors that Iraq intended the spray tanks to be mounted onto a MiG-21 that had been converted into an unmanned aerial vehicle, or UAV. UAVs outfitted with spray tanks constitute an ideal method for launching a terrorist attack using biological weapons.

116   Iraq admitted to producing four spray tanks, but to this day, it has provided no credible evidence that they were destroyed, evidence that was required by the international community.

117   There can be no doubt that Saddam Hussein has biological weapons and the capability to rapidly produce more, many more. And he has the ability to dispense these lethal poisons and diseases in ways that can cause massive death and destruction.

118   If biological weapons seem too terrible to contemplate, chemical weapons are equally chilling. UNMOVIC already laid out much of this and it is documented for all of us to read in UNSCOM's 1999 report on the subject. Let me set the stage with three key points that all of us need to keep in mind. First, Saddam Hussein has used these horrific weapons on another country and on his own people. In fact, in the history of chemical warfare, no country has had more battlefield experience with chemical weapons since World War I than Saddam Hussein's Iraq.

119   Second, as with biological weapons, Saddam Hussein has never accounted for vast amounts of chemical weaponry: 550 artillery shells with mustard, 30,000 empty munitions and enough precursors to increase his stockpile to as much as 500 tons of chemical agents.

120   If we consider just one category of missing weaponry, 6500 bombs from the Iran-Iraq War, UNMOVIC says the amount of chemical agent in them would be on the order of a thousand tons.

121 These quantities of chemical weapons are now unaccounted for. Dr. Blix has quipped that, "Mustard gas is not marmalade. You are supposed to know what you did with it." We believe Saddam Hussein knows what he did with it and he has not come clean with the international community.

122 We have evidence these weapons existed. What we don't have is evidence from Iraq that they have been destroyed or where they are. That is what we are still waiting for.

123 Third point, Iraq's record on chemical weapons is replete with lies. It took years for Iraq to finally admit that it had produced four tons of the deadly nerve agent VX. A single drop of VX on the skin will kill in minutes. Four tons. The admission only came out after inspectors collected documentation as a result of the defection of Hussein Kamel, Saddam Hussein's late son-in-law.

124 UNSCOM also gained forensic evidence that Iraq had produced VX and put it into weapons for delivery, yet to this day Iraq denies it had ever weaponized VX. And on January 27, UNMOVIC told this Council that it has information that conflicts with the Iraqi account of its VX program.

125 We know that Iraq has embedded key portions of its illicit chemical weapons infrastructure within its legitimate civilian industry. To all outward appearances, even to experts, the infrastructure looks like an ordinary civilian operation. Illicit and legitimate production can go on simultaneously or on a dime. This dual-use infrastructure can turn from clandestine to commercial and then back again.

126 These inspections would be unlikely, any inspections at such facilities, would be unlikely to turn up anything prohibited, especially if there is any warning that the inspections are coming. Call it ingenious or evil genius, but the Iraqis deliberately designed their chemical weapons programs to be inspected. It is infrastructure with a built in alibi.

127 Under the guise of dual-use infrastructure, Iraq has undertaken an effort to reconstitute facilities that were closely associated with its past program to develop and produce chemical weapons. For example, Iraq has rebuilt key portions of the Tareq State Establishment. Tareq includes facilities designed specifically for Iraq's chemical weapons program and employs key figures from past programs.

128 That's the production end of Saddam's chemical weapons business. What about the delivery end? I'm going to show you a small part of a chemical complex called "Al Musayyib," a site that Iraq has used for at least three years to transship chemical weapons from production facilities out to the field. In May 2002, our satellites photographed the unusual activity in this picture.

129 Here we see cargo vehicles are again at this transshipment point, and we can see that they are accompanied by a decontamination vehicle associated with biological or chemical weapons activity. What makes this picture significant is that we have a human source who has corroborated that

movement of chemical weapons occurred at this site at that time. So it's not just the photo and it's not an individual seeing the photo. It's the photo and then the knowledge of an individual being brought together to make the case.

130 This photograph of the site taken two months later, in July, shows not only the previous site which is the figure in the middle at the top with the bulldozer sign near it, it shows that this previous site, as well as all of the other sites around the site have been fully bulldozed and graded. The topsoil has been removed. The Iraqis literally removed the crust of the earth from large portions of this site in order to conceal chemical weapons evidence that would be there from years of chemical weapons activity.

131 To support its deadly biological and chemical weapons programs, Iraq procures needed items from around the world using an extensive clandestine network. What we know comes largely from intercepted communications and human sources who are in a position to know the facts.

132 Iraq's procurement efforts include: equipment that can filter and separate microorganisms and toxins involved in biological weapons; equipment that can be used to concentrate the agent; growth media that can be used to continue producing anthrax and botulinum toxin; sterilization equipment for laboratories; glass-lined reactors and specialty pumps that can handle corrosive chemical weapons agents and precursors; large amounts of thionyl chloride, a precursor for nerve and blister agents; and other chemicals such as sodium sulfide, an important mustard agent precursor.

133 Now, of course, Iraq will argue that these items can also be used for legitimate purposes. But if that is true, why do we have to learn about them by intercepting communications and risking the lives of human agents?

134 With Iraq's well-documented history on biological and chemical weapons, why should any of us give Iraq the benefit of the doubt? I don't. And I don't think you will either after you hear this next intercept.

135 Just a few weeks ago we intercepted communications between two commanders in Iraq's Second Republican Guard Corps. One commander is going to be giving an instruction to the other. You will hear as this unfolds that what he wants to communicate to the other guy, he wants to make sure the other guy hears clearly to the point of repeating it so that it gets written down and completely understood. Listen.

(Transmission.)

136 Let's review a few selected items of this conversation. Two officers talking to each other on the radio want to make sure that nothing is misunderstood. "Remove." "Remove." "The expression." "The expression." "The expression. I got it." "Nerve agents." "Nerve agents."

"Wherever it comes up." "Got it, wherever it comes up." "In the wireless instructions." "In the instructions." "Correction, no, in the wireless instructions." "Wireless, I got it."

137 Why does he repeat it that way? Why is he so forceful in making sure this is understood? And why did he focus on wireless instructions? Because the senior officer is concerned that somebody might be listening. Well, somebody was.

138 "Nerve agents." "Stop talking about it." "They are listening to us." "Don't give any evidence that we have these horrible agents." But we know that they do and this kind of conversation confirms it.

139 Our conservative estimate is that Iraq today has a stockpile of between 100 and 500 tons of chemical weapons agent. That is enough agent to fill 16,000 battlefield rockets. Even the low end of 100 tons of agent would enable Saddam Hussein to cause mass casualties across more than 100 square miles of territory, an area nearly five times the size of Manhattan.

140 Let me remind you that—of the 122 mm chemical warheads that the UN inspectors found recently. This discovery could very well be, as has been noted, the tip of a submerged iceberg.

141 The question before us all, my friends, is when will we see the rest of the submerged iceberg?

(Video.)

142 Saddam Hussein has chemical weapons. Saddam Hussein has used such weapons. And Saddam Hussein has no compunction about using them again—against his neighbors and against his own people. And we have sources who tell us that he recently has authorized his field commanders to use them. He wouldn't be passing out the orders if he didn't have the weapons or the intent to use them.

143 We also have sources who tell us that since the 1980s, Saddam's regime has been experimenting on human beings to perfect its biological or chemical weapons.

144 A source said that 1,600 death-row prisoners were transferred in 1995 to a special unit for such experiments. An eyewitness saw prisoners tied down to beds, experiments conducted on them, blood oozing around the victims' mouths, and autopsies performed to confirm the effects on the prisoners.

145 Saddam Hussein's humanity—inhumanity has no limits.

146 Let me turn now to nuclear weapons. We have no indication that Saddam Hussein has ever abandoned his nuclear weapons program. On the contrary, we have more than a decade of proof that he remains determined to acquire nuclear weapons.

147 To fully appreciate the challenge that we face today, remember that in 1991 the inspectors searched Iraq's primary nuclear weapons facilities for the first time, and they found nothing to conclude that Iraq had a nuclear

weapons program. But, based on defector information, in May of 1991, Saddam Hussein's lie was exposed. In truth, Saddam Hussein had a massive clandestine nuclear weapons program that covered several different techniques to enrich uranium, including electromagnetic isotope separation, gas centrifuge and gas diffusion.

148   We estimate that this illicit program cost the Iraqis several billion dollars. Nonetheless, Iraq continued to tell the IAEA that it had no nuclear weapons program. If Saddam had not been stopped, Iraq could have produced a nuclear bomb by 1993, years earlier than most worst case assessments that had been made before the war.

149   In 1995, as a result of another defector, we find out that, after his invasion of Kuwait, Saddam Hussein had initiated a crash program to build a crude nuclear weapon, in violation of Iraq's UN obligations. Saddam Hussein already possesses two out of the three key components needed to build a nuclear bomb. He has a cadre of nuclear scientists with the expertise and he has a bomb design.

150   Since 1998, his efforts to reconstitute his nuclear program have been focused on acquiring the third and last component: sufficient fissile material to produce a nuclear explosion. To make the fissile material, he needs to develop an ability to enrich uranium. Saddam Hussein is determined to get his hands on a nuclear bomb.

151   He is so determined that has made repeated covert attempts to acquire high-specification aluminum tubes from 11 different countries, even after inspections resumed. These tubes are controlled by the Nuclear Suppliers Group precisely because they can be used as centrifuges for enriching uranium.

152   By now, just about everyone has heard of these tubes and we all know that there are differences of opinion. There is controversy about what these tubes are for. Most U.S. experts think they are intended to serve as rotors in centrifuges used to enrich uranium. Other experts, and the Iraqis themselves, argue that they are [ready] to produce the rocket bodies for a conventional weapon, a multiple rocket launcher.

153   Let me tell you what is not controversial about these tubes. First, all the experts who have analyzed the tubes in our possession agree that they can be adapted for centrifuge use.

154   Second, Iraq had no business buying them for any purpose. They are banned for Iraq.

155   I am no expert on centrifuge tubes, but this is an old army trooper. I can tell you a couple things.

156   First, it strikes me as quite odd that these tubes are manufactured to a tolerance that far exceeds U.S. requirements for comparable rockets. Maybe Iraqis just manufacture their conventional weapons to a higher standard than we do, but I don't think so.

157   Second, we actually have examined tubes from several different batches that were seized clandestinely before they reached Baghdad. What we notice in these different batches is a progression to higher and higher levels of specification, including in the latest batch an anodized coating on extremely smooth inner and outer surfaces.

158   Why would they continue refining the specifications? Why would they continuing refining the specification, go to all that trouble for something that, if it was a rocket, would soon be blown into shrapnel when it went off?

159   The high-tolerance aluminum tubes are only part of the story. We also have intelligence from multiple sources that Iraq is attempting to acquire magnets and high-speed balancing machines. Both items can be used in a gas centrifuge program to enrich uranium.

160   In 1999 and 2000, Iraqi officials negotiated with firms in Romania, India, Russia and Slovenia for the purchase of a magnet production plant. Iraq wanted the plant to produce magnets weighing 20 to 30 grams. That's the same weight as the magnets used in Iraq's gas centrifuge program before the Gulf War.

161   This incident, linked with the tubes, is another indicator of Iraq's attempt to reconstitute its nuclear weapons program.

162   Intercepted communications from mid-2000 through last summer showed that Iraq front companies sought to buy machines that can be used to balance gas centrifuge rotors. One of these companies also had been involved in a failed effort in 2001 to smuggle aluminum tubes into Iraq.

163   People will continue to debate this issue, but there is no doubt in my mind. These illicit procurement efforts show that Saddam Hussein is very much focused on putting in place the key missing piece from his nuclear weapons program, the ability to produce fissile material.

164   He also has been busy trying to maintain the other key parts of his nuclear program, particularly his cadre of key nuclear scientists. It is noteworthy that over the last 18 months Saddam Hussein has paid increasing personal attention to Iraq's top nuclear scientists, a group that the government-controlled press calls openly his "nuclear mujaheddin." He regularly exhorts them and praises their progress. Progress toward what end?

165   Long ago, the Security Council, this Council, required Iraq to halt all nuclear activities of any kind.

166   Let me talk now about the systems Iraq is developing to deliver weapons of mass destruction, in particular Iraq's ballistic missiles and unmanned aerial vehicles, UAVs.

167   First, missiles. We all remember that before the Gulf War Saddam Hussein's goal was missiles that flew not just hundreds, but thousands, of kilometers. He wanted to strike not only his neighbors, but also nations far beyond his borders.

168   While inspectors destroyed most of the prohibited ballistic missiles, numerous intelligence reports over the past decade from sources inside Iraq indicate that Saddam Hussein retains a covert force of up to a few dozen Scud-variant ballistic missiles. These are missiles with a range of 650 to 900 kilometers.

169   We know from intelligence and Iraq's own admissions that Iraq's alleged permitted ballistic missiles, the al-Samoud II and the Al-Fatah, violate the 150-kilometer limit established by this Council in Resolution 687. These are prohibited systems.

170   UNMOVIC has also reported that Iraq has illegally imported 380 SA-2 rocket engines. These are likely for use in the al-Samoud II. Their import was illegal on three counts: Resolution 687 prohibited all military shipments into Iraq; UNSCOM specifically prohibited use of these engines in surface-to-surface missiles; and finally, as we have just noted, they are for a system that exceeds the 150-kilometer range limit. Worst of all, some of these engines were acquired as late as December, after this Council passed Resolution 1441.

171   What I want you to know today is that Iraq has programs that are intended to produce ballistic missiles that fly over 1,000 kilometers. One program is pursuing a liquid fuel missile that would be able to fly more than 1,200 kilometers. And you can see from this map, as well as I can, who will be in danger of these missiles.

172   As part of this effort, another little piece of evidence, Iraq has built an engine test stand that is larger than anything it has ever had. Notice the dramatic difference in size between the test stand on the left, the old one, and the new one on the right. Note the large exhaust vent. This is where the flame from the engine comes out. The exhaust vent on the right test stand is five times longer than the one on the left. The one of [*sic*] the left is used for short-range missiles. The one on the right is clearly intended for long-range missiles that can fly 1,200 kilometers.

173   This photograph was taken in April of 2002. Since then, the test stand has been finished and a roof has been put over it so it will be harder for satellites to see what's going on underneath the test stand.

174   Saddam Hussein's intentions have never changed. He is not developing the missiles for self-defense. These are missiles that Iraq wants in order to project power, to threaten and to deliver chemical, biological—and if we let him—nuclear warheads.

175   Now, unmanned aerial vehicles, UAVs. Iraq has been working on a variety of UAVs for more than a decade. This is just illustrative of what a UAV would look like. This effort has included attempts to modify for unmanned flight the MiG-21 and, with greater success, an aircraft called the L-29.

176   However, Iraq is now concentrating not on these airplanes but on developing and testing smaller UAVs such as this. UAVs are well suited for

dispensing chemical and biological weapons. There is ample evidence that Iraq has dedicated much effort to developing and testing spray devices that could be adapted for UAVs.

177 And in the little that Saddam Hussein told us about UAVs, he has not told the truth. One of these lies is graphically and indisputably demonstrated by intelligence we collected on June 27th last year.

178 According to Iraq's December 7th declaration, its UAVs have a range of only 80 kilometers. But we detected one of Iraq's newest UAVs in a test flight that went 500 kilometers nonstop on autopilot in the racetrack pattern depicted here.

179 Not only is this test well in excess of the 150 kilometers that the United Nations permits, the test was left out of Iraq's December 7th declaration. The UAV was flown around and around and around in this circle and so that its 80-kilometer limit really was 500 kilometers, unrefueled and on autopilot—violative of all of its obligations under 1441.

180 The linkages over the past ten years between Iraq's UAV program and biological and chemical warfare agents are of deep concern to us. Iraq could use these small UAVs which have a wingspan of only a few meters to deliver biological agents to its neighbors or, if transported, to other countries, including the United States.

181 My friends, the information I have presented to you about these terrible weapons and about Iraq's continued flaunting of its obligations under Security Council Resolution 1441 links to a subject I now want to spend a little bit of time on, and that has to do with terrorism.

182 Our concern is not just about these illicit weapons; it's the way that these illicit weapons can be connected to terrorists and terrorist organizations that have no compunction about using such devices against innocent people around the world.

183 Iraq and terrorism go back decades. Baghdad trains Palestine Liberation Front members in small arms and explosives. Saddam uses the Arab Liberation Front to funnel money to the families of Palestinian suicide bombers in order to prolong the Intifadah. And it's no secret that Saddam's own intelligence service was involved in dozens of attacks or attempted assassinations in the 1990s.

184 But what I want to bring to your attention today is the potentially much more sinister nexus between Iraq and the al-Qaida terrorist network, a nexus that combines classic terrorist organizations and modern methods of murder. Iraq today harbors a deadly terrorist network headed by Abu Musab al-Zarqawi an associate and collaborator of Usama bin Laden and his al-Qaida lieutenants.

185 Zarqawi, Palestinian born in Jordan, fought in the Afghan war more than a decade ago. Returning to Afghanistan in 2000, he oversaw a terrorist training camp. One of his specialties, and one of the specialties of this camp, is poisons.

186   When our coalition ousted the Taliban, the Zarqawi network helped
       establish another poison and explosive training center camp, and this camp
       is located in northeastern Iraq. You see a picture of this camp.

187   The network is teaching its operatives how to produce ricin and other
       poisons. Let me remind you how ricin works. Less than a pinch—imagine
       a pinch of salt—less than a pinch of ricin, eating just this amount in your
       food, would cause shock, followed by circulatory failure. Death comes
       within 72 hours and there is no antidote. There is no cure. It is fatal.

188   Those helping to run this camp are Zarqawi lieutenants operating in
       northern Kurdish areas outside Saddam Hussein's controlled Iraq. But
       Baghdad has an agent in the most senior levels of the radical organization
       Ansar al-Islam that controls this corner of Iraq. In 2000, this agent offered
       al-Qaida safe haven in the region.

189   After we swept al-Qaida from Afghanistan, some of those members
       accepted this safe haven. They remain there today.

190   Zarqawi's activities are not confined to this small corner of northeast
       Iraq. He traveled to Baghdad in May of 2002 for medical treatment,
       staying in the capital of Iraq for two months while he recuperated to fight
       another day.

191   During his stay, nearly two dozen extremists converged on Baghdad and
       established a base of operations there. These al-Qaida affiliates based in
       Baghdad now coordinate the movement of people, money and supplies
       into and throughout Iraq for his network, and they have now been
       operating freely in the capital for more than eight months.

192   Iraqi officials deny accusations of ties with al-Qaida. These denials are
       simply not credible. Last year, an al-Qaida associate bragged that the
       situation in Iraq was "good," that Baghdad could be transited quickly.

193   We know these affiliates are connected to Zarqawi because they remain,
       even today, in regular contact with his direct subordinates, include the
       poison cell plotters. And they are involved in moving more than money
       and materiel. Last year, two suspected al-Qaida operatives were arrested
       crossing from Iraq into Saudi Arabia. They were linked to associates of the
       Baghdad cell and one of them received training in Afghanistan on how to
       use cyanide.

194   From his terrorist network in Iraq, Zarqawi can direct his network in the
       Middle East and beyond. We in the United States, all of us, the State
       Department and the Agency for International Development, we all lost a
       dear friend with the cold-blooded murder of Mr. Laurence Foley in
       Amman, Jordan, last October. A despicable act was committed that day,
       the assassination of an individual whose sole mission was to assist the
       people of Jordan. The captured assassin says his cell received money and
       weapons from Zarqawi for that murder. After the attack, an associate of
       the assassin left Jordan to go to Iraq to obtain weapons and explosives for
       further operations. Iraqi officials protest that they are not aware of the

whereabouts of Zarqawi or of any of his associates. Again, these protests are not credible. We know of Zarqawi's activities in Baghdad. I described them earlier.

195   Now let me add one other fact. We asked a friendly security service to approach Baghdad about extraditing Zarqawi and providing information about him and his close associates. This service contacted Iraqi officials twice and we passed details that should have made it easy to find Zarqawi. The network remains in Baghdad. Zarqawi still remains at large, to come and go.

196   As my colleagues around this table and as the citizens they represent in Europe know, Zarqawi's terrorism is not confined to the Middle East. Zarqawi and his network have plotted terrorist actions against countries including France, Britain, Spain, Italy, Germany and Russia. According to detainees Abu Atiya, who graduated from Zarqawi's terrorist camp in Afghanistan, tasked at least nine North African extremists in 2001 to travel to Europe to conduct poison and explosive attacks.

197   Since last year, members of this network have been apprehended in France, Britain, Spain and Italy. By our last count, 116 operatives connected to this global web have been arrested. The chart you are seeing shows the network in Europe.

198   We know about this European network and we know about its links to Zarqawi because the detainees who provided the information about the targets also provided the names of members of the network. Three of those he identified by name were arrested in France last December. In the apartments of the terrorists, authorities found circuits for explosive devices and a list of ingredients to make toxins.

199   The detainee who helped piece this together says the plot also targeted Britain. Later evidence again proved him right. When the British unearthed the cell there just last month, one British police officer was murdered during the destruction of the cell.

200   We also know that Zarqawi's colleagues have been active in the Pankisi Gorge, Georgia, and in Chechnya, Russia. The plotting to which they are linked is not mere chatter. Members of Zarqawi's network say their goal was to kill Russians with toxins.

201   We are not surprised that Iraq is harboring Zarqawi and his subordinates. This understanding builds on decades-long experience with respect to ties between Iraq and al-Qaida. Going back to the early and mid-1990s when bin Laden was based in Sudan, an al-Qaida source tells us that Saddam and bin Laden reached an understanding that al-Qaida would no longer support activities against Baghdad. Early al-Qaida ties were forged by secret high-level intelligence service contacts with al-Qaida, secret Iraqi intelligence high-level contacts with al-Qaida.

202   We know members of both organizations met repeatedly and have met at least eight times at very senior levels since the early 1990s. In 1996, a

foreign security service tells us that bin Laden met with a senior Iraqi intelligence official in Khartoum and later met the director of the Iraqi intelligence service.

203   Saddam became more interested as he saw al-Qaida's appalling attacks. A detained al-Qaida member tells us that Saddam was more willing to assist al-Qaida after the 1998 bombings of our embassies in Kenya and Tanzania. Saddam was also impressed by al-Qaida's attacks on the *USS Cole* in Yemen in October 2000.

204   Iraqis continue to visit bin Laden in his new home in Afghanistan. A senior defector, one of Saddam's former intelligence chiefs in Europe, says Saddam sent his agents to Afghanistan sometime in the mid-1990s to provide training to al-Qaida members on document forgery.

205   From the late 1990s until 2001, the Iraqi Embassy in Pakistan played the role of liaison to the al-Qaida organization.

206   Some believe, some claim, these contacts do not amount to much. They say Saddam Hussein's secular tyranny and al-Qaida's religious tyranny do not mix. I am not comforted by this thought. Ambition and hatred are enough to bring Iraq and al-Qaida together, enough so al-Qaida could learn how to build more sophisticated bombs and learn how to forge documents, and enough so that al-Qaida could turn to Iraq for help in acquiring expertise on weapons of mass destruction.

207   And the record of Saddam Hussein's cooperation with other Islamist terrorist organizations is clear. Hamas, for example, opened an office in Baghdad in 1999 and Iraq has hosted conferences attended by Palestine Islamic Jihad. These groups are at the forefront of sponsoring suicide attacks against Israel.

208   Al-Qaida continues to have a deep interest in acquiring weapons of mass destruction. As with the story of Zarqawi and his network, I can trace the story of a senior terrorist operative telling how Iraq provided training in these weapons to al-Qaida. Fortunately, this operative is now detained and he has told his story. I will relate it to you now as he, himself, described it.

209   This senior al-Qaida terrorist was responsible for one of al-Qaida's training camps in Afghanistan. His information comes firsthand from his personal involvement at senior levels of al-Qaida. He says bin Laden and his top deputy in Afghanistan, deceased al-Qaida leader Muhammad Atif, did not believe that al-Qaida labs in Afghanistan were capable enough to manufacture these chemical or biological agents. They needed to go somewhere else. They had to look outside of Afghanistan for help.

210   Where did they go? Where did they look? They went to Iraq. The support that this detainee describes included Iraq offering chemical or biological weapons training for two al-Qaida associates beginning in December 2000. He says that a militant known as Abdallah al-Iraqi had been sent to Iraq several times between 1997 and 2000 for help in

acquiring poisons and gasses. Abdallah al-Iraqi characterized the relationship he forged with Iraqi officials as successful.

211 As I said at the outset, none of this should come as a surprise to any of us. Terrorism has been a tool used by Saddam for decades. Saddam was a supporter of terrorism long before these terrorist networks had a name, and this support continues. The nexus of poisons and terror is new. The nexus of Iraq and terror is old. The combination is lethal.

212 With this track record, Iraqi denials of supporting terrorism take their place alongside the other Iraqi denials of weapons of mass destruction. It is all a web of lies.

213 When we confront a regime that harbors ambitions for regional domination, hides weapons of mass destruction, and provides haven and active support for terrorists, we are not confronting the past; we are confronting the present. And unless we act, we are confronting an even more frightening future.

214 And, friends, this has been a long and a detailed presentation and I thank you for your patience, but there is one more subject that I would like to touch on briefly, and it should be a subject of deep and continuing concern to this Council: Saddam Hussein's violations of human rights.

215 Underlying all that I have said, underlying all the facts and the patterns of behavior that I have identified, is Saddam Hussein's contempt for the will of this Council, his contempt for the truth, and, most damning of all, his utter contempt for human life. Saddam Hussein's use of mustard and nerve gas against the Kurds in 1988 was one of the 20th century's most horrible atrocities. Five thousand men, women and children died. His campaign against the Kurds from 1987 to '89 included mass summary executions, disappearances, arbitrary jailing and ethnic cleansing, and the destruction of some 2,000 villages.

216 He has also conducted ethnic cleansing against the Shia Iraqis and the Marsh Arabs whose culture has flourished for more than a millennium. Saddam Hussein's police state ruthlessly eliminates anyone who dares to dissent. Iraq has more forced disappearance cases than any other country— tens of thousands of people reported missing in the past decade.

217 Nothing points more clearly to Saddam Hussein's dangerous intentions and the threat he poses to all of us than his calculated cruelty to his own citizens and to his neighbors. Clearly, Saddam Hussein and his regime will stop at nothing until something stops him.

218 For more than 20 years, by word and by deed, Saddam Hussein has pursued his ambition to dominate Iraq and the broader Middle East using the only means he knows: intimidation, coercion and annihilation of all those who might stand in his way. For Saddam Hussein, possession of the world's most deadly weapons is the ultimate trump card, the one he must hold to fulfill his ambition.

219   We know that Saddam Hussein is determined to keep his weapons of mass destruction, is determined to make more. Given Saddam Hussein's history of aggression, given what we know of his grandiose plans, given what we know of his terrorist associations, and given his determination to exact revenge on those who oppose him, should we take the risk that he will not someday use these weapons at a time and a place and in a manner of his choosing, at a time when the world is in a much weaker position to respond?

220   The United States will not and cannot run that risk for the American people. Leaving Saddam Hussein in possession of weapons of mass destruction for a few more months or years is not an option, not in a post-September 11th world.

221   My colleagues, over three months ago, this Council recognized that Iraq continued to pose a threat to international peace and security, and that Iraq had been and remained in material breach of its disarmament obligations.

222   Today, Iraq still poses a threat and Iraq still remains in material breach. Indeed, by its failure to seize on its one last opportunity to come clean and disarm, Iraq has put itself in deeper material breach and closer to the day when it will face serious consequences for its continue defiance of this Council.

223   My colleagues, we have an obligation to our citizens. We have an obligation to this body to see that our resolutions are complied with. We wrote 1441 not in order to go to war. We wrote 1441 to try to preserve the peace. We wrote 1441 to give Iraq one last chance.

224   Iraq is not, so far, taking that one last chance.

225   We must not shrink from whatever is ahead of us. We must not fail in our duty and our responsibility to the citizens of the countries that are represented by this body.

Thank you, Mr. President.

[End]

Released on February 5, 2003

Glossary of Common Informal Fallacies

Keep in mind that there are probably other fallacies that do not show up in this glossary, and there are probably other names for some of these fallacies.

ACCIDENT (sweeping generalization, *dicto simpliciter*) concluding that a legitimate generalization necessarily applies to a particular case, so what is usually true of members of a group is necessarily true of a specific member of that group.

AD ANTIQUITATEM a specific type of false sign that reasons that something is necessarily better because it is old or worse because it is new.

ad baculum see APPEAL TO FORCE.

AD CRUMENUM a specific type of false sign that reasons that there is necessarily a direct relationship between cost and quality, concluding that something is necessarily of higher quality because it costs more, or of a lower quality because it costs less, or that someone is necessarily a better person because he or she is wealthy or highly paid, or a worse person because he or she is poor.

ad hominem see ARGUMENT AGAINST THE PERSON.

ad ignorantium see APPEAL TO IGNORANCE.

AD LAZARUM a specific type of false sign that reasons that there is necessarily an inverse relationship between cost and quality, thus concluding that something is necessarily a better value because it costs less, or someone is necessarily a better person because he or she is poor, or a worse person because he or she is wealthy.

ad misericordiam see APPEAL TO COMPASSION.

AD NAUSEAM a form of appeal to the people that involves reasoning that a claim is true based only on evidence that it has been made so often.

AD NOVITATEM a specific type of false sign that reasons that something is necessarily better because it is new, or worse because it is old.

ad numerum see APPEAL TO THE PEOPLE.

ad populum   see APPEAL TO THE PEOPLE.

ad vericundiam   see APPEAL TO TRADITION and ARGUMENT FROM AUTHORITY.

ambiguity   see AMPHIBOLY.

AMPHIBOLY (unclearness, misusing ambiguity, ambiguity)   using language and punctuation in a way that a statement can have multiple interpretations, so it's not really clear what is meant.

ANECDOTAL EVIDENCE   a particular type of hasty generalization in which individual stories are substituted for a larger sample as support for a generalization.

APPEAL TO ANONYMOUS AUTHORITY   a specific form of appeal to authority in which it is argued that a claim should be accepted based only on evidence that unidentified authorities accept it.

appeal to authority   see ARGUMENT FROM AUTHORITY.

appeal to beliefs   see SELF-EVIDENT TRUTHS.

APPEAL TO COMMON PRACTICE   a particular type of appeal to the people that argues that something is right or should be done based only on evidence that other people do it. This fallacy is also often considered a type of the *tu quoque* fallacy.

APPEAL TO COMPASSION (appeal to pity, *ad misericordiam*)   a specific type of appeal to emotion that argues that a conclusion should be made based on feeling sorry for someone when that feeling is irrelevant to the conclusion.

APPEAL TO CONSEQUENCES (*ad consequentiam*)   arguing that something is or is not true because of the results expected from its truth.

APPEAL TO EMOTION   an attempt to gain agreement based solely on the feelings aroused in the message.

APPEAL TO FEAR (scare tactics)   a specific type of appeal to emotion that argues that actions should be taken to avoid negative results when the negative results are exaggerated, unlikely, or irrelevant.

APPEAL TO FORCE (*ad baculum*)   using threats of harm instead of good evidence and sound reasoning to gain agreement.

APPEAL TO IGNORANCE (*ad ignorantium*, burden of proof, shifting burden of proof, evading burden of proof)   arguing that a claim must be true because there is no evidence that it is false.

APPEAL TO INDIGNATION   a specific type of appeal to emotion that argues against a position based only on negative personal feelings toward it.

APPEAL TO JOY   a specific type of appeal to emotion that argues that something should be done only because it will make the person doing it feel happier.

APPEAL TO LOYALTY   a specific type of appeal to emotion that argues that an action should be taken based only on the need to be loyal to someone or to a group.

appeal to pity   see APPEAL TO COMPASSION.

APPEAL TO THE PEOPLE (argument by consensus, bandwagon appeal, *ad populum, ad numerum*)   a form of appeal to authority in which it is argued that a claim should be accepted based only on evidence that a large number of people accept it or should be rejected because a large number of people reject it.

APPEAL TO POPULARITY   a specific type of appeal to emotion that argues that someone should do something only because it will make that person better liked by others.

APPEAL TO PRIDE (flattery, apple polishing)   a particular type of appeal to the people that argues that one should accept a claim based only on evidence that he or she has the favorable characteristics needed to understand the truth of the claim.

APPEAL TO SPITE   a specific type of appeal to emotion that argues that someone should do something only because of ill will toward someone else.

APPEAL TO TRADITION (*ad vericundiam*)   a particular type of appeal to authority that argues that something should be done based only on evidence that it has been done that way in the past, or should be believed only because it has been believed for a long time.

apple polishing   see APPEAL TO PRIDE.

A PRIORI   reasoning that determines the conclusion one wants first, then accepts only evidence supporting that conclusion, or interprets all evidence as support for that conclusion.

ARGUMENT AGAINST THE PERSON (*ad hominem*)   attacking the character or background of the person making an argument instead of responding to that person's claim, evidence, and reasoning.

argument by consensus   see APPEAL TO THE PEOPLE.

ARGUMENT FROM AUTHORITY (appeal to authority, *ad vericundiam*) arguing that a claim is true based only on evidence that an authority figure accepts the claim.

bandwagon appeal   see APPEAL TO THE PEOPLE.

BEGGING THE QUESTION (circular reasoning, *petitio principii, circulus in probando, circulus in demonstrando*) arguing in such a way that a premise is in some way the same as the conclusion.

burden of proof   see APPEAL TO IGNORANCE.

camel's nose   see SLIPPERY SLOPE.

common man appeal   see COMMON PERSON APPEAL.

COMMON PERSON APPEAL (common man appeal)   a form of appeal to the people in which it is argued that a claim should be accepted based only on evidence that a regular person accepts it.

common practice   see APPEAL TO COMMON PRACTICE.

COMPLEX CAUSE   a specific type of false cause that involves mistakenly attributing an event to a simple cause when the cause is really more complicated.

COMPLEX PROPOSITION (compound proposition)   including more than one claim in the proposition and treating proof for one claim as proof for all the claims.

COMPLEX QUESTION (many questions, fallacy of interrogation, compound question, *plurium interrogationum*)   asking a question that includes either an unproven assumption or more than one question, thus making a straightforward yes-or-no answer meaningless.

COMPOSITION   arguing that what is true of an individual part of an object must be true of the entire object.

compound proposition   see COMPLEX PROPOSITION.

compound question   see COMPLEX QUESTION.

CONCOMITANT VARIATION (joint variation, joint effect, *cum hoc ergo propter hoc*)   a particular type of false cause fallacy that reasons since two events happened at the same time, one event caused the other.

converse accident   see HASTY GENERALIZATION.

cum hoc ergo propter hoc   see CONCOMITANT VARIATION.

DIVISION   arguing that what is true of an entire object must also be true of every individual part of that object.

EQUIVOCATION   changing the meaning of a word or phrase from one part of the argument to another, so you're not really referring to the same thing all of the time, even though you're using the same words.

evading burden of proof   see APPEAL TO IGNORANCE.

EVADING THE ISSUE (red herring, irrelevant conclusion)   supporting a claim with evidence or reasoning that is not relevant to the proposition, or responding to another's argument by changing the subject.

EXTENSION   a particular type of false criteria fallacy that argues that something is inferior just because it doesn't do something it was never intended to do.

FALLACY FALLACY   deciding the conclusion of an argument must be untrue because there is a fallacy in the reasoning.

FALSE ANALOGY (questionable analogy, wrongful comparison, imperfect analogy)   drawing a conclusion based on an analogy, when the items being compared are not similar enough to sustain the analogy.

FALSE CAUSE (questionable cause) arguing that one event caused another without sufficient evidence of a causal relationship.

FALSE CONSOLATION arguing that someone is not really harmed because things could be worse, or pointing out what one has to be thankful for.

FALSE CRITERIA (questionable criteria) reasoning that applies irrelevant standards to the subject of the argument.

FALSE DILEMMA (false dichotomy, either-or fallacy, bifurcation, black-or-white fallacy) incorrectly assuming that one choice or another must be made when other choices are available or when no choice must be made.

FALSE SIGN (questionable sign) drawing a conclusion based on sign reasoning when there is not really a direct relationship between the alleged sign and the subject of the conclusion.

FIGURE OF SPEECH confusing figurative language with literal language.

flattery see APPEAL TO PRIDE.

GENETIC FALLACY arguing that an idea should be accepted or rejected only because of its source of origin.

GUILT BY ASSOCIATION a particular type of fallacy of accident that reasons that someone or something necessarily shares all of the same characteristics of those with which one or it is affiliated.

HASTY CONCLUSION (jumping to a conclusion) drawing a firm conclusion without enough evidence to support it.

HASTY GENERALIZATION (overgeneralization, converse accident, *secundum quid*) Arguing that what is true of a few members of a group must be true of all members of a group.

HORSE LAUGH responding to an argument with an expression of derision instead of a counterargument.

HYPOSTATIZATION (reification) treating something that exists only as a concept as though it were a tangible object.

ignorance of refutation see *IGNORATIO ELENCHI*.

***IGNORATIO ELENCHI* (ignorance of refutation)** causing confusion during refutation because of a real or feigned lack of ability to engage in refutation.

imperfect analogy see FALSE ANALOGY.

interrogation, fallacy of see COMPLEX QUESTION.

irrelevant conclusion see EVADING THE ISSUE.

joint effect see CONCOMITANT VARIATION.

joint variation see CONCOMITANT VARIATION.

jumping to a conclusion see HASTY CONCLUSION.

LAUDATORY PERSONALITY a particular type of fallacy of accident that reasons that a person couldn't do something bad, or must have done something good, because he or she has some good qualities or occupies a prestigious position.

LOADED LANGUAGE using emotionally charged language to create an impression about the subject of a claim without making an argument that the language fits the subject.

many questions see COMPLEX QUESTION.

misuse of statistics see SIGNIFICANCE.

misusing ambiguity see AMPHIBOLY.

NATURAL LAW FALLACY a specific type of false analogy that reasons that what is true about nature must be true about humans.

NON SEQUITUR an argument in which the conclusion "does not follow" from the evidence and reasoning. Most fallacies are a *non sequitur* argument in some way, so it can be used as a generic name for many different fallacies.

no true Scotsman see POISONING THE WELL.

overgeneralization see HASTY GENERALIZATION.

overlooked evidence see SUPPRESSED EVIDENCE.

plurium interrogationum see COMPLEX QUESTION.

POISONING THE WELL (no true Scotsman) a way of suppressing evidence that eliminates a source of evidence from consideration by claiming that the source is flawed when there is no true relationship between the alleged flaw and the reliability of the source.

POST HOC *(post hoc ergo propter hoc)* a specific kind of false cause fallacy that argues that because one event preceded another event the first event must have caused the second event.

QUESTION BEGGING EPITHETS a form of loaded language that uses an emotionally charged restatement of the claim, often in the form of name-calling, in place of support for the claim.

questionable analogy see FALSE ANALOGY.

questionable cause see FALSE CAUSE.

questionable criteria see FALSE CRITERIA.

questionable sign see FALSE SIGN.

questionable statistics see SIGNIFICANCE.

questionable use of statistics see SIGNIFICANCE.

red herring see EVADING THE ISSUE.

REDUCING TO AN ABSURDITY **(***reductio ad absurdum***)** characterizing an opponent's position in such a way as to make it, or its consequences, appear ridiculous.

reductio ad absurdum see REDUCING TO AN ABSURDITY.

reification see HYPOSTATIZATION.

REPREHENSIBLE PERSONALITY a particular type of fallacy of accident that reasons that a person couldn't do something good, or must have done something bad, because he or she has some negative qualities or occupies a particular position.

scare tactics see APPEAL TO FEAR.

secundum quid see HASTY GENERALIZATION.

SELF-EVIDENT TRUTHS (appeal to beliefs) arguing that a claim should be accepted based on evidence that is not presented but is asserted to be well known or obvious, when the information is either not well known or is incorrect.

shifting burden of proof see APPEAL TO IGNORANCE.

SIGNIFICANCE (misuse of statistics, questionable statistics, questionable use of statistics) making an argument using statistical evidence when the basis of the statistic is not revealed, is distorted, or the statistics are misinterpreted, innocently or on purpose.

SLIPPERY SLOPE (thin entering wedge, camel's nose) a type of causal reasoning in which it is argued that an apparently small cause will lead to a major effect when there is no evidence of such a causal relationship.

SNOB APPEAL a form of appeal to the people in which it is argued that one should accept an idea or a product based only on evidence that prestigious people accept it or nonprestigious people reject it.

SOLID SLOPE (spendthrift [fallacy]) reasoning that an act, or a series of acts, should be carried out because it will have no significant consequences when there is no evidence for the lack of significant effects or there is reason to that believe there will be significant effects.

SPECIAL PLEADING referring to an act committed by an opponent in negative terms, while referring to the same act committed by the arguer or supporters in favorable terms.

spendthrift (fallacy) see SOLID SLOPE.

STRAW PERSON (straw man) falsely asserting that an opponent made an argument that is easy to defeat, defeating it, and acting as though that does significant damage to that person's actual argument.

STYLE OVER SUBSTANCE reasoning that ideas presented in an appealing manner are correct, regardless of the content.

SUPPRESSED EVIDENCE (overlooked evidence) drawing a conclusion after purposely leaving out known evidence, or intentionally failing to look for likely evidence that might contradict a claim.

thin entering wedge   see SLIPPERY SLOPE.

TU QUOQUE **("you too" fallacy, two wrongs make a right, common practice)**   responding to charges of wrongdoing by saying that the accuser or others do something equally bad.

two wrongs make a right   see *TU QUOQUE.*

unclearness   see AMPHIBOLY.

wrongful comparison   see FALSE ANALOGY.

"you too" fallacy   see *TU QUOQUE.*

Glossary of Key Concepts

a burden of proof   the responsibility of each person in an argument to provide evidence and reasoning for each claim put forth.

abstract language   language that is more vague or broad in its meaning, so it's harder to tell what is meant.

active listening   the act of exerting substantial effort to intentionally listen well and show the other person that you are listening.

advantages/disadvantages   a stock issue of propositions of policy that argues what will happen beyond solving the harm. The advocate of the proposition argues that the plan will create benefits that make it even more desirable. The opponent to the proposition argues that the plan will create unexpected harms that make the plan less desirable.

ambushing   a form of nonlistening in which the listener listens very carefully to the speaker, but only for the purpose of attacking the speaker.

antecedent   the clause in the major premise of a conditional argument that establishes the conditions that will lead to an outcome; the "if" clause in the major premise of a conditional argument.

application   a stock issue of propositions of fact and value that argues that the criteria are met, were met, or will be met, so the proposition is true.

appreciative listening   listening done for the listener's pleasure.

arguer as abuser   an unethical approach to argumentation in which the arguer sees the co-arguer as an enemy to be conquered and tries to win the argument through force, intimidation, fabrication, monopoly of communication channels, or other unfair advantages.

arguer as harasser   a less ethical approach to argumentation in which the arguer sees the co-arguer as an inferior to be ridiculed, belittled, and annoyed into agreement or withdrawal.

arguer as lover   a more ethical approach to argumentation in which the arguer sees the co-arguer as someone deserving of respect and attempts to argue in as honest and open a way as possible.

arguer as seducer   a less ethical approach to argumentation in which the arguer sees the co-arguer as someone to be manipulated for the benefit of the seducer and tries to win the argument by deceiving, withholding information, misusing language, or gaining assent through means other than clear, sound argumentation.

argument₁   arguing in the sense of *making* an argument; putting forth a claim, evidence, and reasoning.

argument₂   arguing in the sense of *having* an argument; an interaction with another person in which each person presents, responds to, and defends ideas.

argumentation   (1) a form of communication in which at least one person explicitly or implicitly puts forth a claim and provides support for that claim with evidence and reasoning; (2) the process of making and engaging in arguments; (3) the study of the process of making and engaging in arguments.

argumentativeness   a positive personality facet exhibited by the willingness to engage in argumentation when appropriate and to argue in a manner that focuses on issues and reasoning and avoids attacking other people's self-concepts.

asking questions to replace statements   a questionable use of language in which an arguer asks questions to get the audience to supply evidence instead of providing the evidence for a claim.

assertion   (1) an unsupported claim; (2) the lowest (first) level on Perella's hierarchy of evidence.

attitudinal inherency   a type of inherency argument that claims that the cause of a problem is the attitudes and motives of the people who perpetuate it.

authoritative definition   identifying the meaning of a term in an argument by referring to authoritative sources such as a dictionary or textbook.

backing   the element in the Toulmin model of argumentation that justifies believing the warrant.

bipolar thinking   a questionable use of language that uses language in a way that leads people to think in either-or dichot-omies instead of recognizing a continuum of choices or a range of options.

brainstorming   a small group discussion technique intended to generate ideas that can be evaluated later by having the group invent as many ideas as it can in a short period of time.

burden of refutation   the responsibility of those opposed to the proposition to dispute the claims, evidence, and reasoning that the advocate has presented.

bypassing   a communication problem that happens when two people think that they're talking about the same thing but really are not.

canons of rhetoric   lesser arts that make up the greater art of rhetoric, including invention, disposition, style, memory, and delivery.

casual evidence   evidence that naturally occurs without anyone trying to create it as evidence.

categorical argument   a syllogism or an enthymeme with a major premise that establishes categories in which the subject of the minor premise will fit. The major premise takes the form "All As are B."

causal reasoning   reasoning that argues that one thing or event in the past caused another thing or event to happen or will cause something to happen in the future, or that an action taken in the future will cause a particular outcome.

certainty   a threatening communication behavior that gives the impression that the communicator knows everything and is always right.

claim   the element in the Toulmin model of argumentation that is the proposition the arguer supports.

clarifiers   questions that an active listener asks to get more information to better explain ideas that are unclear.

classical structure of an argument   the logical form that an argument should take.

cogent argument   another term for a sound argument.

common knowledge   (1) using widely held beliefs as evidence for a claim; (2) the second lowest level on Perella's hierarchy of evidence, along with "judicial notice."

communication rules the procedures that members of a group follow as they communicate with each other.

comparative advantage approach an approach to arguing propositions of policy in which the advocate of the proposition argues that adoption of a plan will lead to advantages over the *status quo,* without arguing that there currently are significant harms.

completeness a test of evidence that refers to whether the source of evidence, or the evidence as presented in an argument, provides enough information so a critically thinking person can accept it.

conclusion the statement in a syllogism that is the inevitable outcome of accepting the major and minor premises. It must be absolute in a syllogism and may be provisional in an enthymeme.

conclusionary evidence testimony in which only a conclusion is stated and does not provide any indication of how the conclusion was arrived at.

concrete language language that is more specific in what it refers to, so it's easier to tell what is meant.

conditional argument a syllogism or an enthymeme with a major premise that establishes what will happen if particular conditions exist. The major premise takes the form "If A then B." Also called a "hypothetical argument."

confirmers questions that an active listener asks to see whether the listener's understanding of the speaker is accurate.

connotative meanings the personal, emotional reactions that individuals associate with words and phrases.

consensus the agreement by all of the members of a group that a particular proposal is acceptable and one that all will support, even if the proposal is not each individual's preferred choice.

consensus of expert opinion (1) the agreement of several people who are experts in a field; (2) the fifth level on Perella's hierarchy of evidence, along with "empirical study."

consensus of lay opinion (1) the agreement of the reasoned opinion of many people, outside of their fields of expertise; (2) the fourth level on Perella's hierarchy of evidence, along with "expert opinion."

consensus of studies (1) agreement among the findings of several well-designed observational research studies; (2) the sixth and highest level on Perella's hierarchy of evidence.

consequent the clause in the major premise of a conditional argument that establishes the outcome if the conditions of the antecedent are met; the "then" clause in the major premise of a conditional argument.

control a threatening communication style in which the communicator tells others what to do.

control group the members of the sample who are exposed to all of the same conditions as the treatment group except for the experimental treatment.

corroboration a test of evidence that asks if other qualified sources agree with the source of evidence, sometimes referred to as "external consistency."

counterplan a refutation strategy for propositions of policy that admits that the *status quo* problems are significant but should be alleviated by making changes other than those called for by the proposition.

counterpropositional (argument) an indirect refutation technique in which the arguer presents arguments that the proposition is *not* true.

created evidence evidence that was purposely recorded for future use as evidence.

credibility the perception of the audience that the speaker is someone to be believed.

criteria a stock issue of propositions of fact and value that seeks to establish how to determine whether the proposition is true or whether a value is being achieved.

critical listening active listening in which the listener applies the principles of critical thinking.

critical thinking the active application of principles of reasoning to your own ideas and those of others to make judgments about communication and reasoning, to analyze arguments, to expose underlying assumptions, to achieve better understanding, and to approach the truth.

critical thinking disposition   the inclination to use critical thinking skills when the situation calls for it.

critical thinking skills   abilities that can be learned to improve critical thinking, including verbal reasoning, argument analysis, thinking as hypothesis testing, using likelihood and uncertainty, and decision-making and problem-solving skills.

data   another name for grounds in the Toulmin model of argumentation.

deductive reasoning   argumentation in which the conclusion is included in the premises; an argument that reasons from what is known with certainty in the premises to a conclusion that is known with certainty.

defensive listening   a form of nonlistening that involves the listener perceiving that he or she is being personally attacked and acting accordingly, when really there is no attack.

definition and distinction   a stock issue of propositions of fact or value that establishes what the proposition does and does not mean.

delivery   the classical canon of rhetoric that helps the speaker use his or her voice and body to effectively deliver a persuasive message.

demographic analysis   the use of categories into which people with similar characteristics can be grouped to try to determine which appeals are likely to influence an audience.

denotative meanings   dictionary-like meanings that people have for words and phrases.

dependent variable   what the researchers expect to be affected by the independent variable.

description   a supportive communication style in which the communicator describes situations or behaviors and how they affect him or her.

descriptive study   research designed to report on what "is," without attempting to draw causal conclusions.

direct refutation   an argument that directly contradicts what was said in favor of a proposition.

discriminative listening   listening to understand the speaker's meaning.

disjunctive argument   a syllogism or an enthymeme with a major premise that establishes alternatives from which to choose. The major premise takes the form "Either A or B."

disposition   the classical canon of rhetoric that helps the speaker decide the order to present ideas in a speech.

dyad   two people engaged in an activity together.

dyadic argumentation   two people arguing together.

empathic listening   listening done to help the speaker.

empathy   a supportive communication style in which the communicator exhibits a caring attitude toward the other person.

empirical study   (1) a well-designed observational research study about a subject; (2) the fifth level on Perella's hierarchy of evidence, along with "consensus of expert opinion."

enthymeme   an argument that is missing at least one part of the syllogism, comes to a probable conclusion, or both.

equality   a supportive communication style in which the communicator shows that he or she believes that others are important and worthy.

ethos   a rhetorical appeal that uses the personal characteristics of the communicator to influence others.

evaluating   the part of the listening process in which the listener decides how much weight to put on what is said.

evaluation   a threatening communication style in which the communicator lets the other person know that he or she is being judged in some way.

evaluative listening   listening responsibly to messages that attempt to influence the listener's attitudes, beliefs, or actions.

evidence   supporting material known or discovered but not created by the advocate.

examples   a form of evidence that consists of descriptions of *individual* events, objects, persons, or places.

experimental study   research designed to draw a causal conclusion about how one variable affects another by controlling and manipulating variables.

expert evidence   evidence that comes from a source who is experienced and knowledgeable in the subject of the evidence.

expert opinion   (1) the reasoned opinion of one within his or her field of expertise; (2) the fourth level on Perella's hierarchy of evidence.

expertise   the audience's perception that the speaker is knowledgeable about a subject, giving the speaker more credibility.

explanation   a form of communication in which statements are presented to clarify ideas and improve understanding rather than to support a claim.

external consistency   see **corroboration.**

facts   a form of evidence that consists of empirically verifiable descriptions of events, objects, persons, or places.

fallacy   an argument that appears to be sound reasoning but, in fact, is flawed.

fallacy fallacy   deciding that the conclusion of an argument must be untrue, because there is a fallacy in the reasoning.

fields of argument   subject-related communities of arguers with argumentative "rules" specific to each community.

figurative analogy   an analogy that compares cases in different classifications.

formal fallacies   arguments that are flawed because they do not conform to the proper structure or form of a valid argument.

formal logic   the study of the logical form arguments should take, including how premises should lead to conclusions, assuming the premises are correct.

formal validity   means that an argument has the correct structure or "form."

general critical thinking   critical thinking about subjects with which one is not very familiar, applying the general principles of reasoning and argumentation to recognize weak or strong reasoning.

grounds   the element in the Toulmin model of argumentation that is the evidence used to support the claim.

harm (also referred to as "need")   a stock issue of propositions of policy that argues that something is wrong and calls for a policy change.

hearing   the step in the listening process in which the listener receives the auditory and visual stimuli.

HURIER model   a model of the listening process that includes Hearing, Understanding, Remembering, Interpreting, Evaluating, and Responding.

hyperbole   figurative language that uses gross exaggeration to make a point.

hypothesis   a prediction of what the researcher expects to find based on what is already known about the subject.

hypothetical argument   another name for the conditional argument.

hypothetical examples   examples that are made up and should not be used as evidence in arguments but are useful to illustrate ideas.

idioms   language that uses phrases that refer to one thing or event in terms of something unrelated, with no implied comparison between the two.

independent variable   an act that researchers have control over and predict will be the cause of a particular effect.

indirect refutation   an argument that denies the proposition without speaking directly to what was said in favor of the proposition.

inductive reasoning   an argument that comes to a probable instead of an absolute conclusion, or that reasons from what is known in the premises to a conclusion that is unknown in the premises.

inferences   statements that are conclusions about something based on information that the person making the statement knows.

informal fallacies   arguments that are flawed because of mistaken assumptions in the premises, errors in language, misuse of evidence, or violation of the principles of argumentation.

informal logic   the study of reasoning from evidence to conclusions, focusing on elements of reasoning other than the form of the arguments.

inherency   a stock issue of propositions of policy that identifies the cause of the harm.

internal consistency   a test of evidence that looks for overt or subtle contradictions within the source from which the evidence comes.

interpreting   (1) the step in the listening process during which the listener decides what the speaker feels; (2) an active listening technique that involves the listener saying what he or she understands the speaker to mean or feel, going beyond what was just said to confirm impressions and encourage further talking.

invention   the classical canon of rhetoric that helps the speaker discover the ideas that might be included in a speech and choose those that he or she will actually use.

irony   using language that says something that is literally the opposite of what is meant.

I statements   statements that identify ideas as personal opinions or perceptions rather than as undisputed facts or claims needing support.

jargon   a questionable use of language that uses language that can only be understood by experts in the field or members of a particular group to hide meaning or intimidate others.

judgments   statements that express a personal opinion, usually explicitly or implicitly evaluating something.

judicial notice   (1) accepting assertions as evidence without requiring proof; (2) the second lowest level on Perella's hierarchy of evidence, along with "common knowledge."

Kant's Moral Imperative   an ethical principle that can be summarized as "act in a way that would be best if everyone acted that way."

language creates and separates communities   a characteristic of language that means that the way language is used helps people think of themselves as sharing membership in a group and helps them think of others as being outside of their group.

language frames experience   a characteristic of language that means that the way we talk about things affects the way we think about them and what we expect.

language is ambiguous   a characteristic of language that means that there are often multiple possible interpretations of utterances.

language is figurative   a characteristic of language that means that the way people naturally use language is often not literal.

language is imprecise   a characteristic of language that means that people often use language that is not very specific when more specific language is available.

lay evidence   evidence that comes from a source who is neither experienced nor knowledgeable in the area of discussion.

lay opinion   (1) evidence that consists of a reasoned opinion by one outside of his or her area of expertise; (2) the third level on Perella's hierarchy of evidence.

listening   an active form of behavior in which individuals attempt to maximize their attention to, and comprehension of, what is being communicated to them through words, actions, and things by one or more people in their immediate environment.

literal analogy   an analogy that compares cases within the same classification.

literal examples   examples that are based in reality and are acceptable as evidence in arguments.

literal listening   a form of nonlistening that involves listening only for the content level of meaning and ignoring the relationship meaning.

local critical thinking   critical thinking about subjects with which you are very familiar so that you can recognize inaccuracies and common faulty thinking about that subject.

logos   a rhetorical appeal that uses reasoning to influence others.

major premise   the part of a syllogism that is an unequivocal general statement about the subject of the argument.

major term   the term in a categorical argument that appears in both the major premise and the conclusion; the category into which both the minor term and middle term fit.

materially true argument   an argument that reaches a truthful conclusion, as much as "truth" can be determined.

memory   the classical canon of rhetoric that helps the speaker remember the ideas, order, and language choices planned for the speech.

metaphor   language that characterizes one subject with terms that literally apply to another subject, making an implicit comparison between the two.

middle term   the term in a categorical argument that appears in both the major premise and the minor premise; the category into which the minor term fits.

minor premise   the part of a syllogism that is a statement about a specific case, covered by the generalization of the major premise.

minor repair   a refutation strategy for propositions of policy that argues that the *status quo* problems can be alleviated by making changes smaller than those called for by the proposition.

minor term   the term in a categorical argument that appears in both the minor premise and the conclusion; the term that fits into the middle term and, therefore, fits into the major term.

mirroring   an active listening technique in which the listener repeats back what the other person said word for word to confirm understanding and to encourage continued talking.

modal qualifier   another name for the qualifier in the Toulmin model of argumentation.

monopolizing   a form of nonlistening that involves dominating the conversation by continually focusing on oneself rather than the other person.

neutrality   a threatening communication style in which the communicator indicates that he or she doesn't care about the other person.

nominal group technique   a small group discussion technique intended to generate ideas that can be evaluated later by having the individuals invent as many ideas as they

can and take turns sharing them with the group, one at a time.

nonpropositional argument   an indirect refutation technique that argues that the advocate's argument doesn't really support the proposition but supports something that's at least a little different from the proposition.

***non sequitur* fallacy**   an argument in which the conclusion "does not follow" from the premises.

norms   the expectations of the attitudes, values, and behaviors that group members have for all members of a group.

not *prima facie*   an indirect refutation technique that argues that regardless of what the advocate did say, he or she left out enough important lines of reasoning that the argument, as presented, shouldn't be accepted.

not proven argument   a direct refutation technique in which the arguer says that the advocate has failed to prove a claim, because the evidence was asserted, is not relevant to the claim, or comes from an inadequate source.

not relevant argument   a direct refutation technique in which the arguer says that no matter how true the claim or evidence is, it has no real bearing on the proposition being argued.

not true argument   a direct refutation technique in which the arguer presents high-quality evidence that clearly contradicts the opponent's claim or the evidence used in support of the claim.

operational definition   identifying the meanings of the terms by the way they are used in an argument or explaining them as they arise.

opinion   a message that presents an individual's personal belief on a subject.

paraphrasing   an active listening technique in which the listener summarizes what the speaker said in the listener's own words, attempting to accurately capture the speaker's meaning to confirm understanding and to encourage further talking.

pathos   a rhetorical appeal that uses emotion to influence others.

peer pressure the influence exerted by a group to get members to conform to that group's norms and rules.

persuasive public speaking oral communication designed to influence the attitudes, beliefs, or behaviors of others in a setting where one person talks to many others at once.

plan a stock issue of propositions of policy that identifies exactly what should be done to eliminate the harm in the *status quo,* and who should do it.

point out contradictions a direct refutation technique in which the arguer shows that the opponent's claims are contradictory.

population the entire group to which a scientific study is intended to apply.

possible rebuttal the element in the Toulmin model of argumentation that is a statement indicating under what circumstances the claim may not be true.

post-test measure of the dependent variable in the entire sample after the treatment.

presumption (1) the principle that a proposition or claim should not be accepted until sufficient evidence and reasoning have been provided to justify acceptance; (2) the recognition that the *status quo* will remain as it is until good reasons have been provided to change it.

pre-test measure of the dependent variable in the entire sample prior to any treatment being done.

prima facie **case** an argument that presents enough evidence and support that a person thinking critically ought to accept the proposition, at least until the argument is refuted.

primary evidence evidence that comes from a source that is closest to the actual happening; the source has firsthand information.

probes questions that an active listener asks to get more information so the listener can more fully understand the speaker.

problem orientation a supportive communication style in which the communicator focuses attention on mutually determining how to solve a problem rather than controlling anyone's behavior.

proposition the declarative statement that an advocate intends to support.

proposition of fact a proposition that states that something is factually true, was factually true, or will be factually true.

proposition of policy a proposition that argues in favor of a particular course of action.

proposition of value a proposition that argues in favor of a positive or negative evaluation about something.

provisionalism a supportive communication style in which the communicator operates from the assumption that he or she doesn't know everything, is not always right, and can gain important information by listening to others.

pseudolistening a form of nonlistening that involves pretending to listen when the listener is really not paying attention.

psychographic analysis analysis of the audience's thoughts and feelings to try to determine which appeals are likely to influence them.

puffery a questionable use of language in which a claim is made to sound more important than it really is.

qualifier the element in the Toulmin model of argumentation that is any term or phrase indicating the strength of the claim.

quarrel a form of interaction about a conflict, often involving anger, hurt feelings, and the misuse of argumentation to achieve victory.

questioning underlying assumptions an indirect refutation technique in which an arguer identifies, and argues against, unstated assumptions in an advocate's argument.

reasoning (1) the thought process that leads to a conclusion; (2) the presentation of support for a claim in an argument.

reasoning by analogy reasoning that makes a comparison between two similar cases and infers that what is known about one is true of the other.

reasoning by criteria reasoning that applies preexisting criteria to a subject and makes a judgment based on how well the subject fits the criteria.

reasoning by example   reasoning that involves inferring a conclusion from specific cases.

recency   a test of evidence that considers when the evidence was produced and if it was from an appropriate time period for the conclusion being drawn.

reflective thought pattern   a small group discussion technique that establishes a process that helps ensure that a group considers major relevant issues in problem solving.

refutation   the act of responding to the other person's argument, trying to deny what he or she said.

reliability   the ability of the measurement device to consistently give the same results when measuring the same phenomenon.

remembering   the step in the listening process in which the listener stores the meaning in memory so it can be retrieved later.

reports   statements of fact that are capable of being verified.

responding   the part of the listening process in which the listener lets the speaker know that the listener is listening and how the listener is understanding the message.

rhetoric   (1) the study of means of persuasion; (2) the act of using communication to influence others.

sample   in the scientific method, members of the population that are actually studied.

secondary evidence   evidence that comes from a source that is at least one step removed from the actual happening; one who has only secondhand information.

selective listening   a form of non-listening that involves focusing only on particular parts of the communication being listened to.

sign reasoning   reasoning that argues that two variables are so strongly related to each other that the presence or absence of one may be taken as an indication of the presence or absence of the other.

significance   a stock issue of propositions of policy that argues that the harm is qualitatively or quantitatively severe enough to call for a policy change.

sloganeering   a questionable use of language that happens when an arguer uses catchphrases to substitute for the content of an argument.

small group   a gathering of more than two people, but not so many that they cannot all interact with all other members of the group.

small group communication   interaction among a small group of people who share a common purpose or goal, who feel a sense of belonging to the group, and who exert influence on one another.

solvency   a stock issue of propositions of policy that argues how much of the harm the plan will eliminate.

sophistical refutation   (1) an intellectual activity engaged in by sophists in ancient Greece that involved attacking and defending a proposition by asking and answering questions; (2) the title of a text by Aristotle in which the concept of fallacies was first analyzed.

sound argument   an argument that is both materially true and formally valid.

source bias   a test of evidence that asks whether the source of evidence has any self-interests that could distort perceptions.

source credibility   a test of evidence that examines whether the source of information is trustworthy and has the background, knowledge, expertise, and opportunity to be relied upon.

spontaneity   a supportive communication style in which communication appears to be a natural, unprepared response to the moment.

statistics   a particular type of factual evidence that consists of quantified descriptions of events, objects, persons, places, or other phenomena.

status quo   existing policies, attitudes, and beliefs.

stock issues   issues that typically arise for various types of propositions. Addressing all of the stock issues for a proposition generally leads to stronger arguments.

strategy   a threatening communication style in which what is said appears to be rehearsed and manipulative.

structural inherency   a type of inherency argument that claims that the cause of a problem is either the laws, regulations, and court decisions that force it to happen, or the lack of laws, regulations, and court decisions to eliminate it.

style   the classical canon of rhetoric that helps the speaker decide how to use language to express ideas in a speech.

superiority   a threatening communication style in which the communicator indicates that he or she is somehow better than others.

supportive communication   verbal and nonverbal messages presented in ways that are unlikely to be perceived as an ego threat.

syllogism   a deductive argument that includes a major premise, minor premise, and conclusion and which comes to an absolutely certain conclusion that is the inevitable result of accepting the premises.

symbol   something that a group of language users agrees stands for something else.

symbols are arbitrary   the sounds and shapes that groups of people agree stand for meanings have no inherent connection to the things and concepts for which they stand.

testimony   authoritative opinion evidence that interprets or judges events, objects, persons, or places.

the burden of proof   the responsibility of the arguer in favor of the proposition to provide sufficient evidence and reasoning to justify acceptance of the proposition.

theory   an explanation of a phenomenon, and a prediction of what will happen in the future, based on the accumulation of well-collected data.

threatening communication   verbal and nonverbal messages presented in ways that are likely to be perceived as an ego threat.

treatment group   members of the sample who are exposed to the experimental treatment. Also known as the "experimental group."

trustworthiness   the audience's perception that the speaker is honest and unbiased, giving the speaker more credibility.

turn arguments   a direct refutation technique in which the arguer accepts what the opponent says as being correct but shows that it actually argues against his or her position rather than for it.

understanding   the step in the listening process in which the listener decides what the speaker means.

valid argument   an argument that is properly structured, in which all of the logical components fit together correctly.

validity   (1) the degree to which an argument is formally valid; (2) the ability of a measurement device to actually measure what it is supposed to measure.

value   a stock issue of propositions of value that argues which value, or set of values, is the most important for drawing a conclusion about the subject of the proposition.

verbal aggressiveness   a negative personality facet exhibited by the inclination to attack the self-concepts of individuals instead of, or in addition to, their positions on particular issues.

verifiers   an element added to the Toulmin model of argumentation that provides justification for believing the grounds.

warrant   the element in the Toulmin model of argumentation that explains why the grounds legitimately support the claim.

weasel words   a questionable use of language that uses language to make it appear as though more is being claimed than literally is.

Works Cited

Aristotle. *On Sophistical Refutations.* Trans. E. S. Forster. In *On Sophistical Refutations; On Coming-To-Be and Passing-Away;* and *On the Cosmos.* Cambridge: Harvard U.P., 1955.

———. *Sophistical Refutations.* Trans. W. D. Ross. in *The Complete Works of Aristotle.* vol. I. Jonathan Barnes, ed. Princeton: Princeton U.P., 1984.

———. *The Art of Rhetoric.* Trans. H. C. Lawson-Tancred. London: Penguin Books, 1991.

Atheism Web. *Logic and Fallacies.* http://www.infidels.org/news/atheism/logic.html, December 28, 1998.

Beebe, Steven A. and John T. Masterson. *Communicating in Small Groups, Principles and Practices.* New York: Longman, 1997.

Best, Joel. *Damned Lies and Statistics.* Berkeley: U of California Press, 2001.

Bitzer, Lloyd F. "The Rhetorical Situation." *Philosophy and Rhetoric,* 1 (1968): 1–14.

Brockriede, Wayne. "Arguers as Lovers." *Philosophy and Rhetoric,* 5 (1972): 1–11.

Brownell, Judi. *Listening: Attitudes, Principles, and Skills.* Boston: Allyn and Bacon, 1996.

Cacciari, Cristina. "The Place of Idioms in a Literal and Metaphorical World." in Cacciari, Cristina and Patrizia Tabossi (eds). *Idioms: Processing, Structure, and Interpretation.* Hillsdale, NJ: Lawrence Erlbaum, 1993, 27–56.

Capaldi, Nicholas. *The Art of Deception.* Buffalo: Prometheus Books, 1987.

Chase, Stuart. *Guides to Straight Thinking.* New York: Harper, 1956.

Cicero, *De Oratore; or, On the Character of An Orator.* Trans. J. S. Watson. In *Cicero on Oratory and Orators.* London: Bell & Daldy, 1871.

DeFleur, Melvin, Patricia Kearney and Timothy Plax. *Fundamentals of Human Communication.* Mountain View, CA: Mayfield, 1993.

De Vito, Joseph. *The Elements of Public Speaking.* (2nd ed.) New York: Longman, 1997.

Downes, Stephen. *Stephen's Guide to the Logical Fallacies* http://www.assiniboinec.mb.ca/user/downes/fallacy/fall.htm, December 28, 1998.

Eemeren, Frans H. van, Rob Grootendorts and Francisca Snoeck Henkemans. *Fundamentals of Argumentation Theory.* Mahwah, NJ: Lawrence Erlbaum, 1996.

Engel, S. Morris. *Fallacies and Pitfalls of Language.* New York: Dover Publications, 1994.

———. *With Good Reason: An Introduction to Informal Fallacies.* (5th ed.) New York: St. Martin's, 1994.

Fisher, Alan and Michael Scriven. *Critical Thinking: Its Definition and Assessment.* Point Reyes, CA: Edgepress, 1997.

Freeley, Austin J. *Argumentation and Debate: Critical Thinking for Reasoned Decision Making.* (8th ed.) Belmont, CA: Wadsworth, 1993.

Freeman, Andrew. "Factual Errors Make Story Void." *The Lumberjack,* 82 (7) October 17, 2001.

Gibb, Jack. "Defensive Communication." *Journal of Communication.* 11 (3) September 1961: 141–148.

Halpern, Diane F. "A National Assessment of Critical Thinking Skills in Adults: Taking Steps Toward the Goal." in U.S. Department of Education, Office of Educational Research and Improvement, National Center for Educational Statistics. *National Assessment of College Student Learning: Identification of the Skill to Be Taught, Learned, and Assessed. A Report on the Proceedings of the Second Study Design Workshop, November 1992.* Washington, DC: U.S. Government Printing Office, August 1994, 24–64.

Hamblin, C. L. *Fallacies.* London: Methuen & Co., 1970.

Huppe, Bernard F. and Jack Kaminsky. *Logic and Language.* New York: Knopf, 1956.

Inch, Edward S. and Barbara Warnick. *Critical Thinking and Communication.* (3rd ed.) Boston: Allyn and Bacon, 1998.

Infante, Dominic A. *Arguing Constructively.* Prospect Heights, IL: Waveland Press, 1988.

Janis, Irving L. *Victims of Groupthink; A Psychological Study of Foreign-Policy Decisions and Fiascoes.* Boston: Houghton-Mifflin, 1972.

Johnson-Laird, P. N. "Foreword." in Cacciari, Cristina and Patrizia Tabossi (eds). *Idioms: Processing, Structure, and Interpretation.* Hillsdale, NJ: Lawrence Erlbaum, 1993, vii–x.

Kahane, Howard and Nancy Cavender. *Logic and Contemporary Rhetoric.* (8th ed.) Belmont, CA: Wadsworth, 1998.

Kant, Immanuel. *Groundwork of the Metaphysic of Morals.* Trans. H. J. Paton. In *The Moral Law.* New York: Barnes & Noble, 1948.

Kearney, Patricia and Timothy Plax. *Public Speaking in a Diverse Society.* Mountain View, CA: Mayfield, 1996.

Labossiere, Michael C. *Fallacies.* http://www.nizkor.org/features/fallacies/, December 28, 1998.

Lakoff, George and Mark Johnson. *Metaphors We Live By.* Chicago: U. of Chicago Press, 1980.

Moore, Brooke Noel and Richard Parker. *Critical Thinking.* (3rd ed.) Mountain View, CA: Mayfield, 1992.

O'Keefe, Daniel. "Two Concepts of Argument," *Journal of the American Forensic Association,* 13: Winter 1977, 121–128.

———. "Justification Explicitness and Persuasive Effect: A Meta-Analytic Review of the Effects of Varying Support Articulation in Persuasive Messages." *Argumentation and Advocacy,* 35: Fall 1998, 61–75.

Paul, Richard. "Teaching Critical Thinking in the Strong Sense." *Informal Logic Newsletter,* 4: 1982, 2–7.

Perella, Jack. *The Debate Method of Critical Thinking: An Introduction to Argumentation.* Dubuque, IA: Kendall/Hunt, 1987.

Rhoads, Kelton V. L. and Robert B. Cialdini. "The Business of Influence: Principles That Lead to Success in Commercial Settings." in Dillard, James Price and Michael Pfau (eds.) *The Persuasion Handbook: Developments in*

Theory and Practice, (513–542). Thousand Oaks: Sage, 2002.

Schwarzenegger, Arnold. "Schwarzenegger: Cut spending, taxes." *San Francisco Chronicle,* October 5, 2003, E5.

Smith, Craig R. *Rhetoric and Human Consciousness: A History.* Prospect Heights, IL: Waveland, 1998.

St. Augustine. *On Christian Doctrine.* Trans. D. W. Robertson, Jr. Indianapolis: Bobbs-Merrill, 1958.

Szabo, Erin Alison and Michael Pfau. "Nuances in Inoculation: Theory and Applications." in Dillard, James Price and Michael Pfau (eds.) *The Persuasion Handbook: Developments in Theory and Practice,* (513–542). Thousand Oaks: Sage, 2002.

Sztybel, David. *Common Fallacies to Avoid.* http://www.epas.utoronto.ca:8080/~sztybel/fallacy.html, December 28, 1998.

Toulmin, Stephen Edelston. *The Uses of Argument.* Cambridge: University Press, 1958.

Warnick, Barbara. "Arguing Value Propositions." *Journal of the American Forensic Association,* 18: Fall 1981, 109–119.

Wilbanks, Charles and Russell T. Church. *Values and Policies in Controversy: An Introduction to Argumentation and Debate.* (2nd ed.) Dubuque, IA: Kendall/Hunt, 1991.

Wolff, Florence I., Nadine C. Marsnik, William S. Tacey, Ralph G. Nichols. *Perceptive Listening.* New York: Holt, Rinehart and Winston, 1983.

Wolvin. Andrew D. and Carolyn Gwynn Coakley (eds.) *Perspectives on Listening.* Norwood, NJ: Ablex, 1993.

Wood, Julia T. *Communication in Our Lives.* Belmont, CA: Wadsworth, 1997.

Index